Legal Control of the Private Military Corporation

Legal Control of the Private Military Corporation

Benedict Sheehy
Senior Lecturer, RMIT University, Australia

Jackson Maogoto
Senior Lecturer, University of Manchester, United Kingdom

Virginia Newell

palgrave
macmillan

First published 2009 by
PALGRAVE MACMILLAN

Palgrave Macmillan in the UK is an imprint of Macmillan Publishers Limited, registered in England, company number 785998, of Houndmills, Basingstoke, Hampshire RG21 6XS.

Palgrave Macmillan in the US is a division of St Martin's Press LLC, 175 Fifth Avenue, New York, NY 10010.

Palgrave Macmillan is the global academic imprint of the above companies and has companies and representatives throughout the world.

Palgrave® and Macmillan® are registered trademarks in the United States, the United Kingdom, Europe and other countries.

ISBN-13: 978-0-230-52231-2 hardback
ISBN-10: 0-230-52231-9 hardback

This book is printed on paper suitable for recycling and made from fully managed and sustained forest sources. Logging, pulping and manufacturing processes are expected to conform to the environmental regulations of the country of origin.

A catalogue record for this book is available from the British Library.

Library of Congress Cataloging-in-Publication Data

Sheehy, Benedict, 1961–
Legal control of the private military corporation / Benedict Sheehy, Jackson Maogoto, Virginia Newell.
p. cm.
Includes bibliographical references and index.
ISBN 0-230-52231-9 (alk. paper)
1. Private security services. 2. Police, Private. 3. Mercenary troops. 4. Security, International. I. Maogoto, Jackson Nyamuya, 1975– II. Newell, Virginia, 1968– III. Title.

K3465.S54 2008
343'.015354—dc22 2008016323

10 9 8 7 6 5 4 3 2 1
18 17 16 15 14 13 12 11 10 09

Printed and bound in Great Britain by
CPI Antony Rowe, Chippenham and Eastbourne

Dedications

Ben dedicates this book to his siblings Paul Sheehy and Monica Bacic, whose social conscience and moral support provide a context for work such as the present one. He wishes to thank Paul in particular for engaging discussions on the topic and suggestions and support in terms of research.

Jackson dedicates this book to his parents, Mary S. G. Maogoto and the late R. Jackson Nyamuya Maogoto Sr. This dedication would not be complete without an accolade to the Anolaks, Greg and Osija Anolak and their daughter Helena A. Anolak, who have supported and motivated him through some of the more difficult moments of his life through the years. Last and by no means least, the continued inspiration of General (Rtd) Anthony P. V. Rogers OBE, Yorke Distinguished Fellow, University of Cambridge—a regular sounding board for his ideas—and Professor Tim McCormack, Australian Red Cross Professor of International Humanitarian Law and Director, Asia-Pacific Centre for Military Law—his mentor: towering intellectuals who are and continue to be a source of intellectual nourishment both through correspondence and their seminal works.

Virginia dedicates this book to Mark Bursler and Jill Newell for their practical support, unfailing encouragement, and superb proof-reading skills.

Contents

Preface

Two years ago a newspaper article of a few paragraphs reporting on an attempted coup caught the attention of the reader. The paragraphs referred to a private military firm being hired to assist in the overthrow of the government. Such an event sat uncomfortably with the reader and led to some informal discussions with colleagues. It did not seem right that a private individual could hire an army to overthrow a government. It goes against the premises of Western liberal worldview in which the state is the center and all powers within its territory are subject to it. It also contradicts the notion that the only violent challenge to a state can come from other states or from a popular or at least domestically instigated uprising. Of course one recognizes the complicity of nations in the overthrow of other governments—the USA's foreign policy executed through the CIA being the most notorious example. Nevertheless, the premise still stands, and indeed as the saying goes, the rule is more honored through the breach than the observance.

We live in a rapidly and greatly changing world. The premises and worldviews with which we have grown and matured are constantly changing, being challenged, and often falling down around us. It is the challenge of this generation to identify and address these changes and remake the world in the midst of it all. To our generation as never before we must do our best to make the world a habitable place not only for ourselves but for those who come after us as well. We hope that this slim volume contributes at least to some thinking as to how that might be done in this small, but important, area of human activity.

BCS

Acknowledgments

The authors gratefully acknowledge each other's contribution to their own ideas, thinking, and professional growth. Jackson and Virginia wish to acknowledge Ben's contribution in revising the whole manuscript in preparation for publication.

We acknowledge the following courtesies and permissions: use of excerpts from Matthew Georgeson's Honours Thesis entitled "It's a Long Way to the Top: Abu Ghraib, Civilian Contractors and Command Responsibility" (2004, University of Newcastle) in chapter 5, sections 5.3 and 5.4.

The special permission of the Texas International Law Review to reprint excerpts from "Corporate Militaries and States: Actors, Interactions and Reactions," Virginia Newell and Benedict Sheehy (2006), *Texas International Law Review,* 41, 68–101.

The kind permission of the *Adelaide Law Review* to reprint excerpts from "Contemporary Private Military Firms under International Law: An Unregulated 'Gold Rush,'" Jackson Maogoto and Benedict Sheehy (2005), *Adelaide Law Review,* 26(2), 245–270.

The kind permission of the Sandstone Press to reprint excerpts from "Re-Thinking Securities Regulation: A Comparative Study of ASX, NYSE, and SGX," Benedict Sheehy (2006), *Corporate Governance Law Review,* 2(1), 191–244.

In addition, we are grateful to the New South Wales Law and Justice Foundation for financial support from its Legal Scholarship Support Fund. We thank our research assistants Than Thi Vu and Shona Freeman for their work well beyond the call of duty. Last and by no means least, this book would not have been possible without the opportunity and support afforded by the publisher—Palgrave Macmillan—and the valuable comments of the anonymous reviewer.

Introduction

0.1 The problem: A transformation in sovereignty

Despite the enduring history of hired military services, they have often been regarded with distrust.[1] In the late eighteenth century George Washington, America's first president and a decorated five-star Army General, warned that "Mercenary Armies…have at one time or another subverted the liberties of allmost [*sic*] all the Countries they have been raised to defend…."[2] More than a century and a half later, in 1961, the United States' thirty-fourth president, Dwight Eisenhower (a former four-star Army General), cautioned: "[i]n the councils of government, we must guard against the acquisition of unwarranted influence, whether sought or unsought, by the military-industrial complex. The potential for the disastrous rise of misplaced power exists and will persist." Several decades later, Eisenhower's statement has changed from a prophecy to the unsettling situation in which we currently find ourselves. Jennings, in her work on the private military industry, writes: "war…always has been a matter of profit and spoils. What is changing is how the profits are distributed."[3]

Another perspective to consider, put forth over a century ago, is the following:

> Our economic analysis has disclosed the fact that it is only the interests of competing cliques of business men—investors, contractors, export manufacturers, and certain professional classes—that are antagonistic; that these cliques, usurping the authority and voice of the people, use the public resources to push their private interests, and spend the blood and money of the people in this vast and disastrous military game, feigning national antagonisms which have no basis in reality.[4]

The phenomenon under discussion, the Private Military Corporation (PMC), may be viewed as a further concentration of their power and facilitator of those antagonisms, itself yet another contender in the competition seeking its own share, through a new focused commodification of violence, in the above noted redistribution of the spoils of war.

The PMC brings violence, money, and suffering in greater quantities and into closer, more direct contact than ever in history. One notes, for example, the comments of Jack London, CEO of California Analysis Center Incorporated (CACI), to investors shortly after the exposure of CACI involvement in the Abu Ghraib scandal. In that first conference after the exposé, four times he states he "feels good" about CACI services and finances[5] without comment on the consequences elsewhere—one cannot but wonder how the families of the Abu Ghraib torture victims felt and what dignity Iraq had on that date.

The end of the Cold War in the 1990s produced dramatic changes in the complexion of international relations. A geopolitical power vacuum replaced the militaristic bipolar international scene, creating an atmosphere for major militaries in the West to downsize their large standing armies. Downsizing of military forces was driven by the purported economic impetus that privatization would improve efficiency and save costs for nation-states. Nevertheless, military spending has continued to increase and the anticipated "peace dividend" resulting from the end of the Cold War did not materialize for other reasons. Long-suppressed ethnic and regional rivalries erupted creating global instability, and a demand for troops and weaponry resulted in downsized governments growing increasingly reliant on off-the-shelf commercial technology and the newly commodified violence/warfare market.

Privatization can take many forms, facets, and techniques. In spite of the lack of a formal definition for privatization, what most characterizes privatization is the reallocation of public ownership, assets, functions, services, management, or tasks to private hands. For the purposes of this book, privatization is defined as the deliberate and policy-based transfer of certain public functions, tasks, or services from the state to private actors who then carry them out on a for-profit basis. Privatization and procurement are core to the issues of engagement and accountability of the PMC and they present several significant legal challenges particularly in matters of sovereignty and democratic oversight. Where they do so they will be addressed; however, it is important to note at the outset that the focus of the book is on the control of the potentially lethal powers of the PMC and not on the privatization and procurement aspects, which are certainly studies in themselves. In line with this focus will be the mention of those aspects of privatization and procurement touching on the more mundane issues of logistics and contract fraud in passing rather than as a focus per se. Mention will be made of those issues as they illustrate the broader challenges to accountability and control and to the extent necessary to be comprehensive in the discussion and proposition of appropriate regulatory solutions.

Private security contractors such as Executive Outcomes, DynCorp, Military Professional Resources Incorporated (MPRI), Blackwater Consulting USA,

Titan, CACI etc. have been variously called mercenaries, security consultants, "hired guns," civilian contractors, PMCs, private security companies (PSCs), private military security companies (PMSCs), and private military firms (PMFs). Regardless of title, these groups provide services ranging from consulting to logistical support to full-fledged armed divisions and are now undoubtedly a part of global politics and the global market. They are operating in some 50 countries around the world. Though this book will address some of the definitional and classification questions related to the use of private military services, for the sake of uniformity the term "PMC" will be used throughout to refer to any private company providing some form of military support across the spectrum from consulting to fielding active combat groups.

Although in some forms resembling mercenarism, contemporary PMCs have developed a sophisticated business model and a modus operandi compatible with the needs and strictures of the post–Cold War, state-based international system. This sophistication has permitted them to gain both implicit and explicit legitimacy. As will be discussed, the utilization of these private agents compromises the strategic and physical security of nations and the confidence of the citizenry in the democratic practices and institutions of the nation. PMCs, though beneficiaries of substantial public dollars, operate at best without public notification, oversight, approval, or other accountability. A particularly disturbing issue is that while economic aims are acknowledged to be one driver of warfare, at least implicitly, it is not accepted by the populace as the only or main or even appropriate reason for going to war. This is owing to the fact that a purely economic war would be socially and politically repugnant to the vast majority in modern times.

The PMC is an institution established to facilitate and conduct war on solely and exclusively economic grounds. This issue has been dealt with historically in the discussions on mercenarism and legal instruments designed to deal with that phenomenon. However, as the industry has boomed, and significant and dramatic military involvements have occurred, the discussion has morphed into a discussion of state and international legal and policy response to the PMC. Predictably, the issues, parties, and position have changed over time. The time is ripe for an in-depth legal analysis of the phenomenon of the PMC.

One of the many significant distinctions between the PMC and the traditional Soldier of Fortune is that unlike the odd or casual mercenary whose participation may be seen as a form of slippage in the regulation of the battlefield but unlikely to significantly alter the outcome of the battle, the corporate form and organization of the PMC allows the massing of resources for conducting warfare, thus placing it in a position to significantly impact outcomes on the battlefield. Despite this, PMC involvement in war is shielded as it occurs as a result of private actors, unaccountable to the public at large and, in many instances, at arm's length from governmental supervision via private contract.

Traditionally, the right to amass for use such extensive resources for war required the scrutiny, approval, and by accountability of government and, indirectly, the populace. However, the PMC allows use of extensive resources to be expended outside of such an accountability framework. In other words, the PMC is inherently antidemocratic. It can be called in where the government is unable to muster sufficient support among the populace for causes or wishes to evade public scrutiny for its actions. It makes no difference whether the PMC is aiding an unpopular dictatorship to maintain control over a restive populace in a banana republic or the PMC is the agent of a first-world government assisting the achievement of its geopolitical aims. When a government intervenes where there is insufficient popular support for military intervention, it suggests that the legitimacy of the aims or objectives for which it is necessary to contract with a PMC is questionable.

A further concern is that whereas wars have been lost on issues beyond economic power, the PMC allows raw economic power to tip the balance in any armed conflict, exclusive of all other concerns including rights, justice, equity, and self-determination. While this principle of "economic might is right" has a long history in warfare, it has not been determinative, and indeed occasionally fails. Yet, the PMC lives on and among other things may unjustifiably raise the cost in human lives of combatants by causing a poorly armed but popularly supported uprising or army to continue a struggle that it may well otherwise have already won based on its wide, "democratic" support. Still another issue from a policy standpoint is the question of the loss of control; for even when contractors do military jobs, they remain private businesses and thus fall outside the military chain of command and justice systems.

There is another variable in the equation involving civilians, national military, PMCs, wealth, and politics. A discussion of the phenomena must take account of the positive contributions of PMCs in certain instances. One notes, for example, the well-known cases of a frontline-fighting-force PMC, Executive Outcomes, in Angola and in Sierra Leone.[6] In both instances the PMC was very effective in bringing an end to civilian deaths, establishing sufficient order and peace in an environment of chaos and killing to allow real and ultimately fruitful political negotiations to occur—as violence is inherently a political matter. Further, the PMC did so at a very reasonable cost, although questions concerning mining concessions remain.[7] A peaceful environment and effective political process are ultimate objectives, and so achieving such should be a priority regardless of whether it involves public or private means. These successful interventions draw particular attention to the important matter of the context in which the PMC is operating; that is to say, whether it is operating in a stable or unstable environment, and whether there is an effective, viable public alternative—matters of particular importance when considering PMC action in third-world states.

Further, it is important to keep in mind that abuses, killings, and coups are perpetrated by national militaries and are not the sole province of PMCs. The distinctive issue for the PMC with regard to this issue, however, is that whereas there is law dealing with national militaries through established national and international legal systems, such a system does not exist for the PMC. It is not to say that the law controlling national militaries is sufficient or even necessarily effective. Rather it is to point out that it exists and to some degree at least is effective. This situation is significantly different for the PMC, as we shall explore in depth throughout this work.

The problems surrounding violence and war are a tangled and thorny set of human, legal, political, and economic issues, and these issues are exacerbated by the introduction of the corporate form, providing the basis for the establishment and growth of the PMC. The corporate form has specific benefits and costs that are very well suited to some aspects, such as ability to amass significant resources for action, secrecy, freedom from public scrutiny, and rapid response, while being exceedingly injurious in such other aspects such as social costs including the damage to democratic oversight, enforcement of unjust resource allocations, and of course, the dominance of raw economic power.

0.2 Aims and rationale

While the rise of the post–Cold War PMC may be seen as a success for the globalized free market place, these "[PMCs] represent a reconstituted form of organized corporate mercenarism that is responding to the need for advanced military expertise."[8] PMCs now support numerous military operations throughout the world and act as crucial components in enhancing the capabilities of countries both in the Third World and in the West. Within the military establishment of countries whether small, medium, or large, thousands of PMC technical experts operate communications systems, maintain military aircraft, fix weapons systems, link troops to command centers, and in several cases train national armies. PMCs are now in a position to amass unchecked power to affect conflict resolution, world economic stability, and geostrategic negotiations.[9] The decentralization of international security from state-organized militaries threatens the traditional Westphalian paradigm of the state as the natural entity in control of the legal use of lethal military force. Although they do not like to admit it, PMC employees' roles range from providing basic services such as food and housing to frontline fighting. As "corporate mercenary" firms become larger, they are entrenching themselves as key players in the crucial sovereign function of use of military force and now stand in a position to influence and engage in decision-making processes traditionally exercised by politicians and government entities.[10]

The objectives of this book are fivefold but focused carefully on the legal issues surrounding the recent development of the PMC—a corporation organized to provide military skills and manpower for profit in support of any armed conflict and, as a result of remarkable growth, now intricately linked to warfare. The first objective of the book is to draw attention to this important development in contemporary war operations and elsewhere. PMCs are businesses providing professionalized military services—corporate bodies specializing in the sale of military skills. PMCs do everything from leasing out commando teams and offering the strategic advice of ex-generals, to running the outsourced supply chains for armies. Some PMCs have worked for democracies, the UN, and even environmental groups, while others have prospered at the other end of the marketplace, working for dictators, drug cartels, and terrorist-linked groups. Legitimacy is hard enough to determine in international politics and becomes more difficult when billions in potential profits come into play, as it does with the involvement of PMCs.

The contemporary PMC has gained prominence in the last two decades; however, its genesis and utility date back to the Vietnam War era.[11] Although the PMC encroaches on powers traditionally reserved for the state, it has operated largely without regulation or publicity. It is an actor in international affairs and policy and is poised for growth. In other words, the PMC has become an integral player. Such corporations, at least at one level, represent the evolution, globalization, and corporatization of the age-old mercenary trade. Despite this importance, they operate without the public scrutiny appropriate for military actors.

The second objective is to contribute to the growing discussion of the PMC as an actor. It contributes to a dearth of pragmatically based discussion which acknowledges the PMC as a phenomenon unlikely to simply disappear.[12] The authors find it unhelpful to engage in attacks on the ethics of those opposed to one's view in the matter—whether for or against the PMC. There are numerous perspectives and voices, as will be seen. Some parties are advocates, others satisfied users of PMC services, and others are reluctant users of services. Other parties are opponents for a variety of reasons including the moral issues surrounding the commodification of violence; political issues relating to notions of sovereignty; and political issues surrounding politics, violence, and distributions. Still other groups study the phenomena and/or are concerned with the protection of society from unnecessary violence—whether resulting from a quicker resort to violence in the PMC, the potential severing from democratic oversight the PMC may represent, or the proliferation of violent potential the PMCs bring. The present work attempts to present various views to varying degrees and to participate in the public discussion, straddling the line between analysts and pragmatic proponents.[13]

This book provides insight by approaching the PMC through a legal lens, examining a number of significant examples of the role taken on by PMCs around the world in shaping policy, conflicts, and outcomes, to suit not only state policy but the ends sought by private actors, not the least of which is the PMC profits. The PMC does not operate in a world devoid of law. The authors seek to place it into the legal fabric of both the national and international legal systems. They provide an in-depth analysis of the PMC highlighting the weakness of national and international regulation. The book seeks to achieve this end by reviewing the history of mercenary activity by contrasting such with the activities of the contemporary PMC. It examines the problems associated with national and international regulation of mercenaries and critiques various models for regulation. What the analysis reveals is that this industry, so central to national and global security, is largely, if not completely, unregulated, and possibly uncontrollable.

The third objective is to identify and examine particular problems that the PMC poses for nations in terms of actual operations and related matters of accountability. Governments stand in a conflicted situation vis-à-vis the PMC. On the one hand, it is politically expedient to condemn it; on the other, the PMC has proved to be highly advantageous in certain circumstances. Still the matter of accountability remains unresolved, in part because of governments' intention to avoid accountability by using PMCs and in part because of the complex nature of the legal form of the corporation. This concern leads to the fourth objective.

The fourth objective is an examination of the effect of the introduction of the corporate form into an already complex legal and political landscape in particular by considering the shield the corporate vehicle provides for its actors, shielding them from the consequences of their actions. Specifically, directors and others may be excused from personal liability for actions of the corporation where those actions were done in the normal course of business. The liability rests with the corporation and not with the people behind the corporate form. This legal characteristic permits those actors to "live to die another day." The problem is that these actors have designed their "other days" for the express purpose of the coordinated killing of others. Furthermore, the corporate form is dedicated to outsourcing social costs and privatizing the profits. Nowhere is this premise more evident than in the case of PMCs. War is far too important to be left to the CEOs.

The fifth objective which runs as a thread throughout the work is examining and considering from various perspectives the potential for PMC regulation. The work examines the law and the phenomena of a corporatized military and examines how the two forces interact having been put into play by government. The focus is on the ultimate objective of controlling violence, put sometimes as the person with the pen controlling the person with the gun. By examining existing legal regimes and doctrines, the book seeks to advance a broad but nuanced understanding of the potential and pitfalls of various approaches to the control of violence as embodied in the corporate PMC.

0.3 Book synopsis

Chapter 1 explores mercenarism, its history, and the origins of the PMC. It will serve to illustrate, as Peter W. Singer puts it, that today's PMCs are not just "the old poison of vagabond mercenaries in new designer bottles." Rather, they are a new significant phenomenon. The chapter commences with a review of the historical context of mercenarism and the state, and then specifically, the historical accidents of the late twentieth century that saw the birth of the PMC. It delimits the discussion by examining the issues surrounding the definition of the PMC, a matter returned to throughout the book. The chapter next looks to distinguish the mercenary from the PMC. This difficult task, in part, sets the stage for the discussion in the second chapter, dealing with the introduction of the corporate form into the supply of military services. The chapter next postulates that the privatization of military functions has introduced a range of constitutional, economic, and strategic concerns that have a significant impact on governmental functions, civilians, and ultimately democracy. Finally, internationally, democratically, and through the private corporate form, it identifies the concerns related to accountability that will be addressed throughout the balance of the book. This background serves as the introduction to both the PMC and the policy and regulatory issues surrounding it.

Chapter 2 examines the significance of utilizing the corporate form for PMCs. With billions up for grabs, PMCs have developed serious networks with military insiders in various capitals in the West by funneling hundreds of thousands of dollars into lobbying. They now have an active role either formally or informally advising governments on various military policy initiatives. The story is much the same elsewhere. This chapter explores the impact of various corporate legal doctrines including limited liability, the corporate veil, director's duties, and personal liability for corporate actions. It also reviews relevant aspects of corporate governance theory and practice. With this background, the rest of the book is put into a different perspective, as the dominance of the debate by the corporate military and the murky and difficult issues posed by the presence of the corporate form are amply illustrated.

Chapter 3 focuses on nation-states and PMCs in the domestic context. It reviews the state's control of force in de jure and de facto terms before turning to evaluate the privatization of military goods and services and the same de jure and de facto controls of a privatized defense service. It examines in that context the state's loss of the monopoly over violence and issues surrounding accountability via an examination of the Rule of Law and the legal tools for control of government violence. It then turns to examine the nation-state's use of PMCs extraterritorially, and particularly as a foreign policy tool. The examination is illustrated by five case studies in the contemporary international context: Iraq, Sudan, East Timor, Equatorial Guinea, and the Balkans. A clear subtext to the chapter provokes thought on the role of PMCs in influencing international law and geopolitical ordering.

Chapter 4 grapples with concerns about PMC regulation in the domestic context. Regulation of PMCs addresses a number of concerns, both of the PMC sector as well as of governments and the public at large. While PMCs argue that the lack of regulation governing their conduct is not a concern as their work is primarily apolitical night-watchman-type security, they only work for "reputable" clients, and furthermore, as responsible professionalized corporate actors, their codes and structures preclude misbehavior. Their activities and the nonviolence presumptions suggest that this "trust me, trust me" approach is inappropriate. PMCs reject claims that they need to be regulated in order to prevent them from interfering with standing democratic governments or in order to protect the rights of individuals in areas of their operations. These myths are burst when one considers that small and medium governments have reason to be wary of PMCs. So vast are PMC services on offer and so well-heeled is PMC equipment that PMCs have the ability to face off militarily with states and dictate, through their involvement, changes in government.[14] The chapter explores PMC arguments for and efforts at self-regulation. It does so with a review of PMC activities as illustrated in the cases of PNG and Iraq. It determines that nation-state regulation of PMCs is preferable and a key to the control of the PMC phenomena on the world stage. It then turns to examine approaches to national regulation in New Zealand, USA, South Africa, and the UK with the central emphasis on the question: can national regulation be effective?

The fifth chapter addresses the conundrum presented by PMCs: "the international laws of war that specifically deal with their presence and activity are largely absent or ineffective." Although the United Nations attempts to regulate the violent behavior of nation-states and their national militaries, it (like international law more generally) has significantly less influence over the activities of private agents. This situation exists primarily because "the existing laws do not adequately deal with the full variety of private military actors. That is, they are specifically aimed at only the individuals working against national governments or politically recognized movements of national liberation." This chapter examines the impact of international law on PMCs. It covers the important ground of international concepts and mechanisms. It considers various international instruments on mercenarism and examines their weaknesses generally, and particularly with respect to controlling PMCs. It also deals with the troublesome 1989 Convention on Mercenaries. This convention, although universally hailed, is in practice universally ignored. It provides an analysis of the doctrine of state responsibility relating to nonstate actors and private persons acting under direction/control of the state. It then examines the doctrine of command responsibility as embedded in international law. Specifically it reviews the elements of command responsibility including the existence of superior/subordinate relationship, requisite knowledge, and failure to act. It does so within the context of general principles of international law and in the context of the appropriate provisions of the International Criminal Tribunal for the former Yugoslavia (ICTY), the International Criminal Tribunal for Rwanda (ICTR), and the International Criminal Court (ICC).

1
Private Military Companies: The New Face of War

1.1 Introduction

There is a widespread general assumption about warfare: military responsibilities fall into the exclusive domain of the state. However, prior to the 1648 Peace of Westphalia and the emergence of the modern nation-state, military entrepreneurship was common. At this time, in fact, war was the biggest industry in Europe. Military businessmen became rich renting out their "armies for hire," and the Thirty Years' War was the "heyday for hired armies."[1] After 1648, the modern state bureaucracy took over the conduct of warfare.[2] Commencing with the Peace of Westphalia, and the dismantling of Wallenstein's 120,000 strong militia,[3] the state increasingly sought to consolidate its grip on military power with the aim of being the central and exclusive protagonist in military matters.[4]

By the start of the nineteenth century, states' aggressive moves to control military violence through centralization and monopolization and building hierarchical structures were bearing handsome dividends with mercenaries being increasingly marginalized. With European states reaching the apex of bureaucratic maturity, their capability to organize military violence had increased tremendously.[5] With the consolidation of central authority in most European states and the maturation of the notion of nation-state sovereignty, the recruitment of foreigners for duty in national armies declined, and the utility of the private military as a tool of state warfare disappeared.[6]

Writing at the start of the twentieth century, sociologist Max Weber crowned the success of state efforts with his assertion that the state was that entity which "successfully upholds a claim to the monopoly of the legitimate use of physical force in the enforcement of its order."[7] Two general reasons accounted for Weber's assertion. Firstly, the rise and maturity of the modern nation-state and its nationalistic credo of patriotic armed forces as a symbol of national security and governmental authority in defending its territory and citizenry. Secondly, the nature of military skill and its underpinnings—the management and deployment of violence—was now underpinned by the state's determination in the nineteenth century to prevent an active role by private entities. The move contributed to the development and crystallization of the position that military skill should not be bought and sold nor be conceived of or treated as a commodity. In light of the ascendance of the state and its success in marginalizing mercenaries, military violence was now viewed as "noncommodifiable."[8]

Despite the marginalization of mercenaries and the dissipation of their significance in warfare, it was only in the course of the twentieth century that the mercenary was finally vilified and outlawed. This was primarily owing to a new kind of soldier of fortune emerging in the 1950s—the independent mercenaries, commonly referred to as "wild geese," or "les affreux" (the dreaded ones).[9] They plied their trade predominantly in postcolonial Africa, rising into prominence on the heel of the turbulence of decolonization, where they complicated already difficult situations. They presented significant threats to many fledgling newly independent African states.

These soldiers of fortune who infested Africa from the 1950s to 1970s were generally individual adventurers without corporate backing and sought excitement as well as money in troubled corners of the earth.[10] They were motley collections of self-seekers operating outside the state system. Like their predecessors one hundred years earlier, the new breed of soldier-for-hire appeared where there had been a breakdown of internal order, and appeared as a source of instant military force and expertise.[11] The sensationalized images of these mercenaries—daring, dangerous, and destabilizing—fueled distrust toward hired private military services.[12] This distrust had merit in light of the fact that some European powers employed them to hinder and arguably thwart liberation movements, while unpopular African governments used them to consolidate their authority.[13]

This new breed of soldier of fortune was vilified despite the acceptance of the commodification of mercenary violence in yester centuries. The new breed was seen as illegitimate when contrasted with legitimate "appropriate" state violence,[14] particularly as the state had moved away from accepting the commodification of violence. As Juan Carlos Zarate notes: "these independent mercenaries, hired outside the constraints of the twentieth century Nation-State system and seemingly motivated solely by pecuniary interests, were seen as a shocking anachronism."[15] Ironically, it was during this period that organizsed corporate actors began their genesis as PMCs during the Vietnam War, providing primarily support services to military efforts. In the 1950s and 1960s the United States and UK governments used PMCs for "overt and covert military missions."[16] In Vietnam the US Department of Defence (DoD) hired civilian contractors to provide traditional military activities such as logistical support to the military, and such services as trucking, port operation, construction, and more.[17] By 1969, PMCs in Vietnam had 9,000 civilian employees and annual contracts totaling $236 million awarded by the United States Army Procurement Agency of Vietnam.[18]

Paradoxically, despite utilizing PMCs during this period, the US and UK governments viewed PMCs as a "subset" of typical "mercenary activity" and acknowledged reports of contractors in Vietnam as being involved in illegal activity.[19] Still, by the 1980s, the position by the US and the UK with regard to PMCs had thawed as the utility of PMCs crystallized, their role gained increasing legitimacy, and their supply of services and goods became increasingly central to military operations. This position is evident in that, by 1985, the US Army formalized procedures for outsourcing logistical support under the Logistics Civil Augmentation Program (LOGCAP), requiring contractors to be ready to provide logistical support on short notice often with few set requirements until well after an engagement had begun. Although not occurring until after the end of the Cold War, the UK passed its *Reserve Forces Act* (Part V) recognizing the deep integration of PMCs into the national defence force to the extent that in conflict situations PMC personnel become "voluntary sponsored reservists".[20]

1.2 Post–Cold War: The entrenchment of the contemporary PMC

In the early 1990s, the end of the Cold War produced dramatic changes in the relationship of the nation-state to the PMC. Three primary factors fueled the growth of the private military industry: (1) large-scale reduction of military forces after the Cold War, which created a surplus of trained military personnel without jobs; (2) the policy shift to privatizing government services whenever possible; and (3) an increase in regional conflicts.[21]

With the demise of an active Soviet military threat, many Western major military powers including the remaining sole superpower—the United States—embarked on an ambitious program of downsizing and privatizing the military. With end of the Cold War, in three years, worldwide military forces shrank by seven million, creating a huge surplus of unemployed military personnel.[22] In addition to the influx of large numbers of unemployed soldiers, the global marketplace also experienced an enormous release of weaponry into channels of commerce.[23] The main suppliers of these weapons were former member states of the USSR and its satellite nations. In particular, German reunification resulted in "essentially a huge yard sale of weaponry, where nearly every weapon in the East German arsenal was sold, most of it to private bidders at cut-rate prices."[24] This arms sale was not limited to light weapons such as grenades, machine guns, and land mines, but included high-ticket items like missile systems and tanks. This increased access to incredibly destructive weapons by nonstatal and corporate entities meant that governments began to lose their monopoly on the means of warfare.

Corporate entities were quick to seize the opportunities offered by government privatization initiatives. At the heart of the privatization initiative (generally in Western countries) was the imperative to reinvent and streamline government, and cut military costs. The net result was that the world's major powers—the traditional actors in regional and intrastate conflicts during the Cold War bipolar era—decreased interference in many conflicts.[25] The consequence was that geopolitical power gradually diffused leaving power vacuums, affording PMCs a golden opportunity to proliferate and fill the same.[26]

With downsizing gathering pace, tighter military budgets which had resulted in the displacement of military personnel and an increase in underutilized military personnel[27] meant retired members of Special Forces and general combatants were readily available, making the easy hiring of robust, effective privatized armies a reality. In an interesting or perhaps inevitable illustration of the free market ideal, there was a rapid proliferation of new PMCs, while existing ones broadened the range of services to harness the surplus expertise. PMCs rapidly drew together the surplus troops and tools offering a wide range of military and security services. The net result of the shifting geopolitical paradigm was evident in weak Third World countries where governments increasingly sought private military resources to fulfill or augment their security needs.[28] Of course, mention must be made of the highly significant strategic use of PMCs by the US in its invasion and occupation of Iraq.

Even international organizations have not been immune to the lure of the array of services offered by PMCs. During the 1994 genocide in Rwanda, with the response of UN member states hamstrung by realpolitik considerations, Executive Outcomes, a South Africa–based PMC offered to respond on short notice and at less cost than a multinational force. Kofi Annan, the then UN undersecretary-general for peacekeeping (and subsequently UN secretary-general) considered the offer. The temptation in the offer is arguably owing to the fact that

> Private companies offer many significant military advantages. A private force can start up and deploy faster than multinational, and perhaps national, forces. Additionally, it probably will have a clearer chain of command and is not subject to the changing political desires or fears of the contributing nations. It will not suffer the national vs. supra-national tensions that plague multinational forces. It may have more readily compatible military equipment training and common language, and possibly greater experience of working together than do ad hoc multinational forces.[29]

Annan concluded that "the world may not be ready to privatize peace."[30] It is significant that he did not discount the matter outright. Not surprisingly, it was not long before UN organs began to hire PMCs to provide security and military muscle in situations requiring rapid reactions and to aid in demining operations.[31] Thus UN's use of PMCs for logistical support and security suggests that the UN employs PMCs much in the same way that countries use them for military operations.[32] The UN is not alone. Other international nongovernmental organizations such as the International Committee of the Red Cross, World Vision, and World Wildlife Fund have jumped on the bandwagon, hiring PMCs for services ranging from protection of facilities and staff in hostile environments to protecting endangered species.[33] PMCs have recognized this large potential market for their services leading to the establishment of the trade group International Peace Operations Association (IPOA), whose members include familiar names in the PMC industry.[34] This means that the industry is well positioned to "lock-in" this niche as well.[35]

There has been dramatic growth in the PMC industry, with a sizable amount of that growth resulting from the invasion of Afghanistan and Iraq. In Iraq alone, armed private security contractors have increased from approximately 20,000 in 2004 to 48,000 in 2007.[36] The size and operational significance of the PMC contingent is such that it rivals some of the world's major military powers. Taking a snapshot comparison, Canada, a major supporter of the United States' invasion of Afghanistan and the 15th most powerful military in the world, has 62,000 active frontline personnel.[37] Australia, home of the 21st most powerful military worldwide—a member of the "Coalition of the Willing" that supported the US invasion of Iraq and its ongoing occupation—has a standing military of 53,000.[38] As an aside, but equally significant on the comparison spectrum, in 2004 Africa, which has the largest concentration of UN Peacekeepers, had approximately 50,000 "blue-helmets" spread over *eight* countries.[39] While it is noted that these parties are not coordinated in the same way a national military may be, that in no way lessens the violence that many armed and trained people can wreak on a civilian population, or the strategic significance they can play in a conflict.

This growth in PMCs challenges the state-based international legal system's three-hundred-year control over military might. PMCs now stand in a position to threaten global order with military force that is less accountable and controllable than state militaries.[40] There is little doubt that the privatization of force affects the role of the state in the regulation of violence and hence one of the basic features of statehood. The failure to have direct regulation of violence means that the state's monopoly over military force is fragmented. In turn the foundations of its authority are, of necessity, shaken as PMCs increasingly shoulder military responsibilities that once belonged to the state.

1.3 Classification of PMCs

From the 1980s to the present, PMCs have been employed in an increasing variety of capacities across the world. For example, corporations have hired PMCs to provide security for their investments in unstable regions and countries, such as Southeast Asia,[41] and the countries Mozambique and Nigeria.[42] Several countries ranging from Saudi Arabia, Hungary, Croatia, and Bosnia to Taiwan, the Philippines, and the US have hired PMCs to train and equip their forces.[43] This trend of training forces often finds employees of PMCs becoming prominent in the actual theater of war, although states are decidedly unwilling to admit that they ever utilize PMCs in battles. However, the reality is that PMCs currently support military operations throughout the world. They have supported peacekeeping efforts in the Balkans, counterdrug operations in Colombia,[44] and the invasion of Iraq. The services PMCs provide cover both traditional and nontraditional niche operations—provision of food and water, military logistical support, and maintenance of armaments. Thus PMCs arguably represent a form of organized corporate mercenarism that, in responding to the need for advanced military, often also presents a new means of disguised efforts by their home states to influence conflicts in which those home states are technically neutral.[45]

From the above, it is evident that PMCs come in a variety of forms, ranging from small consulting firms to massive multinational corporations. They have a variety of purposes and objectives from such things as mundane food and housing supply to strategic foreign policy objectives. They offer a full gamut of military services, many of which have traditionally been regarded as inherently governmental. They not only provide the mundane but also offer training for general or specialist troops; provide intelligence systems; planning and logistical support;[46] lease out military equipment for use on the battlefield; operate weaponry on the battlefield;[47] and, in certain instances, even provide trained, armed soldiers.[48]

Most of the privatization initiatives in the military field are focused on the delegation of support and logistical tasks that were previously carried out by national armed forces. This type of privatization does not appear to be controversial, and many armies around the world have taken steps to privatize these tasks. There is, however, an increasing tendency to contract out certain tasks that involve nonlethal and lethal use of force.[49] For instance, in the 1990s, Executive Outcomes, the South Africa–based PMC mentioned in the introduction, which garnered notoriety for supplying fighting troops that played pivotal roles in the suppression of rebel movements in Angola and Sierra Leone. Several other countries (mainly the US) have chosen to contract out certain "lighter" military tasks, which can also involve the lethal use of force. Such tasks run the range from providing for the security of important buildings or installations in conflict areas, protecting political figures, escorting convoys, and interrogating prisoners to operating weapons on unmanned Predator drones, Global Hawks, and B-2 stealth bombers.[50] Engaging PMCs for this work allows state armed forces to concentrate on the heavier and more earnest offensive tasks. In the course of these PMC activities, "stories of human rights abuses perpetrated by certain contractors, have done much to shape the public image of private military contracting and have led to charges that private military firms are nothing more than bands of thugs operating as modern-day mercenaries."[51]

A 2002 UK government report[52] which lumps PMCs and PSCs together noted that most of the services they provide fall within the areas of military advice,[53] training,[54] and logistic support.[55] The report further notes that PMC services encompass vital military functions and cautions some likely fall within the ambit of combat operations owing to the fact that "the distinction between combat and non-combat operations is often artificial."[56] Logistical support firms, such as the Halliburton subsidiary Kellogg Brown & Root (KBR), handle basic, nonmilitary operations like providing laundry services, catering, sanitation, and transportation personnel.[57] Private security firms, such as Blackwater USA, supply protection to various groups and individuals carrying out reconstruction efforts as well as to various government officials and installations.[58] Examining the wide variety in types, sizes, and services offered by PMCs, it becomes evident that some classification system is necessary.

There are several approaches to classifying PMCs. One widely accepted taxonomy is that offered by Peter Singer, a leading commentator on PMCs. His system is based on a tripartite business typology of service provider, consultancy, and noncore service outsourcing, which squares roughly with proximity to the battle space.[59] Accordingly, Singer has classified PMCs into three subgroups: military support firms, military consulting firms, and military provider firms, with only the third one, military provider firms, providing direct combat services (such as those provided by mercenaries).[60] Singer presents this classification scheme metaphorically as a spear, with the military provider firms comprising the tip of the spear, in recognition that the combat services they offer place them closest to the battle.[61] The metaphor suggests that all PMCs are inherently militaristic, but the small number of military provider firms willing to engage in direct combat pose the most immediate threat. Singer identifies the spear shaft as military consulting firms, which provide advisory and training services. Finally, at the handle end is the PMC providing military support services, which include such mundane services as food supply and basic logistics.

Singer's classification has five strong benefits. First, as mentioned, it is widely accepted. Second, it is a clear and helpful heuristic metaphor identifying for discussion purposes certain types of activities which are, at least potentially, matters of broader concern—particularly the range of services and level of force. Third, it reflects the reality that Krahmann points out in her discussion of developments of UK legislation, namely "a distinction between combat, which remains the prerogative of its national armed forces, and combat support, which may be delegated to private military companies, ... is weakening."[62] Fourth, it merges the PSC and PMC (into the PMF), recognizing the difficulty of sustaining the distinction between the two in many significant contexts—we refer only to the PMC and consider it to include the PSC. Fifth, to a certain extent it recognizes that a new form of warfare has taken the place of the old such that the old notion of a distinct frontline is disappearing,[63] and the distinction between military and civilian in terms of activity is becoming increasingly tenuous.[64]

Singer's taxonomy is lacking, however, in other aspects. For example, it fails to make a distinction between different things that could be the matter of concern. For example, it may be certain weapons, people, contracts, entities, or activities that may draw the concern of the public and the eye of regulators. Failing to identify the thing being classified beyond the corporate form circumscribes certain meaningful dimensions to the discussion, which, while Singer does note elsewhere, fails to call sufficient attention through the typology.[65] Singer's interest goes well beyond the corporate form, as he demonstrates in his masterful discussion of PMC activities, contracting arrangements, and oversight and transparency issues. Further, Singer's classification does not take account of the multiplicity of goods and services that a single corporation may provide. One PMC may do everything from supplying laundry services to military consulting to operating weapons in the theater of war.

Singer's classification roughly accords with the classification outlined by Mark Calaguas who notes that private military contractors can be roughly divided into three categories based on the companies' primary functions: (1) logistical support firms, (2) private security firms; and (3) private military companies.[66] The difficulty in coming up with a definite classification/taxonomy is evident from the fact that Singer and Calaguas are not alone in trying to distinguish among the types of companies and services available within the industry. Despite the aforementioned wide acceptance of Singer's taxonomy and Calaguas's rather similar approach, it does not approach universal acceptance.

Another classification paradigm is proposed by James Davis, a PMC industry professional. Davis offers a classification system whose basis is delineation between legitimate and illegitimate types of mercenaries.[67] According to Davis, "[t]he four legitimate, acceptable categories of mercenaries are the: 1. Regular Foreign Unit, 2. Auxiliary Foreign Unit, 3. Foreign Volunteer; and 4. Private Military Company."[68] Davis elaborates on his classification thus:

> Regular Foreign Units are "long-serving regular formations that exist internally within a larger national military structure activity such as the French Foreign Legion, the Gurkhas, and the Swiss Guards." Auxiliary Foreign Units are units "formed during a conflict and then disbanded on an end to hostilities such as the Flying Tigers." Foreign Volunteers are "foreign soldiers who are not formed specifically into foreign units but are incorporated into regular national formations such as the individuals

> who serve in the Israeli army, and the American Army of the Vietnam era." Private Military Companies are "privately run mercenary organizations that conduct combat or combat support operations who are officially unaligned such as Sandline International and the former Executive Outcomes."[69]

In his important study of PMCs in Iraq, David Isenberg, although following Singer's categorization,[70] seems to implicitly categorize, or at least base, much of his discussion of PMCs on the basis of whether or not they are using UK or US employees as opposed to people from elsewhere. Isenberg is likely doing so as a practical matter in that the UK and the US are those hiring the PMCs in Iraq, and control issues are related back to those countries. Further, although Isenberg catalogs the involvement of personnel from around the world, he clearly states that his interest is "from a U.S. governmental and corporate perspective."[71] Nevertheless, this approach draws attention to the need to be ecumenical in the consideration of the PMC phenomena and to be cautious in thinking about how classification can and should develop.

Other industry participants and observers like to draw the distinction between PMCs on the basis of whether the PMC is acting in a defensive or offensive capacity. For example, Doug Brooks, president of the PMC lobby group (IPOA), suggests that the best term is "Military Service Provider." He then moves on to delineate the differences among them as follows: Nonlethal Service Providers, Private Security Companies, Private Military Companies (Passive), and Private Military Companies (Active).[72] Where the PMC is engaged defensively, they argue that the PMC is actually no more than a private security company, a PSC, such as the company that employs the harmless nightwatchman. This PMC should escape the military classification and the corollary oversight due over a gun-toting mercenary on the battlefield. The only PMC that is a worry, they argue, is the company that supplies fighting troops. All other companies should suffer but the minimum from the spotlight of scrutiny.[73]

This distinction appears to be based on an implicit assumption that there is a real and clear distinction between "good" and "bad" PMCs. The argument appears to be as follows: "Good" PMCs are presumably those that do our good governments' bidding—hence all the patriotic rhetoric and flag waving that comes from them and their advocates. "Good" PMCs support property rights (of multinational corporations and wealthy individuals). "Good" PMCs are "our" PMCs. "Good" PMCs are undoubtedly dedicated to upholding law and order. "Bad" PMCs must simply be the opposite. "Bad" PMCs oppose our government, our foreign policy, and us. "Bad" PMCs do not support MNC property rights. "Bad" PMCs are not committed to upholding law and order. The assumption fails to note that PMCs are blindly maintaining law and order, regardless of how oppressive the law, or unjust and corrupt the order. In other words, it ignores the all important aspect of violence, as "politics by another means."

Further, the distinction is hard to maintain in practice. It is hard to imagine that a PMC that massacred eight civilians including a police officer and wounded thirteen more with heavy automatic weapon fire in a suburb of New York or Sydney or London, as Blackwater did in Baghdad on September 15, 2007, would be labeled anything other than a terrorist group, let alone a member of the "Good" PMC group that had been awarded at least $800 million in security contracts despite previous murdering of civilians.[74] Consider as another example, the "Good" UK PMC, AEGIS. The firm gained notoriety for its "trophy video" showing employees shooting in an apparent random manner at Iraqis.[75] At that time the firm was being awarded one of the most coveted PMC contracts in the Iraq invasion—supervising other PMC contracts totaling $18.4 billion, earning in the process $239 million. Or consider the even more conflicted situation in which Executive Outcomes, the "mercenary army of racist killers," is gratefully greeted in some towns by civilians in Sierra Leone with chanting and cheering, and acknowledged by the humanitarian group "Children Associated with the War".[76]

There appear to be two further assumptions made by PMC advocates. First, they view the commodification of violence as unobjectionable, or at least the lesser of available evils. And second, they see the PMC as an amoral, apolitical provider of technical assistance. The first of these assumptions runs contrary to much political thought, and the second assumption, as we shall see in various places throughout the work, is false except in the narrowest possible sense. It benefits no one to ignore the essentially political nature of violence, whether that violence be for or against a population, a government, or a warlord.

All the above noted distinctions are questionable on their assumptions. As Kathleen Jennings observes:

> The mere fact of the company's employment has a strategic impact regardless of the form of engagement. Additionally, although a client may consider a company's actions on its behalf to be defensive, the population against whom those actions are taken may have a different perspective. The offensive/defensive divide has also broken down notably in places like Iraq, where the situation on the ground can go from defensive to offensive very quickly, such as when private contractors guarding convoys or providing bodyguard services instigate fire against other vehicles in traffic situations. Similarly, companies engaged in pipeline protection in conflict zones (such as parts of Columbia) tend to operate in a grey area of activity that is neither wholly offensive nor defensive. Finally, some companies themselves offer both military and security services, making a strict delineation impossible.

Jennings continues:

> Thus, although it is analytically relevant to difference between companies operating in a theatre of war and offering obviously military services from companies that, for example, provide security guards for the local mall or wealthier neighbourhoods, the military-offensive/security-defensive distinction is overstated and prone to manipulation.[77]

The problem of taxonomy is manifested in a comprehensive definition of the PMC. Consider, for example, the definition offered by Carlos Ortiz: He writes that PMCs are

> legally established multinational commercial enterprises offering services that involve the potential to exercise force in a systematic way and by military means and/or the transfer or enhancement of that potential to clients. The potential to exercise force can materialize when rendering, for example, a vast array of protective services in climates of instability (on land and sea). Transfer or enhancement, on the other hand, occurs when delivering expert military training and other services such as logistics support, risk assessment, and intelligence gathering. It is a "potential" to exercise force because the presence of a PMC can deter aggressors from considering the use of force as a viable course of action.[78]

Similarly and more concisely, Chesterman and Lehnardt define the PMC thus: "PMCs…denotes firms providing services outside their home states with the potential for use of lethal force, as well as training of and advice to militaries that substantially affects their war-fighting capacities."[79] Brooks offers: "legally constituted for-profit company that uses onsite facilities and equipment and non-indigenous personnel to directly and substantially support or enhance a client's security capabilities."[80] All definitions focus on "foreign" activity of corporate entities. Yet, as Schreier and Caparini indicate, this distinction, while possibly of some value at an earlier point in time, is antiquated in any state of the art discussion today. They identify the issues challenging this foreign-domestic distinction as follows:

> It ignores not only the multinational characteristics of the industry and the frequently transborder nature of their activities, but also the ability of these companies to rapidly transfer and recreate themselves as firms across state borders in the effort to find more benign and accommodating corporate environments. Moreover, a majority of wars or conflicts today are internal, thus making it unclear what can be gained by such a distinction.[81]

The "foreign" aspect comes from two areas of concern: first, that those whose land and property are involved have an innate interest, and hence a right to invoke violence to defend that interest. Second, there is the sense that without that right, the issue of violence for profit is morally questionable.

A detailed and thorough discussion of the taxonomy issue is offered by Schreier and Caparini, leading them to a much more sophisticated approach.[82] They propose a set of parameters based on an analysis derived from three spheres of concern, or perhaps more accurately described as multidimensional continuums of privatization, namely, scope of privatization, form of privatization, and purpose of privatization, and then subject the three to a further analysis depending on the dangers involved in the specific privatization. In terms of scope, they examine the breadth and type of work being supplied, and the source of the initiative of the retainer for that work—government or a private group. As to the form, they question whether the form of service is closer to combat or guarding an empty warehouse in a stable country. Their category of purpose places scrutiny on the aggressively political nature of combat services or the quieter building watch, examining the motives of the recipient to determine the purpose. The final variable is a danger analysis. This final analysis sums up and evaluates the dangers presented by the above three continuums, making something of a matrix. Essentially, they find that PMCs are more dangerous when they are retained by organizations other than governments; are operating in a foreign jurisdiction; are offensive in motivations, intentions, aims and goals; are involved in developing countries; replace rather than augment government provided services; have greater power than publicly sponsored neighbors; or are connected to unstable environments.[83] One weakness is that they maintain the distinction between the PSC and the PMC. It is a weakness in that, as they acknowledge repeatedly, the distinction breaks down particularly at critical times—particularly in the critical context of operating in unstable environments. While Schreier and Caparini's taxonomy is perhaps a bit cumbersome for discussion, it is likely the best analysis in terms of both ultimately developing an analysis and evaluation of a specific case and for identifying and sharpening a regulatory focus. Without explicitly identifying it, the reader will note that many of the issues raised throughout this work sound with this taxonomy.

From yet another perspective, the object of concern is neither solely the entity nor the activity, nor location. Such being the case, the focus of discussion, taxonomy, and regulation on entities, activities, and locations misses the point. As Chesterman and Lehnardt observe: "the control of violence through non-state actors should be at the centre of any effort to regulate the industry."[84] While they have certainly identified a central point to the idea of regulation, there are still larger issues on the table. These issues are that violence is a political issue and not solely a matter of firepower, and that the rise of the PMC adds new layers of complexity to the political issue by shifting firepower from the sphere of political debate, making the matter of firepower a simple issue of economics (itself a matter of politics), and those economics being purely private. In other words, the rise of the PMC marks a significant shift on the political landscape, moving the locus of control and accountability for the resort to violence from the public to the private sphere. As Schreier and Caparini observe: "If the control of violence is a fundamental issue in politics, the export of private military and security services is an even more contentious one and therefore ought to be taken very seriously by all democratic states and their governments."[85] Indeed, Kevin O'Brian's taxonomy makes the strategic impact of PMC involvement the crux of proposed regulation.[86]

In considering this broader issue of regulation one must attend to three specific and only tangentially related issues. These are as follows: first, the issue most easily and already identified thus far in the discussion—the imposition of violence on civilian populations and military personnel by armed and privately engaged parties. There is an obvious imperative to control these parties as it runs contrary to the fundamental assumption in favor of peace. Control of these parties acting in a domestic context is usually done through the criminal law and possibly, as will be seen later, through some form of domestic legislation. The issue that a PMC may be acting on a government authorized mission in a foreign jurisdiction in an unstable environment with a weak government in a failing state suggests that the matter is much more complex.

The second issue of concern is the control of suppliers, whether they be the food and housing folk, or the technicians servicing and manning advanced weapons systems operating in a theater of war, or trainers of strategists and troops. The issues here shift into a gray area, that area represented as between Singer's tight categories of tip of the spear but moving to and encompassing the shaft and handle. Certainly a party operating the weapons system of a stealth bomber can wreak more death and destruction in a day than can the "operator" of an AK-47. Further, as identified later in this work, the strategic advice of and training by consultants can be decisive on the battlefield. Policies of what is privatized and no longer supplied by government-controlled entities is a matter of politics, and as we shall see, politics more or less informed by economics. Shifting into the provision of violence support, some form of violence at an arm's length, must be a political decision and accordingly subject to some political, democratic scrutiny. That political scrutiny is one aspect of regulating the supplier PMCs.

Another aspect of regulating suppliers is the matter of accountability for inflicted harm. To date, the answer has been a form of the confidence man's "trust me, trust me" approach. When trouble arises and denial of the incident fails, CEOs shake their heads promising thorough investigations and dealing with the lower level individuals who engaged in unconscionable conduct. In a conference call with investors just after the Abu Ghraib scandal broke, CACI CEO Jack London stated:

> But I want to leave one, main message here. That's that we have not knowingly done anything wrong on any of this. And if we have, in some fashion, we're going to make it right.... We're not aware of any specific charges against any of our people in Abu Ghraib. But if those come forward, we're going to behave in a proper, right and correct fashion. We don't condone or tolerate illegal activity.[87]

Eventually, three employees were implicated. CACI's comment in 2007:

> While three former employees have been cited in various reports in connection with disputed incidents in Iraq, no CACI employee took part or appears in any of the horrific photos released from Abu Ghraib.[88]

In other words, there was no problem because the employees were not in the photos and in any event, even if they were, there is no problem now because they are "former employees." More up-to-date, Blackwater employee shot an Iraqi civilian in May 2007. The company spokesperson Anne Tyrrell offers a classic "trust me, trust me" statement: "Based on incident reports and witness accounts, the Blackwater professional acted lawfully and appropriately."[89] In response to the recent massacre of Iraqis in Baghdad by Blackwater, the company promises a "full investigation." Already there is a spirited dispute about Blackwater's version of the facts.[90] As we note later in the book, Blackwater not only has spirited an employee out of Iraq after he had drunkenly murdered an Iraqi, but the company has also gone to great lengths to avoid liability even for deaths of its own employees. It stretches credulity to imagine that it will conduct or act on anything like a full investigation.

Employees of DynCorp who identified perpetrators of a child prostitution ring in the Balkans to management were labeled whistleblowers and punished.[91] A Triple Canopy supervisor told two employees one morning that he would shoot an Iraqi and then proceeded to do so. The two employees who notified management were labeled whistleblowers and fired.[92] Donald Vance told the FBI that his PMC employer, Shield Group Security, was selling weapons to terrorists. He was imprisoned for 97 days.[93] However, it is not just the PMC that uses the "trust me, trust me" approach. Government finds it most convenient to engage in the same tactics. Again, government use of the approach will be discussed later in the work.

The other aspect of regulating suppliers, which has drawn a significant amount of attention regarding contractor behavior in Iraq, is the matter of war profiteering. Congressional hearings in March 2007 exposed billions of dollars in contractor billings covering such mundane matters as waste to potentially criminal fraud.[94] Certainly the supply of government services requires considerable regulation and oversight. Indeed, the complex procurement and contract management regime has been designed in part to control these issues.

The third issue for regulation of the PMC, implicit in the above argument, is the matter of democratic control of a government in its intention to inflict violence. The PMC supply of services is referred to in the PMC debate as the force multiplier effect. Where a PMC supplies goods and services traditionally provided by a government military, members of the military who were traditionally reserved to supply tasks are now freed up to take up arms and engage in other more lethal duties. This concentration of lethal duties to the military, while outsourcing all other aspects of a government's military adventures, masks and shields the government and major actors in the war machine. Where these tasks are outsourced to PMCs, the amount of resources committed to the war effort are more easily hidden from the populace. People are merely involved in loosely related and apparently domestic or multinational industries—they do not see themselves as supporting a war effort. Further, when the government is able to outsource these activities to civilians, it will need fewer conscripts on the ground to project its violent power. Thus these service provider PMCs allow governments to hide more easily the amount of a country's resources being committed to an objective and reduce the public power to oppose government violence. This subversion of democratic power results from the reduced demand for higher numbers of people to be members of the military, allowing a seemingly smaller military dedicating military personnel on the ground the more widely objectionable activity of getting on battlefield. Further, it shields the government from democratic oversight on many of its activities as it can provide an impenetrable maze of contracts and claims of commercial confidentiality.

Importantly, despite the focus of the discussion so far on government use of PMCs, it should not be forgotten that the PMC has been an important participant in the support of multinational corporations' ability to operate in unstable settings. The legitimacy of those operations may or may not be in question, but again, regardless of the actors and location, the infliction of violence is a political issue and hence subject to political debate and oversight. PMCs operate not only for aboveboard businesses, but have become a means of assistance to terrorists and criminals allowing them to amass significant caches of weapons and train.[95]

In light of the foregoing, we will use a heterogeneous approach to taxonomy, sensitive to context as would seem appropriate from Schreier and Caparini's taxonomy. Singer's paradigm, focused primarily on armed private personnel, weapons operators, and consultants, covers the broad spectrum of suppliers and contexts. Given the special attention to and concern of the primary focus of the present work, namely the control of violence, we will refer to the generally accepted taxonomy of Singer from time to time. In doing so, our heterogeneous paradigm requires the reader to be cognizant of a number of caveats. PMCs can and do shift effortlessly between the various categories; straddle the categories; and as corporate actors, change their characteristics with developments, acquisitions, and spin-offs of subsidiaries.

Further, it should be kept in mind that in certain instances narrower definitions may be unhelpful, such as dealing with corporate conglomerates providing a multitude of goods and services, or where the nature of the activity may cause actors to shift across the boundaries of a system such as Singer's, and hence in the interests of sharper analysis on the control of violence, narrower definitions will be set down. Finally, we believe that it is important in the discussion of the PMC to consider extending Singer's metaphor and applying it to the nature of the interaction between states and PMCs. As is self-evident, a spear requires a thrower (e.g., a state, corporation, or other individuals with the financing necessary to retain a PMC). That aspect of the thrower will be explored in greater detail and at greater length as occasion arises throughout the work. In line with Ortiz's definitional emphasis on force, and for purposes of regulatory focus, the discussion in the book will emphasize particularly those parties (1) organized in a legal corporate form and (2) involved in the delivery of actual or potential force.

One final note concerning the use of the term "contractor" needs to be made before the issue of taxonomy is set down. The term contractor is often used when referring both to the PMC and to the individual human carrying out duties on the ground. This use of the term causes unnecessary and unwarranted confusion. While it may advance the cause of neoliberal values and outsourcing by emphasizing individual choice in contracting for his or her rights and responsibilities, it may not in fact be legally correct as the issue of an individual's relationship with a body corporate, in this case the PMC, may well be found to be employer-employee, regardless of the niceties of the contract of employment. Throughout the current work, the individual humans will be referred to as "employees." By using this term, we emphasize the control the PMC has over those parties it engages regardless of whether a court of law would find those parties to be individual contractors or employees. In addition, it sharpens the focus on the issues under consideration, namely, the PMC. Finally, it acknowledges the reality that individual humans are engaged in at least some of the activities of concern; they may well be mercenaries and hence already addressed by current law.

1.4 PMC centralization in national military operations

Two examples of the extent of contemporary PMC involvement in military activities highlight the significance of the presence of these battlefield contractors. First, America's involvement in the drug and insurgent war in Colombia, and second, its military campaign in Iraq that commenced in 2003. Casting a glance at South America, in Colombia the provision of services by PMCs entails a whole range of services, including flying Blackhawk helicopters in "drug eradication missions"[96] on behalf of the US government as well as manning surveillance aircraft in the Colombian government's military campaign against guerrilla rebels. Turning to the Middle East, the invasion of Iraq by the "Coalition of the Willing" relied on thousands of technical experts, from PMCs dispensed to "operate communications systems, repair helicopters, fix weapons systems and link the computers with the troops to command centres."[97] As mentioned above, the UK recognizes the essential contribution of PMC personnel by creating the "Sponsored Reserves" category.

So enmeshed are private military personnel in the war effort in Iraq that their duties overlap with those of regular military personnel.[98] Armed security guards from firms such as Blackwater Security protect US bases and frequently engage in battles with "insurgents" and other attackers,[99] while California Analysis Center, Incorporated (CACI), a PMC often referred to as "Colonels and Captains, Inc.," by critics,[100] provided a variety of tasks in Iraq, including the debriefing of personnel, intelligence report writing, quality control, and interrogation of detainees.[101] A US Government Accountability Office sets the number of private security providers—i.e., private armed personnel—at 48,000.[102] As a percentage of the armed American presence, PMC personnel are the equivalent of 33 percent of the US troops in Iraq. They outnumber UK troops, the second largest contingent of the Coalition, by a ratio of 6 to 1 and by May 2007 all other coalition partners, whose combined troops number 12,600, or roughly 8 percent of the 145,000 US troops on the ground.[103] While it is noted that these parties are not coordinated in the same way a national military may be, that in no way lessens the violence that many armed and trained people can wreak on a civilian population, or the strategic significance they can play in a conflict.

If one uses a broader definition and includes those providing logistical support and reconstruction, PMCs have approximately 182,000 contractors on the ground in Iraq as of July 2007.[104] They hail from the US, the UK, as well as developing countries as diverse as Fiji, Nepal, Chile, and Iraq, and provide support and logistics services, such as weather forecasting, food preparation, construction, and mechanical work.[105] These security contracts provide significant contingents of armed individuals under the command and control of single private corporate entities. For example, fifteen thousand security contractors are local Iraqis, mostly hired by Erinys, a British security company charged with guarding oil facilities.

While the rise of the post–Cold War PMC may be seen as a success for the globalized free market place, these "[PMCs] represent a reconstituted form of organized corporate mercenarism that is responding to the need for advanced military expertise."[106] PMCs now support numerous military operations throughout the world and act as crucial components in enhancing the capabilities of countries both in the Third World and in the West. Within the military establishment of countries whether small, medium, or large, thousands of PMC technical experts operate communications systems, maintain military aircraft, fix weapons systems, link troops to command centers, and in several cases train national armies. PMCs are now in a position to amass unchecked power to affect conflict resolution, world economic stability, and geo-strategic negotiations.[107] The decentralization of international security from state-organized militaries threatens the traditional Westphalian paradigm of the state as the natural entity in control of the legal use of lethal military force. Although they do not like to admit it, PMC employees' roles range from providing simple services to actually fighting at the "the tip of the spear." As "corporate mercenary" firms become larger, they entrench themselves as key players in the crucial sovereign function of use of military force and now stand in a position to increasingly influence and/or engage in decision-making processes traditionally exercised by politicians and government entities.[108]

1.5 PMCs and mercenaries: Tailored from the same cloth?

Concerns about PMCs, "like concern about mercenaries, pirates, and terrorists, stems from the inherent violence of their profession combined with a lack of control over and accountability for their actions,"[109] particularly where they are acting or viewed as being outside national legal regimes. Matters are not helped by the fact that governments' use of PMCs is rarely transparent and in most cases is deliberately opaque, deniable, and veiled from public and parliamentary view as discussed in detail in chapter 3 of this book. Like the soldiers of fortune of yester years, PMC operations are of questionable legality.[110] Firstly, to the extent that such law can be identified, it provides little guidance regarding the services PMCs provide, whether training or actual combat.[111] Secondly, despite a multitude of declarations and resolutions by the UN and several anti-mercenary conventions (discussed in chapter 5), state practice does not give rise to an absolute international norm banning the use of mercenaries. Lastly, states have been lax in promulgating and enforcing municipal laws that restrict their citizens' ability to serve PMCs (see chapter 4).

A common and appropriate starting point for discussion of the state-PMC relationship is the familiar and less controversial figure, the mercenary soldier—the person who fights neither for patriotism nor legal duty, but for economic gain. Generally speaking, mercenaries are internationally condemned and outlawed, at least nominally.[112] The simple principle is that civilians should not engage in violence independent of state sanction. Indeed, this principle underlies much criminal law. The principle encounters a sharp challenge in the instance of PMCs that carry on activities that seem to fall on the same paradigm as that of "traditional" mercenaries.

The problem, particularly highlighted in chapter 5, is that the international community has not arrived at a unanimous or effective definition of the term mercenary.[113] However, it is clear that it at least includes a person who is foreign to a conflict, participating in combat with the aim of securing personal gain. What makes this definition difficult to apply to PMCs in a blanket way as discussed in chapter 3 above is the wide range of services PMCs offer, including training, consulting, logistical support, technical support, and potentially combat services. At one end of the continuum, the PMC sector overlaps with the military hardware and software providers. These providers now regularly provide staff to maintain, operate, and train in the use of equipment they have sold. At the other end of the continuum, PMCs can provide commando troops supported by fighter jets and attack helicopters.

There are at least four reasons why states do not equate mercenaries with PMCs, despite that some PMCs provide mercenary (combat) services. They do not do so for practical, political, or other reasons. First, the definition of mercenary is aimed at identifying and deterring individual human actors. This aim is evident in the drafting of the 1989 International Convention against the Recruitment, Use, Financing and Training of Mercenaries, which concentrates on the recruitment and use of individual mercenaries or on the status of individual mercenaries if they are captured during battle.[114] The modern-day reality is that corporations, and not individuals, are now providing private military services, including traditional mercenary services—i.e., the provision offense oriented, combat troops. This corporate repackaging is the primary reason why states are unable or unwilling to make direct comparisons between the individual mercenary of old and the new corporate PMCs.

A second reason is that the hallmark of a mercenary—combat for sale—is not a hallmark shared by the majority of PMCs. Only a small number of PMCs provide offensive combat services. To date, states have not attempted to deconstruct the PMC industry by differentiating between the limited numbers of combat ready PMCs and the more numerous PMCs that provide support and/or security services but do not engage in combat as a core business. Accordingly, for states to regulate PMCs they first must differentiate between a broad range of PMCs and distinguish not only between PMCs but also between the activities carried on within a single large PMC that may provide a broad range of services.[115]

A third reason is that the refined marketing, sophisticated lobbying, and professional business practices of modern PMCs lend them credibility and encourages states to treat them differently from mercenaries.[116] While states view "traditional" mercenaries stereotypically as maverick, malevolent, and individual misfits motivated solely by the prospect of gain, they tend to view PMCs more positively. Indeed, as discussed in greater detail in chapter 3, the PMC lobby has been used to provide advice to government. In short, while PMCs are viewed as professional and credible corporate partners, "traditional" mercenaries are viewed by states as unreliable and without credibility. The fourth and final reason why states are reticent to equate PMCs with mercenaries involves economic rationalism and the trend toward policies that seek to increase efficiency in the public sector through the introduction of private sector competition. In this context, states see financial and political advantage in using PMCs as cost effective military service providers.

A stark disparity exists between the international emphasis on prohibiting mercenary activity and the reality of a vigorous and expanding professional PMC industry that provides a full range of defence services. This disparity is significant for states considering how best to integrate PMCs into their national legal framework and whether or not to regulate the PMC industry. A significant tension exists between those who believe PMCs should be treated as just another growing industry able to provide services that were once government provided services, and those who believe PMCs should be treated as pariahs and threats to national and international security—a conservative approach that parallels the historic perspective on mercenaries and opposes the commodification of violence holding to the potential of democratic accountability by maintaining the state monopoly of violence. These four are the main reasons why the mercenary and the PMC discourses have not merged.

Although in form resembling their antecedents, PMCs have developed a *modus operandi* compatible with the needs and strictures of the post–Cold War, state-based international system leading to both implicit and explicit legitimacy. Explicit legitimacy is based on the increasing use of PMCs by countries which lend them a veneer of legitimacy. Implicit legitimacy is derived from both a lack of vociferous condemnation and their participation in normal business activities, including developing industry associations, market formations, training, lobbying, and participation in traditional financial markets. To consolidate their legitimacy, PMCs have taken considerable steps to upgrade the image of what has historically been an unsavory profession. Contemporary PMCs are now incorporated businesses listed on the world's major stock exchanges[117] with employees often recruited from among the most decorated echelons of various military establishments. PMCs form part of a security industry that in 2006 had an annual turnover estimated at $100 billion.[118] It is not surprising that Fortune 500 and S&P 500 companies have taken notice of the potential profits. Regardless of what opinion one has of the PMC industry, one thing is certain: it is growing and profitable. For instance, in the US (one of the key PMC clients), from the 1990s PMCs publicly traded on the stock market saw their stock grow at "twice the rate of the Dow Jones Industrial Average."[119] And indeed, the Iraq war has only boosted that growth. For example, within a year of the invasion of Iraq and as a result of that invasion, revenues of UK-based PMCs had increased from $320 million to over $1.6 billion[120] and the defense market itself has trebled in value.[121]

1.6 Conclusion

In essence the monopolization of force by the state has never been absolute. States have not been averse to incorporating or capturing the "violence of privateers—a form of violence external to the state—and selectively sanctioning it when profitable or expedient".[122] In past centuries, states relied on private organizations with their own military power to undertake foreign ventures. These included founding colonies, which states themselves lacked the revenue to finance or to assist states pursue hegemonic ambitions. The state's monopolization of force is a rather recent phenomenon. Despite the state's right to hold a monopoly on the use of force, there is nothing natural about this arrangement. "Until the mid-nineteenth century, military knowledge and labour were an alienable commodity in an international market. Sovereignty bore little or no relation to the control of organized violence."[123] The reality past and present is that "[as] long as humanity has waged war, there have been mercenaries."[124]

The emergence of PMCs and their formidable financial and military capabilities does not fit into the paradigm of the state as an entity bearing monopoly over military force. Commenting on the decentralization of state control over the use of force, Montgomery Sapone notes: "This change in military relationship between states and private entities suggests that some states no longer exert explicit control over military technology or manpower. Military skill is becoming increasingly privatized and commodified."[125] The dangers of the privatization of force and concerns regarding the dangers of excessive and arbitrary uses of force finally materialized on a large and well publicized scale in the recent invasion of Iraq where PMCs are engaged heavily in a wide range of operations from transport of supplies to interrogation of prisoners. The central claim that private punishment, policing, and military corporations violate human rights and international law obligations more often than public punishment, policing, and military institutions[126] found practical manifestation in the various scandals that engulf the military operation in Iraq as it did in earlier controversies.[127]

As nonstate actors, PMCs enjoy the rights and privileges of private actors, including the privileges of free movement, relatively minor scrutiny of action, and the privacy accorded to citizens, and lack of accountability to the general public. In this new landscape, states are choosing to interact with PMCs—to retain their services and marshal their capacity—and in the process states are themselves changing in character. PMCs are not waiting passively for states to interact with them; rather, PMCs are locating themselves strategically in key militarily strong states and actively lobbying to be retained by states. These interactions between PMCs and states are generally carried out in private without the glare of international public scrutiny that typically surrounds decisions by states to expand, modernize, or mobilize their military capacity.

The heavy reliance on PMCs has contributed to increased private contractor presence on the battlefield. Many states (small and large) now rely on them for long-term support for major defence systems.[128] With technologically advanced systems requiring PMCs to be responsible for long-term support, military establishments are losing the capacity to manage and generate the ability to maintain key components of war, including not only command systems but also military communication systems and surveillance apparatus.[129] PMCs are thus becoming the key supporting actors of military operations, and now stand in a position to threaten global order with military force that is less accountable and controllable than state militaries.[130] Signs of the decline of the nation-state and the growing role of private military companies are symptoms of a large, dangerous challenge to the aspirations of order in the world, an order represented by the system of nation-states and the Rule of Law.[131]

Fundamentally, the real risk of gross misbehavior by PMCs is not their operations in their home states—predominantly Western countries—but rather in the execution of contracts they have in weak or failing states. Local authorities in such areas often have neither the power nor the wherewithal to challenge these firms. With the PMC industry growing dramatically in size and influence, the need for analysis, discussion, and an innovative policy response is now acute. Any proposed response to the PMC phenomenon must take into account the changing international conflict paradigm where economic resources translate into military might as never before[132] and where nonstate actors can finance war as readily as states.[133]

In sum, the meteoric rise of PMCs in the period from the mid-1970s to the present day creates a whole host of legal, moral, and political problems for individual states and the international community. The problems these corporations raise range from such relatively mild matters as the appropriateness of hiring armed security firms to protect humanitarian organizations in countries where dire poverty is the norm[134] to such highly controversial activities as the overthrowing of governments, the suppression of internal rebellions supporting independence and self-determination movements,[135] and the legal and moral responsibility for human rights abuses resulting from PMC activities.[136] It is these critical matters that will be at the heart of discussion and analysis in the subsequent chapters.

2

The Corporate Form and the Private Military Corporation

2.1 Introduction

Among the more prominent PMCs currently engaged in Iraq is Blackwater USA.[1] It claims to be "the most comprehensive professional military, law enforcement, security, peacekeeping, and stability operations company in the world."[2] Blackwater USA comprises five companies: Blackwater Training Center, Blackwater Target Systems, Blackwater Security Consulting, Blackwater Canine, and Blackwater Air (AWS).[3] Blackwater states:

> Our clients include federal law enforcement agencies, the Department of Defence, Department of State, and Department of Transportation, local and state entities from around the country, multi-national corporations, and friendly nations from all over the globe. We customize and execute solutions for our clients to help keep them at the level of readiness required to meet today's law enforcement, homeland security, and defence challenges. Any and all defence services supplied to foreign nationals will only be pursuant to proper authorization by the Department of State.[4]

It notes elsewhere that "in addition, certain defence services or products provided to foreign nationals or supplied overseas may be subject to U.S. rules and regulations requiring licensing and authorization by the U.S. Government."[5] As to the extent of its facilities, it boasts, "over 6000 acres of private land, we have trained and hosted over 50,000 Law Enforcement, Military and civilian personnel."[6] In line with corporate profit-making objectives, Blackwater has hired former commandos from the Pinochet regime who can be paid a (relatively) paltry $4,000 per month.[7]

Military Professional Resources, Inc. (MPRI), boasts 1,500 employees worldwide.[8] It was acquired for $34.5 million by L3 Communications in June 2000.[9] It offers as its mission the following:

> Providing the United States and international clients with programs of uncompromising quality that enhance security, justice and well-being—programs

> that are built on the bedrocks of experience, integrity and the values that flow from a lifetime of service to the nation.[10]

The UK PMC lobby group, the British Association of Private Security Companies (BAPSC), includes in its charter a commitment from members to "Decline to accept contracts for the provision of security services where to do so will conflict with applicable human rights legislation," and "Decline to provide security services that might be contrary to UK values and interests." In other words, UK PMC members of BAPSC are committed to the objectives of respecting human rights and upholding British foreign policy objectives.

One cannot help but note the political rhetoric in these mission statements. Phrases like "service to the nation" beg the question: is service to the nation an appropriate corporate mission or is it a necessary hallmark of a PMC? Is it not equally likely that PMCs will be disservice to the nation, or does it provide a social license for objectionable business? PMC may well increase animosity against the US or UK abroad on account of PMC's defense of US and UK multinational corporate interests. PMCs have intentionally killed local populations opposed to their presence or activities.[11] Equally predictably, PMCs have accidentally killed local members of the population who simply mind their own business, as for example, an elderly scientist recently killed by PMC employees in Baghdad.[12]

Consider also the UK firm AEGIS Defense Services Ltd. and its political rhetoric. Its CEO is Tim Spicer, the well-connected former Sandline CEO, and one board member is Robert McFarlane, who was the National Security Advisor to US President Ronald Reagan. The firm offers the following self-description on its website:

> AEGIS is a London based, privately owned, British security and risk management company with overseas offices in Afghanistan, Bahrain, Iraq, Kenya, Nepal and the USA. We have substantial experience and a worldwide client-base, including governments, international agencies and the multinational corporate sector. We are a registered and active UN contractor, a major security provider to the US government and security advisor to the Lloyds Joint War Risk Committee.
>
> [O]ur clients ... benefit from the extensive capabilities of our personnel, built up through careers in the military, diplomatic and intelligence services, as well as in the police, journalism, the UN, finance and commerce.... All AEGIS activities are conducted with the highest degree of discretion, integrity and client confidentiality within the framework of national and international law, whilst at the same time maintaining complete corporate transparency. AEGIS is committed to proper industry accountability and regulation.[13]

The corporate aspect of the PMC is a significant development in the development of the privatization of violence. As the AEGIS description makes clear, it is a multinational, highly capable of a variety of tasks, very well-connected, private company. It notes one of the many inherent conflicts for PMCs and those who would regulate it—"discretion...whilst maintaining corporate transparency."

PMCs do not see their mission as ending with offering assistance to governments in the execution of good works. They have been advocating a deeper involvement in humanitarian endeavors. In an article bearing the creative and curious title "Ruthless Humanitarianism: Why Ignoring the Private Security Option in Darfur Is a Mistake,"[14] PMC lobbyist Doug Brooks argues that PMCs should be hired for the job. His title implies that unlike humanitarians, PMCs are committed to ending the suffering.

In this chapter we examine in detail the objectives of the corporation, its history, governance, and control.

2.2 The corporate form as the distinctive difference between individual mercenaries and private armies

From a legal perspective, the PMC is not different from any other business corporation in that it has the same structure, rights, duties, and obligations. It is controlled by a board of directors, has shareholders who hope to receive dividends from corporate profit, and engages in activity with the sole purpose of turning a profit. In other words, despite the PMC's attempts to establish itself as a selfless tool of freedom and democracy, placing itself at the feet of a benevolent state, or intergovernmental organization and NGO saving humanity through humanitarian intervention, or simply supporting other corporations' commercial endeavors, the PMC has the single objective function of all business corporations—simply generating profits for shareholders.[15]

What sets the PMC apart from other business corporations is the nature of the service it provides. The PMC is prepared to engage in lethal violence for the right price. In other words, the profitable business it pursues runs parallel to critical political objectives. Further, not only do its methods permit and include killing, indeed, death of enemies may be an explicit, specific objective. In other words, murder or contract killing may be an important part of its mission. As we have seen in chapter 1, the objection that they provide "security" hardly addresses the fact that at least some are engaged with the specific objective of killing "enemies." Furthermore, the gray zone of armed personnel in combat zones and areas of civil unrest makes the distinction between the security provider and combatant irrelevant in important contexts. Most parties would object and indeed suggest that "contract killing" is, or at least ought to be, illegal. Is it the same with respect to corporations engaged in contract killing? This question leads to the central question of this chapter: What does the presence of the corporate form do to alter what in other contexts would be termed mercenarism? A global answer is simple: power.

Whether it is a single mercenary or a group of mercenaries prepared to act as a private army, even where organized into a legal partnership, such a group cannot achieve all it could were it to adopt the corporate form. Peter Singer has identified the distinctive features of mercenaries as the following: foreigners, independent of the organized structured force, motivated by money and not political goals, recruited to avoid legal prohibitions, and focused on combat.[16] Singer notes that the features distinguishing the PMC from the mercenary are the following: corporate structure, business profit driven rather than individual profit driven, public legal entity, wider range and varied clientele, public specialized recruitments, ties to corporate holdings, and financial markets.[17] Singer is certainly correct in his analysis as far as it goes; however, the really distinctive contribution is the far greater power—military, financial, and political—that the corporate form has facilitated.

One distinctive PMC power comes from the corporation's ability to attract significant amounts of capital. PMC market size and growth potential makes them attractive investments, drawing in more capital, fueling yet greater need to sell services, making them more powerful participants in political, business, and military arenas. PMCs, facilitated by the corporate form, have become greater military powers than their client states. Indeed, as noted in chapter 1, PMCs on the ground in Iraq rival some of the world's leading militaries. This size, power, and private form change significantly the political arena in which peoples and states have traditionally operated and been in competition for control over resources. Singer observes that inter-PMC warfare for control of resources is not only a danger without historical precedent, but has already occurred.[18] PMCs, in this context, threaten to become what the UN Special Rapporteur has described as agents for the "multinational neo-colonialism of the twenty-first century."[19]

This statement identifies another set of concerns with respect to the corporate form in relation to combat. As a corporation grows in size, it grows in power. Such power is not likely to be limited to military power. An organization, which can call up its own military force, is unlikely to sit patiently at the negotiating table waiting for settlement while political interests find resolution or economic opportunity passing by. Further, PMCs, both domestically and abroad, need to be looking for opportunities to sell their services—violence to achieve political and economic ends—often inflicted on civilians. Stronger powers such as the US have no shortage of client states or colonies where they wish to interfere to advance their own interests.[20] Where the formal military must be engaged, the previously mentioned transaction costs can be prohibitive. The PMC with its peculiar efficiencies is too tempting an option to be overlooked, particularly when there are lobbyists at work to keep them ever in view of government officials, corporate executives, and international agencies. To answer the question of the significance of the corporate form in greater depth, we first turn to an examination of the corporation from a legal perspective and then to the distinctive implications of the corporate form for the PMC.

The analysis in this chapter requires two caveats. First, the analysis is focused on PMCs providing two types of services: security providers in conflict zones and providers of combat services. As noted in chapter 1, the reality for a host of PMC security providers is that their employees experience a significant "gray zone" between their roles as bodyguards and combatants when operating in conflict zones. This approach has been taken because the problems formed in the provision of those services provide a sharp relief illustrating the acute problems resulting from the introduction of the corporation into the provision of military services. The second caveat which pertains to the law is that legislation and case law is only occasionally mentioned. The reason for this choice is that the doctrines considered in this chapter are generally similar and widely dispersed throughout the world's legal systems as is evidenced in the notes.

2.3 The corporation: History, theory, and the PMC

The origins of the corporation can be traced back to the Justinian Code, the church of the late middle ages, and to the trade concessions granted to groups of itinerant traders. The business corporation was originally formed and recognized as a vehicle for public good.[21] Investors who formed such companies as the Dutch East India Company or the Hudson Bay Company understood that their financial objective coincided with a sovereign purpose: public good.[22] As stated by Sir William Blackstone in his classic eighteenth century *Commentaries on the Laws of England*:

> It has been found necessary, when it is for the advantage of the public to have any particular rights kept on foot and continued, to constitute artificial persons, who may maintain a perpetual succession, and enjoy a kind of legal immortality. These artificial persons are called bodies politic, bodies corporate (corpora corporata), or corporations.[23]

This public good basis for the corporation has been carried forward into the current political and business dialog by a number of different ways, such as advancing the notion that corporations provide increased economic benefits activity. As Milton Friedman put it in his famous article entitled "The Social Responsibility of Business Is to Increase Its Profits,"[24] the business corporation has a social duty to create profit, and where it fails to do so, it is failing its responsibility and hence liable to whatever sanctions (presumably bankruptcy and dissolution or takeover) the market would impose.

Corporations were created originally by the grant of a charter by a sovereign recognizing a group of individuals as working together in a group. These corporations, where focused on business, were much like current partnerships in that they did not have any legal status independent of the investors, and the investors were not protected from claims against the corporation. There was no limited liability. In North America, corporations were used to build public works such as canals and railroads. Their activities were carefully defined and limited by the terms of their charters. Activities undertaken outside of those authorized by the state were *ultra vires*, and actions done in breach of constitutional powers were susceptible to being unwound, and as to the corporation, to have its charter revoked. Early corporate actors engaging in the unauthorized activities could be punished and the defrauded were given a variety of remedies.[25]

Over the course of time, the corporate vehicle changed. For example, instead of requiring any special dispensation from the government, legislation was enacted permitting the creation of a corporation by simple registration and payment of a nominal fee. Further, no longer were corporations restricted in the activities they could carry on. Indeed, it is fair to say that today any legal activity may be conducted by way of the corporate vehicle.

The corporation is a very flexible vehicle used historically by governments, civil associations, and private citizens alike for a variety of purposes. This variety in purposes is reflected to some degree by a parallel in the variety of corporations, including

1. the business corporation designed for profitable enterprises,
2. the corporation sole which is an office held by a succession of individuals,
3. government corporations set up to serve public purposes such as the delivery of public goods and statutory authorities,
4. mutual companies where members own and benefit directly from corporate business activities, and
5. incorporated benevolent associations.

From this wide variety of corporations, only the business corporation is of interest in terms of analysis bearing on the PMC.

In order to understand the various rights and duties of the business corporation and its participants, as well as the nature and role of government in corporate regulation, it is necessary first to have a clearer idea of the nature of the corporation itself. There are a number of conflicting views, reflecting both the legal history of the corporate form and political ideology often as expressed in the language of economics. We turn next to briefly examine these theories.

2.3.1 Concession theory of the corporation

One theory of the corporation is the concession theory. Based on the historical origins of the corporation in which an initial concession of the monarch (by Royal Charter) or government (by passing an Act of Parliament) was necessary to create a corporation, the concession theory holds that the corporation is a member of society by privilege, given special rights and privileges, and accordingly, subject to special duties to and regulation by society.[26] This type of corporation usually had exclusive, monopolistic trade concessions, and was subject ultimately to royal supervision. Essentially, it paid for the concession, or provided some type of public good such as finance of wars or other such royal imperatives.[27] The creation of these corporations was quite restricted and hence alternative corporate forms were invented by creative lawyers. Thus, although in the nineteenth century, there was also the joint stock company—essentially an unlimited liability partnership—in addition to the corporation just discussed, the two forms were merged through legislation in the UK in the 1844 Companies Act, which forced all larger partnerships to be incorporated bodies with separate identities, and permitted the ongoing personal mutual obligations of partners to continue in partnerships limited in size.[28]

The concession that is emphasized in the theory is the concession by the government to a group of people to recognize them as a collective. In other words, rather than a mere gathering of individuals, it creates a collective identity and concedes to that collective a separate legal identity with its own rights and privileges. Those holding to the concession theory have a broader view of the corporation and believe that the privileges of limited liability for shareholders, the protection of corporate officers from suit for actions undertaken by the corporation, and the right to sue and be sued bring with them special duties. They are not convinced that these particular attributes would be agreed to in the market, nor that all bargainers are equal in terms of power and alternatives, nor that all the transactions are completely voluntary, at least in the sense of bargaining.[29] Accordingly, concession theorists look to government for regulation and tend to view government as having a prima facie right and interest in the regulation of the corporations.

One of the important strengths of the concession theory, although no longer actively advocated,[30] is that it sits well with the legal doctrine of the personhood of the corporation or notion of the corporation as an entity separate from the participants. The notion of personhood of the corporation is that the law has created an entity with rights and duties independent of all its participants, be they directors, officers, or shareholders. The person of the corporation is the object of fiduciary duties of directors, of regulation, and of criminal, tort and contractual liability. But the law is highly inconsistent in its invocation of the doctrine of the corporate person. When granting rights and privileges, it easily recognizes the corporate person.

When creating liabilities, or imposing sanctions, however, it tends to ignore the notion of personhood, preferring instead to find individual humans at fault—a reflection of the liberal bias of law.[31] The lack of clarity in law concerning personhood proves to be a major stumbling block in the control of corporations and development of appropriate control measures.[32]

2.3.2 Contractual theory of the corporation

The contractual theory emphasizes the voluntary nature of the participants in corporation. There is no recognition of a separate entity per se. Rather, the corporation is only what parties have or would have contracted given the opportunity. As such, there is no corporate entity, but merely a nexus of contracts. This view portrays the corporation as a spot market (where goods and services are sold on an instantaneous basis) with no corporate existence or center of authority. The following quote from economists Alchian and Demsetz is illustrative:

> It is common to see the firm characterized by the power to settle issues by fiat, by authority, or by disciplinary action superior to that available in the conventional market. This is delusion. The firm...(has no power of fiat, no authority, no disciplinary action any different in the slightest degree from ordinary market contracting between any two people.[33]

If one takes this view, any regulation is hard to justify, regardless of whether one holds the classical liberal's suspicion of the state or not. As Greenwood observes: "Contract is the classic center of the liberal conception of an ideal society of free, equal and autonomous people joining together on the basis of consent and not coercion."[34] State interference in setting or scrutinizing contractual terms between private citizens would be a highly contentious step.

Essentially, the contractual theory views the corporation as mimicking a market. Those of this view believe the market needs little or no regulation, so too the corporation needs no or little regulation. They argue that the markets for corporate control, management talent, and product provide suitable controls.[35] The legal attributes of limited liability, litigation rights, continuous existence, perpetual succession, right to hold property, and have a common seal, are nothing more than what would have been contracted for in the market. Perhaps most thoroughly and convincingly argued by Easterbrook and Fischel, the position that the corporation is merely a network or nexus of independent contractors has gained the upper hand in the argument.[36]

As to the peculiar benefits granted to the corporation, limited liability for shareholders, the protection of corporate officers from suit for actions undertaken by the corporation, and the right to sue and be sued, the advocates of the nexus-of-contracts model simply state that these benefits would have been contracted for in any event and accordingly are not novel.[37] In other words, according to contractarians, everything is as it should be because it all results from freely contracting individuals all seeking their best interests.[38]

To the extent that a corporation is contractual, that contract has been most convincingly explained as a contract that forms a constitution.[39] This view of the corporation is that the members "contract" (in an economic sense of the word, rather than a legal sense) to form a constitution, and that the constitution sets out the powers and relationships between the parties. Legal scholars note that the term "contract" (discussed in the nexus-of-contracts model) is a metaphor for the relationships, and like all relationships, in some sense, an inadequate one at that. They note that unlike all other contracts, the "corporate contract" has a number of peculiarities. For example, the corporate contract can be altered by a majority against individual "contractors" wishes, courts have no equitable jurisdiction in correcting contractual mistakes, there are many hurdles for an individual to mount should she or he wish to enforce rights against the corporation, the contract is not between persons but is attached to the shares, and "contractors" rights to sue a corporation are severely limited.[40] Even a superficial review of this list makes it evident that the corporation is not a mere contractual arrangement, but in fact an independent entity granted limited liability, perpetual succession, and facilitating the separation of ownership from control. Nevertheless the contractual view has a number of benefits: it has rhetorical power, utility in economic modeling, coincides with neoliberal ideology, and is conceptually readily and easily accessible. Finally, and importantly, it is the dominant model among politicians, bureaucrats, and many influential corporate law scholars.

2.3.3 Implications of corporate theory for the PMC

In sum, where the PMC is viewed as a concession from society of whom government is the representative and a separate entity distinct from its members and participants, there is considerable role for regulation. Not only does it recognize the state's right to impose whatever sanctions the state may choose, the nature of the regulation is potentially broader. Such regulations could include things like controlling objects of the corporation (i.e. activities), disclosure of activities perhaps paralleling the financial disclosure rules, and participation in management or direction to name a few.[41] Adopting this theory creates a prima facie case for states to confront, limit, and restrict activities, and hold accountable those entities that fail to follow the law.[42]

By way of contrast, where the PMC is seen as merely a nexus of contracts, it is difficult to insist on oversight, and certainly to justify any restriction on business activity generally. In terms of regulation, however, it may be argued that one benefit of the nexus-of-contracts model is the potentially greater ease in attaching liability to individuals for corporate action. For example, in the case of the PMC where the contract metaphor is pushed into legal form, the directors could potentially be held liable for corporate policy, which results in deaths and injuries of targets as well unintentional casualties.

Interestingly, this argument has been advanced in the US congress recently in hearings concerning the murder of an Iraqi citizen by an employee of Blackwater. The employee was spirited out of the country by Blackwater to avoid Iraqi justice. Congressional Representative Kucinich, upon being advised that Blackwater did not have plans to return the employee to Iraq, stated: "I just want to point out that ... that [it's actions] could actually make [Blackwater's] corporate officers accessories here in helping to create a flight from justice for someone who's committed a murder."[43] While Kucinich is not explicating corporate legal doctrine, he may unwittingly be propounding the precise consequences of nexus of contract taken not as metaphor but as law.

The contractual model is a combination of neoclassical economics and neoliberal political modeling. Neoclassical economics is based on the assumption that the best way to coordinate supply and demand is by permitting parties to pursue their individual economic interests without regard for the interests of others, and without regulation from the state. Further, it focuses on efficiencies and tends to ignore the issue of distribution of goods and harms.[44] Neoclassical economists also tend to and focus on transaction costs (costs—broadly defined—of doing business), which they regard as undesirable and ignore social costs.

In corporate law, the contractarian model views all actors as contracting parties seeking their own interests (equal and free) and as such producing the most desirable outcome in terms of distribution. The corporate form permits them to maximize their benefits with the lowest transaction costs. As such, it has a normative aspect in that it permits the corporate contractors maximum liberty by selecting and maximizing these benefits of transactions they desire. While it may cause others to bear the undesirable costs, should those costs be sufficiently onerous, those third parties are deemed free and able to contract for themselves. As social costs tend to be ignored, there is no need to consider their impact. Should there be any real issue with social costs, those third parties will negotiate appropriate compensation by developing protections through the market.

In essence, the nexus-of-contracts model is a politically neoliberal, economically neoclassical model of the firm. Where that ideology dominates, it creates an obstacle to those looking to regulate corporate behavior. Despite its flaws, it dominates corporate law scholars' attention because of its conduciveness to law's liberalism, coalescence with neoclassical economic theory used in law and economics scholarship, and conformity to neoliberal ideology. By way of contrast, the concession theory and its replacements, communitarianism[45] and later models of trust, offer both better legal descriptions and more opportunities for regulation.[46]

As is evident from the foregoing discussion, the regulation of the PMC from a corporate law perspective requires consideration of the corporate form from a theoretical perspective. Furthermore it is evident that at a theoretical level the fundamentals of corporate law are not free of contradictions, and thus are inevitably unsettled. These fundamental problems preclude dogmatic exclusions of or prescriptions for any particular regulation, at least where the basis for such is purportedly apolitical. Whether and how one regulates the PMC is a question of one's a priori conviction on such matters as values, rights, property, and politics.

2.4 Corporation laws and the PMC

While on the one hand the law recognizes the independent legal entity of the corporation, and grants it broad rights and duties like human persons, on the other hand the rights, duties, and liabilities of the human participants in the corporation are carefully restricted. This section will examine the main legal rights and duties of those corporate participants. It will examine the basic duties and rights of directors in common law jurisdictions which although certainly different in their particulars, as indicated previously, are in essence similar across jurisdictions. Next, it will examine the implications for the PMC's directors. Then it will offer a similar analysis for shareholders, and finally examine an ongoing debate about the rights of various parties to participate in corporate control.

2.4.1 Directors' duties and rights

Although every jurisdiction has its own set of laws dealing with directors' duties, some reasonably accurate generalizations can be made. Director's duties are owed to the corporation itself and not to shareholders or other interested parties.[47] In broad terms, directors have two basic duties in the main common law and civil law jurisdictions: a duty of loyalty and a duty of care.[48] Each of these basic duties has several refinements and variations in the various jurisdictions. These duties have different origins rooted in the history of company law. We turn now to an examination of each of these duties in turn and their implications for the PMC.

The duty of loyalty is a duty arising from trust and agency principles arising from the era in which the directors were partners in the joint stock companies. The duty of loyalty is a fiduciary duty, meaning that it requires good faith in its execution, and breach of fiduciary duties may give rise to the broader equitable remedies than those available under contract. The duty of loyalty precludes, for example, self-dealing, and requires directors to avoid conflicts of interest. It is a jurisprudential doctrine based on trust rather than economics.[49]

In the context of the PMC, the duty will require loyalty to the well-being of the corporation. It may well preclude such considerations as the safety of employees, the welfare of targets, or, importantly, options for nonviolent negotiated settlements where the company earns from imposition of violence as opposed to peaceful settlement. Although in certain states "constituency statutes" have been passed, which permit directors to consider other constituencies such as employees in the context of takeovers,[50] for the most part, directors are constrained to act as fiduciaries focused on the economic well-being of the company, without regard for shareholders, employees, or other civilians.

The duty of care is a nonfiduciary duty, associated with general law principles or statute. It is a duty to use due and proper care in the execution of one's responsibilities. The duty does not require the director to be correct in that the decision proves to be fruitful. Indeed, the Business Judgment Rule is specifically designed to protect directors from liability for decisions taken which prove to be unsuccessful.[51] It does, however, require the director to be reasonably careful in making informed decisions.[52] Thus, decisions to enter into a specific contract or the strategic decision to move the business into a particular area are not matters for which a director who has been reasonably informed will bear liability.

In terms of the PMC, this duty and the Business Judgment Rule would lead one to suggest that the matter before the director is limited in consideration to the economic good of the company. A decision, for example, to move the business of the PMC to providing front-line tip-of-the-spear services, or to enter into a contract for the supply of such services to any government whatsoever or to any corporation adds no special liability to the director for whatever harm or social costs that may ensue. The net effect of these narrowly focused duties is that directors, unlike military personnel, have no incentive to consider the potentially lethal outcomes of strategic decisions.

A further and troubling aspect of the impact of the corporate form on directors is its nature as a shield. Corporate law doctrine is that directors, like all agents, are protected from liability for the consequences of their actions done on behalf of their principals. This effective shielding allows directors a level of comfort that is to encourage an appropriate level of risk-taking. Indeed, the above-mentioned Business Judgment Rule is a manifestation of that larger doctrine. However, it should be noted that the corporation does not solely shield shareholders. It shields to a significant effect the directors as well.[53] Accordingly, despite Representative Kucinich's response mentioned above, it is most unlikely that such a prosecution would eventuate, and even if it did, it would not likely succeed.

2.4.2 Shareholders' duties and rights

Shareholders' rights and duties are quite constrained. Indeed, over time, the importance and power of shareholders has diminished substantially.[54] Despite the relatively recent development of institutional shareholders,[55] the main rights of shareholders have to do with voting for directors, residual claims,[56] and, of course, limited liability. Corporate shareholders were first also granted limited liability well over a century ago.[57] This grant meant that shareholders would be liable solely for the amount of capital they were willing to put at risk. By this legal innovation, shareholders have no liability for the actions or obligations of the corporation, regardless of whether those obligations are to voluntary creditors or to involuntary tort victims. Unlike any other form of organization in which liability attaches to individuals, limited liability allows the shareholder to ignore all but profits of the enterprise.[58] The restrictions they face have to do with their dealings with other shareholders and participation in management.

Obviously, the benefit shareholders seek is some financial return on their financial investment—whether income or capital. The main benefit to the shareholder from the corporate form is the protection from liability for the actions of the corporation and decisions taken in the process of pursuing profit. The shareholder stands to benefit from corporate activity but has no risk beyond the investment for any harm visited on other parties (social costs) by the corporation.

In terms of the PMC, the shareholder has considerable gains to consider. As noted earlier, defense and security industries have grown dramatically since the end of the Cold War[59] and particularly since September 11, 2001.[60] The Department of Defense in the US noted a 35 percent increase in defense expenditure between that time and a mere 5 months later.[61] In the first chapter it was noted that the market turnover in 2006 was estimated at $100 billion. Given the dramatic growth of the industry and the limited liability of the corporation, the shareholder in the PMC has little to fear and considerable reason for hope.[62] Shareholder interest may well spark even further growth in the industry, particularly when one considers the rewards from merger and acquisition activity in the industry.[63] We turn next to the legal doctrine of a separate entity, which is of particular significance to the discussion.

2.4.3 Separate entity doctrine and the corporate veil

The separate entity doctrine in corporate law recognizes the corporation as a legal being independent of any corporate participant, whether director, officer, shareholder, or employee. It became an independent legal entity[64] able to act in its own right without creating liability for those actions with respect to the directing minds.

As such, the corporation, and no other person, bears liability for its actions. The rationale for the doctrine is that it promotes investment by parties and permits managers to act without fear of personal liability for the actions of the enterprise corporation. The implications of this doctrine, however, are hard to overstate. In essence, the corporation's human actors act with impunity to a degree not enjoyed in any other arena of human activity.

The corporation's separate identity will not be stripped away to expose the corporate actors to liability except in exceptional circumstances. This stripping away is referred to as "piercing the corporate veil" or "lifting the corporate veil." It is a seldom-invoked remedy limited to instances where the corporate actors have used or attempted to use the corporate form to perpetrate a fraud,[65] or in some limited instances, where the parent corporation and subsidiary were substantially connected.[66] This remedy has been granted in situations described generally in the US as situations in which the corporate form has been used to "defeat public convenience."[67]

In terms of the PMC, the strength of the legal corporate veil, as noted, allows the directors and other actors a considerable shield in terms of liability for their actions. Although the risks sought to be protected by law are primarily the financial risks associated with normal and ordinary conduct of business, where the business is extraordinary, such as hiring soldiers to kill other people, the corporate form provides a particularly attractive shield, and it is hard to imagine an instance in which a court would pierce the veil for such killing under current corporate law.

The public purposes of corporations alluded to above are not exhausted by the historical examples set out above. Among the contemporary legal tests for piercing the corporate veil is a test of "proper purposes."[68] Generally, in this context, proper purposes will be such things as operating a corporation for the business purpose of making a profit. It becomes much more difficult when the corporation becomes a vehicle for other activities like sheltering income from tax authorities, or in the more obvious abuses such as defrauding creditors, or using them to mislead investors, as in the Enron case with its Special Purpose Vehicles.[69] Generally, courts tend to pierce the corporate veil more readily for torts than other types of actions.[70] But the purposes test is not limited to finance and fraud. The law in Britain, for example, permitted the piercing of the corporate veil where corporate activity was deemed contrary to national interests, including military action.[71] Piercing for this foreign policy objective is an extreme rarity and most unlikely to occur today. Such matters are dealt with through licensing and trade laws that carry no more than financial penalties for their breach.

Of course, to pierce the corporate veil is but one of the means for gaining access to parties responsible and/or potentially liable for corporate wrongdoing. Essentially, as discussed above, the notion of piercing the corporate veil is ignoring the corporate entity and permitting liability to flow from the effected parties to the human actors operating via a corporate vehicle. As put by the court, piercing the veil is appropriate where "[the corporate vehicle has been] used by the defendant to commit fraud or wrong, to perpetrate the violation of a statutory or other positive legal duty, or dishonest and unjust act in contravention of plaintiff's legal right."[72]

The complexity of the discussion is increased exponentially when one considers corporate groups. Much of the litigation concerning the piercing of the corporate veil deals with corporate groups and, in this context, the nature and purpose of the various corporate entities becomes of paramount importance, and legal doctrines of liability founder completely.[73] Are the entities to provide tax advantages, shelter parent corporations, whether nominally or actually in control, from creditors or other harmed parties? The complexity of the discussion at this point should provide a caution[74] against accepting too simply the position of market fundamentalists who advocate regulation by the market and claim that the only thing a corporation does is to provide a venue for capital accumulation.[75] Equally, it militates against the notion of simple regulatory solutions.

Having reviewed the corporation's public purposes and role in society, there is a stronger argument for caution among proponents of PMCs than is generally acknowledged, at least among their supporters.

2.4.4 Liability issues for deaths specific to the PMC

The issue of corporate killing needs further explication in two directions. First, it is not the actual corporation doing the killing. Rather, it is the employees who do the killing and are killed.[76] Second, corporations have killed humans in a multitude of contexts throughout their history.[77] The only novelty in this discussion is that instead of accidentally killing employees, members of the corporation, or members of the public in general, in the context of the armed security providers in conflict zones and the tip-of-the-spear PMC, the corporation maybe specifically tasked to kill others.

As to the first issue of corporate liability for killing, a corporation is in fact a pile of papers with a government stamp on it. Such being the case, it is hard to attach any liability to a corporation per se. From the perspective denominated above as the concession theory, the directors are mere agents of the corporation and so take no personal liability for the actions executed on behalf of the corporate principals. From a nexus-of-contracts perspective, as we have seen, corporations are a mere fiction and can carry no more actual culpability than a daydream or other fantasy. If the nexus-of-contracts theory were taken seriously at law, all actors including directors, shareholders, and employees would be directly personally liable. It is ironic that the corporate law issue most basic to corporate form is stopping liability with the corporate entity itself.

It is generally public outrage that drives legislative reform addressing liability for corporate killing activity.[78] The public is outraged, for example, when a corporate owned ferry sinks drowning nearly 200,[79] or thousands of employees are struck with asbestosis,[80] or other similar instances.[81] What particularly outrages the public is that, in such instances, the regulations usually provide nominal fines.[82] In some instance, victims of corporate injury or death may have access to the tort system, but those instances are generally limited to the shareholders and, through product liability law, to members of the general public injured directly by corporate products and services.

Over time, the law developed a notion of corporate liability for killing; however, liability was limited to the corporation and not to the corporate actors. Interestingly, the court allowed liability for some actions to side step the corporate entity and attach directly to the corporate actors, but only for property offenses,[83] and generally, not extending to include personal injury. The mechanism for circumventing the corporate form is the above-discussed "piercing the corporate veil." As noted there, in certain, carefully circumscribed instances, the courts will permit financially injured parties or involuntary creditors to sue directly the corporate officials who authorized or acted so as to cause the injurious result. If the law, albeit grudgingly, has been forced so as to compensate financially injured members and the public, why should the corporation not be required to compensate members of the public intentionally killed? There seems to be no good legal reason for this political decision.

In the context of the PMC killings, particularly in conflict zones, the matter is complicated by the situation on the ground. In Iraq, for example, protecting convoys, a task often outsourced to PMCs, is done by random firing described as "clearing the ground" ahead of the convoy. It is unknown how many Iraqis have been killed by this procedure; however, military compensation schemes provide some compensation where the killing of the civilian was done by military personnel. By 2006, the US military has paid $20 million to Iraqi civilians,[84] the UK had paid $2.3 million by 2005,[85] and by 2007 the Australians had paid $266,000.[86] Where the killing is done by PMC personnel, the US government simply states, "they are not our employees."[87] To date, it appears there has been no acknowledgment of PMC liability for such killings, and accordingly, we must assume, no payments either. Indeed, Iraqi officials complained in a May 2007 newspaper article of Blackwater employees having shot and killed four civilians,[88] and as we will see below, efforts to obtain compensation have been thwarted.

In the matter of the deaths of their own employees, it would appear that PMCs have no better record. In the famous incident of the four Blackwater employees mutilated and burned in Fallujah, the families of the employees filed suit for wrongful deaths. The PMC has made a successful effort to block the suit, thwarting claims, and preventing the families even from accessing information surrounding the deaths of the employees. Given the potentially high stakes, the PMC has hired topflight lawyers and to date has been wholly successful in blocking the action,[89] and has changed tactics suing the families in a $10 million breach of contract action bringing into arbitration and thereby avoiding media scrutiny.[90] Perhaps it is in this context of the privatized corporate violence of the PMC that the moral outrage expressed in the statement "the corporation has no soul to be damned or body to confine"[91] finds its most poignant illustration.

The second aspect of the question—"who should be liable for corporate killing?"—creates an equally difficult discussion. Normally, the prompt response is "the corporation."[92] As we have just seen, however, this purported answer merely removes the question one step and confuses the issue by a combination of diffusing liability to an additional legal person and at the same time limiting the liability of the human persons. Yet given the presupposition of peace, the public odium for killing, and the problems of the definition and control of the corporate form,[93] combined with the development of laws recognizing the personal responsibility of corporate executives for activities of the corporation in other areas, such as securities,[94] it seems ingenuous to argue that no personal liability should be attached for intentional killing of members of the public.

Killing with intent, the appropriate *mens rea*, in nearly every other context[95] is the criminal offense of murder or, at the very least, manslaughter. In the context of the PMC, the *mens rea* exists de facto. In such instances, it seems ridiculous to suggest that because the corporation had the intent, the directors or employees should escape liability—acknowledging the court's traditional reluctance to accept the notion of vicarious criminal liability[96] or criminal liability of employers for the acts of employees respectively.[97] Accordingly, the next step is an investigation of how the law tends to treat attaching personal liability to corporate executives, first for civil matters and then criminal matters.[98]

The test for attaching personal liability, i.e. "piercing the corporate veil,"[99] is usually tripartite:[100] it requires evidence of control of the corporate entity, a misuse of the corporate form, and a resulting damage.[101] In an action against a PMC for death, none of the defenses normally advanced against such an attack on the corporate veil should work. The first part of the test, establishing control of the corporation, may be fairly simple or exceptionally difficult, depending on disclosure laws in the jurisdiction where the corporation is domiciled. It may be further obscured by the corporate structure. Multilayered, multinational corporations managed to shield identified responsible executives in notorious extraterritorial corporate torts. Further, as experience in Iraq proves, the contracting and subcontracting arrangements among PMCs can be truly Byzantine. Accordingly, this issue of control may present a significant obstacle to piercing the veil.

Even in the event that corporate control was established it would seem that the key issue here is the test of the "misuse of the corporate form." Normally, misuse is in relation to the use of the corporation to perpetrate financial fraud or avoid the legitimate legal obligations of certain parties, such as directors, officers, or key employees. With respect to the PMC, however, a reconsideration of the proper purposes or permitted purposes of corporations would be appropriate. Analogous situations could range from the use of the corporate form to traffic in illegal weapons, to smuggling illegal goods, to tobacco products—each of which has some elements of fraud, violence, public harm, and tort killing. Finally, the issue of resulting damage would seem to be fairly straightforward. Dead bodies and bombed homes and facilities are both tangible and quantifiable.

The net result of piercing the corporate veil is the attachment of liability to corporate directors and executives. This result, it is supposed, would inhibit directors' and executives' ability to benefit personally from their wrongdoing, the corporate intermediary notwithstanding. The question of whether directors and executives should have a duty to avoid killing seems a bit obvious, nevertheless, the PMC raises the question in a new and interesting context. Normally, law has permitted intentional killing in the very limited contexts of self-defense and pursuant to state command in war.

In the PMC context, the director is either directly or indirectly killing or authorizing the killing of his/her employer's opponents. The issue, of course, is, what authority does the director rely on to make such an order legal? Where it is found that such an order is illegal, or where it is based on economic incentive, usually the law universally condemns such; the executioner and the party who aids and abets, or is otherwise an accessory to the crime, are, as Kucinich advanced at the hearing, held liable. From this perspective, interpositioning the corporate vehicle is an irrelevant consideration in the attachment of criminal liability for criminal activities. Should the court introduce the corporate form into the equation and identify it as a participant in criminal activity, it would be added only as a further potential accused.

The matter of corporate criminal law, however, is a separate and difficult area of law that remains inadequately developed and underutilized.[102] It offers two main defenses of "due diligence" and compliance. Due diligence is a matter of the corporation having taken appropriate steps and having appropriate systems in place to avoid criminal activity. In the case of PMCs committing murder, however, it seems difficult to suggest that any form of due diligence could apply. Efforts made to avoid killing may be contrary to the corporate objective, since killing may well be part of the strategy.[103] Compliance works as a defense in corporate crime cases by claiming that the corporation's activity was legal as it complies with stated laws. Given the dearth of regulation for PMCs, "compliance" would offer no defense. Indeed, as the cases of Blackwater illustrate, a major criticism of corporate criminal law is that it merely shifts the blame to individuals on the lower rungs of the corporate echelon.[104]

The two main defenses, "due diligence" and "compliance" would fail. Due diligence in this context would mean making appropriate efforts to avoid killing and injury, yet if killing and injury is part of the mandate, indeed, this is the strategy of imposing costs on opponents and hence reducing their ability to fight, the defense is in contradiction with the objective. Compliance would fail as there is no regulatory regime with which the PMC is to comply.[105] Nor would "compliance" be an appropriate defense as there are no statutes regulating PMC activity.

Putting PMCs into the larger corporate context, it should be noted that corporations whose products are known to maim and kill are permitted to carry on business everyday. For example, an estimated 4.3 million people were killed by corporate tobacco in 2000,[106] or about one in ten deaths.[107] Although lawsuits against tobacco corporations have been successful to the degree that damages have been recovered, the corporations continue to be in business and indeed are looking to expand markets particularly in jurisdictions less favorable to corporate liability.[108] There is no innate legal reason for allowing these corporations or any corporation to continue to provide harmful products. It would appear then to be a simple matter of revenues and political power preventing governments from outlawing them altogether.[109]

It could be argued that this is an incorrect analysis, and that rather than examining the PMC as a killer in civil society subject to domestic sanctions, a more appropriate analysis would be that of a mercenary on the battlefield. How does this analysis lead to a different outcome? On the one hand, the laws attempting to control mercenaries are wholly ineffective (see discussion in chapter 5). On the other hand, where political will exists, law is no obstacle to prosecuting combatants as illustrated by the politically expedient but tortured "legal" designation of "enemy combatant."[110] In other words, legal analysis of the PMC as a mercenary is a pointless endeavor, the outcome of which depends wholly on politics and not at all on law.

Although a wide range of remedies for PMC killings are discussed, the main obstacle is the lack of political will.[111] Other factors, including government co-option by the PMC industry and the daunting costs and complexities of international litigation, make it most unlikely that prosecution by private litigants is likely to have any significant effect on PMCs. That state of affairs leaves it to the government, which suffers the same two factors facing individuals and the largely toothless international law regime (see discussion in chapter 5).

The most effective remedies available to governments would appear to lie only where PMCs breach contractual terms. The current remedies include a termination of contract, a barring from future contracts, and civil and criminal liability.[112] Yet this panoply of remedies is more apparent than real. For example, despite ongoing litigation and investigations, PMCs involved in such scandals are routinely awarded new contracts even while the processes are in course.[113] Recommendations following the Abu Ghraib scandal have yet to bear fruit. It is interesting to note that to date no private contractors have been prosecuted for the infamous torture they inflicted in Iraq,[114] despite the completion of investigation, prosecution, and sentencing of the military personnel involved. Finally, as indicated above, the matter of international corporate killing adds what may be the most complex aspect of the discussion.[115]

2.4.5 The PMC and the contract to kill

One legal threat to the PMC comes from construing security services contract as a contract for killing, and hence an illegal contract. Illegal contracts may be contracts for conduct prohibited by law or those considered to be against public policy.[116] Indeed, a contract to commit a crime is, by this definition, an illegal contract.[117] A well-recognized example of the second type of illegal contract, being a contract contrary to public policy, is "contracts prejudicial to national or international security."[118] It seems self-evident that contracts to kill soldiers or citizens of foreign states ought to be classified as "prejudicial to national or international security." Despite the potentially broad application of the foregoing statement, the illegality of contract applies only to "contracts which impair relations with a *friendly* country."[119]

The effect of a finding of illegality is dependent on the nature of the illegality and the extent to which it flows through the contract. At the very least, the illegal terms are unenforceable. Generally at common law, the contract is void: that does not mean, however, that no further liability may flow.[120] If the contract under discussion is not just the contract for security services but the basic contract that purportedly forms the corporation (that is a nexus-of-contracts model), and that contract is based on corporate ability to inflict lethal violence, then liability may well flow nullifying the benefits of the corporate form, and of course, the benefit of limited liability. If this analysis is correct, there is potential that all members, including shareholders and directors, would be personally liable for the killings contracted for by the PMC. That outcome, however, seems most unlikely as courts shift between recognizing and ignoring the corporate personality without any explicit policy, as they see fit.[121]

2.5 Corporate regulation

As a subset of corporations in general, PMC regulation can be considered from a purely corporate law perspective. In the section which follows regulation of PMCs will be considered only from within the doctrines and perspectives of general corporate law. In the later chapters, PMC regulation from national and international law perspectives will be discussed.

Since the inception of corporations, various parties have sought to control them. Early monarchs sought to limit corporate development, which might challenge imperial power.[122] However, each step taken by government has been countered by a corporate response. The highly restrictive bubble legislation in eighteenth-century England, for example, led lawyers to create joint stock companies, and various types of trusts.[123]

Corporate regulation is a highly contentious topic. Those controlling the corporation have generally been opposed to its regulation, realizing that greater the control imposed on the corporation by outside parties, lesser control is left to them. Those concerned with corporate power and harm, generally outsiders and employees, have attempted to craft and advocate effective regulation for more than a century.[124] More recently, further attention has been drawn to corporate regulation as a result of the increase in size and quantity of multinational corporations (MNCs), greater recognition of corporate harms, dramatic corporate failures, and efforts to control corporations on an international level—all with less than stellar success.[125]

The intensely political nature of the corporate regulation debate makes it difficult at times to get a clear understanding of the issues. Nevertheless, it is clear that believers in market-based solutions reject nearly all regulation, while those more skeptical of the formalist notions of equality and power tend to acknowledge a model of society in addition to individuals acting in a market, and are less reticent to suggest regulation. The political philosophies underlying the regulatory debate are evident in the legal analysis when one notes the liberal bias of law and the equation of the corporation with the individual on the one hand, while on the other hand, one encounters group rights and institutions, including the law itself.

Corporate regulation in the municipal legal context is for the most part inwardly focused. That is to say, corporate law, as we have seen, is concerned with the regulation of the internal structure of the corporation, the rights and duties of shareholders, directors, and officers. To the extent that corporate law does have an external focus, that focus is limited to corporate finance (that is transactions with members of the public).

The idea of regulating the activities of the corporation is inimical to the antiregulatory market believers (usually neoliberals, discussed above) who have created the "corporate ethos" which pervades western legislatures and many international bodies. Their business lobby, concerned with the elite's profit to the exclusion of all other concerns, has effectively opposed many democratically inspired initiatives. The elite concerns dominating corporate law have a long history of success beginning with such things as efforts to block injured worker lawsuits, product liability, environmental liabilities, employees' rights on termination, and any type of effort to control or restrict their domination of the benefits of corporate activities.

Regulating corporations at the international level is the Holy Grail of international lawyers and corporate law scholars. The obstacles are numerous and have yet to be surmounted. There are at least six major obstacles. These are: First, the general weakness of international law in terms of regulating activities of private actors such as corporations. Second, there is a lack of enforcement provision in most international law instruments. Without enforcement, these laws are more political statements than actual controlling rules. Third, there are no international institutions in existence which could regulate corporations on the international stage. Fourth, there are no courts competent to adjudicate on corporations in the international context. Fifth, there are no conventions regulating corporate behavior from an international perspective. Finally, and most importantly, there is a lack of political will to achieve a global regulatory regime focused on the corporate form, and where there has been, the business lobby has successfully lobbied to thwart or co-opt it.[126] This less than impressive list does little to inspire confidence in looking to an international regulatory regime to control corporations and in particular the PMC, and this is indeed the reason national regulation needs careful consideration (see chapter 4). Furthermore, given the multinational character of PMCs, such as AEGIS mentioned above, and even by definition international as Ortiz would have it (quoted in chapter 1), the imperative for international control of the corporate PMCs becomes even more evident and more urgent.

Underlying the difficulty of municipal and international law is the basic issue which lawyers see as a "conflict of laws" issue. What should one do when the laws of one jurisdiction conflict with those of another? This technical approach fails, however, to come to terms with the real question. Corporate law scholar Eric Orts puts it well:

> [It is expected] that a corporation will "obey all the laws of the countries in which we do business." This promise, however, does not account for hard choices that need to be made when laws of different countries conflict....One assumes that loyalty to its "home country" of the United States outweighs conflicting laws of other countries, but this choice requires a moral judgment. It is not merely a technical question of conflicts of laws.[127]

Ongoing concern in the US with respect to the overcharging by private contractors for services in Iraq draws attention to the difficulty of regulating corporations dealing with government contracts, and in particular multinational PMCs party to military procurement contracts. Efforts to regulate PMCs after a spate of abuses is not new[128] and is a worldwide phenomenon, as are efforts to regulate corporations after cycles of corporate collapses.[129] The corporate response is predictable: corporations prefer voluntary codes of conduct over externally imposed regulation. The question of self-regulation within the industry moves the discussion away from matters internal to corporate law, and hence are dealt with elsewhere in this volume (see chapter 4).

The issues discussed above again raise the issue of the correct corporate model, only this time from a slightly different perspective. Should the corporation respond only to shareholders' interests? Or, should the corporation also be responsive to other members of the community? These questions have been examined in corporate law under the rubric of the shareholder-stakeholder debate.

The debate, which first appeared in response to the 1929 Wall Street collapse, moved between the notion that directors were responsible to shareholders and that directors were answerable to society at large as "statesmen." Berle and Dodd initially carried it out in the pages of the Harvard Law Review.[130] Since that time, various parties have taken up the debate and over time it has shifted between the poles of free market libertarianism and welfare capitalism.[131] The particular view advanced depends on the proponents' political, economic, and philosophical values. There are strong arguments for and against the positions. Neither is completely convincing, although the extreme positions tend to lack much persuasive power to those not already convinced.[132] Ultimately, the position one takes is a political decision as much as anything else.

2.5.1 The politics of corporate law regulation and the PMC

As will be evident by now, corporate law is a highly political area of law. The parties advocating various positions—the shareholders, directors, managers, employees, consumers, local populations, and special interest groups of both business/finance interests and environmental interests among others—all have particular interests and political agendas. Each is looking for ways to alter the distribution of goods and harms, rights and liabilities resulting from the corporate form in the operation of its business. Each interested party seeks to justify a greater share of goods and a lesser amount of the costs of business activities.[133] In its simplest form, the corporation is a legal vehicle designed to concentrate the benefit of collective activity by privatizing it, and permitting the public to bear a portion of the costs of corporate activity.[134] This distribution is a political choice, and the laws that facilitate and enforce it are expressions of those political choices.

The politics of corporate law are particularly evident in the metaphors used in the analysis of corporate law and general corporate legal discussion. One would be hard-pressed to improve upon Daniel Greenwood's brilliant analysis of the four main corporate law metaphors: property, market and contract, agency, and personhood. Greenwood writes:

> Corporate law—and political discussion of public corporations generally ...puts publicly held business corporations on the private side of the great public/private divide. [As a result the position advocated claims] corporations, like citizens, need to be protected from the government, rather than being, like cities or administrative agencies, governmental entities from which we need to be protected.[135]

Greenwood goes on to argue that corporations being on the private side are protected from the checks and balances of government, including transparency, accountability, and political input. He reiterates the concern of generations of civil society advocates and scholars[136] that the size and power of corporations suggests that they are not merely one among many equal citizens, but indeed are powers unto themselves. Thus, although they may have amassed "[a] potential of illegitimate power," they have done so with legal protection of private persons, private property, contract, and agency laws. Of greater concern to Greenwood, however, is that corporate powers have amassed this power without a parallel legal development to protect the populace, which had such protection against the other main power in society, namely government. Thus unlike the situation of the populace vis-a-vis government, corporations have grown without the granting of some power to the populace over the direction and decisions of the corporation.

Greenwood continues:

> Liberal democracies sharply distinguish between state and society, government and governed. The state exists to serve the citizenry, not the other way around. The state is subservient to the population, but the population—taken both collectively, as a people, and individually, as people—has rights against the state.

Greenwood protests that as a result of the political decision to classify corporations at law as being on the private side of the public/private divide, corporate activities having significant impacts on society are thus shielded from public input. The consequence he identifies is that

> While governmental bureaucracies in a republican democracy must be responsive to the will of the people (in both senses), individual people and the people as a whole have both the collective right to control the government and individual rights to autonomy from it. The privatizing metaphors of corporate law mean that business corporations are classified on the society side of this great liberal divide. Our law, that is, treats business corporations as values in themselves, entitled to be given the consideration of citizens as ends of government and not merely tools for a greater end.[137]

Thus while corporations are expressly designed instruments constrained by law for profit seeking, they have been granted rights as if they were self-directed, rational, free moral agents seeking happiness or some other form of self-actualization. This division and assignment of corporations to the civil society side of the divide has particular significance in the context of PMCs. One of the PMC's overriding objectives is none other than political: the securing of distribution or the redistribution of resources. It does so by means of force. Accordingly, PMCs promote a particular politics, which might otherwise not dominate, and they do so through violent means. As discussed in chapters 3 and 4 and elsewhere in this volume, PMCs are engaged to oppose local politically motivated populations, to support governments, or to overthrow governments. PMCs rely on their strong political connections and are developing significant policy selling influence.[138] However, as Greenwood's analysis makes clear, by being viewed as a private entity, the private and corporate PMCs have the ability to escape political accountability while being able to shape policy and inflict violence on a scale that would otherwise be restricted to more accountable and transparent government.

This political theme of private law offending democracy is further exemplified in PMC activities in favor of MNCs. MNC's use of PMCs is extensive. From protecting oil wells to pipelines and mines, PMCs engage civilian populations opposed to contested activities and distribution of natural and other resources.[139] Indeed, some PMCs, such as the former Executive Outcomes (and now its still extant subsidiaries), planted stay-on security corporations' subsidiary PMCs. These subsidiary PMCs ensure that the resource assets the parent company received as payment for securing the government to one party or another provide the asset-based revenue stream promised to the parent company in the first instance.[140] Shielded by their private law status, these corporations are free to interfere and impose state level of violence to achieve private corporate ends—profits.

Hence the politics of corporate law, not particularly benign toward democratic interest in general, are stripped bare in the context of PMC practice. The decision to classify the corporation as a private actor needs to be reconsidered, particularly in the context of the PMC. In a nutshell, the politics of corporate law answers "The issue of who is in charge, and what they control." Further politics answer how that "what" is defined—whether a nexus of contracts or a legal entity. As we have seen, the matter has come no closer to resolution than the shareholder-stakeholder debate discussed above. The stakes are too high for either party to move substantially in either direction, at least as matters stand.

It is important to note that despite the foregoing analysis the PMC has not been only a negative force against the populace. Indeed, as discussed elsewhere in this volume (chapters 3 and 4), in certain civil conflicts PMCs have been decisive in bringing peace. The point here is that the politics of corporate law has generally favored private wealth over public good and this has been reflected in PMC deployments against civilians around the globe. Finally, on the matter of the municipal regulation of the PMCs, it is significant that a number of the head offices are domiciled in tax havens and otherwise less than transparent jurisdictions. These choices may speak well of profit savvy management but do little to inspire confidence in matters of ultimate accountability, public good, or optimism in terms of effective future regulation.

2.6 Corporate governance and the PMC

Corporate governance refers to the control of the corporation. It includes considerations discussed earlier under the rubric of directors' and shareholders' rights and duties and other internal control mechanisms, the shareholder-stakeholder debate, external controls, and of course, accountability. The existence of the corporate governance discourse is evidence that the regulation of the corporation cannot be left to blind market forces. Debate has generally focused on the following: the amount of involvement shareholders should have in the direction of the corporation, what if other stakeholders should have any involvement, how to keep government regulatory initiatives at a minimum, and the influence of markets on corporate principals' behaviors.[141]

Corporate governance of the PMC calls for special consideration. The assumptions of corporate governance being a combination of market controls, self-regulation, voluntary codes of conduct (discussed in depth in chapter 4), and the legislation governing all corporate entities is insufficient and inappropriate for the PMC. The distinct difference, which justifies an alternative approach, comes from the distinctive characteristic of the PMC. That distinct difference is that the PMC combines both political objectives and violent or potentially violent methods with the only norm being the profit motive. This potentially lethal mix requires a unique level of oversight.[142]

Given the PMC's strategically significant contribution to outcomes, and the political significance of those outcomes, it must be accountable to the populace. It is not sufficient to be accountable to the politicians alone as the nexus between PMCs and governments in the first place is too close[143] a fact amply illustrated in the case of PMCs in Iraq.[144] Nor is it sufficient to be only accountable to shareholders for the same reason. Accordingly, only some form of direct civilian oversight and independent monitoring will suffice to make the PMC accountable to the populace. This perspective would lead one to suggest some type of nonpolitical, nonmilitary involvement in the corporation's governance in order to at least monitor, if not advise, on the contracts, strategies, and political outcomes under consideration. Interestingly, a variant of this idea was put forward by the now-defunct Sandline, which called for "observers" in the field.[145] Yet another approach maybe that proposed by Desai of having lawyers from Lawyers Without Borders on the ground working with PMCs in Judge Advocates General model (to avoid the yes-man approach) to advise and monitor not only contractual duties but also matters of human rights.[146] Taking the suggestion to the boardroom would be a significant and important shift in the corporate governance of PMCs.

Nevertheless, no corporation, PMC or otherwise, is likely to welcome such suggestions, let alone consider adopting them voluntarily. The obvious and main practical obstacle to the changes in corporate governance will be from the beneficiaries of the *status quo*—the PMCs themselves, and their clients—politicians and MNCs that use them. The current system works well enough for them, as the whole matter of the PMC seems hardly at issue among these participants. As such, changes to corporate governance will have to come as a result of public pressure and exposure.

The main theoretical obstacle to a different model of corporate governance for the PMC is the corporate model. As long as one sees the PMC as but one among millions of other similar business corporations, it seems inappropriate to consider alternative models of governance that apply in a discriminatory fashion to the PMC. If, however, one acknowledges the particular political objectives and potentially violent methods of the PMC as being sufficiently distinctive from other business corporations to remove it from the realm of the average business corporation, then an alternative model of corporate governance does not seem inappropriate. Indeed, it has been argued that defense industry contractors providing weapons "are not just heavily subsidized; [but that] they are uniquely entrusted with the public good of national security and expectations about their behaviour reflect [justifiably] the deterrent and destructive power of the products they manufacture."[147]

As indicated, a new model would have to take into account the political objectives and the violent methods. Neither of these is an absolute bar to the engagement of contracting with the PMC. Rather, it would appear that PMCs have some role to play; however, the accountability, particularly to the public, is severely deficient. A revised model of governance should follow on the financial model. As with finance, corporations are required to file their finances according to the legislation governing public companies, and comply with listing rules. A similar disclosure could be required with respect to PMCs dealing with governments or international bodies such as the UN or NGOs.[148] It is claimed that this already occurs on operations. For example, in the case of Blackwater killing Iraqi citizens mentioned earlier, Blackwater spokeswoman, Anne Tyrrell, declared: "Blackwater investigates any reports of hostile action in Iraq. Per the terms of our US government contracts, as a matter of routine, Blackwater is required to file after action reports on any such incidents."[149] Yet, the government has been frustrated in trying to get to the bottom of the incident. The filing of reports on PMCs' activities, if Blackwater can be taken as representative of PMCs, generally appears to be a claim with little substance. Requiring probing, timely, complete, and truthful reporting activity would go far in addressing the matters of abuse that have come up. However, for this to occur in a meaningful way, it would have to be the responsibility of someone at a high level in the PMC's organization. Really what is needed is a combination of these methods such that some type of independent body or persons needs to be involved to monitor the violence inflicted. Field reports of weapons discharge, injury, and damage should be mandatory, as they are in the police force, and in certain military arenas. These reports need to be submitted to the independent body, signed and authorized by the directors who take personal responsibility for them, just as they do for financial statements under Sarbanes-Oxley.

The new model would also have to address the potentially violent activities of the PMC. Again, such a model would have to include training, monitoring, and measuring for the employees of the PMC.[150] Indeed, some PMCs offer training in international humanitarian law as part of their overall services. The matter of war crimes history of particular employees, managers, and directors, as well as the corporate activity would need careful attention. For example, DynCorp's corporate response to employee rape and enslaving of young girls in the Balkans was to whisk the employees away so as to avoid prosecution,[151] and the previously mentioned case of Blackwater spiriting its murdering employee out of Iraq is yet another instance of the same. This proposal at a corporate governance level differs from similar recommendations by scholars and industry analysts concerning the vetting of personnel. While those scholars and analysts are undoubtedly right that better vetting of gun toting employees is critical, the proposal herein focuses on the records of those party to the strategic control and direction of the PMC.

Rachel Weber, whose work examines defense industry governance in the context of downsizing of the weapons manufacturers in the 1990s, offers an interesting suggestion. She argues that given the public interest in these PMCs, and problems associated with nationalization of industries, a European solution might be promising. She notes the "Golden Shares" held by governments in formerly state-owned enterprises. These Golden Shares permit the government to maintain some fundamental controls over a corporation by allocating certain preemptive rights to Golden Shares. These shares are simply voting shares and do not have equity rights.[152] Although Golden Shares have been ruled as not being in conformity with EU corporate law, that ruling need be fatal to the strategy of granting some form of government control through share structures.[153] Another approach taken in Germany has the government continuing an equity interest.[154]

Given these PMC issues and corporate governance concerns, it may well be that some aspects of military law be introduced into the corporation, modified, of course, to meet the needs in the context. In particular, the chain of command doctrine of military law discussed in chapter 5, which allows liability for decisions and actions of soldiers in the field under command to attach to generals in charge could be transplanted into corporate law regulating PMCs. Decisions of contracted soldiers need to be visited on the directors, the corporate hierarchy and doctrines of independent entity notwithstanding. This step would certainly motivate the PMCs' directors and principals to be much more cautious in the selection, training, and deployment of soldiers in the field—a widely endorsed suggestion.[155]

Finally, the overall contracts need some form of civilian monitoring. At the international level this monitoring could be done by a UN body of some composition. While the UN itself is web of its own political intrigue, a third party to the proposed contract, providing review should provide some comfort and at least some transparency to the otherwise particularly opaque and obscure world of PMC contracting. Again, directors of the corporation should be signing these contracts assuring that the PMC will operate within the scope of the approved contract. At the domestic level, Weber has made similar suggestions.[156] These are ideal solutions—PMCs are engaged in many situations where such administrative procedures may not be feasible.

Nevertheless, without an objective to aim at, nothing is likely to occur. In sum, the PMC is not a mere business organization. It is at least an important political and, either directly or indirectly, violent organization meriting additional oversight and intervention in its internal and external governance mechanisms.

2.7 Should there be distinctive remedies available against corporate bodies engaged in PMC activities?

As previously noted, the usual remedies for corporate misdeeds are fines. Fines are the preferred mode of punishing corporation—preferred by both the corporation and the regulator. They are easier to administer, easier to calculate, and easier to measure, both in terms of the corporation calculating costs of compliance versus profit for noncompliance and in terms of a regulator watching to see whether the fine has been paid as opposed to some more intrusive, resource-intensive monitoring. There is the obvious drawback, however, with a financial penalty regime in that the punishment is paid by the shareholders not the directors or managers instigating the noncompliance in the first place. In terms of the PMC it has been noted that fines, along with other market-based sanctions, are preferred by the industry and are inadequate in relation to certain harms they may inflict.[157]

In some rare cases, discussed above, the directors may hold particular liability. Yet, where assets of members of the corporation are attacked, it is always the case that the assets forfeited are those forfeited in the capacity as officers or participants in some other capacity. Never have shareholders' personal assets been seized for corporate misdeeds. Yet a major argument in the corporate governance debate centers on the monitoring role of shareholders. Shareholders, it is argued, are very concerned about the well-being of the company and are the most diligent overseers of the managers. If one were to transfer that argument into the PMC context, it may be that should PMCs wish to operate, and should they receive such official or semiofficial approval, their duty to operate within strict guidelines[158] ought to be enforced by a real threat to those facilitating the PMC's existence through the contribution of capital.[159] In other words, with the limited range of remedies usually invoked against corporations it may be that other sanctions are more appropriate.

A second remedy, which has been limited to a remedy available to actions by creditors and some internal disputes, is the traditional winding-up or dissolution of the corporation. Where those private individuals adversely affected by the corporation's actions are unable to receive appropriate or just redress, the state will permit them to require the court to dissolve the corporation. In other words, these other interests are considered superior to the corporation's interest to exist or survive. In the context of the PMC, parties injured or killed by the PMC (for example, civilians or employees) would have access to the assets of the PMC by means of a winding-up.

A third remedy, revocation of a charter, is limited to the power of the state. It is not at all clear why this remedy, so carefully reserved to the state, has yet to be invoked with any regularity. Certainly, it may be undesirable to overuse it—it is the equivalent of the death penalty for corporations, although it amounts to no more than a winding-up order. There have been no concerted calls for this remedy as against PMCs. Indeed, the state has refused to use it against corporate serial offenders. Perhaps the most notorious of such corporate offenders is Unocal engaged in some of the exactly same crimes PMCs have committed. A shareholder activist website offers:

> Unocal has been involved in some of the worst oil spills and leaks in California history, and in a polluting sour-gas plant on Lubicon Cree land in Canada, as well as business negotiations with the Taliban militia of Afghanistan, which practices "gender apartheid." Organizations have submitted a petition to the Attorney General of California calling for the revocation of Unocal's corporate charter, due to the company's "environmental devastation", "complicity in crimes against humanity" in Burma and elsewhere, and other forms of corporate misconduct. Called "a company without a country" by Business Week, Unocal is a rogue company. In 1997, Unocal sold its refineries and Union 76 gas stations to Tosco, making it no longer subject to any boycott regarding Burma.[160]

Many of Unocal's business practices have been litigated with varying measures of success. In fact, so egregious is Unocal's record that the National Lawyers Guild, Alliance for Democracy, and the Burma Forum[161] in part citing Unocals PMC-like crimes have filed a petition on September 10, 1998, with the Attorney General of California to have its charter revoked.[162] Given that to date, citizens have been unsuccessful in their actions to access the remedy, it seems unlikely that without a fresh breath of air this remedy will be of much use in controlling PMCs. Nevertheless, were a state to dissolve a PMC for its behavior, it would send a powerful signal to the PMC industry as a whole.

Although an interesting and potentially powerful remedy that the attorneys general of various jurisdictions have expressed an interest in, as a punitive measure, it has yet to bear any fruit. Further, it leaves the other concern outstanding: What to do with the proceeds of a corporation so dissolved? If the objective is to discourage a particular type of behavior, certainly to return the investment to shareholders, which would be the normal outcome of a corporate dissolution after creditors' claims are satisfied, would be counterproductive. If under statutes such as the various statutes dealing with the Proceeds of Crime, assets which owe their existence to illegal activities can be seized by the state, it can be argued, by analogy, that the appropriate remedy should be similar in the case of corporate crime.

It is suggested that such remedies should be in addition to rather than substitution for the traditional remedies associated with breach of directors' duties. Where directors are determined to be in breach of their duties, they are likely to be personally liable. The present instance should brook no exception to this general rule.

Certainly, if there are to be direct remedies against shareholder assets, there ought to be direct remedies against directors as well. Legislators and judges have created exception to the general protection of directors for corporate harms. These exceptions include improperly declared dividends where such may lead to insolvency, unpaid employee wages, taxes, and certain environmental matters. Surely corporate killing is sufficiently significant to merit some such exception. If one accepts the rights, rewards of being a director or CEO in terms of power, compensation, and status, one accepts the attendant risks. Liability for corporate killing ought to be one of those risks.[163]

2.8 Regulatory recommendations

In sum, the implications for regulation from a corporate law analysis focus on the control of corporate actors, namely the corporation itself, directors, shareholders, and employees. In a commercial context, corporate action is guaranteed by bonding. Bonds are typically a percentage of the overall contract, and posted as a guarantee against default on the terms of the contract. They are designed to connect with the specifics of the particular contract ensuring performance and providing both a ready penalty and compensation for adversely affected parties.

As we have seen, corporate law is designed to shield shareholders and tends to shield directors and managers. Corporations have used their considerable assets to spirit away employees involved in inappropriate actions away from the scenes of their crimes, assisting them to flee the jurisdiction and avoid the juridical consequences of their actions. Bonding could be used to address this issue at two levels. First, the PMC should be required to post a bond. Doing so would provide an incentive to the PMC to appropriately vet and train its personnel before employing them. The matter of vetting and providing appropriate guidance and sufficient protection for employees has been a major issue. Second, bonding individual employees will make them both exceedingly conscious of the potential violence of their actions and the importance of their following rules, and provide sufficient incentive to follow the rules.

A second set of recommendations arising from corporate law is the notion of some form of vetting and control of directors. This could be done by setting standards to be required of PMC directors. These standards would require knowledge of more than business or even military matters. It would require a certain standard of understanding of the laws governing war and human rights. Where the directors are directing the utilization of the corporation's assets for such risky, potentially fatal ends, surely something more ought to be demanded of them than a mere nose for business and a sharp eye for profit. Like other professionals taking the lives of others into their hands, they ought to be held to a higher standard—the standard of a professional. Just as doctors and attorneys are required to have particular education and to swear certain oaths to pursue something more than mere profit and self-interest, society could certainly require the same of directors of PMCs. Indeed, given the vast powers bestowed on directors in the common business corporation, there are increasing calls among corporate governance experts for just such a regulatory system to be implemented in various jurisdictions. Experts are suggesting that professional bodies with examinations, regulations, and powers need to be established.[164] And that to be a director one would have to comply with the regulations. Indeed, current law in some jurisdictions precludes certain people from being directors on the basis of prior misdeeds.[165] There is no reason such a framework could not be developed tailored specifically to the issues surrounding PMCs.

A third set of recommendations from a corporate law perspective would involve some change to law, namely, dealing with board composition. There is no reason that board structures cannot be modified to include a representative of those particular civil interests on the board. This may be done by some form of government or humanitarian representation on the board. Simply, some nonbusiness personnel could be placed on the board of directors so as to ensure compliance with at least the minimal norms of international law. This approach has been taken with success in the case of popular efforts to eliminate multinationals' use of sweatshops. In those cases, companies wishing to do business with universities where students took an interest in the activities of the corporations wishing to supply them, they acceded to student representation on the board of directors.[166] In the case of the PMC there is no legal or economic reason that a group such as Amnesty International or the Red Cross-Red Crescent Societies or some other appropriate body could not have a representative on the board of directors—with adequate corporate funding, of course, to ensure that appropriate information is collected and reported in a timely manner.

Further, and especially where direct and overt political ends are to be engaged violently, as always the case as in "tip of the spear" and other offensive action contemplated[167] in PMC operations, there is no reason a political representative cannot be appointed to the board for purposes of public accountability. Certainly this idea cannot be objected to as "foreign" to the nature of the enterprise engaged in by the corporation, for as previously noted, many of these corporations explicitly identify their objectives as being not only closely aligned with government objectives, but indeed parroting word for word the political speech of the day. This approach—having a politician on the board—is part of Chinese corporate law in state-owned enterprises.[168] Although it may not achieve all the ends hoped for in that context, the idea should still provide some comfort and power ensuring government accountability to the populace and an implementation of a commitment to democracy.

Corporate incentives and monitoring implications connected to shareholding can be incorporated into PMC control. Either of the broader EU initiatives of "Golden Shares" or German public-private investment schemes could be used or modified to be appropriate for PMCs. These shareholdings can be used to control many things, not only the control of violence, but also limit the potential for fraud and abuse.

Finally, a remedy available and not to be overlooked is the state's right to dissolve the corporation. Keeping this stick in the spotlight will provide a strong and clear incentive to directors to ensure proper control and shareholders to monitor the board, and allow the broader public good of safety and the presumption of peace some financial teeth.

2.9 Conclusion

Certainly, these solutions do not exhaust the field. Other aspects of corporate regulation could be drawn from more significant changes to the corporate model itself. For example, having employees on the board would provide significant informational advantages, and having employees own a certain percentage of shares may well help achieve a balancing of short and long term interests which would enhance the notions of care to respect law. Such changes, however, are beyond the scope of immediately foreseeable and hence enactable regulatory reform. Certainly, we are not living in the best of all possible worlds; however, there is no reason at law that creative strategies cannot be created to at least mitigate some of the more repugnant activities that one of law's creations may choose to pursue.

3
The State, Control of Violence, and the Private Military Corporation

3.1 Introduction

This chapter examines nation-states and PMCs in the domestic context. It conceptualizes the PMC somewhat differently in that the PMC in the literature follows a taxonomy focusing exclusively on problems associated with foreign activity. While to do so is both heuristically sound and reflective of the majority of concerns about the PMC, to a certain extent it ignores the 800lb gorilla in the room. This chapter conceptualizes the PMC as an organized, armed, well-financed private group in its home state. Such groups are usually referred to as paramilitary, which indeed they are, just as the PMC is. While paramilitaries may have different motivations in addition to profit, they are engaged in the same fundamental activities of changing the distributions of the spoils of war and other violence. The chapter begins with a review of the nation-state and related notions of sovereignty, including the monopoly of violence. It then turns to examine in detail the Rule of Law and constitutional limitations. Next, it reviews the privatization of defense and issues surrounding domestic accountability. Finally, it turns to examine the nation-state's use of PMCs extraterritorially. Assimilated into this analysis is the role of the PMC as a foreign policy tool. The analysis will be underpinned by five case studies in the contemporary international context: Iraq—Supplementing unilateral action, Sudan—Avoiding public scrutiny, East Timor—Honoring international commitments, Equatorial Guinea—Advancing domestic values on the international stage, and the Balkans—Achieving conflicting objectives by sleight of hand. Alongside this analysis, the chapter will provide some insights on the PMC to influence on international law and geopolitical ordering.

3.2 The nation-state

The formation of the nation-state is a study in itself; fortunately for our purposes, a brief review of the nature of the nation-state will suffice. Although the origins of the nation-state can be traced from the Greek city-state, through the Roman Empire and Machiavelli of the middle ages,[1] the nation-state of the twenty-first century, as it is known to us, is a creature of the seventeenth century, resulting ultimately and in a crystallized form from the Peace of Westphalia.[2]

The nation-state as defined by law in the twentieth century is "a person of international law [and] should possess the following qualifications: (a) a permanent population, (b) defined territory, (c) government, and (d) capacity to enter into relations with other states."[3] This traditional definition, however, has found itself challenged in the tumultuous times following the collapse of colonial powers and the disintegration of the Soviet Union, and even more so in the efforts to settle matters following the dismantling of Yugoslavia.[4] The weakness of the population-territory-foreign relations formula results in the necessity of states, or would be states, or other international actors to rely on other, more traditional indicia of statehood: violence.

One of the fundamental and traditional indicia is the ability to inflict sufficient levels of violence to establish independence from other parties who would control the population and territory, and govern. These indicia were first seen in the establishment of the nation-states as legal entities independent of the auspices of the church conjoined with the Holy Roman Empire.[5] This establishment of statehood on the basis of violent rebellion combined with an unrelenting insistence on independence has been a hallmark of states ever since, as seen in such disparate circumstances as the secession of the Thirteen Colonies to create the United States of America, the rebellions of the Spanish colonies in South America creating the states of modern-day Latin America, and more recently the decolonization of Africa.[6] From this perspective, the need and ability to inflict violence and hence to limit the effect of other violent behavior is at the foundation of the state.

States by definition are sovereign. That is, they are self-contained entities, not defined by reference to other existing orders, or other parties—although as noted, recognition by other states is an important part of the claim to statehood. The idea of sovereignty as initially conceived of by the sixteenth-century French thinker, Jean Bodin, was unlimited.[7] That is, there was no lawmaker or law above the state as embodied in the monarch except the laws of God and Nature.[8] Over time, the notion of sovereignty was transferred from individual monarchs to parliaments and modified to make it subject to law and in particular a constitution. As Maogoto puts it:

> One thing is clear and unanimous: sovereignty embodied the supreme authority of a State within its territorial sphere excluding dependence on any other authority, and particularly the authority of another state. In essence, sovereignty is independence.... It is internal independence with

> regard to the liberty of action of a State inside its border. As comprising the power of a State to exercise supreme authority over all persons and things within its territory, sovereignty is territorial supremacy.[9]

The basis of this independence is the state's ability to impose its will by force. And it is this ability that gives rise to the discussion of the monopoly of violence.

3.3 The nation-state and the monopoly of violence

Implicit in most commentaries concerned with the proliferation of PMCs, and explicit on some occasions,[10] is the belief that the state should have a monopoly over the use of violence. The modern formulation of the idea is attributable to Max Weber.[11] However, in states with a common law tradition, one finds earlier manifestations of the principle such as the 1688 English Bill of Rights which states "[t]hat the raising or keeping a standing Army within the Kingdome in time of peace unless it is with consent of Parliament is against law."[12] A major achievement in the English Bill of Rights was the reinforcement of the state's monopoly over violence by ensuring that there were no standing armies in Britain that were not controlled by the state.

It is the state's monopoly of violence that underpins the international legal system and justifies the emphasis on state sovereignty.[13] It is on this basis that states are recognized as having the right and capacity to declare war, act in self-defense, sign peace treaties, etc.[14] A second dimension of the doctrine of sovereignty is that states have the responsibility for protecting individual rights, a function they could not purport to fulfill if they did not enjoy a monopoly over violence. Third and often implicit in the discussion is the notion that in some way the violence of the state is somehow limited by or answerable to the populace. Accordingly, any nonstate actor engaging in violence, including mercenaries, PMCs, and terrorists, can readily be classified as a threat to state sovereignty, and hence illegitimate.

Given that violence has been the state's ultimate guarantee of sovereignty, violence has traditionally been carefully regulated within the borders of states. On a practical level, states have insisted on the de facto control of violence. That is, the state's monopoly of violence has been guaranteed by the development and institutionalization of state-sponsored, nationalist-based, standing armies, and the development of state-controlled armaments manufacturers. By controlling both the personnel engaged or prepared to engage in violence and the weapons they would use, the state secured to itself control of the means of challenging its sovereignty, and so ensured its continued existence at least as against those under its control.

On the legal level, constraint on the use of violence has been through a combination of constitutional law, administrative law, and the important related legal principle, the Rule of Law, as it pertains to the state. Criminal law is the other legal control on violence as it pertains to private actors. (Control of PMCs under domestic law via regulation is treated in detail in chapter 4 of the present work.) The discussion now turns to an examination of the two forms for controlling violence within a sovereign state, namely, practical or de facto control and legal or de jure control, first of the state and then the PMC.

3.3.1 Nation-state and de facto control of armed groups and armaments

Since the decline of mercenarism (discussed in chapter 1 and a topic returned to in chapter 5) and the development of standing armies, the nation-state has had greater confidence in its ability to defend its sovereignty. Indeed, it may be that one of the few lessons of history ever learned is the necessity of dealing carefully with mercenary armies, as the ultimate dealings with Wallerstein's 120,000 strong militia demonstrated.[15] As previously noted, since the mid-seventeenth century, English states have been most reluctant to tolerate the existence of organized, armed groups within their territories.[16] Accordingly, the only armed and organized groups generally permitted to exist openly in modern-day states are government sponsored and controlled armed groups such as police and military.

In asserting its de facto control over these groups, states have ensured that the groups are clearly identifiable, trained, and accountable. Both the personnel and their weaponry are carefully regulated. Care is taken when the personnel are recruited, trained, and disciplined (within the means of the state in question of course), and the selection of high-ranking officers is done with consideration given to political as well as strategic abilities. The weapons they are given to use are also carefully registered and controlled. They are assigned to limited, restricted areas where they are permitted to amass, train, and discharge weapons. Even with this care in recruitment, training and discipline, and the control of weapons, history is replete with examples of state armies rebelling, overthrowing governments by way of coup d'etat, and inflicting violent agendas on civilians.[17] Police history manifests a similar tendency, particularly with respect to violent dealings with local populations. This violence has been used at times to support and to oppose the government, its policies, and the populace. It is important to remember that the value provided by personnel is not limited to pulling a trigger. Strategic advice from well-trained advisers can be just as important, if not more so, as the weaponry itself,[18] as services by major PMCs MPRI and CACI illustrate.

The other de facto strategy for controlling violence within the nation-state has been by control of armaments and weapons industries. States have put forth various reasons for controlling or at least dominating the weapons industries. Much, if not all, of the major weaponry of the twentieth century was developed under the auspices of the state. From fighter jets and stealth bombers to the Internet, to precision-guided bombs and missiles, and to nuclear armaments, governments have sought to control the development and distribution of weaponry in all its forms.[19] This strategy has a long history, and indeed, archaeological excavations in ancient Crete have unearthed jars of weapons stored in the floors of royal palaces, indicating the recognition of the strategic importance of control of amassed weapons by rulers thousands of years ago.[20] Arsenals of various sorts have been major enterprises of nations and indeed have been described as "the major industrial undertaking of medieval Europe"[21] in the twentieth century. The formerly denominated military-industrial complex—now New Military Industrial Complex[22]—remains a major force in business and government around the world. The 2008 budget of the Department of Defense of the George W. Bush administration is seeking $100 billion for weapons acquisition,[23] just under 10 percent of the 2006 annual worldwide military expenditure of $1204 billion.[24]

The state, however, can no longer rely on de facto control over personnel and weaponry for the regulation of armed groups, including the PMC. One cause of the loss of de facto control is the end of the Cold War, when, as previously mentioned, much of both the personnel and the weaponry previously so carefully controlled and regulated escaped sovereign reigns, and both creating and entering a market for just such goods and services.[25] Efforts to control the black market in weapons have arguably been unsuccessful.[26] As Peter Marsh observes, "Almost all firearms in the black market were originally manufactured under government control, came from military stockpiles, or were bought from licensed gun dealers."[27] In other words, a large and burgeoning black market for weapons has made governments' de facto control not practically possible. Many of the weapons, at least, have entered the black market. This removal of the superpowers' cap on weapons, the loss of traditional markets for weapons manufacturers, combined with the explosion of transnational organized crime have contributed to the development and growth of a black market.[28] In addition to the obstacle represented by the black market, de facto control is not feasible because modern states have never eliminated the private manufacture and distribution of weapons. Furthermore the changing nature of weaponry is such that contemporary advanced weaponry may be made from components that may be dual use and/or sourced through a long obscure supply chain.[29] Finally, despite various efforts at regulation of the arms trade, weapons manufacturers as profit-driven businesses will find ways to sell and distribute arms wherever they find markets.

Accordingly, de facto control of armed groups and weapons is no more than a political fantasy. We turn now to examine the other means of control over the exercise of the state's monopoly of violence, namely legal or de jure control.

3.3.2 Nation-state and de jure control of armed groups, weapons industries, and violence

Nation-state control of armed groups and weapons industries is not only de facto but also de jure. That is to say, the laws of the nation create not only the existence of the armed forces and police, but create a regulatory framework allowing the government to ensure the safe, appropriate, and legal use of violence—at least in theory. Having a framework in place, monitored by government, accountable to the populace (again theoretically),[30] and subject to judicial scrutiny and determinations, the independent ability of such armed groups to control or inflict violence on a society is curtailed.

As previously noted, the English parliament made private standing armies illegal in 1688. In other words, only the state military was a legitimate military organization: other militaries were illegal, and to organize or maintain or attempt to do so would be illegal. After the Peace of Westphalia, as nation-states developed institutionally they shifted from a reliance on mercenaries to standing armies, and developed the law governing the existence, activities, and uses of those armies contemporaneously.[31]

Interestingly, the situation in the US led to different view of the matter, and may be a bit of an exception to the general rule. Indeed, even today the issue of legalities of private militias is not settled at law. As a result of the Second Amendment, which reads: "A well regulated Militia, being necessary to the security of a free State, the right of the people to keep and bear Arms, shall not be infringed," Americans have the right to bear arms, and despite ongoing litigation, judicial interpretation of the amendment is not settled. Accordingly, two different circuit courts have held conflicting views on whether the right is an individual right or a collective right/militia to bear arms.[32] Nevertheless, even in that nation-state it is well established that the right of private militias to parade and exercise in public is quite restricted.[33] Still it is universally accepted that the military should be subject to government legislated control.

The issue of police regulation is quite similar. Police are not free to act and inflict violence as they see fit. Instead, with the development of modern policing, arguably with the London constabulary reorganized under Robert Peel in 1829,[34] police have been held accountable by law for their actions.[35] Police can be liable to both criminal and civil prosecution for violent acts carried out in the course of their duties.[36] Police use of force is carefully circumscribed by law, as is the wearing of uniforms, and the display and discharge of their weapons. Where police violate these laws, they will be subject to legal sanction like any other member of the public. Just as the other organized armed group in modern society, the military, the police are subject to de jure control.

Private policing has a longer history than public policing in the modern state. Indeed, policing was a private matter until the early nineteenth century.[37] In the US and subsequently elsewhere, names such as Wells-Fargo,

Burns, and Pinkerton have become well-known. These and other private police providers have lesser legal powers than public police. Like public police, however, they are subject to the laws governing the behavior of nonpolice actors, and generally, further, in many instances, their status as private police officers does not offer them additional protection from the liabilities of their policing actions. In addition, they may be subject to regulation where they interact with the public in an official capacity, wear a uniform, or carry otherwise restricted weapons.[38] Thus police, whether public or private, are in theory subject to high levels of legal accountability. It is important to note that one of the world's leading experts on policing describes these common notions of police accountability and control as "myths." Philip Stenning writes:

> A...prevailing myth about private police is that they are not [as] accountable as public police are. This is...particularly troubling...because it misleads us about the public police as well as the private police. The public police are not as effectively accountable as this myth would have us believe, and private police are certainly not as unaccountable as the myth suggests.[39]

Although private police are at least as accountable as public police, they have considerably more power than is commonly acknowledged. Again, Stenning is worth quoting:

> A more accurate description of the powers of most private security personnel would be that they have no fewer powers than...other powerful persons and institutions in society whose agents they are. Even a moment's reflection will make it clear that these people and institutions are able to wield power over the lives of ordinary citizens which far exceed those we accord to the public police, let alone ordinary citizens themselves.[40]

In most developed countries, neither the military nor the police are granted independent discretion as to when they choose to inflict violence on the populace, and they certainly cannot do so without some accountability to both the government and the populace. Of course, in countries where the police and military are more corrupt, accountability to and control by government and the populace in general is not nearly as pervasive. However, such corruption does not invalidate the principle. Rather it illustrates the point that armed groups need to be closely watched and accountable to protect civilian interests, create an environment of safety and peace, and enhance governability of the state. Nevertheless, in the last decades of the twentieth century governments took steps back from immediate control by engaging in an exercise of privatization, including the privatization of defense services. We turn now to examine privatization generally before turning the discussion to the privatization of defense specifically.

3.4 Privatization: A historical and policy perspective

Privatization does not describe a single government initiative, rather, it consists of a host of government initiatives based upon neoclassical economics, economic rationalism, and neoliberal free market ideology. In the supply of public benefits, this commitment translates into the contracting out of government services, the commercialization of government departments, and the sale or partial sale of public enterprises.[41]

The privatization of the public sector is a trend in institutionally and economically strong states that has been dominant since the Reagan-Thatcher era. It is driven by the basic belief noted in the previous chapter that governments are inefficient suppliers of goods and services, and by a political commitment to the philosophy that such government activity impinges on the liberty of citizens. The result of such privatization initiatives is that functions and roles that were once exclusively provided by the state and which were viewed as fundamental to its identity are now being provided by the private sector.[42]

Broad statements such as the following from the Australian National Audit Office are illustrative:

> Where feasible the right to deliver government services should be open to a range of private sector providers. In cases where direct competition in the delivery of government services is not feasible because it is more economic to have only one provider, the right to provide the government service could be put to tender. Such potential competition would provide strong incentives for improved performance by public sector managers.[43]

Where states have resisted the privatization agenda they have at times been unsuccessful. Weak states have often been forced to follow the neoliberal agenda through the structural adjustment programs of the World Bank and the IMF.[44] In these cases, the governments have no choice but to surrender to the demands of financiers, cutting all government services, including defense. Where this has happened and the complying states find themselves in need of defense services, they may have no choice but to contract for services in the newly created PMC market, dominated by large American firms.[45]

Unfortunately, the anticipated efficiencies of outsourcing have not been realized in the private sector, where one would have most certainly expected to see the savings.[46] That being the case, it seems less than logical to expect those efficiencies to have occurred in the public sector, and indeed, as noted previously with respect to defense costs in the USA at least, they have not.[47]

Another important issue for consideration when discussing the privatization of public goods is the issue of accountability. While the word "accountability" can have a wide variety of meanings in the context of privatization, it means being responsible for the timely delivery of sufficient quantity and quality at reasonable cost. Lacking public accountability, corporations frequently fail to operate facilities and offer services with an eye to the public good. While they can hardly be faulted for this—after all, public good is not their province—they are responsible and should be held accountable for failing to fulfill properly their contractual obligations. Unfortunately, such has not always been the case. Further, the failure to fulfill these contracts has had significant negative consequences for the governments and populations that have relied upon privatized service providers, in terms of both immediate and practical consequences as well as economic consequences. Where fresh water,[48] electricity,[49] roadways,[50] or other services have not been provided, the population has suffered, the government has lost credibility, and the great expenditure of economic resources[51] and government resources used to privatize has been wasted.

Privatization does not result in the sudden dissolution of the supplying entities or organizations supplying or in the dispersion of the supply of these goods and services widely through the population. Rather, these opportunities are taken up by a select number of prepared parties. These parties are groups of investors, former bureaucrats and government officials, industry executives, and other insiders working through corporate entities and structures. These corporate entities, whether newly purpose-formed enterprise-specific entities, or add-ons to existing corporate groups, have the potential to become major forces as significant actors in the marketplace, and powerful corporate citizens in the political sphere.[52]

Privatization, therefore, does not necessarily result in new efficiencies or a democratization of goods and services or a new level of transparency or accountability. Rather, if anything, it results in the opposite, at least in respect of the latter two. Privatization results in a concentration of formerly publicly provided goods and services into the hands of a few privately held entities, protected from public scrutiny by laws protecting commercial secrets. We turn in the next section to examine the privatization of defense services.

3.5 Privatization of defense services: Historical trajectories and market drivers

Privatization of defense follows from two historical trajectories. The first is the series of events, as previously mentioned, associated with the end of the Cold War.[53] These events include the discharge of vast numbers of employees from militaries of the Communist Block and the corollary release of all types of weaponry formerly belonging to national militaries. Coincident with this release was a second phase of decolonization marked by the independence of various former soviet republics and satellites.[54] (The first phase of decolonization is of the last century resulting from the combination of expulsion and withdrawal of European powers from former colonies around the globe.) Many of these newly formed states both republics and former colonies have been unsuccessful in establishing their sovereignty through any means, including the failure to establish effective national armed services.[55] Combined, these facts have proved to be significant market drivers and created both a great supply and a huge demand for violent services.

The combination of personnel and resources seeking economic opportunities in a destablized world coincided with the other second major historical trajectory, the neoliberal commitment to privatization. Neoliberal policy makers, as indicated above, argue that the government is an inefficient means of providing goods and services, and that government involvement in their position limits individual opportunity or liberty to participate in the market. So from a liberal to the greatest extent possible government should withdraw from the provision of such. Instead, those services should be sourced and purchased from the market, including military services.

Indeed, a democratic-capitalist political perspective, other than the previously discussed theory of state monopoly over violence, there are no ideological reasons to categorically preclude the privatization of violence. The incentives that motivate states to contract out existing defense roles to PMCs, or more radically to commercialize their own defense forces are largely political and economic. As privatization is currently both ideologically and politically in vogue, it follows that states have legislated to facilitate privatization, including defense.

There are a number of reasons that could explain why states such as the United States and the United Kingdom, over the last 20 years, have been so receptive to privatization and, in particular, outsourcing aspects of their defense sectors. First, there is a long history of private military providers and therefore a sense of familiarity.[56] Second, as a result of the Reagan-Thatcher changes from the 1980s onwards, there was a nascent military service market ready to compete with the public defense sector.[57] These military provider firms, which were primarily providing military hardware up until that time, from that period onwards, provided logistical support services as well as military equipment.[58] Indeed, services make up majority of privatized defense spending. Third, there was the Vietnam War experience, which marked a significant increase in contracting and saw the start of the trend of senior military personnel moving to the private sector and providing services back to their former employment.

Finally, the Gulf War accelerated the privatization of defense services. The vivid television coverage of the Desert Storm campaign brought home the harsh realities of modern warfare and the value of outsourced military services. After that war, US government commissioned studies to explore ways in which private companies could increase their participation in military operations by selling more services to US armed forces operating in combat zones.[59] In the wake of the Gulf War, the 1990s saw a proliferation in the size and number of PMCs worldwide with the value of publicly listed PMCs growing at twice the rate of the Dow Jones Industrial Average.[60] Earlier estimates suggested that the total value of the PMC market would rise from $33.6 billion in 1990 to $202 billion in 2010;[61] as of 2006 the market had reached an estimated $100 billion.[62] This exponential growth in the PMC sector suggests that states are increasingly willing to entrust PMCs with the delivery of defense services. Indeed, it is to be expected that the market would boom when the then US Secretary of Defense, Donald Rumsfeld, publishes a piece in Foreign Affairs advocating a privatized defense policy.[63]

3.6 Control and accountability of privatized defense forces

One of the most significant challenges to the privatization agenda is maintaining control and accountability. In the case of controlling privatized defense capabilities including controlling the PMCs, the record, including the case of Iraq discussed in detail later in this chapter and mentioned throughout in passing, is appalling. In other contexts as mentioned previously, this weakness of accountability and control has surfaced where private corporate-controlled services have failed to public expectations. They have breached commitments to maintenance, operation, and development of areas previously operated by governments.[64]

In the context of the privatization of defense, as will be shown, the situation is different making the matter of accountability of PMCs a matter of urgent concern. When public militaries and governments interact, the interactions have not always been peaceful. Drawing from the history of such interactions, one should certainly conclude that a public military does not always act in the public interest. History is replete with instances in which a military has seized control and been unwilling to give up power.[65] Nevertheless, public militaries often can and do surrender to public will, particularly when the basis for their legitimacy rests on some notion of public accountability and maintenance of the Rule of Law. The privatized defense industry, however, has no such constraints, and indeed history is replete with examples of PMCs running amok.

Consider the example of the US-sponsored PMCs supporting the Contras' attacks on the democratically elected government of El Salvador. That debacle, which was finally brought to an end by public scrutiny and disclosure of what came to be known as the Iran-Contra Affair, left El Salvador in shambles with gangs and paramilitaries running rampant.[66] One may also consider the example of DynCorp's activities in the Balkans,[67] or lesser known events such as Spearhead Ltd.'s training of the Colombian drug enforcers whose list of victims included mayors, provincial governors, judges, presidential candidates, and civilians massacred in terror causing bombings,[68] the activities of which have left whole regions in ruins.

This set of problems raises the issue of accountability of PMCs in the domestic context. These are that (1) the defense services provided by the PMC the objectives whether cast as contract specifications or broader policy objectives, (2) the services are performed within the bounds of the law, (3) the activities undertaken are fully and truthfully reported, and (4) all breaches of obligations create appropriate avenues of liability and compensation.

Perhaps the greatest challenge of accountability has to do with violent actions taken by a PMC extraterritorially in the name of a nation without corollary accountability to the people of that nation. Unlike other privatized services, which may be provided extraterritorially, PMC services may well include intentional death or injury, and challenge the sovereignty of another people. Services of this nature and potential consequences require a distinctly higher level of accountability to a nation's people than say the provision of privatized transport services. Indeed, Rachel Weber, in her detailed study of the defense industry, argues for a thoroughgoing revision of the government's approach to defense industry contractors in essence removing industry participants from the strictly private sphere based on the nature of their work, subsidies received, and the level of importance to the nation.[69]

Thus the basic challenge of control and accountability is exacerbated when a state privatizes the delivery of defense services. Given the nature of defense services and the consequent need for vast sums of money, secrecy, and power, the importance of control and accountability as well as the risks associated with privatization are exponentially greater.

There have been a shocking number of serious abuses by PMCs of their de facto powers. These include fraud and corruption discussed in chapter 2, and include not only failing to warn a government it has been hired to protect, but in fact, participating in the overthrow of that government in favor of a preferred government.[70] Other incidents related to their deployment in Iraq discussed throughout, and of course the exploitative compensation demands including mineral rights put to cash strapped governments. As the Iraq experience demonstrates, there have been few if any lessons learned when dealing with PMCs. Companies that have murdered civilians, as we saw, have not only not been penalized but have been awarded additional contracts.

Singer sets out the nub of the problem thus: "With PMCs, clear tensions always exist between the security goals of clients and the firms' desire for profit maximisation. For governments, the public good and the good of the private companies are not identical."[71] Indeed, Singer, writing in 2003, seems prescient concerning problems encountered with PMCs in Iraq when he goes on to identify the three main obstacles to effective control of PMCs in the domestic context. First, among the obstacles he identifies the problem of monitoring. From the contract drafting and tendering process to the implementation, evaluation, and renewal process, the contracting process is complex. While these problems have the potential to occur in any contract, they pose a particular quagmire for governmental contracting with the PMC. PMC contracts may be predetermined or in a highly specialized niche market that precludes actual competition, and so avoid market scrutiny. Contracts with PMCs often take place in highly secret contexts, such as in the course of war. In fact some types of monitoring have been precluded in Iraq by the shortage of personnel available to PMCs. Further PMCs as private actors, dealing with private contracts and having access to military secrets, are well shielded from public scrutiny. Such being the case it is obvious that PMC contracts may well go unobserved by public authorities.[72] Monitoring is further challenged in the field when the chain of command is not clear, a complaint made by military officials, leaving it unclear to which the PMC is accountable and for what.[73] On the issue of accountability, one may ask about the PMC's accountability from activity in the field to such things as accountabilities in the office for expenditures, and ultimately for military success. The question of accountability becomes even more difficult when parties' accountabilities are in conflict, as in the case of the PMC. The conflict of profit and security is not a minor matter as was illustrated in a recent incident when the airport in Baghdad was shut down by the firm engaged to guard it over a pay dispute,[74] and also in Blackwater's threat to refuse to guard US diplomats when Iraq wished to "cancel its license." The more specific discussion of the vagaries of the PMC contract will be saved for later in this chapter.

A second concern Singer identifies is the profit motive. Whereas one of the neoliberal government's objectives in the use of privatized defense service is the reduced expenditure, the PMC's objective is the opposite. What is particularly different in the PMC-government nexus, however, is that the nature of the services provided puts the government in a vulnerable position in two senses. First, where a government has privatized its defense services, it is no longer in position to substitute its own resources in the event of PMC failure. Accordingly, it is in a very weak bargaining position particularly vis-à-vis an entrenched PMC providing service in a niche market. Second, services as opposed to goods are harder to measure and monitor, and indeed are easier to supply at less than agreed levels than goods, and again particularly so in the supply of military services.[75] PMCs have encouraged outrageous and notorious cost overruns, including overcharging, billing for ghost employees, encouraging unwitting military officers whose focus is on strategy rather than expenditures to take more expensive alternatives, and even outright fraud.[76] These outrages have occurred to such an extent in Iraq that a Senate hearing, "Combating War Profiteering: Are We Doing Enough to Investigate and Prosecute Contracting Fraud and Abuse in Iraq?" was organized. Senator Leahy reported "untold billions [were] unaccounted for"[77] and the Office of the Inspector General was only able to report that $9.8 million had been repaid in restitution.[78] The ten largest PMCs in Iraq have collectively repaid $300 million in penalties.[79]

These two issues have bearing on the efficiency claim supporting the neoliberal privatization policy agenda. As noted in chapter 2, Markusen's study indicates that the predicted efficiencies have not been realized.[80] She wrote: "No one has been able to evaluate fully the long-term costs and consequences of extensive privatization of national defense, and the sheer inability to do so should give pause to advocates of outsourcing anything other than the most routine functions."[81] Indeed, while standing armies are expensive, the less accountable and corporately shielded PMCs will almost certainly prove to be more so,[82] even without counting the costs to democracy and its institutions.

The third question for the PMC as Singer identifies is, "Why fight hard?"[83] He notes the incentives to prolong contracts, protect one's weapons and employees. Other concerns include the firm's potential reluctance to fight on the basis of protecting its own commercial interests in certain areas, preferring to protect its land-based assets over the government's strategic needs and objectives, or divided loyalties where its employees wish to avoid engaging in combat against former comrades working for PMCs on the other side of a conflict, as appears to have happened in Ethiopia.[84] While Singer notes these negative examples, PMCs have engaged in firefights apparently beyond contractual obligations in certain instances in Iraq.[85] Although these PMCs have conducted themselves admirably under fire in Iraq, what the norm is cannot be determined. There is an interesting alternative perspective. That perspective places the onus on the government to be a smarter client.[86] The USA Department of Defense has taken a number of steps in that direction with some success, however, at least the Pentagon's ability has been outsourced to the extent that it can be a smart buyer may be compromised.[87]

Achieving PMC accountability to the nation-state in both the domestic and international contexts may well require some radical rethinking of traditional approaches to control of PMCs, as well as reform to corporate and contract law and regulation. The foregoing discussion of the complexities of accountability and control associated with the privatization of defense sets the stage for a fresh analysis of the nation-state-corporate-PMC relationship and potential for the de facto and de jure control of the PMC to which we turn next. It should be noted that in terms of the accountability for violence inflicted extraterritorially one cannot but be pessimistic. Laws and courts have been remarkably otiose in constraining governments in their foreign adventures. Given such, control of PMCs in that context by legal means is not likely to produce much result.

3.7 Control of the corporation as creature of the state

It is the basis and nature of the state, as an independent, self-creating, self-perpetuating entity to be able to enforce its desires on those other entities or bodies within its territorial jurisdiction that gives it its claim to control, regulate, and enforce its regulations. Among the regulated entities is, of course, the military and all corporations, including the PMC.

Although the legal nature of the PMC has been discussed in detail in chapter 2, a brief note here will establish it in its relation to the state in the domestic legal context. Today, most corporations are created by a simple registration process. They need not have carefully proscribed objects, but instead are given an unlimited range of powers and activities in which they are permitted to engage so long as they abide by the law. As creations of the state-sponsored legal system, they exist by authorization of the state. In other words, their very existence at law is dependent on the prior existence of and recognition by the state. This fact of their existence lays out clearly the nature of the relationship between the state and the corporation at law. The latter is dependent on the former not only for its existence, but also for its rights and powers.

Most states have a legislative framework and extensive regulatory regime which controls corporations. From the initial enabling provisions of a statute to the registration, reporting, internal governance, and winding up of the corporation, most corporate acts are controlled or at least addressed by a statutory framework. This framework is in addition to the rules governing human persons, which, by large, also apply to corporations. Thus, the corporation occupies one place in the state's overall legislative schema, which regulates and controls the activities of actors within its internal sovereign sphere.[88] It follows logically from this that the corporation ought not to dictate to the state, and morally, that the corporation ought not to threaten the state with violence.

Nevertheless, corporations do dictate to states regularly in the political arena through various corporate lobbyists' contractual terms and political influence. Of particular concern in the discussion of the PMC is the corporation dictating to the state backed up with the threat of violence. This is not an idle threat. As previously noted, PMCs have dictated to the state which governors it will accept, and have used force or abetted others against its own client when it preferred those others for its own ends.[89] In this context, the state faces an ironic and peculiar dilemma in that it has created an independent entity and outsourced its sovereign monopoly of violence to it and then that subject entity purports to challenge the validity of the state, which enabled its creation. As stated, control of the PMC is done by the state through four areas of law—contract, corporate law, procurement law, and regulation aimed at the industry generally. The section which follows will deal only with the first type, contract, as corporate law and the PMC are dealt with in chapter 2 and regulation of the industry is dealt with in chapter 4.

3.7.1 De jure control of the PMC—Law of contract

Contract law is the primary means by which the state controls the PMC, provided, of course, that the state has not outlawed the PMC outright.[90] Contracting with PMCs, however, is replete with difficulties. Among other things the Defense Industry Initiative, an American process started in the 1960s, although purported to be a means of improving accountability and reducing fraud in defense procurement, is first and foremost a measure by the industry to improve its public image by promoting accountability, and as such prima facie evidence of the problem.[91] Contractor fraud and abuse in Iraq is so notorious that further evidence is redundant. The US tends to prefer no-bid, costs-plus, indefinite delivery contracts. These contracts allow the government to rely on suppliers to attend to government needs without a constant renegotiation, allowing the supplier to be assured it will receive payment, and the military to rest assured it will receive the support it requires without constant referral to high-ups for obvious, urgently needed goods and services. Suppliers given this golden credit card arrangement tend to oversupply.[92] The alternative approach to widely drafted, open-ended contracting has been taken by the UK. The UK has set rigid, capped contracts; how- ever, as its experience in Kosovo demonstrated, contracts of this type tend to be more cumbersome to deal with and more costly as well.[93]

While contracting for goods may be a challenge, contracting for services is even more fraught with difficulty.[94] Given that the majority of defense spending (in the US at least) is for services, the issue becomes more pressing. One important issue is whether it is possible to draft contracts between states and PMCs with the necessary specificity to achieve objectives. For example, one may ask: can an objective such as "winning the hearts and minds" be drafted with sufficient specificity to form a contractual objective? The question is not facetious as indeed this is the oft-repeated military objective certainly as subject to privatization as any other. This question is separate and distinctive from the issue of whether trained and experienced and armed foreign personnel (whether PMC or military) can interact with local populations (they can). The question is focused on the issue of sufficient levels of legal certainty in a contract to determine matters of fulfillment, of breach, and enforcement. The objective, of course, is to avoid being void for uncertainty, and hence, unenforceable. Such specificity is necessary as it permits, at least potentially, the state to evaluate and control the PMC by making the PMC subject to damages for breach. The state must be able to describe or define the services it wants from a PMC and be able to stipulate appropriate specificity to achieve the objectives of the contract, stipulating performance standards and benchmarks to ensure that all of the overall objects of the contract have been met.

An example illustrates the point. Mike McNamara, principal adviser, Logistics Projects, Department of Defense in Australia observed: "we know how to buy guns, boats, trains and planes, but are less good at buying services."[95] Consider a specific request for tender (RFT) from the Australian

Department of Defense in relation to the provision of information technology (IT) services: "Defense seeks a partnership-oriented cooperative longer term relationship where the contract is able to flexibly provide the services needed by Defense in the rapidly changing IT environment."[96]

McNamara argued that the RFT was not a "motherhood statement," rather it clearly indicated to potential contractors that the Defense Department "was not going to want to look at the fine detail of the contract every day of the week." What the Department of Defense sought was to develop a "close working relationship." Without providing any specifics, McNamara stated that the prospective contractors put forward very robust and viable arrangements to achieve Defense's stated objectives.[97]

One can understand the Australian Department of Defense's objective—it wanted to ensure that the contract arising from the RFT provided maximum flexibility with respect to IT in a fast changing environment and that negotiating a ceaseless stream of minor variations to the contract would be unnecessary. From a contractor's perspective, however, it may not be desirable to build such flexibility into a contract as it raises the risk of unquantifiable deliverables or unknowable performance measures. Were a contractor to accept such flexible terms, the contract price would need to be very high to allow the contractor to meet numerous contingencies and still make a profit. If it is difficult and time-consuming for the Australian government to draft a suitable contract for the delivery of IT services in the defense context, then it will be even more difficult for states to draft effective contracts for the retention of PMCs generally and particularly when violent activities or events are anticipated. Not only is it difficult to contract for the "unknown unknowns," to use Rumsfeld's infelicitous phrase, and set sufficiently specific or even appropriate objectives in that context, second-tier specificity setting appropriate methods, procedures, and rules could only be described as nightmarish.

Other concerns arising in the contract negotiation and preparation phase are illustrated in the Papua New Guinea (PNG) contract with Sandline. There are two points of particular interest in the contract. First was the nature of the negotiations between Sandline and the PNG government over payment of the contract. Sandline drafted the contract and was not willing to reconsider any of the contractual terms except the payment terms. Sandline recognized the government's vulnerable position and commenced hard bargaining. Second, Sandline indicated that in relation to payment it was willing to consider accepting "part repayment with mineral concessions" in Panguna Copper mine.[98] Yet it was exactly corporate and government control over the mine that was a critical issue in the indigenous revolt illustrating, of course, the political nature of violence.[99] The PNG government did not agree to make payments of this kind: however, Sandline's interest in payments in the form of future rights in the national resources of PNG, a common practice of this PMC, is indicative of a broader problem—if PMCs accept economic interests in a state's natural resources, then they may be unwilling to leave that state at the end of the contract if to do so means forfeiting their payment, or security of payment. It also compromises the notion of the disinterested PMC. A PMC that counts on payment only in the event of one outcome in a civil war becomes a political warrior and not merely an economic actor. As well, it exposes the untenable views that PMCs are readily distinguishable as "good" or "bad" and that they are merely suppliers of technical solutions in political contexts.

Consider in addition the contractual concerns raised by Singer and discussed earlier. Although a contract may call for "fighting hard," putting weapons, personnel and other resources at risk to achieve strategic ends, this contractual obligation is diametrically opposed to the business ends. While Brooks argues that PMCs fight hard to increase profitability to keep fixed costs down, there are certainly other and more pressing contract and profitability concerns.[100] For the business, the preservation of these critical resources is necessary for the preservation of the business itself. The PMC does not earn money on the basis of the number of its weapons that are destroyed, or the number of personnel injured or killed as a result of the fulfillment of contractual obligations. In fact, the loss of weapons and injury and death of personnel are likely to be significant legal and financial risks[101] on the company and are inimical to its corporate survival. In the regime where unspecific objectives, no-bid, costs-plus service contracts are being granted to opaque profit-driven PMCs, the notion of contractual accountability and control is simply risible. There is no turning from the fact of dramatic, deep, and intractable conflicts of interests.

Singer identifies a further series of concerns and solutions in the context of PMCs supporting UN peacekeeping missions where the PMC is controlled by contract. He identifies the following risks: "premature withdrawal by the forces, without consideration for the political costs and risks to those depending on their protection or, even worse, the firm acting to extend a contract by prolonging the conflict." In other words, the issues illustrated above in the Sandline Affair only worsen. He recommended:

> There must also be assurances of corporate independence (i.e., only using firms expressly unlinked to other business networks that might warp their motivations); the maintenance of competition to ensure quality and replacement; clear standards to ensure a quality product; outside vetting of personnel; the attachment of independent observer teams; and, the requirement that firm personnel place themselves under the jurisdiction of international tribunals for any violation of the laws of war.[102]

Surely, these recommendations are suitable for a wide array of PMC deployments and not just for peacekeeping. In light of experience in Iraq, Singer seems prescient. One sees, for example, PMC work stoppage in Baghdad airport, mentioned above; Blackwater's threat to withdraw from Iraq, stranding US diplomats and civilian officials in the Green Zone, if its contract was cancelled; the notorious corporate-government linkages like CACI and MPRI; non-bid contracts; failure of oversight; failure of enforcement; failure of vetting; and deliberate avoidance of international legal obligations, all manifest in Iraq. Although not a matter of contract, the right given to PMCs to possess all manner of weaponry and military skill and control their use cannot but be a risk to any country where they are permitted. While outlawing is no guarantee that they will not be amassed and turned against either the government or the civilian population, the permitted existence cannot but heighten the risk. In sum, the current faith in de jure control by the nation-state of the PMC by contract is misplaced faith. We turn next to examine the nation-state's other potential means of control, namely de facto.

3.7.2 De facto control of the PMC—Materiel and services

As previously noted, governments struggle with limited success to impose de facto control over violent groups and public-owned weapons. The difficulty of imposing de facto is exacerbated in the case of the PMC as the PMC's, with its private legal status, ability to amass considerable financial and personnel resources and abilities to move and hide mobile or leased weaponry is most likely to escape any form of de facto control whatsoever. PMCs can and have moved their resources out of jurisdictions to avoid governmental control and have accessed both governmental and private materiel for the purposes of carrying out their contractual obligations.[103] In one sense, this is a peculiar and significant danger of the PMC to governments and civilians alike. The danger to the government is that it can be overthrown; to the civilians, it is inflicted violence with neither accountability nor redress, and loss of the benefits of control over resources.

The ability to control the PMC by controlling weapons and training of military personnel has been unsuccessful. Major weapons manufacturers, such as Boeing, Lockheed Martin, and General Dynamics have long histories and many aspects to their businesses other than weapons production. This history and multifaceted business makes more comprehensive business regulation difficult to justify. Further, many of their products and services, and the products and services of many other manufacturers can be described as dual purpose. That is, those products and services can be used for both peaceful and military purposes. The ultimate use of goods or services depends on the end user, rather than the innate nature of the goods or services itself. For example, an armed security guard may guard a building in Iraq or the UK, although seemingly an identical service their contracts make them very different. The guard in Iraq is better characterized as a defender of occupying army interests and a representation of foreign powers whereas a guard in the UK represents a supplemental policing of settled accepted domestic law. To recognize the diversified nature of the business of these corporations with the multiplicity of dual use products and services is, in effect, to prelude de facto control of the PMC.

In some countries, such as previously noted case of the US, civilians have a right to bear weapons. Major caches of weapons and training grounds are legal. As mentioned earlier Blackwater boasts of its 6,000-acre training facility. Further, as previously noted, a thriving black market in weapons has a long history, and the attempts to control weapons sales on the international front have been largely unsuccessful and ineffectual. Finally, some countries, such as Cambodia, have allowed private business operators to make the firing of former military weapons a tourist attraction. Efforts of states to restrict the distribution of weapons are, at least to some extent, fruitless and certainly limited in the scope in the types of quantities of weapons that they could reasonably hope to control.

For the PMC, the government's lack of ability to control the materiel is a bonus. It allows the PMC to acquire weaponry inexpensively. Singer notes, for example, "Missile attack boats went for $200,000, while light machine guns went for $60.... A T-55 tank, retrofitted with the latest reactive armour, costs $40,000, less than a SUV."[104] Similarly, the government's lack of ability to impose de facto control of the provision of PMC has been a cause and effect of civil war and chaos. A prime example is the security provider PMC paramilitaries operating in Southern Colombia. Those PMCs whether acting for landowners or drug cartels have been successful in wresting control of a sizable territory away from the government in addition to terrorizing the population as a whole. In fact, this is not the first time as the PMC has assisted terrorists and criminals amass weapons and train while operating as legitimate security businesses elsewhere.[105]

The government's lack of ability to establish de facto control of weapons and services within its territory of sovereign jurisdiction has had ultimately dire consequences in various instances where those weapons have been used against it and/or its citizens. We turn next to examine legal controls on nation-state government's decisions to resort to violence via militaries by extension PMCs.

3.8 Legal myths about control of the state's use of the monopoly of violence

The dual objectives, at times implicit and at times explicit, throughout this discussion are effective control over government use of violence and of private contractors performing violent acts. The objectives are of great importance to the populace as they may be victims of governmental violence, the perpetrators of violence where a government purports to inflict violent acts in their name, and certainly the financiers of government activity. Notionally, at least, a legal framework ideally set out in some form of constitution restrains governments. The constitution in turn is interpreted and applied by the judiciary. This idea is the notion that forms the basis for the Rule of Law: that exercise of government power is always subject to scrutiny, and in this context that violence is not perpetrated without appropriate political debate and accountability. In essence, the Rule of Law should work to protect the populace from its government, including its violence.

3.8.1 Understanding the Rule of Law

Control of the state by nonviolent internal mechanisms has been the ever-elusive goal of philosophers, political scientists, and lawyers for millennia. Indeed, Aristotle, writing 2,400 years ago, proposed something we would recognize as the Rule of Law—the settling of matters beforehand by the establishment of rules.[106] At its most basic, the idea behind of the Rule of Law is that the whims of a few individuals cannot be permitted to rule a people. It follows from this proposition that human society must rely on something higher to control, regulate, and guide the hand of the governors and that higher something is the Rule of Law.

The Rule of Law, although erroneously used as a synonym for "law and order," is a much broader idea that all power within a state must be exercised according to law.[107] The Rule of Law is premised on the state's respect for the citizens,[108] the state's respect for law, and an independent judiciary. As Professor R. Peerenboom, who has written extensively on the topic, puts it:

> At its most basic level, Rule of Law refers to a system in which law is able to impose meaningful restraints on the state and individual members of the ruling elite... [through] a government of laws, the supremacy of the law and equality of all before the law.[109]

Bringing the concept of the Rule of Law to the issue at hand, namely, the state's decision to resort to violence whether by its standing army or by retaining a PMC, it is then up to the people of that state to challenge that decision through the law. Further, should the court so decide, law would prevent the government from sending out the army or retaining PMCs.[110] We now turn to examine the practicality of this legal approach to control of government decisions.

3.8.2 Legal challenges to government action

This section provides an overview of the legal mechanisms for bringing a challenge to government decisions. For the Rule of Law to be effective, governments must have not only laws under which they are accountable, but also a means by which their actions can be challenged and if necessary denied. At law, this is accomplished by means of judicial review. An understanding of judicial review requires at least a basic understanding of two additional doctrines: justiciability and political questions. We turn now to examine these concepts and their application in the context of government resorting to violence and then specifically, the use of PMCs.

3.8.2.1 Judicial review, justiciability, and political questions

The basic notion of judicial review is that the judiciary will review a decision taken by the government and make a determination as to whether the government is following the law.[111] This essential function of the judiciary requires, as noted, an independent judiciary of the government and a government prepared to submit to its authority. While good in theory there are a number of other matters, practical and political, which have bearing on the issue. As a practical matter a government cannot function if its every decision must be defended in court. Furthermore, the courts recognize not only the impracticality of such, but also the legitimate scope of governmental discretion. Accordingly, not every action or decision of the government is subject to judicial review. Judicial review is limited to those actions and decisions determined to be "justifiable."[112] That is, the courts will hear only a limited type of complaint about government actions and decisions, and specifically those actions and decisions usually of an administrative nature, or those issues not properly assignable to another branch of government.[113]

One important and further limit on justiciability is the doctrine of "political questions." That is, the court will abstain from entertaining applications for judicial review of executive action where that action is characterized as solely or primarily political. This judicial deference to political decisions by the executive is appropriate where government is representative of the populace; it is particularly marked with respect to matters of war, violence, and security, and has a long history.[114] As Lord Roskill observed:

> The courts are not the place wherein to determine whether a treaty should be concluded or the armed forces disposed in a particular manner....The courts have long shown themselves sensitive to the assertion by the executive that considerations of national security must preclude judicial investigation of a particular individual grievance.[115]

With this background, we turn now to examine how courts have interrupted the law and constitutions in particular as a control on state resort to violence.

3.8.2.2 Rule of Law and constitutional limitations on the use of violence: Militaries and PMCs

Section 8 Clause 11 of the first article of the Constitution of the United States of America states unequivocally that Congress has the power "To declare war, grant letters of marque and reprisal, and make rules concerning captures on land and water."[116] Nevertheless, despite more than a century of litigation on this article, the court has not been successful in restraining executive fiat calling the troops out, endangering both lives at home and abroad. A separate resolution was passed in 1973, the War Power Resolution, to address the problem of executive use of the military in execution of foreign policy without Congressional approval. The decision to invade a country and start a war killing millions, leaving a toxic, defoliated landscape, and a legacy of related genetic disorders, from a legal perspective, never happened. The invasion of Vietnam was never approved by Congress, the president never formally declared war. With few exceptions, presidents have called out the military without consulting Congress.[117] One may rightly ask: "how have the governments avoided the courts and so avoided implementation of the Rule of Law on this matter?"

The courts have taken a wide range of positions from attempting to restrain presidents to practically granting them carte blanche at the other. Consider the following two judicial opinions on the matter. Judge Leventhal, an example of an effort to reign in presidential power, wrote:

> executive would have it that the Constitution confers on the executive absolute discretion in the area of national security. This does not stand up. While the Constitution assigns to the President a number of powers relating to national security, including the function of commander-in-chief and the power to make treaties and appoint Ambassadors, it confers upon Congress other powers equally inseparable from the national security, such as the powers to declare war, raise and support armed forces and, in the case of the Senate, consent to treaties and the appointment of ambassadors.[118]

At the other end of the spectrum, the judiciary has wholly excused itself from reviewing presidential decisions with respect to foreign policy, including war. Consider the opinion of Justice Jackson speaking for the court:

> The President, both as Commander-in-Chief and as the Nation's organ for foreign affairs... [and], the very nature of executive decisions as to foreign policy is political, not judicial. Such decisions are wholly confided by our Constitution to the political departments of the government, Executive and Legislative....They are decisions of a kind for which the Judiciary has neither aptitude, facilities nor responsibility and which has long been held to belong in the domain of political power not subject to judicial intrusion or inquiry.[119]

Jackson's view has ruled the day, and as a result, at least since Truman's time, the decision to mobilize the largest military in the history of the world is subject to the decisions of one man, without regard to democratic or Congressional oversight, to the extent that he claims the right to this power even contrary to the express laws on the issue.[120]

The Bush administration not only followed this transaction but also extended it purportedly within the law. In advising the president, as he was making the decision to invade Afghanistan and Iraq, the administration's lawyers took an unprecedented position following the political decision. As early as September 25, 2001, legal counsel wrote a Memorandum of Opinion for the deputy counsel to the president entitled "The President's Constitutional Authority to Conduct Military Operations against Terrorists and Nations Supporting Them." That memorandum makes clear the position of the administration that it needs no Congressional or other approval before invading another sovereign state.[121] In other words, regardless of the wishes of the American Congress, the administration had taken the power to instigate a war away from democratic oversight and ignored the express provisions of the constitution.

The same issue of constitutional limitation on the use of government's violence, but more narrowly focused on the use PMCs, has been illustrated in the south Pacific. Although referred to earlier in passing and discussed more fully in chapter 4, a short reference to the case of PNG serves as an illustration here. The PNG constitution has an express provision preventing the government from retaining the services of mercenaries. (The wording of the section is broad enough to include PMCs.) The constitution was put to test in what has become known as the Sandline Affair. The Sandline Affair which occurred in 1997, as noted, resulted from a government decision to retain PMCs to quell a rebellion by indigenous people on Bougainville Island.[122] In that contentious and well-publicized event the constitutional limitations in the PNG constitution essentially failed to limit the actions of the PNG government. Again, the essential question is, how?

The PNG government circumvented the constitution by granting all Sandline personnel status as "special constables," making them members of the PNG defense force.[123] Doing so avoided the constitution by bringing Sandline personnel within its bounds. Coincidentally, the PNG government's decision also protected Sandline personnel from liability under international law prohibiting with mercenaries.

During the controversy, a human rights advocacy group, the Individual and Community Rights Action Forum,[124] and another by Rimbink Pato, an independent PNG lawyer, mounted constitutional challenges against the government's decision to retain the PMC. Neither action was ultimately decided as they were overtaken by events. The government sought to circumvent the constitution and was only checked by a popularly supported military insurrection. It may be put that although the constitution was circumvented, the people were not.[125] The conclusion to draw from the Sandline Affair is that express constitutional provisions, designed to ensure that only state-sponsored military operations are legal in PNG, were easily avoided. It also draws attention to the serious concern of PMCs being hired by a state to act against a state's own citizens. Again, the issue of the legitimacy of government action where that government cannot use its own military is brought into question; although certainly not a guarantee of legitimate action, a military failing to follow government directions may well be representative of popular will. Indeed, the subsequent popularly supported military revolt that led to the PNG government's overthrow illustrates the point further; to have retained the PMC Sandline to produce the opposite result supports the view that the PMC is far from a possibly neutral technical service provider. Rather, it is intimately connected to achieving political outcomes determined by the elite able to pay its bill.

3.8.3 Conclusion concerning the Rule of Law and restraint on government's resort to violence

It is difficult to conclude that the Rule of Law will restrain aggressive governments in any context or form—whether such governments are acting internally against their own citizens or on foreign soil, whether acting through militaries or PMCs. The cases above illustrate such in the domestic context as Law Professor John Yoo, a member of the Bush government's Office of Legal Council and supporter of the invasion of Iraq, observes:

> The consensus view among most international legal scholars is that the recent American interventions in Kosovo and Iraq, and the Bush administration's announced plans to use force pre-emptively against rogue nations and international terrorist organizations, violate core principles of international law.[126]

The Bush administration's (and the administrations of many of his predecessors)[127] blatant refusal to honor international law and the cases above leads one to suggest that the Rule of Law, a restraint on violent power, is naught but a figment of judicial minds, lawyers, political scientists, and political philosophers. As Foucault put it: "Humanity does not gradually progress from combat to combat until it arrives at universal reciprocity, where the Rule of Law finally replaces warfare; humanity installs each of its violences in a system of rules and thus proceeds from domination to domination."[128]

3.9 The PMC challenge to monopoly of violence-based sovereignty

If it is accepted that one essential feature of a state's sovereignty is that it possesses a monopoly over sanctioned violence within the state, then how does one reconcile the historical reliance of states on the services of mercenaries[129] and the modern-day reliance on PMCs? Does the interaction undermine the sovereignty of a state?

A state's reliance on PMCs will undermine national sovereignty, if the absolute monopoly over violence is viewed as a key hallmark of sovereignty. It is likely that the risk of PMCs undermining national sovereignty will decrease if (a) the state retaining the PMC is institutionally and economically strong and (b) the PMCs being retained are not providing tip-of-the-spear services.

Large PMCs generally limit their engagements to contracts with internationally recognized states.[130] It is therefore possible for such PMCs to argue that because their actions are instigated, determined, and sanctioned by the state, they do not undermine the sovereignty of the state.[131] This argument raises theoretical and practical problems. At a theoretical level, is the delegation of an essential element of sovereignty at least a partial surrender of sovereignty? Is a state's sovereignty compromised if PMCs are responsible for, or essential to, a state's security? Some would argue that such outsourcing of defense services is evidence of an abdication of a state's responsibility to its citizens. Others would argue that it is evidence of the government taking seriously its responsibility for providing defense services. They would argue: Does not the real control rest with the state that is paying the PMC? At a practical level, the degree to which PMCs can be viewed as agents of a state depends on whether it is conceivable, under the circumstances, to view the government of that state as having the capacity to control the PMC. Consider the following point of view espoused by the British government in its Green Paper canvassing the options for regulating PMCs:

> The idea of a state relying for its security on a foreign force is contrary both to this reasoning and to our concept of citizenship. Nevertheless, the fact that a force is private or foreign does not prevent it from being under the control of the state. Although such arrangements may not be ideal, they may be far less damaging to sovereignty than an unchecked rebel movement.[132]

The argument that PMCs need not be viewed as an intrinsic threat to the sovereignty of states is supported by academics such as David Shearer, who worked with the UN Department of Humanitarian Affairs and advised in relation to the crises in Liberia in 1995 and Rwanda in 1996.[133]

A contrary view has been expressed by Enrique Bernales Ballesteros, the Special Rapporteur of the Office of the United Nations High Commissioner for Human Rights:

> The fact that a Government hires mercenaries or turns to "qualified" companies that provide mercenary services for its own defense and to strengthen positions during armed conflicts should not be invoked in claiming that its action is legal. A Government is endowed with legitimacy in order to work within its constitutional framework and that of

> the international treaties to which it is a party. Under no circumstances, however, may they use that power entrusted to them to engage in acts that are contrary to self determination, to jeopardize the independence and sovereignty of the State itself or to consent to acts that may do irreparable harm to the life and security of the inhabitants.[134]

The British government has dismissed Bernales Ballesteros' argument as "an extreme point of view."[135]

Indeed, the two points of view above are not readily reconcilable. On the one hand, from the perspective of the British government (which does not need to retain the services of PMCs to buttress its internal security but which chooses to retain the services of PMCs for training and support services), the concern over PMCs is to ensure the effective regulation of a troublesome but useful industry. Accordingly, Britain's primary concern is to facilitate the work of "reputable" PMCs and to control "disreputable" and "unsavoury" PMCs through the introduction of an appropriate regulatory regime.[136] This dichotomy is a government use of the "Good" PMC versus the "Bad" PMC discussed and discredited in the first chapter. On the other hand, and in contrast to the situation in Britain, the Rapporteur visits many states where both security and sovereignty are threatened by the intervention of, or reliance on, PMCs. Given his mandate to report on international mercenary activity, the Rapporteur is particularly concerned with the military provider, tip-of-the-spear firms, and it is in this context that the adamant nature of his comments resonates. Between these two extremes are the concerns related to and consequences of MNC use of PMCs in weak or poor states where their rights are contested as part of a general opposition to a corrupt regime or an unjust status quo.

There is a third perspective on the issue left out of the discussion of sovereignty and that is the perspective of those on the receiving end of the PMC. Africans complain about the lack of control over American PMCs operating in their countries, particularly as those PMCs operate on instructions from a foreign country. They see those PMCs as a challenge to their sovereignty.[137] The same issue has arisen in Iraq where the interior minister spoke on national television concerning the Blackwater massacre of September 15, 2007. "We are implementing the law and abide by laws, and others should respect these laws and respect the sovereignty and independence of Iraqis in their country."[138] This issue, interestingly enough, has arisen recently in the US. DynCorp has made an effort to obtain a contract to provide Border Control Guards. The issue has been put directly: "From a political perspective, if we privatize a basic function of government such as border protection, it questions our view of territorial sovereignty and how we want government to work."[139]

In institutionally and economically weak states, particularly where sovereignty is contested, the intervention of a PMC will undoubtedly provide a significant boost to the side that has retained the PMC. The question is whether this type of PMC intervention can be viewed as compromising the independence and sovereignty of a state. For example, if an incumbent government retained a PMC but the government did not enjoy the support of the majority of the citizens, then the PMC's intervention could be seen as undermining popular sovereignty within the state. The problems with this type of analysis are twofold. First, the ultimate test of the legitimacy of a government's decision to retain a PMC is only discernable in hindsight, depending upon the view of sovereignty one chooses to adopt and only if there is agreement as to the collective will of the citizens. It is with such thorny and subjective conundrums in mind that Bernales Ballesteros and the United Nations have urged the international community to maintain the view that all mercenary activity (i.e., combat-related interventions in foreign countries for gain) are illegal and to accept that will necessarily mean that at least some PMC activities are illegal.

3.10 Domestic PMCs and international influence—Lobby and geopolitical outcomes[140]

The extraordinary growth of the PMC sector suggests that it will be undertaking all the normal channels for increasing its business, and particularly, with government being a main client, a heavy reliance on lobbyists. The political connections of PMCs are numerous and well-known. From Sandline International's connections with the British government to MPRI's relations with the US Army, to the AEGIS—US-CACI and US links, PMCs need to court favor with the governments. Indeed, the connections between the PMC and government in case of Iraq have been so close that there has been considerable concern expressed among scholars and media alike. Isenberg, for example, makes "Political Connections," leadership, political donations, and lobbying of PMCs the first items of concern in his chapter entitled "Issues of Concern around PMCs."[141]

The size, power, ambitions, and objectives of the lobby should not be underestimated. In 2005, a Blackwater subsidiary put on a by-invitation-only convention for diplomats, oil companies, and weapons manufacturers. The promotional literature described the PMC as "an international security services company that offers your country or organization a complete solution to your most pressing security needs."[142] In other words, the PMC offers unlimited range of military services to the highest bidder. In another attempt to drum up business PMC lobbyists have engaged in calling for the retaining of PMCs in Darfur. Doug Brooks, as mentioned in chapter 1, is the president of the PMC lobby group International Peace Operations Association. Brooks avers that westerners fail to grasp the reality of weak, inept, corrupt African militaries.[143] There are the well-known cases where PMCs Executive Outcomes and Gurkha Security Services made significant positive contributions to end the brutal civil wars in Angola and Sierra Leone, respectively. And indeed, it is inappropriate to rule out some tip-of-the-spear PMC assistance in certain interventions. But it is not at all clear that a few cases produce a norm. Nevertheless, Brooks argues that without this important information about Africa non-Africans incorrectly assume that African militaries can attend to African peacekeeping.[144] In line with this views, Brooks wrote an article for popular consumption advocating surrendering the problem in Darfur to PMCs.[145] Unsurprisingly, among a rather significant lobby,[146] Blackwater has made known its interest in securing a contract for services in Darfur, making its case in the media in March 2006.[147]

Although the gruesome killing and desecration of the four Blackwater employees in Fallujah leading to the assault on the city and a swell of patriotism and support for the occupation of Iraq is well-known, Blackwater's capitalization on the event is not. The day after the incident, Blackwater retained the well-connected lobby firm Alexander Strategy Group. Of course, the information shared and services rendered are confidential and hence one must be cautious in drawing inferences or conclusions. However, the record is that two months later Blackwater had won a coveted international security contract valued at $300 million.[148]

Professor Anna Leander identifies the issue in its broader, sociopolitical context thus:

> The political processes establishing for what purpose what kind of force is used are fundamental and PMCs do take part in them and do shape them....PMCs are increasingly present as a new cast of efficient, competent, and apolitical security experts. In this context, the...way PMCs (as specialists on violence) shape politics is readily swept aside and forgotten.[149]

Leander's concern is more than a worry; it is a reality. A relatively significant amount of opinion and advice on PMCs, given to Congress in a 2007 research report, is based on the opinions of the above-mentioned Doug Brooks. In that research report, "Private Security Contractors in Iraq: Background, Legal Status, and Other Issues," Brooks is cited ten times, which is more than the combined input of the world's four leading PMC experts.[150] This industry lobby reflects not only a particular ideology concerning governance, but obviously an agenda to increase the PMC market through further commoditized violence.[151]

In the African context, it has been described thus: "[PMCs] interpret political instability in Africa as a market issue, and position themselves perfectly in that market."[152] Indeed Brooks, when advocating PMCs' peacekeeping, sees the problem in Africa as a technical issue, and hence subject to his exclusively technical solution. For the most part, politics escapes the discussion except as lamentable obstacles to the PMC solution. Brooks does make mention of a mediation group as part of a pre-PMC deployment procedure,[153] and notes that in the African context "There are too many factions involved, too many warlords, and too much money in the offing for the winner,"[154] but fails to address who should get the support of the PMC or on what basis. The extreme emphasis of advocates is on how PMCs "crave legitimacy" and value their good names so highly that there is little or no cause for concern,[155] social benefits of PMCs, economic benefits of PMCs, humanitarian assistance, discussions of "capacity building" that sound like PMCs are interested in charity work,[156] it is difficult to remember that under discussion is a group of armed people whose job it is to fight. Further, this picture does not echo with the views and experiences of some employees on the ground with the same famed PMCs on the missions in question.[157]

The efficacy of the PMC lobby has drawn academic comment. Markusen observes: "Their congressional success makes it difficult for the nation to adapt to new security realities and to shift resources toward new approaches such as peacekeeping missions, negotiated settlements, and economic development in place of regional warfare."[158] This effective lobbying activity calls attention to a dangerous and fundamental problem with PMCs: there is a combination of commercial imperative with its marketing spin and disregard of (if not outright opposition to) political process and worldview that violence is the solution. The limitation of a worldview is encapsulated in the old adage, "to the man with a hammer, everything looks like a nail." This dangerous combination of issues suggests that PMC industry's activities, connections, and advice to home governments and in the international community should be subject to scrutiny and any advice considered and taken only with utmost caution. The "trust me, trust me" of the PMC lobby should be looked at most skeptically. After all, policy makers do not turn to tobacco companies for advice on health issues.

It is unrealistic to characterize the relationship as one-sided, however, for as we have seen in chapter 1 and in section 3.5, as a result of government outsourcing, governments have come to rely more and more on PMCs for essential military services. Not only have PMCs increased supply of less controversial services such as logistics, but as noted, PMC specialization has become critical to the operation of hi-tech weapons which form part of nations' strategically significant arsenal.[159] Indeed, it is questionable whether the Iraq invasion could have occurred without the support of PMCs, given that weapons-toting PMC employees exist in a ratio of 1 to 3 vis-à-vis military personnel. This interdependency is at least as strong in the sector's relations with third-world governments where PMCs may be the only true power the governments are able to use to project their authority.[160]

In its move to the mainstream of business, and perhaps too, as a result of growing public awareness from their involvement in the Iraq war, PMCs have begun to work more carefully on their public images, creating and publicizing international codes of conduct (examined in detail in chapter 4), setting up industry websites, and showing themselves in the public realm. Their role has certainly expanded from the provision of fighting forces to many other endeavors, including supporting UN missions and humanitarian aid. On the one hand, the PMC has brought considerable benefit, while on the other the costs are still being counted,[161] not the least of which is the accountability issues raised here and elsewhere in this work.

3.11 PMC as foreign policy tool: Five case studies

When a state retains a PMC to act on its behalf extraterritorially, it is using the PMC to further its foreign policy objectives. It is important to consider all the dimensions of such a decision. Why would a state choose to retain a PMC to further its foreign policy objectives rather than use its own armed forces? A state could choose to retain a PMC to act for any number of reasons, including: (1) the state's armed forces could be overstretched, (2) the PMC could be in a position to provide the defense services more cost effectively than the state's armed forces, (3) the PMC may have good contacts within the retaining/deploying government, (4) the PMC could have good contacts within the operating/receiving government, (5) it could form part of its foreign aid package, and (6) the PMC could have technical specialization which may be lacking in operating/receiving state's military.

From a state's perspective, one of the key advantages of using PMC contractors extraterritorially to further foreign policy objectives is that when something goes wrong the state can disavow responsibility for the problem by turning the blame onto the PMC.[162] For example, the United States uses a PMC called Aviation Development Corporation to provide reconnaissance for the CIA in South America. In 2001, the PMC identified a plane as possibly belonging to cocaine traffickers, and consequently the Peruvian Air Force shot the plane down. Unfortunately, the intelligence from the PMC was faulty, and a US missionary and her daughter traveling on the plane were killed. When questions were asked in Congress about the incident, the CIA directed the enquiries to the company.[163]

On a much larger and more significant scale, use of private contractors has allowed the American government significant political advantages in its invasion and occupation of Iraq. The killing of the Blackwater employees that triggered the massive American attack on Fallujah[164] was a result of Blackwater's failure to provide the necessary, more expensive armored vehicles.[165] The complex arrangements of contracts allowed Blackwater and the Department of Defense to avoid scrutiny of the matter by Congressional hearings of the Oversight and Government Reform Committee for more than eighteen months.[166]

Use of PMCs has given the Bush administration a psychological advantage over American people by employing PMCs. The Bush administration, which does not count private contractor deaths in its statistics, was able to delay the announcement of the death of 1,000 Americans in Iraq.[167] As Jeremy Scahill, author of the authoritative 2007 work, *Blackwater: The Rise of the World's Most Powerful Mercenary Army*, testified on May 10, 2007, in a Congressional hearing:

> Through the US Department of Labor, we have been able to determine that at least 770 contractors had been killed in Iraq as of December 2006 along with at least 7,700 wounded. These casualties are not included in the official death count and help to mask the human costs of the war. More disturbing is what this means for our democracy: at a time when the administration seems unwilling to subject its war strategy to oversight by the Congress, we face the widespread use of private forces seemingly accountable to no effective system of oversight or law.[168]

Indeed, the ability to oversee the military's action is critical. As Congressional representative Jan Schakowsky put it: "Having a third or a quarter of [the forces] present on the ground not even part of the debate is a very dangerous thing in our democracy, because war is the most critical thing that we do."[169] Yet the use of PMCs has shielded the government's action from democratic oversight.

Institutionally and economically strong states such as the United States are increasingly choosing to retain PMCs to advance their foreign policy objectives when intervening extraterritorially in the domestic affairs of weak states. Such interventions are often cloaked as offering foreign aid but may work as a means of achieving foreign policy objectives without attracting the level of scrutiny and attention that should occur when a state mobilizes its armed forces extraterritorially. As the examples below will illustrate, all of which involve the retention of PMCs by the United States and Australia, there are a variety of domestic and foreign policy imperatives that lead institutionally and economically strong states to retain PMCs for use extraterritorially. The examples considered below include Iraq, Sudan, East Timor, Equatorial Guinea, and the Balkans.

When one state[170] pays for a PMC to intervene in another state, there is a serious risk that the intervention will be resisted by the recipient state and viewed as an aggressive act. A situation could arise where one state retains a PMC in order to launch a war by proxy against another state or, less dramatically, to exert some control over the foreign state or its resources in order to further its own foreign policy objectives. Perhaps requiring states to answer the following three questions would help to determine whether one state is justified in retaining a PMC to intervene in another state: (1) Was there a request for assistance from the state in which the PMC is operating?[171] (2) Has the UN decided that military intervention in the state is necessary for humanitarian reasons? and (3) What is the motive of the state that has retained the PMC services as determined by disinterested third party evaluations of likely outcomes?

3.11.1 Iraq: Supplementing unilateral action

The occupation of Iraq has been termed "the first privatised war."[172] Although historically incorrect as noted in chapter 1, the invasion does exemplify the new trend in military activity. The US was unable to obtain UN approval for its invasion. Accordingly, the US, in a bizarre attempt to spin on the international stage its explicit commitment to unilateralism into some form of multilateralism, created a "Coalition of the Willing."[173] Without such approval, it has been difficult to muster sufficient troops as there were only minimal contributions to troop numbers by the subsequently formed "Coalition of the Willing." It is uncontroversial to assert that without PMCs the US would not have been able to invade Iraq,[174] and General David Petraeus, commander of the Multi-National Force-Iraq, acknowledged that PMCs were an important part of his confidence in military success there.[175]

This body is indeed a significant contingent but there is a real worry, for as 2007 research report states: "There is no count of the total number of contractors or subcontractors who carry weapons while performing services contracted for by the United States,"[176] part of the reason being that the Department of Defense has not released information about the number of private security contractors.[177]

Indeed, a memorandum of the Committee on Oversight and Government Reform sets the number at 48,000, a figure put forward by the Private Security Company Association.[178] As a percentage of the armed American presence, PMC personnel are the equivalent of 33 percent of the US troops in Iraq. They outnumber UK troops, the second largest contingent of the coalition, by a ratio of 6 to 1[179] and by May 2007 all other coalition partners, whose combined troops number 12,600, or roughly 8 percent of the 145,000 US troops on the ground.[180]

It may be that the PMC phenomenon is evidence in part of a shortfall of recruits in the US. Essentially, the 48,000 PMC personnel are the 48,000 who were not or could not be recruited by the military. Indeed, the US Army sought to increase recruits by 30,000, but given the challenges it had in meeting its basic recruiting goals, increases have been a virtually impossible.[181] As its alternative, to invoke conscription, the US government would have had to enact very unpopular legislation instating a new draft.[182] By using PMCs it has avoided this significant political hurdle.[183]

The PMCs in Iraq supplement American unilateral action by carrying out a variety of tasks. While the US government and the PMC lobby emphasize less controversial tasks, including maintaining machinery and weapons systems; training Iraq's new army, paramilitary, and police, which they have indeed done,[184] PMCs have engaged in much more active combat roles. Illustrative of the military nature of the work undertaken by some PMCs in Iraq is a story published in an Australian newspaper about local ex-police officers working in Iraq on lucrative contracts with a "private security company."[185] One of these new recruits was regularly emailing diary entries to the newspaper (and his local pub) and reported that a week after crossing onto Iraqi soil from Kuwait, he was dressed like a US Marine, was armed with M16s and 9mm Berretta pistols, and was being shot at and returning fire while supporting a US Marine convoy. He wrote, "[t]he insurgents, radicals, criminals etc. try to disrupt the supply convoys moving around the country [and w]e tag along [with the convoys] to provide further fire power and to ensure the goods get there."[186] He later elaborated on what he meant by "providing further firepower," explaining that it involves shooting when under attack with the aim of "neutralising the source."[187]

Stories such as the one above illustrate the supplementing role played by PMCs and explain why the Iraqi resistance forces are not differentiating between PMC personnel and military personnel when selecting targets. The story also suggests that many PMCs currently operating within Iraq would, arguably but for the support of the recently elected Iraqi government, meet the international definition of mercenaries discussed above.

The US-sponsored Iraqi authorities are currently playing catch-up and attempting to control the quality and behavior of the PMCs.[188] The notion of the Iraqi government being prepared to deal with PMCs is naive. The recent massacre by Blackwater mentioned earlier, in which eleven Iraqis were killed and another thirteen wounded, is a case in point. On the day the event occurred, September 15, 2007, the Iraqi government declared the license would be revoked and the company expelled from the country. By the 18th of the same month, the Iraqi government spokesman was saying: "We are not intending to stop them and revoke their license indefinitely but we do need them to respect the law and the regulation here in Iraq."[189] Indeed, as Isenberg observes, "from the viewpoint of the PMC sector, doing business with the relevant Iraqi ministries is extremely difficult, if not entirely ridiculous."[190] It is not unfair to assume the corollary. Further, given the extreme difficulties the US is having controlling and accounting for PMCs and their personnel, it seems unlikely that Iraqi authorities will do much better, relying as they are on US expertise in these matters. Repeated attacks on PMC personnel in Iraq demonstrate that Iraqi insurgents consider them to be hostile to Iraqi sovereignty and self-determination.

The US determination to invade Iraq without the approval of the UN demonstrates clearly that this military engagement was undertaken in furtherance of US foreign policy interests. It may well be that the unilateral nature of US action has forced the country to rely on PMC services, some of which would undoubtedly, in other instances, have been supplied by other UN member states.[191] With PMCs forming the largest contingent of non-USA military personnel, it is fair to say that they are indeed supplement for unilateral action.

3.11.2 Sudan: Avoiding public scrutiny

Using PMCs permits governments to implement foreign policy by military action and project power on foreign soil without oversight by or accountability to the public. In other words, using PMCs allows democratic governments to breach the presumption in favor of peace without explaining or justifying their actions to those they purport to represent. They circumvent the democratic institutions of popularly elected representatives by not relying on the state military. Instead, governments call forth an armed force by a stroke of the proverbial pen on the state's checkbook and retain the PMC of their choice to execute foreign policy away from the public eye. Singer, in his evaluation of PMCs' post-Iraq occupation refers to it as "Public Policy through Private Means."[192] Although public opinion may not have the limiting effect often claimed by democratic theorists, at least some form of public scrutiny cannot be a negative in the efforts to restrain governments' proclivity for violent means.[193] The issue is illustrated in the case of US retaining PMCs in Sudan in furtherance of foreign policy.

In late 2004, Sudan agreed to accept a peacekeeping force from the African Union comprising 4,500 Rwandan and Nigerian soldiers. The peacekeepers received logistical support from the United States via two PMCs: DynCorp and Pacific Architects & Engineers (PAE).[194] The joint contract between DynCorp and PAE and the US State Department is valued at $20.6 million and is described as an "indefinite delivery, indefinite quantity" contract.[195] The contract was entered into pursuant to a five-year task order issued in 2003 by the State Department, which allows for the use of these two PMCs anywhere in Africa.[196] There are two aspects to this contract that should draw the observant person's attention.

First, given the difficulties the nations of Africa have had in their efforts to build up cooperation and coordination, where they have been successful in doing so, most certainly support for those efforts should be a paramount objective of foreign policy. However, as noted in the April 2007 edition of the Africa Research Bulletin, American PMCs work contrary to the stated objects. As the Bulletin reports: "Africa stresses the role of African forces in solving African conflicts. But...another model, dependent on US private military companies,...may challenge basic AU precepts."[197]

Second, the amount of $20.6 million does not meet the $50 million dollar threshold at which an export of defense services expenditure requires Congressional approval. Accordingly, there was no legal obligation on the administration to notify Congress. The retaining of the PMCs to implement violent foreign policy where the cost is less than $50 million could therefore be done by the hawkish Bush administration, without resort to the public institution of Congress.

Two further aspects of the United States' action are troubling. First is a further concern about the United States' strategic decision as to how it will use the PMC. The Bulletin reports: "US-backed Ethiopian forces took the lead role in a region where they are not seen as neutral—they have long been engaged in hostilities with Somalis over the Ogaden region—and the US has sent in one of its biggest private security companies, DynCorp, to train and back the AU force."[198] In other words, the US decision to send in DynCorp with Ethiopian troops emphasizes the political nature of PMC involvement, in this case skewing the balance of power in local hostilities and the fallacy of considering peacekeeping training as harmless intervention.

The World Security Institute' Arabic online newspaper, Taqrir Washington, sets out the concerns succinctly in its recent article:

> Recent history of US involvement in Sudan suggests that the [DynCorp] contract may be predicated on a more complicated set of foreign policy goals than the demobilization and integration activities outlined by DynCorp officials. The US government has long been sympathetic to the opposition groups operating in southern Sudan....US government support for Sudanese opposition groups—intensifying after the 1989 coup which brought to power an Islamist-oriented regime—[suggest] some skepticism may be warranted[199]

Indeed, the comments of Al Rigney, DynCorp's vice president for International Business Development, in the *Sudan Tribune* indicate a confused set of objectives, not to put too fine a point on it. In explaining DynCorp's mission he stated: "They [former rebel army] ought to be taught that use of weapons should be structured through proper chain of command, and not used to settle disputes."[200] And "We need to get them walking and talking like professionals."[201] It seems that Rigney sees the issue as a mere technical problem resulting from the silly Sudanese failure to know the right way to use weapons to resolve disputes as opposed to the wrong way to use weapons to resolve disputes. In addition, the Sudanese are evidently lacking in fashion sense and social graces in the carrying out of military activities. This analysis goes along well with the public story of humanitarian decision of the US to send in an apolitical PMC into an apolitical landscape. Again, Rigney: "The US government has decided that a stable military force will create a stable country."[202] The obvious issue of what has caused the instability in the first place, certainly a political issue, the elephant in the room, has simply been dropped from view. Among other issues is an oil-rich south, home of the US supported rebels acting against an Islamist government in the north. US involvement in the causes and support of violence cannot be overlooked and swept under the rug under the guise of supplying apolitical PMC services to create some mysteriously absent stability.

Second, the reluctance of the United States to contribute defense force personnel to the peacekeeping mission in Sudan could reflect that its public may oppose further military engagement or that military resources are overstretched by the current invasions and occupations of Iraq and Afghanistan.

A hawkish president's decision to send more soldiers to yet another country would be most difficult to sell to the public. Bush had already spent considerable political capital in the invasions of Afghanistan and Iraq, and it would be most unlikely that he would be successful in garnering support for a third military engagement. Without political engagement he would not be able to call out the military.

The matter of the military resources being stretched was side-stepped when Charles Snyder, the State Department's senior representative on Sudan, said that the United States uses PMCs out of preference because "[p]rivate companies can do the job more quickly and efficiently in the short term than a government bureaucracy."[203] Given the questionable efficiency of PMCs discussed above, it seems likely that other factors are at play. The fact that this particular contract was entered into by the executive arm of the US government leads commentators to conclude that the real reason behind the US decision to utilize PMCs in Sudan is to indirectly exert influence without attracting Congressional oversight.[204]

The voices of those on the ground and on the receiving end of the political decision to send in a PMC see it as neither neutral nor harmless. DynCorp's ongoing involvement in this troubled area is concerning. The foregoing discussion as part of the US Department of Defence's decision to raise its profile in Africa with US-based PMCs[205] provides strong support for the view that the PMC is being used as a tool of foreign policy avoiding wider public scrutiny.

3.11.3 East Timor: Honoring international commitments

Foreign policy is advanced at times through honoring international commitments. Doing so enhances a country's status in the international forum, and importantly with neighboring states. To honor those commitments militarily adds prestige by demonstrating a country's ability to project power extraterritorially. It demonstrates an excess of capacity in terms of not needing those violent resources domestically. In a very real sense it signals to neighbors the seriousness of a country's military might. In this light, honoring such commitments may be viewed as a veiled threat.

From another point of view, it promotes a view of goodwill of a sending state toward its neighbors, indeed the opposite of a threat. It creates political capital useful in developing persuasive power where political determination of issues is preferable. It provides legitimacy for a claimed right to participate in regional affairs.[206] Finally, where that power is expressed through outsourced PMC, it can communicate a commitment to neoliberal governance.

East Timor had been part of Timor, a colony of Portugal since 1702. The western half was transferred to the Dutch in the nineteenth century, which surrendered its colonies in the aftermath of the Second World War. West Timor devolved to the newly created Indonesia leaving East Timor a

Portuguese colony. Portugal, preoccupied with its own internal problems as well as more important external problems in Angola and Mozambique, essentially abandoned East Timor, creating an opportunity for the former colony to claim independence. This step, which it took on November 28, 1975, was the impetus for an invasion by neighboring Indonesia.[207] The Indonesian invasion was explicitly supported by the US and Australia [208] and formed part of Australia's "Jakarta first" policy.[209] That policy led Australia to oppose independence for East Timor and even assist in attempting to suppress criticisms of Indonesia at the UN.[210]

In 1999 the Howard government, in its second consecutive term in Australia, did a complete about-face on the issue and declared its support for an independent East Timor.[211] This about-face, whether driven by political, economic, or moral concerns set the stage for Australian humanitarian intervention in East Timor. After an initial supply of some 3,000 troops, Australia committed to assisting the development of policing in the new country. To fulfill that commitment, the Australian government contracted with Chubb Security Australia (Chubb).[212] At the time Australia sent Chubb to East Timor, the country was not internally stable and hostility still existed between Indonesia and pro-Indonesian rebels on the one hand and the East Timorese on the other.[213] Indonesia's withdrawal had left governance void in East Timor—there were no elected leaders or public servants, and there was no working legal system. In this environment, Chubb was retained to provide security personnel, some of whom were armed, to guard key infrastructure, equipment, warehouses, and supply routes. The internal instability in East Timor and the scope of the security work carried out by Chubb demonstrate that it was operating as a PMC in East Timor,[214] although Chubb does not view itself as a PMC but rather as a personal security provider. In its ongoing work in East Timor Chubb's own legal documents contradict this claim. After employees claimed that Chubb's termination of security personnel protecting the World Bank offices in Dili was unlawful, Chubb defended itself by claiming that as a provider of essential services—policing—its workers have no right to strike.[215] In other words, it was not a mere provider of personal security. It identified itself as engaging in essential policing operations. Indeed, this may well be a more accurate description of its work there. Such being the case, should it not be subject to the public scrutiny and accountability of essential public service providers, particularly when those service providers are armed with potentially lethal force?

As part of Australia's commitment to the development of East Timor's institutions, the retaining of the PMC Chubb accomplishes a number of important Howard government goals. It furthers such foreign policy objectives as supporting the government's claims of engagement in the region; establishing the legitimacy of Australian intervention in neighboring states; giving basis for a claim of international citizen; demonstrating a commitment to peace, law, and order; and more broadly, public institutions such as police. The specific use of the PMC in this context allowed Australia to fulfill this commitment, as its own federal police force did not form an International Deployment Group until 2004.

3.11.4 Equatorial Guinea: Advancing domestic values on the international stage

A major impetus for foreign policy of many countries has been the reproduction of domestic values abroad. Doing so facilitates the smoother operation of international cooperation and coordination on matters such as trade and commerce, peace and security, and human rights. The importance of advancing those values has increased as economic globalization increased and multinational corporations extended their reach, as well as the contemporaneous linking of civil society's information through the innovation of high technology.

One significant component of foreign aid has traditionally been the provision of military assistance. In many instances where governments and their countries have been deemed worthy of aid on the basis of the geopolitical strategic agendas of wealthy nations, aid has often been provided in the form of military assistance supporting those governments. Given the various drivers of and restraints on governments interested in violent intervention in affairs of other nations, the growing PMC market, and the spread of neoliberal governance, the PMC is likely to take an increasingly prominent role in the pursuit of the foreign policy agenda of advancing domestic values abroad. One instance where that has occurred is Equatorial Guinea.

In 1998, the government of Equatorial Guinea approached MPRI to evaluate its defense systems and to determine whether it was in need of a coast guard to protect its oil reserves. MPRI duly applied for a license from the US government to carry out the work. The Clinton administration initially rejected the application on the grounds that the regime in Equatorial Guinea had an appalling human rights record.[216] MPRI lobbied the Pentagon and the State Department with a view to having the license granted; in 2000, the State Department reversed an earlier determination. One US State Department official who was initially opposed to the granting of the license to MPRI changed his mind after hearing that the proposed training would include human rights training. The same official was also reported as saying that "These private military companies, if properly directed by US government officials, can in fact play positive roles."[217] The policy reversal provides another example of the use of PMCs as a tool for implementing foreign policy objectives and, in this case, advancing domestic values.

The United States' self image as a model for all other states to follow, and the subsequent implications for US foreign policy, are well documented. As the *New York Times* writer David Sanger has observed:

> For more than half a century, the United Nations has been the main forum for the United States to try to create a world in its image, maneuvering its

allies to forge global accords about human rights, nuclear tests, or the environment that Washington insisted would mirror its own values.[218]

Having used up much of its political capital at the UN through its decision to act in Iraq regardless of UN approval, its rejection of the Kyoto Protocol, and abandoning of the Nuclear Non-proliferation Treaty, the United States has arguably abandoned the substance of the agenda, although not the objective of recreating the world in its own image. Reviewing US history and these recent events, including the legislation making Iraq a home of one of the world's most liberal trade laws,[219] some commentators would argue that the driving force behind US intervention is nothing other than the economic demands of its financiers, thinly cloaked in the language of Wilsonian idealism.[220] Regardless of the substance of the agenda, in both Equatorial Guinea and Iraq, it would appear that the US has utilized PMCs for the purpose of advancing its values abroad.

A discussion of US involvement in Equatorial Guinea would not be complete without mention of the following facts. It is the second wealthiest country in the world in terms of GDP per capita[221] and has the highest purchasing power parity per capita in Africa, but the populace suffers extreme wealth inequality.[222] It has a population of a mere 500,000 and a notorious human rights abusing president, Teodoro Obiang Nguema Mbasogo, who has been elected in fraudulent elections since 1993 after coming to power by a coup in 1979. Spain, France, and the US have worked together to provide an appearance of democracy.[223] It also has significant oil and gas reserves for which American oil firms have paid over $500 million to accounts controlled by the dictator.[224]

3.11.5 The Balkans: Achieving conflicting objectives by sleight of hand

Operating in a conflict zone, particularly one where there is international consensus and scrutiny by independent observers, can make it exceedingly difficult to achieve foreign policy objectives, which may be contrary to those observers or bearers of alternative consensus, or objectives. Nevertheless, foreign policy objectives do not evaporate as a result of scrutiny. The anonymity of PMCs' sponsors allows states to pursue their foreign policy objectives through PMCs while nominally at least keeping their reputations free of the opprobrium associated with breach of international consensus—at least in such smaller situations where the expenditure of political capital is not worth the anticipated benefit—or the opprobrium associated with partisanship when neutrality is the order of the day. One example of this can be seen after the breakup of the former Yugoslavia, where the UN banned the provision of military assistance to either Serbia or Croatia. Despite the ban, during the Bosnian conflict, the US State Department issued two licenses to MPRI to carry out contracts in the Balkans.

The first contract, entered into in 1994, involved MPRI's provision of training to the Croatian army. The United States' foreign policy objective in granting a license to MPRI involved ensuring that the Croatian army became an effective counterforce to the dominance of the Serbian forces and president Slobodan Milosevic.[225] Kassebaum sets the complexities of matter clearly:

> In 1995, the United States decided to increase its involvement in the ongoing efforts to stop the Bosnian war. The United States faced a difficult problem. While it was possible for it to intervene militarily to halt the ongoing destruction, the United States did not want to keep a military presence in Bosnia for more than a few years. To allow US troops to leave, it was decided to develop a balance of power between the warring sides, to equalize military power between the Muslims and Croats on one side, and the Serbs on the other. In order to achieve this balance of power, the United States had to support one side over the other, which would prevent it from being able to deal with all sides as a neutral party. Even if the United States tried to be neutral, any support it gave would be perceived as partisan.... After several months of negotiations and debate, the Dayton Peace Accords were reached in December 1995, implementing part of the solution to these problems.[226]

Following the instructions of the party signing the check, MPRI insists that the contract did not require it to provide combat training, but in August 1995, after benefiting from MPRI's services, the Croatian army launched Operation Storm. The operation was a very efficient and bloody four-day assault that saw the Croats regain the Krajina region from the Serbs. In many respects, this outcome could be seen as consistent with the US foreign policy objective of establishing a strong Croatian army able to counter Serbian forces.

Having signed the Dayton Peace Accords in late 1995, the State Department issued another license to MPRI the following year, this time to train and equip the army of the Federation of Bosnia and Herzegovina (the Croat-Muslim army).[227] The contract was paid for by moderate Arab states[228] and the US State Department donated $100 million worth of equipment without restricting its distribution or use.[229] This approach fulfilled the dual US foreign policy objectives of remaining ostensibly neutral while at the same time ensuring that the military balance between the Muslims and Croats on the one side and the Serbs on the other was relatively even.[230] The intervention was considered cost effective[231] and, as mentioned, had the added advantage of reducing the need for direct US military engagement.

The increased maneuvering room that PMCs give governments in pursuing foreign policy in awkward contexts is certainly a benefit to that government, and potentially to the recipients. In the case just discussed, it may be argued that the provision of PMC services served to promote peace by introducing a more balanced situation between the parties, thereby avoiding further violence or even a complete genocide. The other side to the issue is that it undermines the potential for multilateral control and direction of international violence, as well as undermining and circumventing the domestic political process. It is for precisely the purpose of supporting the presumption against violence that the ban on mercenaries was made part of international law, yet in the PMC there is the perfect vehicle for avoiding that law and countering the presumption in matters of foreign policy. It creates the pretense of acceptance of the norm while allowing its breach simultaneously. It allows foreign governments to feign neutrality while acting covertly on one side or another. In effect, it continues in yet another form the ruse perpetuated on an unsuspecting public and the world at large of a government's clean and indeed beneficent hands promoting humanitarian ends and democracy on the one hand while on the other acting as ruthlessly as it always has through internal agencies such as secret police, spy agencies, and others which may have higher levels of scrutiny and accountability than a PMC.

3.12 Regulatory recommendations

The discussion in the foregoing identifies significant weaknesses in the nation-state's control of violence and the severe limitations of the populace to control the state's decisions concerning the implementation of violent solutions to political problems. We have seen the problems associated with the use of law as a restraint on government's decisions and power with respect to utilizing the ultimate and most powerful tool in its political toolbox—that of organized, group-inflicted violence. As put pithily by Professor Philip Allott: "All governments are conspiracies with a constitution as an alibi." What this suggests is that the system of laws as it stands is inadequate, that indeed a constitution may be no more than a pretext, and that citizens of a state are largely unprotected by law despite the rhetoric to the contrary. It suggests that one should be cautious to avoid an overconfidence in law's ability to shield citizens, deliver democratic oversight and accountability, or restrain government's exercise of its sovereign rights of violence. It also leads to the suggestion that any instrument that improves or in some way advances the causes of peace and democracy, putting power into the hands of the people should be considered with an open mind and explored to the fullest extent possible.

More specifics of regulation have been offered by Schreier. Of particular interest are those pertaining to a licensing system. Schreier recommends a three-fold system of licensing.[232] This system would require (1) licensing a company for a range of activities in a specific list of countries, (2) licensing the service capabilities of companies requiring them to obtain licenses to undertake contracts for services abroad, and (3) licensing for or notification of individual contracts, essentially requiring companies to notify a governmental federal agency of each contract prior to tendering/bidding.

In terms of establishing criteria for determining whether a license will be granted, Schreier recommends an evaluation of the potential of the service to produce any of the following six impacts: (1) jeopardize public security and law and order, (2) undermine economic development, (3) increase instability and human suffering, (4) augment a perceived threat as viewed by neighboring countries, (5) contribute to or provoke internal intervention or external aggression, and/or (6) violate international embargoes.[233]

Finally, in establishing a transparency framework, Schreier suggests a public record disclosing details of the following: ownership; shareholding and financing arrangements; declaration of board members and responsibilities, perhaps in some form analogous to the financial disclosure statements suggested in chapter 2; an identification of the PMC's headquarters; a disclosure of corporate or firm structure with divisional activities; information about joint ventures and partners; disclosure about subsidiary and subcontractor ownership and interests; and finally, information concerning contracts for outsourced services and clients.[234] This level of disclosure would go a considerable distance in providing the information to design and implement appropriate regulation.

3.13 Conclusion

The PMC is up-and-coming. It is a force to be reckoned with on the domestic front, as it challenges many of the long-held beliefs and practices concerning the state's monopoly of violence. The traditions of state control, both de facto and de jure, of weapons, weapons manufacture, and armed groups is a tradition with strong and purposive roots. These traditions are not traditions that should be set aside without careful consideration and caution. They reflect the wisdom of millennia of human experience. Where those traditions are to be set aside, it needs to be done carefully and with sufficient and appropriate mechanisms for achieving the ends achieved (or at least attempted) by those traditions. A simple, reductionistic view presented by certain economists is not a sufficient excuse for unleashing on society the mechanisms of unprecedented violence currently in the hands of the PMC.

Markets and contracting are particularly inadequate controls on PMCs. Identifying appropriate objects for contracts, monitoring and holding PMCs accountable at the end of the day by contractual means has proven to be nigh well impossible. Further, we have seen that neither governments nor PMCs themselves seem particularly inclined to follow the wishes of the populace. PMCs serve both their own ends and government ends that do not and need not comply with the views of the populace. In fact, PMCs facilitate a governmental flight from democratic accountability.

Further, consideration of law as a control of the state's use of violence should leave members of civil society feeling unsettled. We have seen that the Rule of Law is a mythical restraint easily brushed aside by determined governments and their agents. Even where the judiciary finds itself sufficiently courageous to stand up to politicians on these grave decisions concerning violence, politicians are just as likely to run slipshod over the judges as they are to follow their rulings.

In this chapter we have also seen the use of PMCs extraterritorially. Their use in these contexts illustrates the complexities of the geopolitical landscape and their potential as forces of good and evil, or perhaps more accurately, forces providing protection and inflicting harm. The PMC is well and truly embedded in the foreign policy of provider nations, yet they are subject to exceedingly low levels of public scrutiny and accountability, particularly in these contexts.

All of these factors combined with the general observation that considerable potential violence has been on the increase while national powers have been in a state of decline. Furthermore, we have seen that the state's ability to control the PMC in either de jure or de facto terms is nearly nil. Conversely, PMC's ability to control states has been demonstrably clear. They have indeed installed the governments of their choice to protect their own economic interests without regard to the interests of opponents, civilians, or even the parties with whom they have contracted.

The PMC-government nexus is potentially fraught with intractable conflicts of interest. How these are avoided is unclear and likely in many cases, insoluble. Difficulties seem to arise at every stage of the contracting process and some of the most basic and important aspects of contracting—monitoring and measuring compliance—appear to be, in some cases at least, beyond the scope of or in contradiction to the terms of the contract. While PMCs are likely here to stay, and governments are pleased to use their services, the citizens appear to remain unshielded from one more violent group belonging to the national terrain of the twenty-first century. Such being the case, the necessity for regulation is abundantly clear.

Regulatory designers will have to ensure that their focus remains on the main guiding principles dealing with violence, whether state- or PMC-inflicted. Those principles include the protection of the citizens and control by and accountability to the citizens. The system itself will have to be tailored to the particular states party and take account of the circumstances of the proposed host country.

4
National Regulation of Private Military Companies

4.1 Introduction

Acknowledging the utility of PMCs to states in this age of privatization, the increasing reliance placed on PMCs by states as they strive to maintain an adequate defense capacity and the simple fact of their existence, states stand in a difficult and conflicted situation vis-à-vis the PMC industry. While it is often expedient for a state to condemn the actions of a given PMC in a foreign state, the same state will undoubtedly be reliant on a raft of other PMCs (or perhaps the same PMCs) for the successful implementation of its defense policy. Accordingly, the fundamental question to be addressed in this chapter, expressed pragmatically is, how can states impose consistent controls on PMCs that will simultaneously stymie the actions of rogue PMCs and allow the state to further its policy objectives via PMCs and not jeopardize the utility of PMCs to that state's defense agenda?

In this chapter we first examine issues surrounding regulation and regulatory design. After a review of the potential of self-regulation, we examine two voluntary codes as attempts at self-regulation. Then we examine the broader argument for regulation using the cases of PMC activity in PNG and Iraq. The remainder of the chapter considers the variety of regulatory regimes that have been advocated and adopted by various states, namely New Zealand, US, UK, and South Africa, and assesses the pros and cons of each model in terms of whether they effectively achieve their regulatory goals and their potential contribution to developing appropriate and effective regulation of the PMC on the national front.

4.2 Regulation and regulatory design

Regulation is a controversial topic. Even what is meant by "regulation" is disputed. Generally, regulation can mean any one of the following: to govern according to rules; to have state activity controlling other activity; an instrument of policy (as contrasted with incentive-based instruments); an instrument for shaping of markets to include incentives, and legal rules in a command-and-control schema possibly including some form of delegated authority.[1] In the discussion of the regulation of PMCs that follows, the term will be used in the second, third, and fourth senses: that of state control of market activity, an instrument of policy, and an instrument of market-based incentives.

Regulation is controversial because of the philosophical commitments it reflects, not only with respect to economics, social policy, and social philosophy, but also because of the views of constitutionalism it entails. As to the first set of disputes, scholars and legislators committed to neoliberal views tend to regard regulation with the same suspicion that they view all government.[2] Those scholars and legislators who have a preference for a social democratic model believe that markets, like many other parts of society, function better with some level of regulation.[3] In the situation at hand, a total free market in PMCs would be the same as a Hobbes all-out war of all against all, while at the opposite extreme the government provides and controls all aspects of military, from buttons to bullets and plunder to peace talks. Clearly, the situation in which we find ourselves is somewhere in the middle.

The issue of regulation is controversial among legal scholars because of commitments concerning constitutional law. Following Dicey's dual foundation model composed of its parliamentary or legislative supremacy and Rule of Law, regulation which involves the delegation of powers to nonparliamentary bodies is immediately problematic and suspect[4]—not to reiterate the concerns with the whole notion of the Rule of Law, discussed in the previous chapter. Accordingly, regulation, where it is considered a delegation of parliamentary oversight activity, runs contrary to the legal doctrines identified by Dicey.

Once one has made decisions concerning the above matters, decisions still need to be made concerning the empowering legislation: Will it be form-based (legal rules) regulation or economic effect-based (outcome) regulation,[5] or some newer type of regulation[6] such as "beyond incentive"-based regulation which capitalizes on parties' voluntary efforts to coordinate and solve problems.[7] And still other questions about the structure and view of the regulator will remain.[8] For example, will the regulator be an independent agency or mere governmental department, or some type of an external self-funded agency?[9] Decisions concerning the nature of the regulation and regulatory model need to be made to determine whether it will follow an inquisitorial, or adversarial,[10] or ombudsman model;[11] follow policy or address matters ad hoc;[12] and finally, whether control of the agency will be ministerial or by judicial oversight.[13] In sum, it is not a simple matter to conceptualize and design appropriate, effective regulation. This level of difficulty is identified without having identified the substantive issues of the regulation, of objectives and entities. Once these are identified and considered, they both assist in clarifying options but simultaneously may add complexity. With these preliminary considerations of regulation set out by way of background, we now turn to the substantive issues of regulation of PMCs. We turn first to the simplest option, self-regulation.

4.3 Is self-regulation of the PMC industry feasible?

There is currently much debate, in the context of corporate responsibility, about how and when self-regulation of any industry is appropriate in a privatized, globalized world.[14] The public fear is that the power of corporations is expanding while the government's ability to regulate, and the public's concomitant ability to influence the content of those regulations, is ebbing. As discussed in chapter 2, self-regulation is often a preferred approach.

Self-regulation, although not a new idea, is a model that has become increasingly popular for a number of reasons. Participants in the industry are deemed to be the most knowledgeable about the challenges and proper practice of their particular occupation and hence argue that they are in the best position to design implementation and administration of the regulation. Further, it is considered to be cheaper. Not only does government avoid the cost involved in creating the regulation, but also avoids the costs of funding administration of the regulation. Were these the only concerns of governments, industries, and public, self-regulation would be the only system in existence. There are other issues and motivations that are equally, if not more, important.

Industries will be motivated to self-regulate in a number of instances. These are when they are facing industry-wide problems such as problems with public image; distinguishing its goods or services from competitors; facing undesirable pending government regulation; concern about consumer collective action; as well as seeing the potential gains from cooperation, including enhanced profits from better processes, enhanced profits from limiting competition in the market, and in instances where an industry tends to create social capital—that is, where an industry's members move freely among various market participants, sharing technical expertise and know-how.[15]

Bringing this analysis to bear on the PMC we note the following. The industry has a serious problem with public image. Not only has the public not accepted the commodification of violence, the issue of PMC legitimacy has also not been settled. It is not likely to be settled ever as the PMC market poses an inherent challenge to notions of sovereignty. The issue is manifest by the PMCs' significant efforts on a number of fronts: it emphasizes its potential benefits; creates spin by such things as naming its industry association International Peace Operations Association (IPOA); emphasizes its support of humanitarian ends, condemning as "Ruthless Humanitarians" those trying to solve problems through the political process; emphasizes loyalty to national foreign policy; emphasizes patriotism; and insists on framing the discussion in terms of "rebels," "private contractors," and "security" rather than "civilians," "employees," and "violence."

Further, the PMC must distinguish its goods and services from competitors. Competitors to the PMC are mercenaries and government. PMCs are eager to distinguish themselves from mercenary services in order to gain any legitimacy at all, and for the utility of governments who use them as we have seen as guise claiming them to be entities distinct from the foreign policy arms of the government. Additionally, the PMC industry needs to distinguish itself from publicly provided, potentially violent services of military and police in order to create market space, yet in some manner it seeks to identify with those public services to gain whatever legitimacy it may yet be able to obtain from the connection.[16]

There is no outspoken objection to pending regulation. Indeed, quite the opposite has occurred with the IPOA, among other industry participants, in calling for regulation. This shows that the industry has identified reasons for regulation. Certainly one such reason is that any government regulation other than an outright ban implicitly legitimizes them, acknowledging their right to exist. Another important reason is that the PMC industry wishes to prevent a proliferation of proscriptive state regulatory systems. Certainly the growth and unregulated nature of the PMC industry, and the broader security industry, is causing governments, the public, and users of security services to become nervous. The PMCs have picked up on this concern and have, over the last ten years, acted preemptively to professionalize their industry. The formation of industry representative bodies and codes of conduct has been one of the most visible manifestations of this new professionalism.

Next among the noted motivations for self-regulation, potential collective consumer action (i.e., government or multinational corporation boycott) does not appear to be an issue. Finally, there may be certain advantages from cooperation in terms of process. One can see that cooperation among PMCs could enhance the safety of their members' employees in the field, cooperation in obtaining larger contracts by coordinating the supply of services, etc.

This analysis does not settle the matter of self-regulation for the PMC. For self-regulation to be effective it must address three other particular challenges. Self-regulation tends to be inappropriate and ineffective the larger the group.[17] Further, self-regulation tends to be difficult and/or ineffective unless consumers or peers can identify and punish breaches of code.[18] Finally, as Gunningham and Grabosky observe, self-regulation is only appropriate in that "minority of cases in which industry interest and public interest are sufficiently coincident for self-regulation to be a viable regulatory strategy."[19] There is a peculiar motivation not mentioned in general regulatory discussion because it is unique to the PMC industry and that is that it wishes to avoid prosecution of its members. Industry advocate Doug Brooks discusses this as PMCs requiring "a great deal of latitude in their operations."[20] This is too a version of "trust me, trust me" and should be treated with utmost caution.

These three pose formidable challenges to the PMC industry's self-regulatory aspirations. The industry, as we have noted, is large and dispersed worldwide. Further, given the nature of its business, it is a secretive industry. Such being the case, the lack of information does not make it a good candidate for self-regulation at the outset. Finally, as to the coalescence of public interest and private interest one must note that while one party wants free peace and safety, the other party is prepared to engage in violence for profit.

The PMC industry has developed industry associations which include elements of self-regulation to one degree or another. The primary industry body, the IPOA, is located in the US, and a number of regional industry bodies such as the British Association of Private Security Companies, the Private Security Company Association of Iraq, and South African Special Forces League are located elsewhere as their names suggest. In the next section we look at the role played by the IPOA in developing and implementing a voluntary regulatory code for the PMC industry and then delve into the Voluntary Principles on Security and Human Rights, which were developed by companies, governments, and NGOs to govern their retention of PMCs.

4.3.1 The International Peace Operations Association

IPOA is a trade association that draws its members from the "Peace and Stability Industry" who in turn provide services in the "peace sector."[21] IPOA acknowledges that the "private security industry"[22] is a subset of its membership. The private security industry is defined to include a firm that provides at least some armed security services outside of their country and in a conflict zone.[23] The mission of the IPOA is as follows:

> The International Peace Operations Association (IPOA) is an association of military service companies that support international peace and stability operations around the world. This includes companies that do everything from mine clearance, to armed logistics, to emergency humanitarian services, to the provision of specialised equipment, to actual armed peacekeepers. The association was founded to institute industry-wide standards and a code of conduct, maintain sound professional and military practices, educate the public and policy-makers on the industry's activities and potential, and ensure the humanitarian use of private peacekeeping services for the benefit of international peace and human security.[24]

IPOA members have voluntarily agreed to abide by the *IPOA Code of Conduct* (the Code).[25] The Code, like most voluntary industry codes, is written in very general terms and is not enforceable in any meaningful way. There is no complaint mechanism in the Code, which decreases the likelihood that any breach of the Code will be reported. There is also no mention of a compliance officer or a regular audit process. The Code does include a clause requiring members to only work for "legitimate, recognised governments, international organizations, non-government organizations and lawful private companies."[26] If a member breaches the Code then the only sanction they face is, perhaps, being dismissed from the IPOA.

The limitations of the Code can be illustrated by looking at what the Code has to say on compliance with international humanitarian law. Up until December 1, 2006, there was a clear directive in clause 1.3 that members follow all rules of international humanitarian law and human rights law:

> 1.3 Signatories agree to follow all rules of international humanitarian law and human rights law that are applicable as well as all relevant international protocols and conventions, including but not limited to:
>
> 1.3.1 Universal Declaration of Human Rights (1948)
> 1.3.2 Geneva Conventions (1949)
> 1.3.3 Protocols Additional to the Geneva Conventions (1977)
> 1.3.4 Protocol on the use of Toxic and Chemical Weapons (1979)
> 1.3.5 Voluntary Principles on Security and Human Rights (2000)

The above laudable obligation on PMCs must have been viewed as too onerous as it was removed from the Code itself and added to the nonbinding preface to the code, though the wording had changed significantly. What had been clause 1.3 now reads: "[a]dditionally, Signatories are *encouraged to* follow all rules of international humanitarian law and human rights law.... [emphasis added]."

The reason behind the watering down of the requirement for IPOA members to comply with international humanitarian laws is not explained. However, in the industry journal immediately following the adoption of the new Code, there is a brief congratulatory mention that the 1975 Convention against Torture had been added to the Code.[27] It was not mentioned that the Convention against Torture has been added, along with the revised clause 1.3, to the nonbinding preface. Is it possible that the IPOA and its members balked at accepting a binding obligation to abide by the Convention against Torture and it was therefore necessary to quietly move the whole of clause 1.3 from the binding to the nonbinding section of the Code?

It is more likely that the IPOA and its members moved 1.3 into the nonbinding section of the Code because they realized that it conflicted with clause 2.2 and 3.1. Clause 2.2 pertaining to transparency reads:

> Signatories engaged in peace or stability operations pledge, *to the extent possible and subject to contractual and legal limitations,* to be open and

> forthcoming with the International Committee of the Red Cross and other relevant authorities on the nature of their operations and any conflicts of interest that might in any way be perceived as influencing their current or potential ventures [emphasis added].

Similarly, clause 3.1 in relation to accountability reads:

> Signatories support effective legal accountability to relevant authorities for their actions and the actions of company employees.... Signatories pledge, *to the extent possible and subject to contractual and legal limitations,* to fully cooperate with official investigations into allegations of contractual violations and violations of international humanitarian law and human rights law [emphasis added].

Had clause 1.3 not been moved to the nonbinding preface, IPOA members would have been, on the one hand, obliged to abide by the rules of international humanitarian law, and on the other hand, by virtue of clauses 2.2 and 3.1, able to avoid complying with 1.3 if it conflicted with the contractual terms under which they are operating. It is possible that the removal of clause 1.3 was simply an acknowledgment by the IPOA and its members that it was ridiculous to include a strongly worded obligation that was readily able to be circumvented.

If the PMC industry wishes to implement an effective voluntary regulatory regime it will need to revise the Code by removing the words "to the extent possible and subject to contractual and legal limitations" from clauses 2.2 and 3.1 and reintroduce a requirement to abide by international law and international humanitarian law. The Code would need to be further amended such that members would be prohibited from entering into a contract that is contrary to the Code. It is simply not acceptable for PMCs to argue that they are effectively self-regulated if they are not obligated to follow international humanitarian and human rights law or to abide by their code of conduct if it conflicts with their contractual obligations.

We turn now to examine a more broadly representative and broadly applicable piece of self-regulation by parties who contract with PMC dealing with, among other things, human rights.

4.3.2 Voluntary Principles on Security and Human Rights

The *Voluntary Principles on Security and Human Rights* (Voluntary Principles) were first released in December 2000 and were sponsored by the US and UK governments; extractive companies such as Chevron, Shell, and BP; and NGOs such as Amnesty International, Human Rights Watch; and unions. These voluntary principles do not seek to directly regulate PMCs. Rather, the Voluntary Principles seek to govern the manner in which signatories (states, mining companies, and NGOs) retain security firms, including PMCs. It is noteworthy though that IPOA members are encouraged to abide by the Voluntary Principles in their Code of Conduct.[28]

The Voluntary Principles acknowledge a company's need for "public security "and, where this is inadequate, for "private security."[29] Public security refers to the security provided by the state in which the PMC is operating.

> The primary role of *public security* should be to maintain the rule of law, including safeguarding human rights and deterring acts that threaten Company personnel and facilities. The type and number of public security forces deployed should be competent, appropriate and proportional to the threat [emphasis added].[30]

Private security refers to PMCs:

> Consistent with their function, *private security* should provide only preventative and defensive services and should not engage in activities exclusively the responsibility of state military or law enforcement authorities. Companies should designate services, technology and equipment capable of offensive and defensive purposes as being for defensive use only [emphasis added].[31]

The Voluntary Principles comprise, as the title suggests, generally worded statements of intention ("should" and "may") rather than binding obligations and prohibitions ("must" and "must not"). The document is, in its entirety, expressed in aspirational language, with no attempt to draft clauses that could be interpreted in a legal sense. It is perhaps oxymoronic to say that there are no enforcement mechanisms or sanctions to be found in the Voluntary Principles.

Amnesty International has been agitating for the Voluntary Principles to be made more rigorous by incorporating a "reliable reporting mechanism."[32] Amnesty's concern over the efficacy of the Voluntary Principles was heightened in 2005 after it completed a report on mining in the Niger delta[33] and concluded that signatories to the Voluntary Principles had retained PMCs that had committed breaches of the Voluntary Principles. Amnesty was concerned that signatories had been able to vicariously breach the Voluntary Principles (via hired PMCs) while being in technical compliance.[34] Mining company representatives and some business groups have also expressed concern about the difficulty in implementing the Principles and the confusion over how to report breaches of the Principles.[35] The fact that concerns have been voiced by both the corporate and an NGO sector suggests that the Principles are not functioning optimally. There is no indication on whether the US and UK governments are content with the Principles as currently drafted.

At the 2006 Voluntary Principles Plenary Meeting, the NGO signatories[36] raised the issue of governance of the Voluntary Principle process and the introduction of effective reporting requirements. When the issues were not resolved during the plenary they wrote a letter of protest, which included the following warning:

> The Voluntary Principles process is at a critical crossroads and its long-term sustainability and credibility is contingent on the implementation of these criteria as a minimum but essential measure of adherence by participants. We strongly encourage the Plenary, Steering Committee, and the relevant working groups to quickly and expeditiously develop robust reporting guidelines on the implementation of the Principles, and an effective process for appointing investigative panels and recommending remedial measures for non-compliance. These systems should be operational by 2007 at the latest, must affirm the importance of all three institutions represented in the Plenary, and should be intended to maximise the effective implementation of the Principles in order to avoid complicity in human rights abuses.[37]

If the NGOs were to withdraw their support from the Voluntary Principles, then their efficacy as a self-regulatory tool would be severely undermined. It is the imprimatur of the NGOs that makes adherence to the Principles attractive to governments and companies—it is a guarantee to citizens and consumers that the Principles are meaningful and appropriate and not mere corporate gloss and government spin.

4.3.3 Can self-regulation work?

Experience in other industries controlled by voluntary codes suggests that the rational company response to the introduction of a voluntary code is to sign up and enjoy the benefits until such time as compliance conflicts with the company's operations or becomes too expensive. If the costs involved in adhering to a code are too high then the economically rational company will not sign up to the code until noncompliance becomes a liability. There is no reason to suspect that PMCs are anything less than economically rational. Of course, it is possible that a *status quo* can be reached within an industry such that noncompliance with a Code of Conduct becomes a liability and compliance costs are viewed as just another cost of doing business. This compliance *status quo* is typically only achieved if the Voluntary Code is backed by an industry body that is patronized by the majority of industry members (not the case with IPOA), has an enforcement mechanism with a degree of independence and substantial penalties, and is monitored by an outside body (for example, government looks to compliance when considering registration or authorizations or a watchdog reports on breaches).

These two codes, the IPOA's and the Voluntary Principles, illustrate the opposing principles at work in a self-regulatory approach. IPOA's role, as one of the key PMC industry bodies, is to strive to ensure that the costs of complying with the code are kept to a minimum while the benefits, in terms of an improved reputation for its members, are maximized through publicity. With respect to the Voluntary Principles, the hope within governmental and nongovernmental organizations is that the introduction of a voluntary code binding PMC customers will have a normative effect within the private security industry such that, after a number of years, compliance becomes essential to doing business within that industry. There is little if any empirical evidence demonstrating that this is a well-founded hope.

The introduction of a voluntary code of conduct for the PMC industry and voluntary principles to be adhered to by customers of PMCs serve one major purpose: they highlight the need for compulsory regulation of PMCs. A secondary benefit is that, until such time as compulsory regulation is in place, they are a mechanism that allows the more professional PMCs and PMC retainers to establish their bona fides.

In 2002 a meeting was convened by a working group of the International Peace Academy to delve into the options for promoting social responsibility among companies working in conflict zones. Its conclusions focused on the limitations of voluntary regulation and the likelihood that the PMC industry would follow a typical regulatory progression from voluntary to governmental regulation:

> Generally, private sector participants favored voluntary measures rather than legally binding obligations. Conversely, many outsiders argue that voluntary measures alone are ultimately insufficient to ensure that private sector activities do not directly or indirectly contribute to armed conflict, as they lack rigorous enforcement and broad coverage. There is an emerging interest—predominantly among NGOs, but also within some governments and industry groups—for a more overarching and robust approach to complement self-regulation, for example, a global minimum standard of conduct on the responsible use of natural resources and on norms of fiscal transparency. The most likely trend in the near future is the fine-tuning and standardization of existing voluntary international measures, combined with improved national legal and regulatory enforcement.[38]

4.4 The case in favor of regulation

Those arguing against greater state regulation of PMCs place great emphasis on the fact that PMCs are subject to the same laws as every other citizen and typically operate within, and work for, states that are governed by the Rule of Law (the reader is referred to chapter 3 for a thorough analysis and critique of these claims). This integration within a state should entitle PMCs to be treated in the same as any other corporate citizen. Furthermore, those opposing PMC regulation would argue that the time and cost involved in establishing an effective PMC regulatory regime is unjustified both in terms of the real risk posed by PMCs and the benefits that will accrue to the state. Finally, they argue that the market will regulate through its competitive forces, constraints, and incentives, creating, among other things, appropriate self-regulation.

Further, as discussed above, among PMCs themselves and the IPOA there is a call for regulation. The now defunct Sandline called for regulation back in 1998 in a document entitled "Should the Activities of Private Military Companies be Transparent?"[39] David Claridge, the managing director of Janusian Security, a PMC working in Iraq has stated: "most of the serious players are quite supportive of bringing in some degree of regulation... Iraq is forcing the industry to grow up and consider how the industry should be regulated."[40] Accordingly, regulation is not inconsistent with the intentions of the industry itself.

The arguments in favor of greater state regulation of PMCs can be reduced to simple propositions: first, states are concerned that PMCs have been, are now, and will be involved in unsanctioned acts of violence or aggression. States need only look to the recent past to document a litany of inappropriate PMC activity that has caused anger and embarrassment and has challenged their ability and duty to protect life, maintain security, and uphold sovereignty. States look to Iraq and are awed and slightly daunted by the sheer number of PMCs engaged in that theater of war and the largely uncoordinated, unreported, unaccountable role they are playing. Finally, states look to the future and surmise that an unregulated PMC industry based in their territory could potentially pose a risk to the state and/or its citizens. The risk could be limited to international condemnation for providing safe haven to rogue PMCs or could be more far reaching, for example, where PMCs threaten a state's internal sovereignty. To the extent that PMCs are operating within a state there is pressure, domestically and internationally, for that state to move preemptively to impose regulatory controls over those PMCs that fall within its jurisdiction. Second, given the breakdown of the demarcation between the frontline and supply, the deep penetration and integration of PMCs into the defense forces[41] and even the most basic concern of national security demands some form of regulation.

Two high-profile incidents involving PMC activities in PNG and Iraq are explored in the following section and will suffice to demonstrate the type of PMC activity that clearly should be curtailed because it endangers state sovereignty, is contrary to international law, and/or compromises good relations between states. The incidents were chosen with a view to exploring two threshold questions pertinent to the design and efficacy of any regulatory scheme for the control of PMCs. Those questions are (1) what precisely should a state regulate (a company, an activity, a contract) in order to effectively constrain an industry and (2) to what end (to protect state sovereignty, to preserve the presumption of peace, to avoid human rights abuses, to protect state interests)?

4.5 Papua New Guinea: The Sandline Affair

In 1997 there was a national crisis in PNG when the government, led by Prime Minister Julius Chan, retained the services of a PMC, Sandline International (Sandline), for deployment to Bougainville Island. The plan was to deploy Sandline in order to bring an end to a rebellion by Bougainvilleans who, among other grievances, were opposed to the environmentally devastating mining practices at the Panguna mine, in which RTZ-CRA held a 53 percent shareholding.[42] Sandline entered into a subcontract with another PMC, Executive Outcomes, to provide personnel and military hardware.[43] The response within PNG was an unequivocal rejection of the government's action in retaining PMCs. In March 1997, one month after the contract with Sandline became public, there was a military revolt that was popularly supported by the citizens of PNG. Brigadier General Jerry Singirok, who was in charge of the PNG defense force, terminated the proposed military solution, which was to involve both the PNG Defence Force and Sandline.[44] Sandline personnel were subsequently expelled from the country.[45] New elections were held in July 1997 and Chan and a number of other politicians implicated in the affair lost their seats in Parliament. Ultimately the PNG government was forced to compensate Sandline for its contractual losses.[46]

The bare facts set out above do not convey the intrigue that accompanied the Sandline Affair. As Dorney has noted in *The Sandline Affair*, from the beginning, "none of the normal rules were followed."[47] For example, the government, as noted in chapter 3, was aware that its actions were in breach of section 200 of PNG's Constitution, and took steps to circumvent the constitutional limitation by deputizing Sandline's personnel as "special constables" of the PNG defense force.[48] This course of action we have indicated avoided any possible conflict with subsection 200(1) of the Constitution by bringing the Sandline officers within the bounds of subsection 200(2). It also served to protect the Sandline personnel from liability under any international laws dealing with mercenaries. Furthermore, the PNG government was aware that it was acting contrary to the fiscal accountability framework that existed in PNG in that the contract sum was not authorized by the correct PNG authorities and was in excess of what the government is permitted to pay without adhering to an open tender process.[49] Perhaps the only bright note to the whole affair was the apparent refusal by the PNG government to agree to pay Sandline in kind by assigning to it future entitlements to the Panguna mine,[50] though it seems that this was the carrot that first attracted Sandline and Executive Outcomes to PNG.[51]

This PMC intervention was also an embarrassment for the Australian and New Zealand governments who had been sponsoring peace talks between PNG and the Bougainville Resistance Army (BRA) that had broken down. They were caught completely unprepared for this turn of events despite the fact that Chan had earlier sought military assistance from Australia and New Zealand that had not been forthcoming. Britain was also embarrassed by the actions of Sandline, which was a PMC based in Great Britain.

The Sandline Affair encapsulates the type of PMC activity that is in need of regulation. Firstly, it should not be possible for a PMC to enter into contracts with the executive government of a state that is contrary to the domestic law of that state. To allow such contracting undermines the Rule of Law in that state and, ultimately, undermines a state's legitimacy. Secondly, it is contrary to international law[52] and should therefore not be possible for states to retain PMC assistance to suppress self-determination movements such as the one on Bougainville, especially given that some headway had been made toward resolution of the issue.[53] Thirdly, it should not be possible for a state to retain a PMC within its own territory, particularly for tip-of-the-spear type of actions without parliamentary approval. A brief summary of regulatory approaches, objectives, and alternatives are canvassed next.

What type of regulatory prohibition, administered by which state, would have averted the Sandline Affair? At the time of this catastrophe, Sandline and Executive Outcomes were headquartered in the UK though the former was incorporated in the Bahamas and the latter in South Africa.[54] A regulatory regime administered by the UK could be made applicable to PMCs incorporated or operating from the UK and could therefore capture both PMCs. Alternatively, South Africa could introduce regulation that caught the activities of Executive Outcomes, however the regulations would need to be drafted in such a way that they caught PMC subcontractors and required a subcontractor to produce the head contract (between Sandline and the PNG government) for scrutiny. If a Sandline Affair was to be averted, then the regulatory regime would need to prohibit PMCs entering into contracts that were inconsistent with the domestic laws of the state where the PMC activity was to take place; or inconsistent with international law; or had not been approved in a parliament. Given the PMCs' obvious interest in securing future mining royalties, it may also be advisable for the regulatory regime to stipulate additionally that the contract sums be expressed in dollars rather than in terms of mining options or ongoing mining royalties. A PMC that counts on payment only in the event of one outcome in a civil war (that is, when a mine that has fallen into rebel hands has been recaptured) is a political warrior and not merely and economic actor.[55] A more comprehensive analysis of implemented PMC regulatory regimes is conducted later in the chapter.

We turn now to the second example of PMC activity that should be curtailed as being a threat to sovereignty, contrary to international law and/or compromising good international relations.

4.6 Iraq: CACI and Titan

It is well-known that individuals working for PMCs were involved in the human rights abuses perpetrated at Abu Ghraib prison in Iraq (discussed from an international perspective in chapter 5). A report by Major General Antonio Taguba[56] into the military police at Abu Ghraib has named two private companies that provided interrogation services, CACI International (CACI)[57] and Titan Corporation (Titan). Janis Karpinski, previously army reserve brigadier general, who had been in charge of the Abu Ghraib prison in 2003 when the infamous torture photos were taken, spoke about the role of private contractors in the abuses and the failure to integrate effectively the contractors into the chain of command. She described the importation of "aggressive" interrogation from Guantanamo Bay amounts to torture. She said:

> [W]hen you take those same techniques and put them in the hands of irresponsible and non-accountable people like these civilian contractors were, you are combining lethal ingredients. You get civilian contractors who have a playground, and they get out of control.[58]

Karpinski has stated that the majority of the interrogators had previously worked in either Guantanamo Bay or Afghanistan prior to working in Iraq for CACI[59] or Titan. In her own words the situation was as follows:

> So now you have a deadly mix. You have people who have been exposed and who have used these techniques first-hand in other locations. They know that there is no supervision or control. They have been directed, using whatever words, to get Saddam, get the information and get these prisoners to start talking, use more aggressive techniques.... And it got out of control. It clearly got out of control.[60]

This example clearly raises the issue of the accountability of private contractors, but it also illustrates a further issue that requires serious consideration before the development and introduction of a new regulatory regime for PMCs. What should the indicia of a PMC or a PMC activity be so that a PMC will fall within the scope of a regulatory regime? The issue raised earlier, in chapter 1, regarding the classification of PMCs becomes important in this context. Should CACI and Titan be categorized as PMCs given that the predominant business activity of both companies is the provision of information technology services as opposed to security or weapons-related services?[61] Of course, regardless of whether or not it comprised a core business activity,[62] both CACI and Titan chose to provide information, interrogation, and intelligence services in Iraq in relation to "high value" prisoners in a high security jail run by the military police. These services while not tip-of-the-spear military services are core military services.[63] Perhaps the answer is that the regulatory system should catch individual "military service" contracts entered into by any company rather than attempting a definitive definition of a PMC company. Alternatively, should the relevant regulatory criteria be the nature of the organization or body to which the PMCs provide its services? CACI states on its website that 73 percent of its work is for the US Department of Defense.[64] Is this preponderance of work for the premier military organization in the US enough to render CACI a PMC, regardless of the services it provides?

As a postscript to this example, while it is technically possible for individual contractors to be prosecuted in the US under various domestic laws, to date there has been only one successful prosecution of a private contractor and that was for possession of child pornography.[65] That action was taken under the Military Extraterritorial Jurisdiction Act (MEJA). A dry-eyed review and assessment of the law potentially applicable to PMC personnel, undertaken by the Congressional Research Service in 2007, is less than optimistic. Essentially, although MEJA and the Uniform Code of Military Justice could potentially apply, because of the limitations in definitions and legal precedents, in all likelihood they would not.[66] Actions in relation to the abuses at Abu Ghraib are purportedly still pending three years later and after all of the outstanding military prosecutions have been completed and verdicts reached.[67] As Scahill observed in his testimony before Congress:

> In four years, there have been no prosecutions for crimes against Iraqis committed by contractors and not a single known prosecution of an armed contractor. That either means that we have tens of thousands of boy scouts working as armed contractors or something is fundamentally wrong with the system.[68]

Scahill's evaluation would appear to be a fair summary of the situation. The difficulty is not in identifying the type of contractor behavior that is unacceptable in hindsight, it is in devising a regulatory scheme that is able to recognize in advance when a particular PMC, or a particular employee, or a particular contract entered into by PMC, or particular purchasing party that warrants particular regulatory scrutiny.

4.7 Can state regulation be effective

Despite the rapid growth of the PMC sector (discussed in chapter 1) and its involvement as a nonstate actor on the international security stage (discussed in chapters 3 and 5), the international community has not acted to regulate the PMC industry to control the manner in which it interacts with states. The International Convention against the Recruitment, Use, Financing and Training of Mercenaries (the Convention on Mercenaries) is of limited utility as it is covers only a relatively narrow range of mercenary activities as discussed in detail in chapter 5. This lacuna in international law means that individual states are being left to tackle the issue of PMC regulation on an ad hoc basis.[69]

A Green Paper by the UK government in 2002 focused on the options for regulating private military companies. It noted that there were two primary arguments favoring regulation of the PMC industry,[70] the first was the need to keep nonstate violence under control, and the second was the recognition that the nature of the transactions entered into by PMCs are atypical commercial transactions with the potential to impact the stability of a country or region. Accordingly, regulation was necessary for PMCs to be held accountable.[71] Both of these reasons demonstrate the state's concern to reestablish its monopoly over violence.[72]

Commentators are divided over the efficacy of national regulatory efforts. Commentators such as Zarate believe that regulation at the national level is important for securing accountability of PMCs,[73] while others, such as Singer, believe that regulation at the national level is doomed to fail.[74] Zarate has noted that PMCs tend to be based in, though not necessarily incorporated in, militarily advanced countries.[75] On a practical level, this allows PMCs ease of access to military expertise and networks of retired military officers. On a strategic level, it allows PMCs to claim some form of state endorsement as the state has either tacitly agreed to the PMC's operation within its territory or it has expressly regulated the PMCs headquartered in relation to its contracts.[76] If a state has introduced a regulatory regime to control PMCs, then it should be able to exert a degree of control over the activities of PMCs incorporated or headquartered within its territories.[77] The matter of regulatory control over PMCs in countries where they are operational is a distinct matter dealt with as we have seen by those courts and legal systems.

As discussed in chapter 2, Singer and other commentators are skeptical of a state's ability to regulate PMCs. They note the ability of PMCs, as corporate entities, to dissolve, reform, and move across borders with minimal effort.[78] Other impediments to effective state regulation are, firstly, the difficulty of defining precisely what the PMC is and what it is about PMCs that is in need of regulation, as discussed in chapter 1. And secondly, the practical difficulties of designing and enforcing regulation that requires extraterritorial application.[79] Despite his skepticism about PMC regulation generally, Singer notes that among the choices national regulation of PMCs offers hope of superior legal definitions and enforcement. Likewise Isenberg, in his study of the Iraq PMC debacle, calls primarily for increased national power.

Echoing these perspectives, states advocating the regulation of PMCs need to clearly articulate which elements of the work undertaken by PMCs require regulation. Before this task can be tackled it is necessary for a state to identify its regulatory objective: Does it want to prohibit all private combat soldiers or perhaps all armed soldiers who are doing anything other than guarding an object or person? This type of regulatory focus would help address the issue of mercenarism, but again the definitional problems mentioned in chapter 1 and the disappearing frontline make the focus problematic. Alternatively, a state could choose to tackle PMCs generally by controlling the type of contracts that companies are permitted to enter into. In other words, states will have to delimit the appropriate realm of activity for PMCs and then decide on the appropriate criterion for regulation. Going to the heart of the discussion the issue of delimitation is highly contentious. Are these military services core government activities such that they cannot be outsourced without compromising sovereignty?[80] For purposes of discussion, the assumption must be made that indeed they are.[81] The criterion for regulation, or regulatory trigger, as suggested by an expert panel, could include one or more of the following aspects of PMC activity: (1) the nature of the PMC services being rendered, (2) the identity of the customer retaining the PMC and their motive for retaining the PMC's services, (3) the suitability of the PMC providing the services, or (4) the physical location in which the PMC services are rendered.[82] A further trigger could be the proximity to or control of potentially lethal force. This latter trigger may be a key in the debate and design of regulation as it is the infliction of violence that is the main matter of concern and hence potentially the critical activity for regulatory focus. The efficacy of the respective regulatory triggers would depend on the state's ultimate regulatory objective, and most importantly, its political will.

In the following sections we will look at the way that a number of states have approached the issue of PMC regulation. In each instance we will endeavor to identify the regulatory objective and the regulatory trigger and identify whether the law achieves its objectives. However, before turning to that discussion a cautionary note must be sounded to avoid an unwarranted enthusiasm and hope for effective legal control.

It is important to note the government's complicity in assisting PMCs to avoid regulation aimed at controlling arms trade. The UK government, for example, refused to prosecute Sandline International for the 1998 shipment of rocket launchers, assault rifles, machine guns, and ammunition to Sierra Leone, despite Sandline's contravention of UK law. The UK government claimed Sandline's actions were in the UK's interests.[83] In 2007 the UK government was again making headlines, this time related to stifling an investigation into bribes involved in the export of weapons manufacturer BAE's Eurofighter Typhoon warplanes to Saudi Arabia.[84] It goes without saying that governmental decisions to enforce and ignore laws on the basis of political interests undermine the legal order and expose both the fallacy of the notion and the political nature of de jure control of PMCs, whether supplying hard weapons, support services, strategic skills, or frontline fighting troops.

4.7.1 New Zealand: National regulation consistent with International Treaty

Although the limitations of the *International Convention against the Recruitment, Use, Financing and Training of Mercenaries* (the Convention on Mercenaries) are discussed in detail in chapters 1 and 5, a brief consideration of the Convention is necessary here.[85] The fundamental problem with the Convention on Mercenaries is that it was drafted prior to the ascendancy of PMCs. Accordingly its preoccupation with mercenaries is now anachronistic. While the recently formed UN Working Group on Mercenaries does not shy away from labeling certain PMC activities as a new form of mercenarism,[86] the more widely held view among states is that the Convention on Mercenaries is obsolete with respect to PMCs.

While many states have refused to sign the Convention on Mercenaries for the reasons outlined above, the treaty has been in force since 2001[87] and at the time of writing this chapter had 29 signatories.[88] The UK, US, South Africa, France—home-states for the bulk of PMCs—are conspicuously missing from the list of signatories. Articles 5–7 and Article 9 of the Convention on Mercenaries requires states to act to give effect to the Convention. Below we will consider the manner in which one of the signatories, New Zealand, has legislated to give effect to the Convention on Mercenaries and we will consider whether the legal framework has any purchase with respect to regulating PMCs.

New Zealand acceded to the Mercenary Convention in September 2004 and has enacted the *Mercenary Activities (Prohibition) Act 2004* (Map Act) to give it domestic force. The introduction of the MAP Act in New Zealand was accompanied by acrimonious debate in Parliament and in the wider community.[89] There was concern that the scope of the Act was too broad and would criminalize many essential security services provided by the private sector overseas, particularly by New Zealanders working for PMCs in Iraq. Those opposing the introduction of the legislation were generally in favor of proscribing mercenary conduct (though definitions of what activities were included within the range of prohibited conduct varied). However, they were not in favor of proscribing "legitimate" security and military service providers. The Foreign Affairs, Defence and Trade Committee, that considered the Bill, commented that the Convention was never meant to cover all types of mercenaries but rather was directed at "a small group of so-called 'true' or 'traditional' mercenaries: unaffiliated individuals prepared to fight wars."[90]

The definition of "mercenary" included in the MAP Act follows the definition in the Convention on Mercenaries very closely. The definition catches any person who is recruited in order to take part in hostilities in an armed conflict and whose purpose includes making private gain and who is promised compensation substantially in excess of that promised or paid to combatants of similar rank and functions in the armed forces of that party. The term "armed conflict" is undefined and will, presumably, take its content from international law. The definition of mercenary also includes a person recruited to commit a concerted act of violence and who is paid material compensation. The MAP Act definition has many exclusions most notable of which is that a mercenary is not a person on a peace mission or working for the UN, a mine clearer, a humanitarian aid worker, or a person providing domestic policing duties or similar work involving the protection of individuals or property (that is, domestic security work).[91] Recruiting, using, financing, and training mercenaries are prohibited consistently with the Convention on Mercenaries.[92] Finally, section 13 provides for extraterritorial operation for the Act where there is a nexus to New Zealand.

The one notable deviation from the definition in the Convention on Mercenaries is that the requirement that a mercenary "fight" in an armed conflict has been changed and broadened in the MAP Act to a requirement that the mercenary merely "take part in hostilities" (not defined). This amendment was supported by the major parties and was designed to ensure that the Act applies only to those persons involved in wars as combatants.[93] If the words, however, are given their plain meaning then it is hard to see how the phrase "take part in hostilities" is more likely to net a combatant than the word "fighting." In fact, it is possible to argue the opposite. A PMC could be characterized as "taking part in hostilities" by providing transport services; providing weapons, by providing logistical support, but these same PMCs could not be characterized as "fighting." The definition of mercenary in the MAP Act differs from that in the Convention on Mercenaries in one other significant respect: it includes a number of additional negative attributes. Specifically the aforementioned exclusions of a person taking part in a peace support mission; the detection, clearance, and so on of mines; the delivery of humanitarian aid; or "domestic policing duties or other lawful activities of a similar kind involving the protection of individuals or property."[94]

The question then is, who, in the wake of the enactment of the MAP Act, falls within the definition of mercenary in New Zealand? Many PMC employees who have a nexus to New Zealand will potentially fall within the scope of the Act but only if they cannot avail themselves of one of the many "outs." Firstly, they can argue that they are not really operating in an "armed conflict." Secondly, they can argue that they are not providing services that could be characterized as contributing to the *continuation* of hostilities (a likely interpretation of what "taking part in hostilities" means). Thirdly, PMC employees will be able to avoid being labeled a mercenary if they can characterize their work as the delivery of humanitarian aid. If we consider that the War in Iraq has, at various times, been characterized by the coalition members as a humanitarian mission to save the Iraqis from a dictator; a mission to support a transition to democracy; or a mission to prevent civil war in Iraq, then it is a relatively simple step to assert that PMC services, perhaps even combatant services, could be characterized as a form of humanitarian aid. Arguably, larger loopholes exist in the form of the "protection of individuals or property" and "domestic policing duties"—exceptional activities engaged in by most PMC workers. Many PMCs are engaged in Iraq in roles that essentially involve them defending people or property in the form of members of the fledgling Iraqi Parliament, convoys, pipelines, and the like. These defensive duties all too frequently involve the PMCs directly in hostilities,[95] yet employees carrying out these duties will avoid being labeled mercenaries under the MAP Act.

The dearth of defined terms in the MAP Act in conjunction with the expanded list of exceptions means that prosecutors will have difficulty proving that many PMC employees operating in Iraq with the coalition forces or many other parts of the world where PMCs are operating in areas of civil unrest are mercenaries. Moreover, the MAP Act, like the Convention on Mercenaries, is aimed at proscribing the behavior of individual mercenaries and will be of little, if any, utility in tackling corporate PMCs and their coordination of potentially lethal activities.

Furthermore, the MAP Act will not catch individual New Zealanders who are career mercenaries, such as David Pemberton. Pemberton was retained by a mother to abduct her two children who were in their father's custody in Lebanon. After the successful abduction mission Pemberton was captured by Lebanese authorities and charged with kidnaping, though those charges were later dropped and replaced with a charge of obstructing the course of justice. Pemberton and his fellow security consultants have consistently been labeled mercenaries in the press,[96] yet his activities will not be captured by the Act as their mercenary activities were not undertaken in the context of an international armed conflict. To date, and unsurprisingly, there have been no prosecutions under the MAP Act.

Instead of legislating to regulate PMCs, New Zealand chose to legislate to proscribe a very narrow range of mercenaries as defined in the Convention on Mercenaries, and then further narrow that by the inclusion of additional exceptions. The Foreign Affairs Defence and Trade Committee, that considered the bill before it was considered in Parliament, acknowledged the shortcomings of the MAP Act and foreshadowed the need for more specific legislation to regulate PMCs. It stated:

> This bill does not purport to deal with all issues associated with mercenaries. It is aimed simply at implementing the Convention. Its passage would not therefore preclude the taking of further measures in the future to recognise a role for and regulate the activities of private military companies. However, the manner in which these companies should or may

> be regulated raised a range of issues that are beyond the scope of the present bill to consider.

Legislation in the form of the MAP Act, enacted to give domestic force to the Convention on Mercenaries, is not a model that should be promoted for dealing with modern-day PMCs. At best this type of legislation draws a line in the sand and indicates that a state will not tolerate the traditional, individual, dog of war. The issue of whether or not PMCs should be regulated, and if so, to what end, is a debate that New Zealand is yet to have.

4.7.2 United States: Registration and licensing

For more than 20 years, the US Department of state has issued export licenses to American PMCs in accordance with the United States' Arms Export Control Act and International Transfer of Arms Regulations.[97] The system of regulation equates the export of security and military services with the export of arms. The system has been described as idiosyncratic since input from the state and Defense Departments varies from contract to contract.[98]

One of the criticisms directed against the US licensing regime is that, pursuant to the International Transfer of Arms Regulations, Congress does not need to be informed of a contract in advance of the issuance of a related license unless the contract is valued at over $50 million.[99] Another criticism is that once a company receives a license, there are very limited oversights or reporting requirements.[100]

The pros and cons of a US-type regulatory system were considered by the UK in the previously mentioned Green Paper. Its authors concluded that the primary drawback of a US-style licensing system was that in order for it to be effective, the regulating state had to be prepared to expend money on policing and enforcement.[101]

A further drawback of licensing regulatory schemes is that some may interpret the issuance of a license as evidence of state sanction for a particular PMC activity. Singer, for example, refers to a national regulatory scheme involving licensing as providing a "safe harbor" for PMCs insofar as the licenses obtained by PMCs through the schemes can be touted as evidence of state endorsement.[102] The other side of this argument is that a licensing scheme allows a state to pursue its foreign policy objectives though the management of PMC deployments. The example of Equatorial Guinea,[103] discussed in chapter 3, illustrates how the United States makes use of its PMC licensing scheme to influence the activities of PMCs operating from within the United States and which governments may be supported by the US. As mentioned, the United States refused to issue MPRI a license to operate in Equatorial Guinea reportedly because of that state's poor human rights record. The US refusal to issue a license continued until the nature of the engagement included human rights training. Having spent a considerable amount of time and money securing the license from the US government, MPRI could now claim with some justification that the United States had endorsed its intervention. By hosting PMCs within its borders, the United States has been able to further its foreign policy objectives and successfully influence PMC activities, all at little expense to taxpayers. The downside to this arrangement, as Singer has noted, is that the process places the imprimatur of state approval on PMC activity.

It is evident that the US licensing system would be a more effective tool for regulating PMCs if the licensing application process was more rigorous, more transparent, and monitored. However, in the absence of more effective national legislation in other states, the US model is often held up as the preferable model of regulation.[104] The US model of regulation has its strengths. By concentrating on exports it offers some control of PMCs that are operating in weak states unable to exercise any effective control. It sets some minimum standards for PMCs using the US as their home state, although it must be acknowledged that in substance those standards appear to be no more than the whims of the president in power.

The debate in the US and UK, as illustrated by Congressional hearings, has not focused directly on the efficacy of the regulatory scheme itself but rather on the broader issue of the accountability of PMCs retained and deployed. In other words, the emphasis has not been on controlling when PMCs are utilized, where they are deployed, or the services they offer, but simply on how they can be held accountable when they behave criminally, or contrary to foreign policy.

The apparent regulatory objective in the US is to be aware of the overseas activities of all PMCs using its territory as a base and, as noted, where PMC activity does not fit with US foreign policy, to prevent deployment. To achieve this regulatory objective the US has legislated to require all PMCs who wish to accept a contract to work outside of the US to apply for a license. The regulatory trigger therefore is the offer of a contract to work overseas. The regulatory method achieves the regulatory goal and to that extent the scheme is successful. However, as a model for other regulatory schemes, or as a means of addressing the broader regulatory objectives throughout this work, the model is woefully inadequate.

4.7.2.1 Proposals to create a Civilian Reserve Corps

Finally, a brief note on nascent plans that, if realized, could have a bearing on the interaction between the PMC industry and the US. In his State of the Union Address in January 2007, President Bush renewed his call for the creation of a Civilian Reserve Corps.[105] The aim is to ease the burden on the US Defense Forces by creating a corps of volunteers with the skills needed on US reconstruction and stabilization missions. This is not a new idea. In addition to the UK Act[106] it has US precedent. Prior to the Democrats gaining control of Congress the Senate had, on May 25, 2006, passed the Reconstruction and Stabilization Civilian Management Bill which provided for the State

Department and the US Agency for International Development to jointly develop "an effective expert civilian response capability to carry out reconstruction and stabilization activities in a country or region that is at risk of, in, or is in transition from, conflict or civil strife."[107] It was envisaged that the "response readiness" corps would have up to 250 personnel on active duty and 500 volunteers, drawn from within the executive and from the public, on reserve duty.[108] An appropriation authorization for USD 80,000,000 for 2007 was included in the Bill.[109] After being passed by the Senate, the Bill was referred to the House International Relations Committee and languished there until it lapsed with the Democrat win at the mid-term election.

Given the current Democrat-led Congress, it is far from certain that the Civilian Reserve Corp will be realized. If, however, a Civilian Reserve Corp was to become a reality it would add a further layer of complexity to the conundrum of PMC regulation. Would PMC companies be able to act as personnel providers for the corps? Alternatively, would PMC companies themselves be able to join the corps by guaranteeing to deploy a certain number of experts in certain fields as and when required? Lastly, would the creation of a corps significantly reduce the US reliance on PMCs or simply serve to reinforce the role of PMCs in furthering US foreign policy objectives?

We turn now to a third example of a national PMC regulating regime.

4.7.3 South Africa: Prohibition, registration and executive authorization

The military/security industry is a multibillion dollar industry in South Africa[110], and the South African Department of Foreign Affairs has estimated that at least 4,000 citizens are currently working in conflict areas around the world: some commentators believe the number may be closer to 20,000.[111] Given the apartheid history of South Africa and the pool of available military and security personnel, the statistic is not particularly surprising. When considering how best to deal with PMCs, the South African government is committed to ensuring that its foreign policy agenda is transparent, ethical, and consistent with the constitution, [112] which at section 198(b) affirms that South Africa is to live in peace and harmony and that no South African citizen is to participate in armed conflict except as provided for by South African law. The practical issue for the South African Parliament is how to ensure that private military and security personnel do not endanger the new democratic order in South Africa, do not engage in unethical military activities abroad that would be contrary to its foreign policy, and do not embarrass it internationally.[113]

The South African Parliamentary response was to adopt an approach that achieved two objectives. First, it sought to ban outright mercenary services (defined to include many military services). Second, and more generally, it aimed to delegitimize PMCs[114] and PSCs. To achieve these objectives, it designed regulation creating the implementation of a registration and licensing scheme designed to severely curtail South African involvement in the international security sector. South Africa passed its first law regulating PMCs in 1998: the *Regulation of Foreign Military Assistance Act 1998*. At the time of writing, the Act was still in force though deliberations on a replacement law, the *Prohibition of Mercenary Activities and Regulation of Certain Activities in Country of Armed Conflict Bill*, were reaching their conclusion and it seems likely that the Bill will be passed in the near future. In the circumstances it may be prudent to discuss both laws.

4.7.3.1 Regulation of Foreign Military Assistance Act 1998

In 1998, South Africa enacted the *Regulation of Foreign Military Assistance Act*, which prohibits individuals and companies within South Africa, and all South African individuals and companies outside of the country, from "direct participation as a combatant in armed conflict for private gain."[115] The Act also prohibited the recruitment, training, and financing of mercenaries.[116] The legislation established a license-based regulatory scheme. A person or company wishing to provide military-related services had to first register with the National Conventional Arms Control Committee (NCACC), obtain government approval to offer foreign military assistance, and then receive authorization to enter into a specific contract with a third party for the provision of these services.[117] The decision on whether to grant authorization or approvals lay with the Minister of Defense acting on advice from the NCACC.[118]

The strength of the Act is that it bans mercenary activity and regulates the provision of foreign military and security services abroad, specifically in armed conflict. The weakness of the Act is that it bites off more than it can chew. In the process of regulating those offering "foreign military assistance" it is in effect regulating all manner of service providers operating in armed conflict situations. There is widespread agreement among commentators that the definitions for "foreign military services" and "security services" in the Act are too broad and, to the extent that they seek to regulate activities that are clearly not military in nature, they compromise the integrity of the Act.[119] Taljaard argues that the Act needs to be radically amended so that it is triggered not by consideration of "where" the services are destined for (that is, whether or not the services will be provided in a conflict zone), but rather by the "nature of the assistance offered" (that is, whether the service is military in content or not).[120] A further concern expressed by Singer is a concern that placing the regulatory scheme in the hands of the executive limits effective parliamentary oversight.[121]

For the above reasons, the Act has not been well received by the PMC industries in South Africa and it seems that PMCs and PMC employees have largely decided to ignore its terms. This comment is not made flippantly. During its period of operation the Act has not prevented South African citizens and companies from providing a range of military services in Iraq in blatant breach of the Act. The NCACC formally declared Iraq a conflict area for the purposes of the Act approximately 12 months after the invasion of Iraq, which clearly indicated to South African PMCs and employees of PMCs that their ongoing presence in Iraq would be unlawful if they did not secure a license. Two South African companies applied to the NCACC for licenses, arguing that their services were not military services. They were not granted licenses.[122] Furthermore, while the Act has been in force, South African PMCs have been involved in lurid security scandals in the Ivory Coast and in Equatorial Guinea, yet there have been only a handful of prosecutions and those that have been successfully conducted have typically relied on plea bargains to secure convictions.[123] We turn next to discuss the second attempt at legislative regulation.

4.7.3.2 Prohibition of Mercenary Activities and Regulation of Certain Activities in Country of Armed Conflict Bill

President Mbeki announced that the *Prohibition of Mercenary Activities and Regulation of Certain Activities in Country of Armed Conflict Bill* would be drafted in his State of the Nation address in 2005 in response to the obvious failure of the Act to regulate effectively the operations of PMCs in Iraq.[124]

The original draft of the Bill was breathtaking in its scope and was roundly criticized from organizations as disparate as Amnesty International[125] and the UK High Commissioner to South African Catholic Bishops' Council.[126] As a direct result of the public hearings and the debate in the Defence Committee, the Bill was radically amended[127] to reduce the scope of the extraterritoriality provisions, to reduce the scope of the prohibition on unregistered humanitarian organizations working in countries where there is armed conflict,[128] to remove the provision that would have made an exception for groups fighting for national liberation, and by allowing South Africans authorized to enlist in foreign armies to be deployed to conflict situations.

The Bill prohibits mercenary activity, which is defined broadly to include not only participation for private gain in an armed conflict but also recruiting, training, and financing a combatant in an armed conflict; and participating directly or indirectly in furthering an armed conflict.[129] The Bill now seeks to regulate PMCs by dictating when juristic persons, citizens, or those permanently living in South Africa (and foreign citizens to the extent they commit offenses within South Africa) can provide "assistance" or "service" of military, military-related, or security nature in an area of "armed conflict."[130] Taljaard has commented that the Bill is "plugging any loopholes in the [*Regulation of Foreign Military Assistance Act 1998*] and is grappling with the thin line between PSC activity in conflict zones and 'tip-of-the-spear' PMC activity, if not modern-day mercenarism."[131] Furthermore, because of the tendency of PMCs to pose as humanitarian organizations the Bill also regulates humanitarian assistance offered by South Africans in a country where there is armed conflict.[132] While the extension of the Bill to cover humanitarian organizations has been controversial, judging by media reports and public submissions, the plan requiring South African citizens seeking to enlist in the armed forces of another State to obtain authorization is even more so.

At the time of writing, the *Prohibition of Mercenary Activities and Regulation of Certain Activities in Country of Armed Conflict Bill* (the Bill) had not passed the upper chamber of the South African Parliament, the National Council of Provinces. The Bill has already successfully passed through a public hearing process initiated by the Defence Committee and the Select Committee on Security & Constitutional Affairs.[133] Until such time as the Bill is passed, the *Regulation of Foreign Military Assistance Act 1998* (the Act) remains in force.[134]

The Bill does not attempt to rectify the definitional or enforcement-related problems with the Act; instead it simply broadens the regulatory net even further by capturing South African humanitarian services providers and those South Africans wishing to join foreign armed forces. While definitions have changed slightly they have not been overhauled and there has been no attempt to refine the regulatory trigger, which remains the presence of "armed conflict," either objectively or as proclaimed by the government.[135] Importantly, South Africa's regulatory objective is clear. It appears to be to ban or drastically curtail the operations of PMCs. For example, the preface to the Act states:

> The Constitution of the Republic of South Africa, 1996, provides in section 198(b) that the resolve to live in peace and harmony precludes any South African citizen from participating in armed conflict, nationally or internationally, except as provided for in the Constitution or national legislation. In order to implement aspects of this provision and in the interest of promoting and protecting human rights and fundamental freedoms, universally, it is necessary to regulate the rendering of foreign military assistance by South African juristic persons, citizens, persons permanently resident in the Republic and foreign citizens who render such assistance from within the borders of the Republic.[136]

While there is no express denouncement of PMCs the anti-PMC sentiment is palpable. The Preamble in the Bill is similarly worded, though longer given the need to justify its increased scope. As noted, regulatory schemes require cooperation between the regulator and those being regulated to work optimally. The alternative, if those being regulated feel that the scheme is unfair, is a high degree of regulatory noncompliance that results in the state incurring increased costs to secure compliance. If South Africa has the stated regulatory aim of severely curtailing the PMC industry then the PMC industry can rightly suspect that the licensing scheme will be implemented in such a way as to limit PMC activity. If, as is the case with the Act, the enforcement mechanism is difficult to administer, relying as it does on an ability to collect evidence outside of South Africa, then the state is left with a high level of noncompliance and unacceptably high costs to secure compliance.

States often make the mistake of equating tough regulation with effective regulation. For a regulatory system to work there must be either the metaphoric big stick or big carrot in play. Neither the Act nor the Bill has an effective big stick, as demonstrated by the difficulty the South African authorities have had prosecuting breaches. A big carrot could be incorporated into the regulatory scheme but only if South Africa is prepared to modify its regulatory objective.

If South Africa reconciled its commitment to maintaining an ethical foreign policy with the ongoing existence of the PMC industry in South Africa, albeit a PMC industry that operated to higher standards, then a regulatory compromise is possible. South Africa must implement a regulatory scheme that offers the PMC industry an incentive of some sort. If South Africa does not intend to allow the PMC industry to continue in any meaningful way, then it would be better off prohibiting all PMCs (leaving aside the fact that an illicit market for PMC services would be sure to develop). South Africa will not be able to secure regulatory compliance from the PMC industry unless the regulatory scheme offers the PMC industry some incentives and operational certainty.

A South African compromise regulatory scheme could take many forms and we outline but one possibility. South Africa could legislate to prohibit PMCs that offer frontline combat services but work with the remainder of the PMC industry to draft an enforceable code of conduct. The code would need to stipulate that PMCs are responsible for ensuring that all service contracts comply with a set of agreed standards (the standards would cover matters such as what type of services can be offered to whom and in what circumstances). PMCs would then be required to submit all contracts to a central government body for approval. To ensure timely government response approval would be deemed to be granted if not forthcoming within a designated period of time. That same government body would be empowered and well resourced to undertake audits of certain PMCs or certain contracts. Some thought would need to be given to the most effective sanction to impose on PMCs found to be in breach. The costs of running, monitoring, and enforcing the scheme could be offset by charging a fee to PMCs submitting contracts based on the value of the contract. While far from ideal, this form of regulation offers the prospect of achieving the regulatory objects of removal of the most offensive PMCs and some degree of government oversight of the entire PMC industry. Furthermore, the introduction of a code of conduct that incorporates enforceable minimum standards allows the African National Congress to ensure that its ethical foreign policy is not compromised.

4.7.4 United Kingdom: "Light footprint" regulation, if any

In 2002, the Foreign and Commonwealth Office published a Green Paper entitled "Private Military Companies: Options for Regulation" (the Green Paper).[137] As outlined in the Green Paper, the UK has considered regulating PMCs in a variety of ways. Proposals have included enacting a complete prohibition on their activities, imposing a licensing regime on the provision of military services, or permitting the PMC industry to self-regulate through a voluntary code of conduct.[138] The major argument put forward in support of self-regulation is that it is "a relatively unburdensome form of regulation" from the perspective of the British government, which would nonetheless help establish standards of behavior within the industry.[139] Furthermore, self-regulation would not require the British government to police "unenforceable legislation or regulation," which could arise if the law attempted to define or specify the types of PMC activities being regulated.[140]

After collecting public submissions, the Green Paper was sent to the UK's Foreign Affairs Committee for consideration. The committee formulated a number of recommendations for the British government's consideration. The recommendations suggest support for a limited form of regulation that would not disrupt the legitimate activities of the PMC industry.[141] The recommendations encouraged the government to choose appropriate criteria for regulation that would distinguish reputable from disreputable PMCs and facilitate the business of the former while curbing the latter.[142] In a rather generous assessment of the industry, it seems that all activities short of dealing in arms or engaging in combat are to be considered reputable activities of PMCs, a much more catholic view of "good" PMCs.

Some commentators would suggest that the UK benefits directly from a close working relationship with disreputable PMCs and that British firms need these disreputable PMCs to further their business interests in countries that do not offer security.[143] Such hypotheses are difficult either to establish or disprove. However, if benefits truly are forthcoming, the phenomenon would explain Britain's "poor luck" with PMC scandals and its preference for light regulation. Light regulation of the PMC industry allows Britain to suggest that it is cleaning up the industry while at the same time benefiting from the widespread availability of unfettered PMCs. Light regulation also allows the UK to avoid expenditure on regulatory oversight. Other reasons why the UK is likely to opt for a light regulatory approach are listed by Walker and Whyte and include embarrassment over past PMC activities such as the "Arms to Africa" scandal that involved Sandline, the UK's unwavering and unrelenting commitment to economic rationalism, disenchantment with international law approaches to private military actors, fear that the horse has already bolted and that regulation is the only way of constraining PMCs, and the UK's reliance on PMC independence.[144] Regardless of speculations concerning motives, the UK preference for light regulation fits well with the neoliberal, laissez-faire ideology that seeks to, as far as possible, leave the market to regulate itself.

The UK has not taken any further action to regulate the PMC industry since 2002. If the Green Paper and responses can be taken as accurate indicators of political will, it seems likely that at some time in the future the UK will introduce regulations designed to protect and facilitate the economic viability of what are considered to be reputable "good" PMCs. It seems likely that the design of this "light footprint"[145] regulatory scheme will most closely resemble that in place in the US. The impetus to place PMC regulation back on the political agenda is not likely to occur until the end of the Iraq war. It is conceivable, however, that the issue could be catapulted to center stage if there is a fresh scandal involving PMCs based in or retained by the UK, or if there is European Union interest[146] in the issue. In the meantime, it seems that the only pressure for the introduction of effective regulation of PMCs is being driven by the private security companies[147] (who distinguish themselves from PMCs by limiting their role to security of property or people).[148] ArmorGroup, for example, has proposed a regulatory scheme for PSCs, which builds on the existing scheme in place domestically in relation to the provision of private security services.[149]

In the meantime, the PMC industry based in the UK or working for the UK need only abide by the laws of the land, including the *Foreign Enlistment Act 1870* which prohibits UK citizens from enlisting in foreign armies or recruiting others to enlist in foreign armies (there have been no successful prosecutions under this Act), *the Export Control Act 2002* (aimed at equipment not services), and the recent proliferation of terrorism-related legislation that has the potential to tangentially impact on PMCs.[150]

4.8 Regulatory recommendations

As previously noted, self-regulation is inappropriate for the PMC sector. The PMC lobby group, IPOA, itself recognizes this and is one of the voices calling for regulation. Citizens groups and governments are calling for regulation. All that is left is for governments to form the political will to attend to these calls and develop an appropriate response. It is not an easy issue from the government perspective. As noted throughout in this book in anecdotes and case studies, government has a conflicted stance toward PMCs. In considering prerequisites for regulatory design, Jennings' two caveats are significant hurdles for effective PMC regulation. These are "that the state actually has a clear and desired regulatory end, and that the definitional issues...are more or less resolved. Neither condition applies to the private military industry."[151] Yet it may be that Jennings is overly pessimistic in this conclusion.

It seems clear that the objective of nonviolence is certainly one clear objective. Further, the control of parties who collectively control the potential to inflict lethal force is certainly a necessary and corollary objective. Next the issue of accountability and transparency come to mind, particularly as the PMC as we have seen is not a mere provider of technical services but is inevitably the potentially violent implementer of politics, and hence a political instrument. In explication of the foregoing analysis, the regulatory objective is the protection of civilians from and the appropriate control of parties able to create a credible threat of violence whether on domestic citizens or foreigners, and giving control over such parties to the civilian population.

In terms of definition, again, mentioning the context of civil unrest (whether foreign or domestic), the control of potentially lethal force, the profit motive, and the collective corporate organization should suffice. It would be broad enough to encompass the main area of concern and the actor, the PMC, yet narrow enough to allow lesser actors to escape overly burdensome and expensive oversight, an issue agreed by most participants and regulators alike.

Taking these objectives and definitions and combining them into a piece of legislation would provide a template along the following lines. First, the legislation would prohibit the controllers of weapons from effecting control from within that state signatory or of weapons with the potential to strike at targets within the territory of that signatory state without supervision by agents of the state. Second, the legislation would prohibit the retaining of a PMC by the government or acceptance of PMC services paid for by another state, unless such a proposed deployment of the PMC had been put before the popular representatives in a parliament. Clearly the nature and scope of activity, including remuneration, would have to be put out into the open. This condition would satisfy many of the issues surrounding basic democratic accountabilities. Third, there would have to be a consent to and means provided for the monitoring and enforcement of the contract. Fourth, and critical to the whole issue of PMC activity, is that the PMC and by extension all employees and subcontractors would be subject to all the laws of the host country.

Recognizing the lack of a "silver bullet" piece of regulation in most instances, and rather that a combination of overlapping regulatory terrains is the more realistic and preferable option, there is no need to assume that the one piece or type of regulation will cover the regulatory landscape. Rather, various forms of regulation will likely have to exist. State regulation would likely be most effective if there were a statutory regulatory body. That body would best be wholly independent of the PMC industry lobby. It would be tasked with regulating and administering the bonding scheme mentioned in chapter 2, and have responsibility for overseeing the vetting of personnel and directors. It would be charged with the development of further regulation, the investigation of complaints and incidents, the conduct of independent spot audits, and the provision and re-sourcing of observers (to avoid observers in the field being dependent upon those under their scrutiny). No form of co-regulation is appropriate because of the dangers of regulatory capture. Co-regulation would permit a dangerous shift in the focus away from public safety and democratic accountability.

In this instance, given some of the significant benefits of self-regulation, a form of self-regulation should be encouraged to coincide with the legislated regulation and form part of the regulatory framework. Self-regulatory bodies will assist by providing their expertise in identifying issues that should or should not be subject to regulation, identifying parties seeking to avoid regulation, identifying parties who breach codes, engage in disciplining those members in breach of the code, and assist in the development of codes.

It will be important to keep a clear space between the self-regulatory body and the legislative scheme and regulatory agency for the obvious danger of regulatory capture inherent in close industry-regulator relations. Given the clear danger to the populace from PMC activities, the protection of the populace must always be given priority over PMC interests, and the PMCs must be kept at arm's length and communication between a regulator and the PMC always open to public scrutiny. Certainly the PMC lobby will complain about this issue claiming, among other things, commercial confidentiality. Given the lives at stake, presumption against violence, the threat to sovereignty, and the absolute choice left to the PMC to not engage in that business activity, it seems ingenuous to make the claim that it is inappropriate to have public scrutiny of those communications and contracts should it choose to engage in the activity. After all law, including corporate and commercial law, is designed for the benefit of the public.

This proposal clearly needs much further debate and development, but as a suggested way forward, it does not fall into the narrower traps set by either the definitional or taxonomic debates identified in chapter 1 and throughout the work.

4.9 Conclusion

We have argued in this chapter that regulation of the PMC industry is necessary in order for a number of reasons, first and foremost is the safety of civilians. Second, to ensure that PMCs are accountable for how, why, and where they operate and for their compliance (or lack of compliance) with national and international law. Some will argue that PMCs should simply be proscribed and that states alone should monopolize the delivery of military services. The authors have not given these arguments serious consideration because, as previously stated in the outset, the "horse has already bolted" and that a return to a time without PMCs is no longer conceivable. We have attempted to deal pragmatically with the unique regulatory challenges faced by states wishing to exert some level of control over PMC deployment and mode of operation.

Self-regulation by means of a code of conduct is a useful starting point but is of limited efficacy in terms of improving accountability and ethical operating procedures particularly if it is lacking in meaningful reporting, enforcement, or monitoring provisions. Industry codes of conduct can, however, serve a useful role in supplementing national regulation.

As argued above, an effective regulatory scheme needs to be consistent with a state's overall regulatory objective vis-à-vis its interaction with PMCs. If a state's regulatory objective is to ban all mercenaries in accordance with the UN Convention on mercenaries as we have seen in the case of New Zealand, then national legislation can quickly be drafted and enacted but will only affect a handful of individuals working for PMCs. We suspect that New Zealand will rarely, if ever, find the need to prosecute anyone under the *Mercenary Activities (Prohibition) Act 2004* precisely because it has been drafted to capture a historical figure who is unlikely to be found in great numbers, matching that description of "mercenary," anywhere in the world.

If, like South Africa, a state's regulatory objective is to ban or closely regulate a wide range of PMCs, then a broader definition of mercenary and/or of PMCs must be used in the legislation. Of course, the broader the definitions used, the wider the scope of the law, the more PMCs will be affected, and the greater the resistance to the introduction and implementation of the law. The regulatory system implemented in South Africa in 1998 graphically illustrates this point. Unfortunately, the new regulatory system proposed for South Africa will not secure greater compliance or greater effective oversight of the PMC industry in South Africa because it does not tackle the shortcomings of the earlier Act.

Finally, if a state's regulatory objective is to utilize PMCs to further its foreign policy objectives but to do so in a way that encourages compliance with some minimum operational standards, then an executive-run licensing scheme, such as exists in the US, is ideal. By tasking the executive with oversight of the regulatory scheme, the US ensures the maximum level of flexibility and secrecy and a minimal level of Congressional oversight. We do not endorse the US style of regulation specifically because it is secretive, subjective, and largely unaccountable to the public. However, the US model of regulation with its commitment to advancing US foreign policy illustrates one important point. States do not have to implement a wholly objective regulatory system because PMCs arguably are not providing essential services (although Chubb claimed to in East Timor in chapter 3). They are providing military services or military-related services, which are unique services that should only be rendered in support of sovereignty. A sovereign state has the right and perhaps the duty to ensure, not that PMC regulation is objectively fair, but that PMCs are not deployed in circumstances that pose a threat to state sovereignty or otherwise in a manner contrary to international law or international humanitarian law.

The UK was considering the options for regulation, but with the last PMC scandal a dim memory in Downing Street, it is likely that the UK will delay introducing any regulatory scheme until the European Union decides on an appropriate regional regulatory approach. While the US model of regulation is undoubtedly attractive to the UK, their system of responsible government would make executive control of the regulatory scheme less secretive and more open to scrutiny.

In order to develop a workable regulatory framework, states and the United Nations need to concentrate on the basics. The starting point is to acknowledge the impossibility of returning the genie to the jar. Although PMCs will always be distasteful to some, in certain instances, they may have a legitimate role to play. States need to identify their objectives in regulating PMCs, which should be to ensure that the services offered by PMCs are used to strengthen, not weaken, civilian power and security, strengthen and not weaken nation-states and their institutions, and that PMCs operate in a manner wholly consistent with national and international law and are held accountable for any breach of such laws. To achieve these objectives a regulatory scheme must be able to distinguish between the type of services being offered by different PMCs and the context in which they propose to offer those services. States, and the international community at large, need to move away from the Convention on Mercenaries and its unhelpful definitions and focus instead on how best to regulate the full spectrum of PMCs. Finally, states need to cooperate with each other to ensure maximum efficiency in monitoring and enforcing national schemes regulating PMCs and, ideally, in designing an overarching international regulatory scheme for PMCs, which we consider in the next chapter.

5

Private Military Firms under International Law

5.1 Introduction

In Angola, Executive Outcomes, a South Africa-based PMC, used fuel air explosives—a highly effective but particularly tortuous weapon;[1] in Iraq the use of untrained PMC personnel in interrogation resulted in the widely publicized Abu Ghraib prison scandal. Even the "War on Terror" has not been spared. The tentacle of the PMC is manifest in the emerging practice of the United States government labeled "extraordinary rendition"—an insidious scheme involving the transfer of terrorism suspects to third countries that harbor no qualms about using all manner of processes and procedures to "extract information."[2] As in the case of the Abu Ghraib abuse, various international norms were violated, including the Convention against Torture (CAT) and the 1949 Geneva Conventions which prohibit governments from taking such actions. However, the ambiguous legal status of PMCs under existing international law offers leeway for countries to not only bend but also occasionally breach their international legal obligations, thus threatening the very fabric of the international legal order.[3]

The incidents outlined above are but a tip of the iceberg of a wider range of incidents around the globe[4] that raise a host of complex legal issues. Rights and duties that exist between the military and its contractors constitute an uncertain, legal gray zone and so substantially reduce the potential for military to observe international legal obligations. The fundamental problem is that command and control so essential for military operations in a theater of conflict is unclear with regard to private military personnel. As the debacle that unfolded in the aftermath of the recent invasion of Iraq in which PMCs were central and integral players demonstrates, often local military commanders are unaware of the daily actions of firms in their zones of responsibility. As one former Special Forces veteran said of the role of PMCs in Iraq: "The military really can't tell you [PMCs] how to do your job—they can advise you, but they really have no control over you."[5] This ambiguity and its consequent problems have been identified by military jurists themselves. They note that

> by ignoring the well-thought-out doctrine on civilians' role in warfare, contractors now operate in a legal no man's land, beyond established boundaries of military or international law. The reality of the fact is that since contractors do not fall within the formal military hierarchy, they are generally self-policing entities.[6]

As the case of Iraq demonstrates, there are numerous issues pertaining to the operations of, contracting with, and rules governing the operation of PMCs. This is more so since their largely unregulated activities span a number of fields ranging from police, paramilitary, and military training to logistics and protection of installations and officials.

The multibillion dollar question then is whether this new trend and growth in global security falls within the ambit of national and international law, and if so whether adequate regulatory and accountability mechanisms exist. Chapters 2, 3, and 4 have grappled with the domestic dimension of regulation and accountability of PMCs. The central focus of this chapter is a review of the limitations of international law in dealing with PMCs and articulation of possible avenues to hold PMCs accountable.

There are three potential approaches in the international schema for controlling the conduct of interstatal violent conflict and violence, which have bearing on the international regulation of PMCs. These three are the applicability of the laws dealing with mercenaries and mercenarism, being laws dealing with the conduct of war as contained in various international conventions; the laws pertaining to state responsibility for private actors; and the laws governing the military, specifically the laws surrounding command responsibility. This chapter turns to look at each of these in turn.

5.2 PMCs and the mercenary regime: Peeling a legal onion

This section reviews attempts by the international community to control mercenarism. It first reviews General Assembly resolutions and then turns to specialized mercenary conventions.

5.2.1 General Assembly resolutions

The authors wish to commence this section by noting that the initiatives to ban mercenaries have not been solely driven by the UN General Assembly, but also by UN Security Council. Various resolutions by the Council have sought to ban the recruitment, use, and training of mercenaries aimed at destabilizing national liberation movements.[7] However, in light of the fact that Council resolutions are all highly particularized, prompted by specific incidents the chapter chooses to dwell on Assembly resolutions. Admittedly, some of the Assembly's resolutions bear the same weakness as Council resolutions—particularization to specific incidents. However, a number of them are of a more general nature, paving the way for argument that the Assembly's numerous resolutions on the matter as well as its broader constituency, unlike the Security Council, evidences emerging *opinio juris*.

Formal activities of the General Assembly in relation to mercenarism date back to 1968. In Resolution 2395, condemning Portugal's failure to grant independence to the territories under its domination,[8] the Assembly appealed to all states:

> to take all measures to prevent the recruitment or training in their territories of any persons as mercenaries for the colonial war being waged in the Territories under Portuguese domination and for violations of the territorial integrity and sovereignty of the independent African States.[9]

In the same year, the General Assembly made its first general foray into the regulation of mercenary activities in postcolonial regimes through the adoption and passage of Resolution 2465—the Declaration on the Granting of Independence to Colonial Countries and Peoples.[10] In paragraph 8 of the resolution, the Assembly declared that

> The practice of using mercenaries against movements for national liberation and independence is punishable as a criminal act and that the mercenaries themselves are outlaws, and calls upon the Governments of all countries to enact legislation declaring the recruitment, financing and training of mercenaries in their territory to be a punishable offence and prohibiting their nationals from serving as mercenaries.[11]

Subsequently, the General Assembly reiterated its position on the question of mercenaries in Resolution 2548.[12] In the resolution the General Assembly reaffirmed that "the practice of using mercenaries against national liberation movements and sovereign States constitutes a criminal act and that the mercenaries themselves are criminals."[13] The resolution went on to exhort governments of all countries to enact legislation that would declare "the recruitment, financing and training of mercenaries in their territories, and the transit of mercenaries through their territories, to be punishable offences, and prohibiting their nationals from serving as mercenaries."[14] Further, it rested the responsibility of enforcement at the feet of the states concerned to take the necessary measures to prohibit transit of mercenaries on their territory and to prohibit their nationals from serving as mercenaries.

In 1970 the General Assembly passed a resolution recognizing the legitimate right of "liberation movements" to use "all the necessary means at their disposal"[15] to achieve their objectives while at the same time declaring the use of mercenaries against national liberation movements was recognized as a criminal act. In the same year, the General Assembly indirectly addressed the matter when it adopted the Declaration on Principles of International Law concerning Friendly Relations and Co-operation among states in accordance with the Charter of the United Nations.[16] In this declaration, the UN stated once again that "the practice of using mercenaries against national liberation movements in the colonial territories constitutes a criminal act." In the same year, the Assembly directly addressed the matter in Resolution 2708 which was passed specifically to implement the Declaration on the Granting of Independence to Colonial Countries and Peoples.[17] The resolution largely echoed the sentiments declared in previous resolutions which criminalized mercenary activity and urged the passage of domestic legislation to this effect. Equally, Resolution 2727 of December 14, 1970, emphasized what had become a familiar chorus—using mercenaries against national liberation movements was a criminal act.[18]

In late 1973, the General Assembly returned yet again to the theme of regulating mercenary activities in postcolonial regimes with the passage of Resolution 3103.[19] The resolution entitled "The Declaration on Basic Principles of the Legal Status of the Combatants Struggling against Colonial and Alien Domination and Racist Regimes" noted that

> The use of mercenaries by colonial and racist regimes against the national liberation movements struggling for their freedom and independence from the yoke of Colonialism and alien domination is considered to be a criminal act and the mercenaries should accordingly be punished as criminals.[20]

In 1979, the General Assembly took a decisive step in the outlawing and control of mercenaries. In Resolution 34/140 it decided to consider the drafting of an international convention to outlaw mercenarism in all its manifestations.[21] "The Assembly at that time stipulated that 'mercenarism' is a threat to international peace and security and, like murder, piracy and genocide, is a universal crime."[22] With this language, the Assembly went further than ever before in its condemnation of mercenaries.[23]

In addition to commencing the drafting process of the International Convention, which got underway in the early 1980s, the United Nations continued to issue a series of resolutions addressing mercenarism.[24] In these resolutions, the United Nations continued to emphasize that the activities of mercenaries are contrary to the fundamental principles of international law, such as "non-interference in the internal affairs of States"[25] and "territorial integrity and independence."[26] The resolutions further explicitly condemned mercenarism, and like their predecessors, emphasized the criminality of the activity, placing an obligation on individual states to enact the necessary domestic legislation.

5.2.1.1 *Problems with General Assembly resolutions*

It may be argued that the multitude of the UN General Assembly's resolutions and their repeated appeals for governments to restrict the supply and demand for mercenaries is evidence that states have obligations under international law to both criminalize and punish mercenaries. However, the utility of these resolutions against mercenaries is questionable and in terms of its drafting wholly misses the corporate organization, the PMC. The concern of the General Assembly arises principally from the rise in the use of mercenaries in Africa, where they have had a deleterious impact on the ability of states to maintain order and encouraged the militarization of civil society and rapid growth in small arms markets. However, in the often frustrating and politically driven law-making process in the international system, matters are not as clear-cut as this. A number of factors militate against the argument that the resolutions posit legal obligations. First, many of the General Assembly resolutions address particular conflicts. Second, the General Assembly resolutions are broader in scope than established, customary international norms. Third, "under the UN Charter, the General Assembly has no authority to enact, alter, or terminate rules of international law."[27] Last, "General Assembly resolutions do not necessarily constitute international law. Instead, resolutions from the General Assembly…may only represent the crystallization of customary international law or evidence of State practice and *opinio juris*."[28]

Overall and especially in relation to contemporary PMCs, the narrow focus of General Assembly resolutions adopted in the process of outlawing mercenarism is significant. Despite mercenarism dominating the UN agenda as evidenced by a multitude of resolutions, the importance of the issue has been singularly tied to the context of national self-determination. The initiatives focus largely on the relationship between mercenary activities and the stifling of the right to self-determination. This necessarily means that contemporary PMCs operating internationally and outside the specific context of wars of national liberation fall outside the limits of General Assembly initiatives. The importance of a clearer legal definition of mercenaries and context of operations thus remains an open question.

5.2.2 Specialized mercenary conventions

5.2.2.1 *Regional instruments*

In 1971, the Assembly of Heads of State and Government of the Organization of African Unity Convention (OAU) declared that mercenaries represented a threat to the "independence, sovereignty, territorial integrity and the harmonious development of Member States of the OAU" and condemned the use of mercenaries as inimical to the sovereignty of member states.[29] The following year, the process of crafting of the Convention for the Elimination of Mercenaries in Africa commenced. Five years later this initiative resulted in the signing of the Organization of African Unity Convention for the Elimination of Mercenaries in Africa.[30] The Convention directly codifies a ban on mercenaries.[31] Article 1 of the draft convention stated:

> [A] "mercenary" is classified as anyone who, not a national of the State against which his actions are directed, is employed, enrols or links himself willingly to a person, group or organization whose aim is:
>
> (a) to overthrow by force of arms or by any other means the government of that Member State of the Organization of African Unity;
> (b) to undermine the independence, territorial integrity or normal working of the institutions of the said State;
> (c) to block by any means the activities of any liberation movement recognized by the Organization of African Unity.[32]

The definition clearly reflects the limited concerns of the drafters. In their concern to limit interference with African peoples' right to self-determination, free from interference by white minority regimes, and the protection of those states once established, the drafters created a definition of mercenary dependent in the first instance on his/her relationship to the state. That is, a mercenary must be someone foreign and hence unable to argue the legitimacy of participation in the fight by claiming to be fighting for self-determination. In other words, fighters within their own states cannot be classified as mercenaries and are instead classified as rebels. Once this test has been passed, it must be proved that their aims are to overthrow governments; to undermine independence, territorial integrity, and institutions of governance (i.e., the three hallmarks of sovereignty), or who otherwise seek to block independence. This carefully crafted narrow definition allowed the states to have their cake and eat it too—as the representatives of the most powerful group upon the successful expulsion of colonial powers, they could ban mercenaries from without and continue to express their power from within against those who would represent a challenge to their newly found sovereignty. The narrowness of the definition would make it useless in dealing with the challenge posed by today's PMCs. The convention that came into force, however, adopted the UN Convention's definition mentioned and discussed above.

As the Special Rapporteur on Mercenarism noted in 1988,[33] this was the first instrument of international law which was applicable in the territory of the states' party to the Convention and to all persons covered by its provisions. It was also notable because it imposed well-defined obligations on each of the parties and stressed the need to adopt appropriate measures in each state's domestic criminal law. The Convention was intended to control the use of mercenaries by insurgent groups and coup-makers. Under the

Convention, mercenarism was confined to acts committed by states or individual actors who have the "aim of opposing by armed violence a process of self-determination, stability or the territorial integrity of another State."[34]

The Convention has two significant drawbacks. Firstly, it does not prohibit states from hiring mercenaries. It defines mercenaries only as those men who sold their services to a "person, group or organization" engaged in insurgency against a state.[35] It only prohibits governments from hiring mercenaries to suppress movements of national liberation, but does not proscribe the hiring of mercenaries by acknowledged governments, nor the hiring of mercenaries for purposes that do not compromise the "independence, territorial integrity or normal working of institutions."[36] There is hypocrisy in two levels in this position, despite the reality that mercenarism is a pernicious problem in Africa. The first is answered in part by Montgomery Sapone's observation that "By permitting their own use of mercenaries, while controlling circulation among non-State actors, States established a pool of legitimate purchasers of military manpower."[37] This decision was based in part on the desperate weakness of many African states, whose security forces were and still are often either ineffectual, or oppressive, or both, and the appeal of the nascent PMC industry both to African politicians and to Western businesses and governments.[38] The second allows governments to retain such private militaries as they see fit for purposes other than the suppression of independence movements.

The net result set the stage for the frequent use of PMCs to crush insurrections and secure mineral sites, allowing states to continue to monopolize the market for alienable military skills while disapproving the use by nonstate sanctioned entities.[39] The second significant drawback to the Convention is its status as a source of international law regarding mercenarism. Its regional character, which localizes and particularizes the problem to postcolonial African soldiers of fortune, serves in part in its being viewed as a regional convention addressing regional issues. This regional character denies it playing a more significant role in creating added impetus in international circles toward criminalizing and punishing mercenarism. Finally, it too wholly misses any provisions that may be extended to apply to PMCs.

5.2.2.2 International instruments

In 1989, after seven long years of delicate negotiations and drafting, the International Convention against the Recruitment, Use, Financing and Training of Mercenaries was adopted by the UN. It was the first convention of international scope against mercenarism.[40] The Convention defines a mercenary in Article 1 as

1. A mercenary is any person who:
   (a) Is specially recruited locally or abroad in order to fight in an armed conflict;

(b) Is motivated to take part in the hostilities essentially by the desire for private gain and, in fact, is promised, by or on behalf of a party to the conflict, material compensation substantially in excess of that promised or paid to combatants of similar rank and functions in the armed forces of that party;
(c) Is neither a national of a party to the conflict nor a resident of territory controlled by a party to the conflict;
(d) Is not a member of the armed forces of a party to the conflict; and
(e) Has not been sent by a State which is not a party to the conflict on official duty as a member of its armed forces.[41]

The Convention establishes an expansive definition of mercenary.[42] Coming at the end of a long unbroken series of General Assembly resolutions stretching back into the 1960s, it also appears to crystallize the customary international law regarding mercenaries.[43] The Convention reflects an emphasis on the punishment of mercenaries themselves[44] as well as those who promote or organize mercenary activities.[45]

Significantly, states' responsibilities go beyond merely recruiting, using, financing, or training mercenaries to include duties to prevent offences under the Convention and notification of the UN or affected states parties to establish jurisdiction over the Convention's offences. In addition, the Convention obligates states to apprehend suspects, to extradite suspects under certain circumstances and, in cases where the state does not extradite the suspect, to "submit the case to its proper authorities for the purpose of prosecution."[46] The Convention, if followed by states, will help guarantee the right of peoples to self-determination and ensure stability to lawfully constituted governments. As the UN Special Rapporteur on Mercenarism noted in his 1991 report:

> The formulation of broader, more comprehensive and more precise international regulations updated to take account of the forms which mercenarism has assumed in recent years with the aim of overthrowing Governments and undermining the constitutional order or territorial integrity of States highlights the importance of this new multilateral instrument and the necessity and desirability of its prompt entry into force.[47]

The anti-mercenary conventions (both regional and international) discussed above have five primary weaknesses. Firstly, despite their emphasis on punishment of mercenaries, the criminal jurisdiction granted to states is very restrictive falling within the traditional nationality or territoriality link.[48] It is the linkage between the mercenary and the state that is crucial to providing governments with the basis for jurisdiction. Unfortunately, this linkage, even if it can be established, is impractical insofar as states themselves are complicit in the activities of mercenaries through the use of their services. Further, it is unclear how the conventions would challenge corporations such as PMCs or their principals and investors particularly where the bulk of the activities of the PMCs is extraterritorial, thus effectively placing the burden of prosecution on a local government which often has only rudimentary or a seriously compromised administrative and criminal justice structure. Finally, the extraterritorial nature of PMC actions allows governments (usually Western where many major PMCs are domiciled) to fend off criticisms in relation to accountability issues.

Secondly, the primary definition under the UN Mercenary Convention would exclude state actors sent by their home state (a third party, neutral state) if they were "on official duty as a member of [the sending State's] armed forces."[49] In this regard, Todd S Milliard, a Judge Advocate with the US Army, notes that "In addition to covering service members, this exclusion would likely extend to military technical advisors who were government employees or government-sanctioned contractors of the sending State." The secondary definition would exclude state actors sent by their home state, provided they were on "official duty."[50] Therefore, this exclusion would cover any sending state government employee or government-sanctioned contractor, whether or not considered a member of the sending state's armed forces, in addition to the sending state's actual service members. Thus, a PMC acting on sending state instructions or sanctioned by the sending state is exempt from legal sanction, as presumably would be its employees.

Thirdly, the anti-mercenary conventions address the use of mercenaries almost exclusively where used as a means of violating human rights and impeding the exercise of the right of peoples to self-determination in post-colonial Africa. The proliferation of dozens of PMCs offering services focused on recognized governments as opposed to PMCs focused on suppressing rebels have displaced the "gangs of misfit professional soldiers" and as a result they manage to effectively fall through the cracks of the various anti-mercenary conventions even though some of their activities may have some mercenary traits.

Although PMCs provide military services, the majority do not "take direct part in hostilities," and hence the definitions of mercenary services slanted toward netting traditional mercenaries are at best ambiguous and of little help in controlling PMCs. These entities evade the international definitions of a "mercenary" by their close ties to states and in light of the fact that they gain government authorization for their contracts they can claim official state sanction effectively placing them outside the conventional definitions of mercenarism.[51] The secondary definition of "mercenary" in the Mercenary Convention excludes persons "sent by a State on official duty."[52] This exclusion would cover government-sanctioned contractors. Indeed, as

Millard points out, when a state sends a state-sanctioned PMC to a requesting state, or hires such a PMC, "the definition is nearly worthless."[53] Fourthly, as PMCs are juridical persons, it is unclear how the conventions would be applied to such persons and/or the human parties involved in them, or what the control, penalty, enforcement provisions would do to control and punish PMCs.

Finally, and perhaps most importantly, the conventions focus on the protection of the state. As an important focus of the present work is the protection of civilians from organized violence, the conventions' focus limits their utility in this particular and important sense. Although they provide an incentive to would be mercenaries to reconsider a proposed venture into for-profit violence, by stripping them of combatant status, they do not make them susceptible for war crimes—certainly a significant concern in practice and indeed the underlying first principle of the Laws of Armed Conflict (LOAC), restraint. Another approach to control PMC activity through international law would be through the laws pertaining to war. We now turn to consider this.

5.2.3 The Law of Armed Conflict

Given the misery left by warfare through the centuries, warring nations have developed customary practices seeking to ameliorate its devastating effects. As the customs of war have evolved into the customs and laws of war, the dominant objective underlying the law as it relates to military force has remained constant and can be summed up in one word: restraint. We turn now to discuss the main instruments commonly referred to as LOAC and their potential application to PMCs.

5.2.3.1 Hague Conventions

The LOAC conventions adopted in 1899 and 1907 at The Hague provide, to this day, the backbone of international regulation governing the means and methods of warfare. These eighteen treaties attempted to fulfill four main purposes: first, they sought to identify those who may lawfully participate in war and define the duties and rights of those individuals; second, they sought to regulate means and methods by which states could lawfully conduct warfare; third, they sought to describe the conditions and manner under which belligerents could bombard or besiege; and fourth, they sought to regulate truces, capitulations and armistices, and the military government of occupied territories.

The Hague Conventions of 1907 represent the first international effort aimed at regulating mercenary activities. The Convention Respecting the Rights and Duties of Neutral Powers and Persons in Case of War on Land (Hague V)[54] aspires to "lay down more clearly the rights and duties of neutral Powers [toward belligerents] in case of war on land."[55] This convention is geared to codifying customary international law to the satisfaction of the states' plenipotentiaries attending the drafting conference. The articles of the convention that are relevant to the issue of mercenaries are Articles 4 and 6.

Article 4 of Hague V provides: "Corps of combatants cannot be formed nor recruiting agencies opened on the territory of a neutral Power to assist the belligerents."[56] Article 6 continues: "The responsibility of a neutral Power is not engaged by the fact of persons crossing the frontier separately to offer their services to one of the belligerents."[57] Article 4 is based on the doctrine of state responsibility under customary international law. This doctrine holds that a state is normally responsible for those illegalities which it has originated.[58] However, a state does not bear responsibility for acts injurious to another state committed by private individuals when the illegal deeds do not proceed from the command, authorization, or culpable negligence of the government.[59] One may thus conclude that under Article 4 a neutral state must allow neither mercenary expeditions to be formed nor mercenary recruiting to take place on its territory.[60]

Similarly, one sees strong echoes of state responsibility in Article 6. When one considers that the concept provides that if the state neglects the duties imposed by vicarious responsibility it incurs original liability for the private acts and is guilty of an international delinquency. However, no state bears absolute responsibility for international illegalities committed by individuals acting on its territory.[61] Thus Article 6 obviates the state's regulatory obligation placing no duty on it "to prevent individuals—whether its citizens or another State's citizens—from crossing its borders to serve as mercenaries for a belligerent."[62]

From the analysis above it is evident that the provisions of Hague Convention V have a fuzzy quality to them. Though a neutral state must prevent domestic mercenary recruitment or staging activities under Hague V, it is not required to outlaw the mercenary per se. In this way, "[t]he individual mercenary himself was only indirectly affected [through Hague V], by means of the implementation by a State of its obligations as a neutral."[63] The end result is that in spite of the fact that the Hague V recognizes mercenarism as a problem, it neither criminalizes the activity nor sets out any substantive obligations on the part of the states other than an exhortation not to assist or participate in the process of assembling such outfits.

5.2.3.2 Additional Protocol I

The 1949 Geneva Conventions serve primarily as protection for individuals suffering as a result of armed conflict. Those employing the term "humanitarian law" as the preferred reference for the law of war often seem to have the Geneva Conventions principally in mind. This perspective follows from the simple observation that the 1949 Conventions highlight the international interest in ensuring that warfare respects the human person to the maximum extent possible.[64] At this point it is important to note that LCAC establishes a difference between civilians who are taking a direct part in hostilities thus losing their protection and those who are only making a contribution to the war effort and who do not thereby lose their protection.[65] Significant for this section of the chapter is the 1977 Protocol Additional to the Geneva Conventions of 12 August 1949, and Relating to the Protection of Victims of International Armed Conflicts (Additional Protocol I), which provides the international community's definitive statement on mercenaries.[66] Article 49 defines a mercenary as any person who:

> (a) is specifically recruited locally or abroad in order to fight in an armed conflict;
> (b) does, in fact, take a direct part in the hostilities;
> (c) is motivated to take part in the hostilities essentially by the desire for private gain and, in fact, is promised, by or on behalf of a Party to the conflict, material compensation substantially in excess of that promised or paid to combatants of similar ranks and functions in the armed forces of that Party;
> (d) is neither a national of a Party to the conflict nor a resident of territory controlled by a Party to the conflict;
> (e) is not a member of the armed forces of a Party to the conflict; and
> (f) has not been sent by a State which is not a Party to the conflict on official duty as a member of its armed forces.[67]

The interplay of the differentiation between mercenaries and soldiers in Article 49 is significant when one considers that Article 47 of Additional Protocol I removes the protection of combatant or prisoner of war status from mercenaries and provides a definition of a mercenary.[68] However, other than simply depriving mercenaries of the status as participants in armed conflict, and protections afforded to other combatants, the provision does not seek in any way to regulate the international military market, or restrict consumption to certain categories of consumers.[69]

Those who object to the more radical aspect of PMC claim that their employees may fall under the definition of mercenaries in Article 47 of the Additional Protocol I:

> The employees of SCs [PMCs] are foreign military soldiers specially recruited abroad and paid in excess of what the military personnel of the contracting State are paid; they engage in fighting; and they are not sent on official duty of the armed forces of another State.[70]

From a substantive perspective, three significant hurdles to classifying PMCs and their employees as mercenaries arise under Article 47. To begin with, as David Kassebaum observes, "[t]his definition of a mercenary is cumulative; all requirements must be met before a person can be labelled a mercenary.

Even then from a law-enforcement viewpoint, the requirements lack specificity."[71] Secondly, paragraph 2 of Article 47 imposes criteria as to a mercenary's motivation[72] and relative compensation.[73] As the UK Report of the Committee of Privy Counsellors Appointed to Inquire into Mercenarism noted over three decades ago, these elements are extremely difficult to prove, thus limiting a state's legal basis to deprive mercenaries of lawful combatant and prisoner of war status.[74] The report went on to note that the international definition of "mercenary" based on the motivation of the combatant was not viable, as it is difficult to determine exact motivation in the legal realm. The report concluded that the flawed definitions meant that "to serve as a mercenary is not an offence under international law."[75] These observations have not changed throughout the years and remain just as true in the 21st century. As recently as 2002, in considering the definition of mercenary in its entirety, as per Article 47, the United Kingdom's Foreign and Commonwealth Office concluded that "[a] number of governments including the British Government regard this definition as unworkable for practical purposes."[76] Although it is uncontroversial to state the PMC's motivation as financial, its corporate status combined with limited definition of mercenary makes it difficult to see how the hurdle would be surmounted in an Article 47 prosecution.

Secondly, active combatant status is also required under Article 47. Section 2 requires that mercenaries take direct part in the hostilities[77] and "excludes mere advisers by requiring that to be a mercenary, one must in fact take a direct part in hostilities, that is, become a combatant [*sic*], albeit an illegitimate one."[78] It is clear under the law of armed conflict that experts who do not take direct part in combat are regarded as civilians under international law.[79] Thus at first glance, PMCs in general appear to fall outside the conjunctive definition of Article 47 since they tend to restrict their activities to training government troops only. But circumvention of Article 47 is questionable when considered in the light of some of the operations of PMCs. Advances in remote-operated weaponry capabilities make it difficult to identify which combatants are taking "direct" part in the hostilities.[80]

The most dramatic example of the slippery nature of classifying the combat status of PMC employees is offered by PMC activity in Colombia. As noted in chapter 1, numerous PMCs are working under contracts with the Colombian government, the United States Department of Defense, and the United States Department of State. They make up roughly 20 percent of the American military personnel working in Colombia. Their operations include flying Blackhawk attack helicopters and manning surveillance aircraft to assist Colombian security forces in the ongoing military campaign against drug cartels and Marxist guerrilla rebels. These actions—which are essential to the military operations—can only be classed as of a combat nature.[81]

Thirdly, Article 47 (1) (f) of Additional Protocol I also identifies a mercenary as a person who has not been sent by a state which is not a party to the conflict on official duty as a member of its armed forces.[82] In view of the complicity of states in the use of PMCs, it can be argued that a PMC, which receives authorization from its home state to operate abroad (through a licensing process or more informally), is "sent by a State which is not a party to the conflict on official duty" and that the PMC represents a member of that state's armed forces.[83] The contractual nature of the services provided also provide ample basis for characterizing employees of PMCs as civilian contractors, who although not regarded as a member of the military force in the field are assimilated and may thus claim some official status.[84] Accordingly PMCs can be regarded as contractors of their home states or of their employing states. In any case, PMCs would be tied to state actors and would fall outside the definition of a mercenary in this aspect as well.

In sum, Additional Protocol I does not prohibit the use of mercenaries by states or other entities. Part of the weaknesses of the Protocol is owing to the fact that it singled out a particular kind of mercenary, the soldier of fortune, who emerged and rose to prominence in the 1950s to 1970s to wreck havoc in Africa. The provisions were specifically tailored to address this problem. They were branded as criminals, regardless of who employed them or on whose behalf they fought. As Montgomery Sapone notes:

> The Protocol I definition is so restrictive that almost no one will fall into the category. One military historian remarked that, "any mercenary who cannot exclude himself from this definition deserves to be shot—and his lawyer with him!"[85]

Even beyond the inadequacy of the provisions dealing with mercenarism under the law of armed conflict, they certainly would not catch the PMC. In any event, given that it is often states who retain them, it is clear that PMCs are not mercenaries, particularly because state accountability is the key to distinguishing mercenaries from other combatants. PMCs are tied to states in various unofficial ways:

1. PMCs are legal entities, bound to employing States by recognized contracts and to home States by laws requiring registration, periodic reporting, and licensing of foreign contracts in most cases.
2. Most PMCs are willing to share information with their home governments because the home governments tend to be large, repeat customers that appreciate voluntary cooperation.
3. PMCs try to act in their home States' interest abroad, thereby making the PMCs quasi-State agents.
4. PMCs are long-term market players (unlike most individual mercenaries).[86]

The reality is that existing international law neither regulates nor forbids the activities of mercenaries, but rather proposes a definition and specifies their legal status only under certain conditions. As Enrique Ballesteros, the UN-appointed expert on the subject, acknowledged several years ago, defining mercenaries is extremely difficult, if not outright impossible, and certainly of no assistance in dealing with the PMC industry.[87]

International legislation is even troublesome when it comes to prosecuting the "traditional" form of mercenary. As the UN Special Rapporteur on Mercenaries lamented in 1997, "there is no appropriate legal definition or legislation under which [mercenaries] can be prosecuted."[88] As noted above, Geneva Protocol I[89] and the UN Mercenary Convention[90] make the most decisive attempts at defining and regulating the activities of mercenaries. However, not only do these documents lack any real enforcement measures, their definitions are too loose to encompass the complex, modern, and international PMC.[91] The net result is that the various international initiatives offer limp definitions which contribute to the difficulty of regulating PMC activities instead of assisting. Despite the occasional charge that PMCs are "nothing but the old poison of vagabond mercenaries in new designer bottles,"[92] current international mercenary treaties are a dead-end avenue as a means of control.

The leaky regulatory framework spun by existing relevant international instruments regarding mercenaries largely misses PMCs, perhaps the better option would be to link the actions of PMC personnel to other international law paradigms. In any case, as the analysis in chapters 2 and 3 has demonstrated, the domestic regime is equally leaky necessitating a concerted effort at both the national and international level. The international dimension is even more important in light of the extraterritorial nature of PMC activity. The chapter now turns to consider two avenues, state responsibility and command responsibility. On the one hand, state responsibility would be an avenue for activating states' accountability for the use of PMCs since it invokes international law, allowing liability to flow both to the individual actor and to the responsible state. On the other hand, command responsibility could help to expose and curb the actions of PMCs through the "control and direction" standard. This approach would provide the necessary jolt for governments to utilize the means at their disposal to take regulatory action.

5.3 State responsibility: Snaring governmental and PMC duplicity

In March 2003, the United States, assisted by a "coalition of the willing,"[93] invaded the State of Iraq. A month later, after it had ousted Iraq's dictator, Saddam Hussein, the US became the country's occupying power. About a year later, on April 28, 2004, the CBS news magazine program *60 Minutes II* aired photographs depicting detainees in Iraq's Abu Ghraib prison suffering gross abuse at the hands of American military personnel. As the well-publicized and sensational prisoner scandal at Abu Ghraib in Iraq unfolded it became evident that the United States military had hired private intelligence personnel from CACI, a PMC, to interrogate prisoners. The personnel were hired under a standing "blanket purchase agreement" between the Department of the Interior and CACI, negotiated in 2000.[94] The contracts, however, did not require CACI to comply with international law norms. This omission was brought to light in 2004 after an investigation by the United States Army Inspector General which concluded that 35 percent of CACI's Iraqi interrogators did not have any "formal training in military interrogation policies and techniques."[95] More damning was the revelation by one of the interrogators that "cooks and truck drivers" were hired because the private company was "under so much pressure to fill slots quickly."[96]

In the case of Abu Ghraib prison, the presence of civilian contractors and increasing reliance on civilian contractors to perform military operations meant that this anomalous model will become more and more typical and continue to present critical problems for international human rights and humanitarian norms. These may well be problems that can be addressed through the spectrum of state responsibility.

5.3.1 State and nonstate actors

It is a customary and "well-established rule of international law"[97] that breaches of international law committed by individuals classified as state organs will engage state responsibility.[98] A state is also responsible for *all* the conduct of its armed forces, even if the forces exceed their authority[99] and even if the acts are performed privately;[100] this is a *lex specialis*—a special law—that creates an exception to the usual legal rule of responsibility.[101] It is universally accepted that states owe non-derogable obligations to other states and often to the world at large—especially in the area of international criminal and human rights law.[102] The doctrine of state responsibility entails the international responsibility of a state for international wrongs, such as breaches of international customary or treaty law (primary rules), and permits legal consequences to flow (secondary rules).[103]

The doctrine of state responsibility depends primarily on the link that exists between the state and the person or persons who actually commit the unlawful acts and requires some form of relationship between the persons and the government of the state purportedly responsible. Although typically the conduct of nonstate actors, such as private persons or corporations, are not attributable to the state, in a variety of situations international decision makers have sufficiently likened the actions of private entities with those of state agents to result in attribution to the state. The state responsibility doctrine recognizes that a state may breach its international obligations through a range of actors, not necessarily limited to those who are its obvious agents. Just as humanitarian law holds accountable those in formal positions of authority and those who wield de facto power, a state may be responsible for violations of international law perpetrated by private actors who are considered its de facto agents.[104] Employees of PMCs—although ostensibly private actors—may in certain circumstances be sufficiently connected with an exercise of public power for their actions to be deemed actions of the state.

A second approach to state liability is found in the International Law Commission's Articles on State Responsibility.[105] State responsibility in this view comes from a state's decision to delegate "governmental authority." The test here is not on the nature of the party carrying out the particular task—whether public, private or some other combination—rather, the test focuses on the nature of the task being carried out. Private actors can be regarded as special types of state actors because they carry out tasks or functions that are arguably of a public nature "governmental authority" mentioned above (e.g., extracting information from prisoners and prisoners of war for military purposes in a confined environment—a prison—thus serving a public need). US military guidelines appear to consider the tasks carried out by these contractors to be inherently governmental since they require knowledge and skills acquired primarily through military training. Because these activities are also very closely linked to the public interest—the information to be extracted was supposed to help save US soldiers and counter the Iraqi insurgency—and have been made possible through publicly sanctioned military guidelines that allow these activities to be contracted out, it stands to reason that the actors carrying them out can be considered state actors for the purpose of applying human rights norms.[106]

Still, as Lehnardt points out, the utility of this doctrine in the control of the PMC is difficult for two reasons: first, what constitutes "governmental authority" is a shifting sand, and second, what PMC services offer from among a wide array of services on offer are equally unclear.[107]

Under international law, responsibility principally attaches to the state (as a subject) for human rights abuses by the personnel, officers, or entities under its direction and control. Post-World War II elaborations of human rights law have also expanded the obligations to cover individual actors so that they may be held accountable for offenses such as war crimes, crimes against humanity, and torture. Various treaties encode these standards.[108] However, a problem emerges when states act through corporate entities. Tiny steps have been taken toward attaching international liability to companies. For example, in the 1950s, American courts tried various German industrialists for their complicity in Nazi war crimes, as the "flesh-and-blood" persons existing behind the scenes in companies.[109] In the process, the courts considered the illegal activities and breaches of corporate duty committed by the companies.[110] However, at present, private firms—even when they are multinational entities—remain unrecognized as subjects of international law.[111] This fact stymies the flow of liability to the company and its principals for the offenses of contractors and employees.

5.3.1.1 Private persons acting under direction/control of state— "quasi-state actors"

The test for attributing the actions of nonstate actors to a state remains somewhat unclear. In the *Nicaragua* case, the International Court of Justice (ICJ) considered the US responsible for the actions of various nonstate actors in Nicaragua during the 1980s.[112] In order to impute the acts of the nonstate actors to the US, the ICJ required the US to have "effective control of the military or paramilitary operations in the course of which the alleged violations were committed."[113] The strict test effectively required the US to have financed and coordinated or supervised the acts of the private actors. In addition, it must have issued specific instructions concerning the commission of the unlawful acts.[114] The ICJ found a sufficient nexus existed between the US and certain individual Latin American operatives, or "Unilaterally Controlled Latino Assets" (UCLAs). The UCLAs carried out tasks in Nicaragua, such as the mining of ports. Though not as official agents of the US, they operated under the instructions of US military and intelligence personnel and received payment. The US was responsible for the acts of the UCLAs due to the provision of payment, supervision,[115] and specific instructions.[116] Ultimately, however, the ICJ held that the link was *insufficient* for the Contras' acts to be imputed to the US[117] According to the court, even if the US "generally controlled" the Contras and the Contras were "highly dependent" on the US, the Contras' acts would not necessarily be attributable.[118] This decision was criticized for its "painstaking examination" of specific acts—an approach still reflected in Article 8 of the International Law Commission's Draft Articles on State Responsibility and which demands proof of state authorization for each and every act of the private actors before conduct can be attributed to the state.[119] The "all or nothing" approach to state responsibility demanded a high level of proof; in its absence, the US government escaped all responsibility for the Contras' actions.[120] This was despite considerable evidence that the actors were simply "US-run terrorist forces"[121] operating as part of United States' tenacious and scarcely concealed offensive against the Nicaraguan government.

Unsurprisingly, the "effective control" formulation in *Nicaragua* attracted criticism when the matter next came up for consideration in an international judicial tribunal. In the *Tadic* case,[122] the International Criminal Tribunal for the former Yugoslavia (ICTFY) Appeals Chamber found the test "unconvincing... [given]... the very logic of the entire system of international law on State responsibility."[123] In order to find that the Serb militia operating in Bosnia and Croatia constituted part of the armed forces of Serbia, the Chamber preferred an "overall control" test.[124] It considered that the acts of an armed group are attributable to a state, provided the state "has a role in organising, coordinating or planning the military actions" of the group.[125] Notably, this standard does not require control of the group's particular operations and, in light of past cases and scholarly writings, is more sensible and legally sound.

Although the exact standard required for attribution of private actors remains uncertain, and the difference between the two tests may turn out to be "negligible,"[126] it is clear that the touchstone of the *Nicaragua* and *Tadic* approaches is that states must *direct or control* the private actors; supporting, encouraging, or condoning their actions is insufficient.[127] If the actors are of a military nature, it will be significantly easier to attribute the group's acts to the state.[128] This brings us to the question: If the state is complicit in the actions by engaging the corporate entity, can the actions of employees be linked to the state and thus operationalize international law? International law undoubtedly may hold a state responsible for violations of international law, as well as the individual perpetrators. In this fashion, if the state were the responsible body for the actions of PMCs, international law could hold the state and any of its guilty officials liable for international offences, and also punish the individual perpetrators. As Professor Steven Ratner explains, "State (or quasi-State) action elevates violations of human rights to the international plane."[129]

It is a highly contested proposition that multinational companies should continue to evade liability under international law for abuses[130] and the international community is not only beginning to voice concern about the connections between corporations and human rights abuses,[131] but also edging toward extending responsibility for protecting rights to non-state actors.[132] However, states still constitute the greatest danger to human rights.[133] State complicity in PMC activities bridges the gap between corporate responsibility and international law, rendering both the state and the individual liable. State complicity in PMC activities is a potential trigger for operationalizing international law and, in view of the breaches of international customary law; it should trump the protective corporate veil forming a new basis for lifting the veil as discussed in chapter 2.

It is to be borne in mind that the Human Rights Committee (the predecessor to the Human Rights Council), the body that supervises compliance by states with the International Covenant on Civil and Political Rights (ICCPR)[134] as in the past, concluded that serious physical abuse with the intent of extracting information from a detainee is a breach of the prohibition of torture under Article 7.[135] Significantly for the discussion in this section of the book, the Human Rights Committee has concluded on a number of occasions that a state *"is not relieved of its obligations under the Covenant when some of its functions are delegated to other autonomous organs."*[136]

The observations of the Human Rights Committee are bolstered further by the Committee against Torture, the body entrusted with the supervision of the CAT.[137] Notwithstanding the strict division between "torture" as defined in Article 1 of the CAT and "other ill treatment," the Committee has concluded that the combination of certain techniques used during interrogation, including hooding, violent shaking, and sleep deprivation, amount to torture.[138] Of importance with regard to state responsibility is Article 16 of the CAT which asserts explicitly that *States have to prevent in any territory under their jurisdiction such acts if they are committed by or at the instigation of, or with the consent or acquiescence of, a public official or other person acting in an official capacity.*[139]

Evidence points to state responsibility as an effective solution to corporate accountability where international law is violated. The weaknesses and deficiencies of domestic and international mechanisms, and the status of corporations as objects rather than subjects of international law, makes a strong case for state responsibility—particularly in light of states deliberately seeking to exploit this state of affairs. In general, the authors postulate that there are sufficient connections between PMCs and states to engage state responsibility and allow liability to flow to both the home and contracting state. These include personnel connections, their use for foreign policy operations discussed in chapters 3 and 4, and their close participation in military operations. Countries, particularly in the West, appear to use PMCs as quasi-state agents and are therefore complicit in PMC behavior. This is more so considering that on paper they have developed systems of oversight, licensing, and control, though these systems are rarely managed effectively or utilized honorably. This recalcitrant attitude often renders articulated regulated systems and processes useless.

5.4 PMCs and command responsibility: A new avenue for an established doctrine

This section of the chapter looks at another possible avenue of holding PMCs accountable—command responsibility. Command responsibility, generally, is concerned with the accountability of superiors for war crimes committed by their subordinates. It is a doctrine steeped in military culture and was once unique to the military hierarchy. Historically, the doctrine could be broadly defined as the "responsibility of military commanders for war crimes committed by subordinate members of their armed forces or other persons subject to their control."[140] This extant definition is today complemented by developments that extend the doctrine to both military and nonmilitary superiors, touching individuals from the military, the government, and the general populace.

Post–World War II tribunals were the definitive launch pad for modern command responsibility; however, the doctrine has echoed through centuries of history. Over two thousand years ago, during the time of Sun Tzu, a commander's liability could flow from allowing troops to commit crimes to giving improper orders, and failure to control or punish troops.[141] More

Western principles foreshadowing the modern doctrine are discernable in the 17th-century work of Hugo Grotius—the "father of international law"—whose work was preoccupied with universal rules for state behavior.[142]

The modern advancement of command responsibility has occurred in sudden, seismic shifts, typically lurching forward in close connection with some of history's worst atrocities. The international military tribunals at Tokyo and Nuremberg were created in reaction to the terrible events of World War II, reanimating the doctrine after a long, dormant period. Recently, the jurisprudence of the ad hoc war crimes tribunals, created in response to the surge of war crimes in the former Yugoslavia and Rwanda, reinvigorated the doctrine. Command responsibility, like the other laws of war, continues to evolve to fit these shifting patterns. Despite its explicit recognition under domestic and international law, the precise application of command responsibility to different forms of superiors remains inchoate and it is unclear how it could apply to complex scenarios involving soldiers and civilian security personnel. It is this very thorny issue that the next sections of the chapter will grapple with.

5.4.1 Embedding command responsibility in international law

It was not until the aftermath of World War II and the decisions of the post–World War II tribunals that the doctrine of command responsibility became embedded in international law. At this time, no treaty codified command responsibility; there was no substantial body of interpretive jurisprudence for the tribunals to draw upon and neither of the tribunals' charters explicitly articulated the doctrine. The decisions were therefore based on the laws of war as they were held to exist in customary international law. Following the bloody atrocities of World War II, the victorious Allies doggedly pursued and prosecuted war criminals. The most relevant criminal trials were those conducted by the International Military Tribunal at Nuremberg (Nuremberg Tribunal) and by the International Military Tribunal for the Far East (Tokyo Tribunal). These were supplemented by various tribunals established under Control Council Law No.10. The post–World War II trials were a turning point for international law and state sovereignty. The tribunals demonstrated unprecedented enthusiasm for expanding the enforcement of individual responsibility for international crimes and were determined to try any high-ranking public officials or military officers regardless of their status[143] with one important exception, only members of Axis forces and governments were prosecuted for war crimes loosely defined.

Nevertheless, in practice, the post–World War II tribunals demonstrated a willingness to apply command responsibility to civilian superiors, including senior politicians and even leading industrialists,[144] with vigor equal to its application to military commanders. Many of these cases were premised on the principle of de facto control: that is persons are responsible for those under their power, whether they are serving a military or civilian function.[145] However, the lingering criticisms of the tribunals and their vacillating nature make these cases a mere "guide for establishing that civilian leaders can be held culpable for certain acts of subordinates."[146] Eventually in 1977, the international community enacted Additional Protocol I to the Geneva Conventions of 1949, previously discussed in reference to mercenaries, to explicitly articulate command responsibility and provide some clarity to the doctrine on the international plane.

Additional Protocol I was the first international treaty to codify the doctrine of command responsibility.[147] The Protocol filled a troublesome lacuna in codified law and purported to express the customary law of command responsibility.[148] Article 86(2) clearly sets a standard of actual or constructive knowledge: superiors can be responsible for a breach of the Geneva Convention by subordinates if the superiors "knew, or had information which should have enabled them to conclude in the circumstances at the time" that the subordinate was committing or was going to commit the breach. In this instance, a superior must take "all feasible measures within their power to prevent or repress the breach." Article 87(1) extends the duty of military commanders to include not only forces under their command, but also "other persons under their control." The provision thus renders military commanders responsible for the actions of civilians under their control.[149]

Additional Protocol I has had a significant influence on the codification of command responsibility in the statutes establishing the extant international criminal tribunals—International Criminal Tribunal for the former Yugoslavia (ICTFY) and the International Criminal Tribunal for Rwanda (ICTR). The influence of the Protocol has also spilled over into the statute of the International Criminal Court (ICC), the world's first permanent international penal tribunal. To prosecute the perpetrators of the humanitarian catastrophes in the Former Yugoslavia and Rwanda adequately, the statutes of these tribunals encode the command responsibility doctrine. Article 7(3) of the ICTFY and Article 6(3) of the ICTR statute house these provisions in an almost identical manner. Under these provisions, even if a superior did not order or participate in the crime of a subordinate, she/he may be personally liable for that crime if she/he "knew or had reason to know" that the subordinate was about to commit the crime, or had done so, and she/he fails to take "necessary and reasonable" steps to prevent it, or fails to punish the perpetrator once it has been committed.[150] "Necessary and reasonable" replaces the "all feasible measures within their power" standard in Protocol I. "Knew or had reason to know" also parallels the Protocol I standard of knowledge.

In drafting and adopting the ICC Statute, the international community shed further light on the status of command responsibility by accomplishing the challenging task of defining a standard of command responsibility culpability for the Court. Article 28 of the ICC Statute is the most recent expression of the doctrine. The text of the article articulates the established elements to the command responsibility doctrine. These are:

(i) The existence of a superior/subordinate relationship;
(ii) The superior knew or had reason to know that the criminal act was about to be or had been committed; and
(iii) The superior failed to take the necessary and reasonable measures to prevent the criminal act or punish the perpetrator thereof.

5.4.2 A new calculus: Should command responsibility embrace civilians?

Some commentators see serious problems with a definition of command responsibility that encompasses civilians, particularly nongovernment civilians, citing the intrinsically military nature of the command responsibility doctrine.[151] Despite this, it is now clear that the doctrine also applies to civilian superiors. Civilians in the military chain of command—for example civilian heads of state or government—are indisputably subject to the coalescing command responsibility standards outlined above.[152] The doctrine also applies to other civilian leaders, though the civilian doctrine is a mere "skeleton" that should be fleshed so as to clearly include civilians engaged in military activity. In this regard, Additional Protocol I created an opening to civilian responsibility by referring to "superiors" in Article 86, in contrast to its later limiting specification of "military commanders."

As the International Committee of the Red Cross (ICRC)—"guardian" of the Geneva Conventions and their Additional Protocol—point out in their influential commentaries, the Additional Protocol allows command responsibility of civilians because "[t]he concept of a superior is broader and should be seen in terms of a hierarchy encompassing the concept of control."[153] Although some commentators remain unconvinced that the sole occurrence of "superior" lends enough credence to this theory,[154] ICTFY and ICTR judges have used identical reasoning in their interpretation of the similar ICTFY and ICTR statutes.[155] Both civilians and military individuals can incur criminal responsibility under command responsibility based on de jure or de facto authority.[156] In such cases, the court will focus on the "requisite 'degree of authority' necessary to establish individual criminal culpability" present in each individual case.[157]

The enthusiasm for the civilian standard, however, continues to waver. For instance, the ICTR has remained reluctant to express a general rule by which command responsibility would apply to civilians and has often applied the doctrine reluctantly.[158] The ICTFY has taken a less hesitant approach, unequivocally holding that the command responsibility doctrine applies to military and civilian superiors.[159] It is, however, heartening to note that the ICC Statute does explicitly include civilian superiors, albeit with a lower *mens rea* standard for civilian superiors than for military superiors, requiring nonmilitary superiors to have known, or "consciously disregarded information which clearly indicated that the subordinates were committing or about to commit crimes."[160]

Taking the Abu Ghraib scandal as a test scenario, the authors argue that although command responsibility finds its clearest application in the case of standard military hierarchies, it can extend responsibility (under the international doctrines of state and command responsibility) for the crimes at Abu Ghraib beyond the impugned soldiers to private military personnel and the PMC and to its principal—the US—for complicity in acts that violate international law. Persons (whether military or civilian) implicated in the Abu Ghraib prison atrocities should and ought to be held individually responsible and corporately for their crimes under international law.

5.4.3 Abu Ghraib: State and command responsibility: Belling the corporate "devil"

Abu Ghraib prison was home to numerous breaches of Geneva Conventions (GC) (III) and (IV). Some of the interrogation methods used there included hooding, beatings, solitary confinement, threats (of ill-treatment, execution, harm to family members, etc.), forced public nudity, acts of sexual humiliation, and exposure to excessive noise and temperature extremes.[161] In light of the abuses at Abu Ghraib, a number of military and governmental investigations have occurred.[162] The abuses are now well documented and acknowledged to be violations of international law.[163] Military personnel involved have been identified and punished, although action against senior US government officials is yet to take place. However, civilian contractors who were also implicated in the abuses have escaped largely unscathed. This could be explained by the prominence of soldiers from the 372nd Military Police Company in the released photographs. Most importantly, US officials also have an interest in minimizing the attention paid to their practice of military outsourcing, particularly since this is the first time the privatization of interrogation and intelligence-gathering has been outsourced to PMCs.[164]

The investigations into the Abu Ghraib documented a number of deaths with many more deaths still under investigation.[165] Several of these deaths appear to be torture-murders.[166] The 2004 Fay Report into intelligence activities at Abu Ghraib documented allegations of rape, which it labels "abuse," even though it is well accepted that rape actually constitutes torture—an international criminal offence.[167] Subsequent to the report, General George Fay, the author of the Report, admitted in a Pentagon news conference that "there were a few instances when torture was being used."[168]

Common Article 3 of the Geneva Conventions of 1949 forbids cruel treatment and torture, as well as other "outrages upon personal dignity," such as humiliating and degrading treatment, in armed conflicts recognized by the

ICTFY.[169] Additionally, according to Article 13 of Geneva Convention (III) and Articles 27 and 32 of Geneva Convention (IV), together with Article 76 of Geneva Convention (IV), prisoners of war, as well as other detainees, must at all times be humanely treated. Article 13, in conjunction with Article 130 of Geneva Convention (III), stipulates that acts of commission or omission perpetrated by the "Detaining Power" (in this case the United States), which are harmful to the health and life of prisoners of war, amount to a grave breach of the Geneva Conventions.[170] Antenor Hallo de Wolf notes:

> In light of the nature of the abuses that took place in Abu Ghraib prison there can be little doubt that these abuses amount to torture and other cruel treatment as defined by the ICTFY as understood by common article 3 to the Geneva Conventions, article 13 of Geneva Convention (III), and articles 27 and 32 of Geneva Convention (IV), and thus a "grave breach" of these two conventions.[171]

The abuses committed in Abu Ghraib prison also amount to human rights violations, particularly with respect to normal detainees who are not prisoners of war. The most important rights at stake under these circumstances are the right not to be subjected to torture or to cruel, inhuman, or degrading treatment or punishment found in Article 7 of the ICCPR[172] and Article 1 of the CAT, and the right of a person to humane treatment while deprived of his liberty as protected by Article 10 of the ICCPR.[173] Similarly, Article 2, paragraph 2 of the CAT provides that "[n]o exceptional circumstances whatsoever, whether a state of war or a threat of war, internal political instability or any other public emergency, may be invoked as a justification of torture."[174]

Not only were civilian contractors directly involved in much of the abuse, the abuse was alleged to have been "requested, encouraged, condoned, or solicited" by military and other intelligence personnel.[175] Although the breaches can give rise to contractors' personal liability, the breaches of the contractors also must be attributable to the PMC itself and the US. In this way it can be said that the contractors and PMCs acted as individuals *and* as actors of the state, and command responsibility can attach to the PMC and the state via the doctrine of military chain of command.

5.4.4 Corporate actors in the chain of command

Contractors implicated in the abuse at Abu Ghraib were employees of two US-based PMCs, CACI and Titan Corporation. CACI provided contract interrogators and Titan provided contract linguists. They formed part of the special Joint Interrogation and Debriefing Centre (JIDC) military intelligence unit at Abu Ghraib, which was set up for the purpose of extracting intelligence from detainees. Contractors implicated in human rights violations are connected to PMCs. However, unlike the Nicaraguan Contras who operated for the US behind a buffer of detachment, the contractors have the closest type of connection with the US: the contractors were under an actual contract to work for the US government.

These contracts, like typical PMC contracts discussed in chapters 2 and 4, are not simply contracts for the provision of a standard commercial service. If this was the case, liability for offenses committed by contractors would simply trace to the company through the standard doctrine of vicarious liability employee acts. These contracts coordinate PMCs and government by integrating personnel and resources to achieve outcomes. The contracts insert the PMC into the military operation as both a buttress and a bridge. It buttresses the military by providing support in the form of instruction and supervision for lower level military personnel in its sphere of influence. It provides a bridge for information between the Army and detainees. Thus the PMC both receives orders from the military hierarchy above and provides instruction and supervision to military below. CACI's work orders, for example, were funded by the US Army and were awarded through the Department of the Interior. The contract for interrogation services specifies that CACI employees are to be "directed by military authority" and that "the contractor is responsible for providing supervision of all contractor personnel."[176]

The contractors were classified as Military Intelligence (MI) personnel.[177] Rumsfeld testified before the Senate Armed Services Committee that civilian interrogators in Iraq are "responsible to military intelligence who hire them, and have the responsibility for supervising them."[178] Contract personnel were also managed by a "contracting officer," who was a member of the military.[179] The contracts and information from the official investigations make clear that contractors at Abu Ghraib were officially under the control of the US military. In this regard Antenor Hallo de Wolf notes:

> Delegating the interrogation of prisoners and prisoners of war to CACI and Titan contractors was made possible through official U.S. military guidelines and policy. This was endorsed and affected through the signing of official contracts with these companies. Considering that the interrogation of prisoners and prisoners of war can be regarded as an intrinsic and inherent task of the state, due to the fact that these tasks or functions require military knowledge and skills that are essential for attaining their goals and that these tasks also require extensive familiarity with international legal standards in the field of international humanitarian law and human rights.[180]

A key problem identified by the Fay Report was the lack of "credible exercise of appropriate oversight of contract performance" exercised by the responsible contracting officers.[181] Poor and inefficient performance characterized this task of supervision and control, though this in no way alters the fact that the US was officially responsible for directing and controlling the private actors. In Abu Ghraib, private contractors had effectively been assimilated into the US armed forces and could no longer realistically be categorized as private actors. Indeed, as Ken Johnson, President of US Operations, with Jack London, CACI CEO and veteran with 12 years experience, commented in a conference call in 2004:

> I believe every general officer who has talked indicates that we the contractor community work under the direct supervision in the prosecution of our tasks by military people whether it's a warrant officer or a senior noncommissioned officer or in some cases an officer.[182]

Arguably, contractors occupying positions of authority and influence may also be liable for command liability for failing to act to prevent crimes that occurred. The primary challenge though is that civilian contractors appear to be outside the normal chain of command at Abu Ghraib. This complicates the process of proving that a superior-subordinate relationship existed between them and the actors. While de jure command is inapplicable owing to the location of the contractors in the official military hierarchy, the well-established de facto command doctrine is relevant.

Contractors' control over the perpetrators appears to have been effective and hence de facto. General Taguba explained to the Senate Inquiry that although contractors "were not in any way supervising any soldiers... those who were involved, looked at them as competent authority."[183] Command responsibility is enlivened further by the use of subordinates with inadequate training.[184] An army memo written in 2000, for example, strongly counseled against the use of private contractors in intelligence roles, explicitly explaining:[185]

> the contract administration oversight exerted over contractors is very different from the command and control exerted over military and civilian employees... reliance on private contractors poses risks to maintaining adequate civilian oversight over intelligence operations.

From the Taguba and Fay reports, one can infer that the US military apparatus was aware that private contractors were being used for translation and interrogation purposes (in fact, it would appear to have been policy).[186] The US, however, appears to have neglected to adopt sufficient precautions and supervisory mechanisms to monitor and restrain the activities of these private actors despite several US military personnel purposely striving to create a suitable environment for extracting information from the detainees. In such instances, a state may trigger state responsibility by a failure of due diligence. As was made clear in the Corfu Channel case, the Albanian government's failure to ensure a passage clear of mines led to the state being found liable.[187] Whereas in the case at hand the chain of command is so intertwined, the private actor is carrying out duties normally done by a government authority, and the government has failed to exercise due diligence, one would certainly expect some form of liability to flow back to the government, regardless of the PMC interposition.

5.5 Regulatory recommendations

Some form of international convention seems to be an important and inevitable part of the solution to regulating PMCs. Compensatory mechanisms of holding states accountable for individual actors, as desirable as they may be, are insufficient for two reasons. They are retrospective, focusing on the compensation once harm has occurred, rather than prospectively seeking to avoid the harm in the first place. While certainly knowing that compensation may be extracted for harms inflicted may be a deterrent in the deployment of PMCs and providing instructions, in the first instance, surely a preventative approach is to be preferred. Second, efficacy of state responsibility depends on a highly contestable assumption, namely, that states will abide by international court rulings. Perhaps the classic example of the problem is Nicaragua v. United States (Merits) which was heard before the ICJ in 1986. In that the US refused to acknowledge the court's jurisdiction as it became evident that the US was going to lose.[188] Further, and perhaps more importantly, the US has failed to comply with the court's ordered compensation. Such being the case, further consideration must be given to an international convention.

Additionally, as Peter Singer observes, "given the ability of PMCs to globalize and escape local regulation, [a system to regulate PMCs] must be international to be effective."[189] He advocates a registration process to screen firms and establish "initial qualifications of firms." He suggests some international body operating under the auspices of the UN as designed and informed by "governments, the academy, NGOs, and the firms themselves, could establish the parameters of the issues and lay out potential forms of regulation, evaluation tools, and codes of conduct."[190] This body, says Singer, would be charged with auditing PMCs and would appeal to the PMCs by providing legitimacy and less odious to non-UN clients. A fundamental element of Singer's plan is that the body reviews licensed PMCs' contracts in order to prevent PMCs from being retained by "unsavory clients or engage[ing] in contracts that are contrary to the public good."[191]

In line with the concerns of democratic oversight and accountability, Singer's body would have the power to demand operational oversight and appoint observers who would be tasked with ensuring the LOAC and contract terms are not breached. Importantly, Singer recommends the power to punish to be extended beyond mere market remedies particularly where human rights violations are found. Singer suggests that one effective way to implement this would be requiring the PMC to submit to host state jurisdiction or agree to extradition to third party states empowered with universal jurisdiction having a body such as the ICC to decide the matter.[192]

To implement sufficient support for such a convention and to give it efficacy, one would need to think a bit unconventionally. As we have seen, the US, UK, France, and South Africa, the main mercenary providers are not signatories to the Mercenary Convention. Their failure to sign has had a significant impact on the efficacy of the convention. It will be necessary to build in incentives for these major PMC suppliers to become parties to the convention. Accordingly, attention will have to be given to designing the regulation to create incentives to the countries to become signatories. Drawing on regulatory theory, we can see that implementing some form of market incentives would be most appropriate. That can be done by designing the regulation to prohibit PMCs headquartered, based, or having offices in nonsignatory states from operating in those states signatory to the convention. In other words, PMCs domiciled, having headquarters, offices, or operations in US, UK, France, and South Africa, should those countries fail to be signatories, would be prohibited suppliers of PMC services to the rest of the world. Such PMCs would not be eligible for the lucrative contracts in Africa, the Middle East, or elsewhere until their home countries are signatory. PMCs would be able to use their close connections and significant lobby power to induce the regulatory regime they, among others, are calling for.

Certainly, there will be the objection that it is unfair for the PMCs so located. Why should they be penalized and prevented from exercising their commercial rights simply because the governments of those locations where they are operating from have refused to sign? The issue is analogous to immigration rights of humans. Why should a particular human be prevented from entering another country simply because he or she is of one nationality or another? Indeed, it is much more difficult and complicated to change nationalities than it is for a company to relocate. Further, in weighing the competing interests, personal security versus commercial opportunity, the balance would seem to tip clearly in favor of the former over the latter. Accordingly, this objection is of little weight. Further it recognizes the regulatory imperative of implementing social norms.

5.6 Conclusion

A great deal of genuine alarm has been generated by the lack of oversight of PMCs and their ever-increasing role in the prosecution of war. As the Iraq invasion demonstrates, there are numerous issues pertaining to the operations, contracting, and rules governing the operation of PMCs. This is complicated even further as their largely unregulated activities span a number of fields ranging from police, paramilitary, and military training to logistics and protection of installations and officials.

PMCs' amassed unchecked power stands to affect conflict resolution, world economic stability, and geostrategic negotiations.[193] Indeed, as corporations become larger—both economically and politically—corporate managers increasingly engage in decision-making traditionally exercised by politicians.[194] The decentralization of international security from state-organized militaries not only threatens the traditional Westphalian model of state-monopolized force,[195] but also accentuates the inability of international law to hold private actors accountable.[196] PMCs are thus in certain ways modern evolved form of the traditional mercenary and are quite different in important ways. They are motivated by "business profit" rather than individual profit.

The conundrum presented by PMCs is that "the international laws of war that specifically deal with their presence and activity are largely absent or ineffective."[197] Although the United Nations attempts to regulate the behavior of nation-states and their national militaries, it (as is often the case with international law) has comparatively little influence over the activities of private agents.[198]

Conclusion

Taming the Wild Dogs

As we have demonstrated throughout this work, the phenomenon of the PMC raises a number of thorny, complex, and perplexing problems. The PMC raises not only such relatively mundane matters as who should cook and do laundry for soldiers, but also such highly controversial matters as who should be permitted to guide missiles at enemy targets and who should be liable for the massacre of civilians in an unstable area. We have also drawn attention to the central role of economics in violence and the role of politics in the development and enforcement of laws. Further we have demonstrated that the PMC far from being a mere provider of technical services is by its very nature a provider of strategic advantage, a political power in any struggle. This strategic adviser role has become critical in the new battlefield where there are no frontlines. We have examined the PMC's great utility to governments of all stripes for a number of legitimate and not so legitimate uses. We have noted the various areas of law and legal regimes which have bearing or potential bearing on the PMC, as well as the efforts of various countries to regulate them. We have examined the complexities and perplexing problems in those laws and regimes when attempting to unpack them and understand their applicability to the PMC. We have seen that from a number of different perspectives regulation is desirable, yet how and to what ends such regulation is to be created, designed, and implemented remains far from being clear.

As a starting point we noted the newness of the phenomenon, although the history of paid warfare is of considerable antiquity. We also noted the considerable difficulty in developing an appropriate taxonomy. This difficulty has been manifest throughout the work as the PMC has shown not only its shapes and talents, but also its abilities to transform, evade sharp definitions, and avoid liability. We reviewed the nature of the corporation and the problems as well as the potential corporate law presents for regulation. We considered in particular how it contributes in some significant ways to the development of the PMC phenomena.

We then examined the various means for controlling them through existing law and arrangements. We examined de facto and de jure control of armed groups and the role of the courts in the control of government resorting to violence. It was noted that none of the laws or practices are particularly effective for the control of violence. Next examined were the efforts at regulation already in place. Specifically, we reviewed self-regulation and the regulatory regimes of New Zealand, the US, the UK, and South Africa. We found that none of those schemes were particularly effective for dealing with the phenomena in question. In the last chapter we reviewed the extant and potential of the international legal system to reign in the PMC. The review on the international level was not a greater cause for optimism than were the previous regimes and systems. Yet at the end of each of chapters 2, 3, 4, and 5 we noted a number of recommendations for potential regulation. The potential identified in these sections and the growing public awareness, combined with PMC interest and government attention to PMC regulation, suggest that cautious optimism may yet be the order of the day.

It needs to be recognized that there is no silver bullet of regulatory innovation that will solve these issues. No single, simple form of regulation can cover the regulatory landscape necessary to deal with the PMC phenomenon. As in most instances, a combination of overlapping regulatory regimes is the more realistic and preferable option, and hence, various forms of regulation will likely have to coexist, cognizant of each other, working in conjunction, and in a complementary manner. In light of the foregoing discussion, there are some contours that can be identified which would be crucial to the development of legislation regulating PMCs. These contours, when combined with the insights provided by contemporary regulatory theory, suggest that a combination of corporate law reform enacted nationally, self-regulation and international regulation, may be necessary to achieve desired outcomes. Accordingly, we sum up and suggest that a broad range of regulation and regulatory reform on the lines set out in the regulatory recommendations sections may be the best option.

In terms of proposals for regulation we noted at the end of the previously mentioned chapters the following. Corporate law could be reformed to allow oversight at the board of directors level to ensure compliance with laws governing the supply of military services, and in particular to ensure the proper and timely disclosure of matters of concern to the community at large. Further, such a member of the corporation could be tasked with ensuring appropriate system to respect human rights laws were in place. Reforms could be implemented to control the directors of PMCs requiring them to be licensed. PMCs could be structured to have political representation on the board or some form of shareholding permitting greater government accountability. Finally, we suggested that the powerful incentive dissolution would pose to shareholders to oversee the activities of the corporation.

State regulation needs to be enacted such that the maximum level of oversight and accountability is put into the hands of the public. These recommendations were made in light of the ineffective nature of the constitutions and courts in restraining governments bent on violence. While putting power into the hands of the people may not serve the cause of nonviolence much better, where it is up to the courts to ultimately adjudicate on the matter, yet providing the public with such increased rights of oversight and making governments more accountable cannot be but a good thing. This good would be particularly important in the case of PMCs and their influence as a lobby and in the case of government use of PMCs abroad as a foreign policy tool, for, as was demonstrated, state involvement in the affairs of other states tends to be a most suspect activity and hence should be subject to the highest levels of scrutiny.

State-level regulation should be clear in terms of objectives. It should be focused upon the control of potentially lethal force and accountability to the populace. A licensing regime, as suggested by Schreier, may well serve, provided the caveats of supervision of weapons controllers, a prohibition of contracting with PMCs without parliamentary review, adequate monitoring and enforcement and subjection to host state jurisdiction. This regulation should be coordinated with self-regulation of the industry which would be charged with, among other things, the vetting of personnel. Finally, we noted the importance of an independent regulator.

At the international level, we noted the importance of a regime with a high level of accession. Hence, an international treaty would have to be designed with this particular issue in the forefront of drafters' minds. Some form of international overseer would need to be established and have power beyond mere fines or market power. That body would need additional powers, including resort to some internationally recognized body.

We recognize that this study is preliminary and that there are considerable areas for ongoing research. In particular, we note the lack of political will in the enactment and enforcement of laws in this area. In order to have effective law in this crucial area, further research needs to be done on that matter. Further, we have noted the difficulties related to international prosecutions. Where these involve multinational corporations, the resources and complexities can and will be daunting. Further research needs to be conducted on how investigations and access to MNC assets to enforce judgments can be made sufficiently efficacious to deter, compensate, and punish. Additional work on the taxonomy issue is outstanding and critical for effective regulation to be developed. Finally, the actual design and regulatory costs involved for various types of regulation needs research.

On a broader level, PMCs raise the thorny issue of the future of the military itself. The armed services have long seen themselves as engaged in a unique profession, set apart from the rest of civilian society, which they are entrusted with securing. The rise of PMCs, and their recruiting from within the military itself, challenges that uniqueness by allowing encroachment on those services by the creation of a civilian market for such services. As we have seen, PMCs now compete directly with the government, drawing employees from the military by offering higher pay, which ironically comes from public funds. This reality is particularly poignant when one considers that even the US military, the world's most dominant force, has become dependent on PMCs.

Given their profit motive, it should not be surprising to see their activities on all sides—morally and politically—of any activity and indeed we do. With this incentive, the PMC identifies power with wealth in a way and to a degree never seen before. Further, the wide range of services they offer suggests at least some level of restraint to be exercised in the design and implementation of regulation.

As this volume has amply demonstrated, the legal systems, both national and international, are woefully inadequate to deal with the PMC. Further, given the high stakes and lack of alternative methods of dealing with them, PMCs must be subject to some form of law. States and the members of the international system must respond to this imperative by some form of regulation. Further, given the problems of international regulation, every country whether home to PMCs or contracting with, or susceptible to PMC intervention needs to address them through some form of regulation. The nature and depth of this regulation, whether it be constitutional amendment or merely some form of subsidiary regulation, is a matter for the particular jurisdiction. However, no responsible government can ignore this new, violent, and potentially nation-threatening institution. This position finds support in David Shearer's argument that the focus should be on the normative framework in which the actors operate. He suggests that instead of turning away from military companies dialog should be opened between them and other members of civil society.[1] We believe that dialogue must be opened with an eye to making the world a safer place for everyone.

Clausewitz feared that "political, social, economic, and religious motives" have become "hopelessly entangled."[2] Perhaps it has always been that way. Nevertheless, this comment alerts us to an important reality. Humanity is not driven by a single overriding concern, whether capitalism's economic dominance, communism's brutal equality, or Nietzsche's will to power. Rather, humans are complex creatures and the drive to live a decent life should not be adumbrated by the will of a few with economic power, who are prepared to pay others committed to the delivery of efficient violence to assist the wealthy achieve their own narrow goals without due regard for the rest of the population.

As Isaac Asimov's character, Salvor Hardin, states: "Violence is the last refuge of the incompetent." Although we should be in no rush to legitimize raw economic commoditization of violence, PMCs do exist and are in demand, serving a variety of better and worse ends. Further, violence forms not only a basic part of the human condition, but also human society. Failing the best of all possible worlds where neither violence nor PMCs exist, what second choice exists?

Notes

Introduction

1. See Niccolo Machiavelli, *The Art of War*, 13–14 (ed. and trans. Peter Bondanella and Mark Musa Penguin Books, 1995) (1521).
2. Reid v. Covert, 354 U.S. 1, 24 n. 43 (1955) (omissions in original) (quoting 26 The Writings of George Washington from the Original Manuscript Sources 388 (John C. Fitzpatrick (ed.), 1944)).
3. K. Jennings, "Armed Services: Regulating the Private Military Industry," FAFO Report 532, 2006 http://www.fafo.no/pub/rapp/532/index.htm, last accessed, September 1, 2007.
4. J. A. Hobson, *Imperialism: A Study* (London: James Pott and Co., 1902), quoted in K. Nelson, "The 'Warfare State': History of a Concept," *Pacific History Review*, 40 (1971), 127, p. 133.
5. M. David Dragics, "CACI International Inc CAI Unscheduled Material Events (8-K) Exhibit 99" (USA, 2005).
6. H. Howe, "To Stabilize Tottering African Governments," *Armed Forces Journal International*, 18 (1997), pp. 32–48.
7. Ibid.
8. See J. C. Zarate, "The Emergence of a New Dog of War: Private International Security Companies, International Law, and the New World Disorder," *Stanford Journal of International Law*, 34 (1998), 93–103, pp. 81–2.
9. T. Garmon, "Domesticating International Corporate Responsibility: Holding Private Military Firms Accountable under the Alien Tort Claims Act," *Tulane Journal of International and Comparative Law*, 11 (2003), 325, p. 327.
10. E. W. Orts, "Corporate Governance, Stakeholder Accountability, and Sustainable Peace: War and the Business Corporation," *Vanderbilt Journal Transnational Law*, 35 (2002), 549, pp. 556–7.
11. See e.g. Deven R. Desai, "Have Your Cake and Eat It Too: A Proposal for a Layered Approach to Regulating Private Military Companies," *University of San Francisco Law Review*, 39 (2005), 825, 831; Deborah Avant, "Privatizing Military Training," 7 *Foreign Pol'y: In Focus*, May 2002, http://0-www.fpif.org.library.newcastle.edu.au:80/pdf/vol7/06ifmiltrain.pdf (last visited June 20, 2007); Michael J. Davidson, "Ruck Up; An Introduction to the Legal Issues Associated with Civilian Contractors on the Battlefield," *Public. Contract Law Journal* 29 (2000), 233, 235.
12. Noted in F. Schreier and M. Caparini, *Privatising Security: Law, Practice and Governance of Private Military and Security Companies* (No. Occasional Paper—6) (Geneva: Geneva Centre for the Democratic Control of Armed Forces (DCAF), 2005), p. 12.
13. Ibid., p. 10.
14. Consider for example the "rent-a-coup" scandal involving the son of a former British prime minister where Logistics, a British–South African PMC, was accused of plotting to overthrow the Equatorial Guinea government for profit motives. In the same vein, some "failed" or "failing" states have relied almost exclusively on private actors to perform both international and domestic roles of government.

1 Private Military Companies: The New Face of War

1. P. W. Singer, "The Ultimate Military Entrepreneur," *MHQ: Quarterly Journal of Military History*, 15 (2003), 6–15.
2. Ibid., 6–15.
3. Ibid., 9–15.
4. At least, this is Weber's argument in M. Weber, *The Theory of Social and Economic Organization* (New York: Free Press, 1947), p. 154; See also J. N. Maogoto, *State Sovereignty and International Criminal Law: From Versailles to Rome* (New York: Transnational publishers, 2003), pp. 15–31.
5. J. C. Zarate, "The Emergence of a New Dog of War," pp. 94–5.
6. Ibid., pp. 94–5.
7. M. Weber, *The Theory of Social and Economic Organization.*
8. M. Sapone, "Have Rifle with Scope, Will Travel: The Global Economy of Mercenary Violence," *California Western Journal of International Law Journal*, 30 (1999), 5.
9. J. C. Zarate, "The Emergence of a New Dog of War," p. 87.
10. C. Wrigley, "The Privatisation of Violence: New Mercenaries and the State" (1999). Retrieved September 15, 2004, from http://www.caat.org.uk/information/issues/mercenaries-1999.php.
11. J. C. Zarate, "The Emergence of a New Dog of War," p. 82.
12. Deven R. Desai, "Have Your Cake and Eat It Too," 825, 830.
13. G.A. Res. 3103, U.N. GAOR, 28th Sess., Supp. No. 30, at 142, U.N. Doc. A/9030 (1973).
14. H. M. Howe, "Global Order and the Privatization of Security," *Fletcher Forum of World Affairs*, 22 (1998), 4.
15. J. C. Zarate, "The Emergence of a New Dog of War," p. 87.
16. Deborah Avant, "Privatizing Military Training."
17. Deven R. Desai, "Have Your Cake and Eat It Too," 825, 831.
18. See Michael J. Davidson, "Ruck Up," 233, 235.
19. Deborah Avant, "Privatizing Military Training."
20. Discussed in E. Krahmann, "Private Military Services in the UK and Germany: Between Partnership and Regulation," *European Security*, 14 (2005), 277, pp. 281–2.
21. See Nelson D. Schwartz & Noshua Watson, "The Pentagon's Private Army," *Fortune*, March 17, 2003, at 100, 103, available at 2003 WLNR 13891324.
22. See David Isenberg, "Soldiers of Fortune Ltd: A Profile of Today's Private Sector Corporate Mercenary Firms," Center for Def. Info. Monograph, available at http://0-www.totse.com.library.newcastle.edu.au:80/en/politics/us_military/armylove.html (last visited July 10, 2007).
23. P. W. Singer, *Corporate Warriors: The Rise of The Privatized Military Industry* (Ithaca: Cornell University Press, 2003), 53–4.
24. Ibid., 13.
25. J. C. Zarate, "The Emergence of a New Dog of War," p. 76.
26. T. Garmon, "Domesticating International Corporate Responsibility," 325, p. 327.
27. Ibid., p. 329.
28. D. Shearer, "Outsourcing War," *Foreign Policy*, 68 (1998), 70.
29. H. M. Howe, "Global Order and the Privatization of Security," p. 4.
30. Traci Hukill, "Should Peacekeepers Be Privatized?" *National Journal*, May 15, 2004, 1526.

31. De-mining operations alone, which the UN routinely outsourcers, has an estimated market of $400 million. Foreign Affairs Committee, "Private Military Companies: Options for Regulation," 2001–2, H.C. 577, pp. 56–9, http://www.fco.gov.uk/Files/kfile/mercenaries,0.pdf.
32. Foreign Affairs Committee, "Private Military Companies: Options for Regulation," 2001–2, H.C. 577, pp. 56–9, http://www.fco.gov.uk/Files/kfile/mercenaries,0.pdf.
33. P. W. Singer, *Corporate Warriors: The Rise of the Privatized Military Industry* (2003), 82.
34. See Int'l Peace Operations Ass'n, Members, http://www.ipoaonline.org/background/members.htm (last visited May 30, 2007).
35. In 2006, the G-8 countries pledged to train 75,000 African peacekeepers over 5 years to fulfill the proactive mandate of the African Union with its vision to play an active and decisive role in the numerous humanitarian crises in that continent that have often gone unchecked due to lack of political willpower or indifference by the West. In all likelihood, PMCs will do the training.
36. D. Isenberg, "A Fistful of Contractors: The Case of a Pragmatic Assessment of Private Military Companies in Iraq," British American Security Information Service, Research Report 204.4, September 2004, p. 29.
37. Global Fire Power, "Canada Military Strength," httlp://www.globalfirepower.com/country_detail.asp?country_id=27, last accessed, September 14, 2007.
38. Global Fire Power, "Australia Military Strength," httlp://www.globalfirepower.com/country_detail.asp?country_id=31, last accessed, September 14, 2007.
39. J. Guehenno, "A Continent in Crying Need of Peacekeepers," *International Herald Tribune*, October 15, 2004.
40. H. M. Howe, "Global Order and the Privatization of Security," p. 7.
41. D. Isenberg, "Security for sale," *Asia Times*, August 14, 2003, http://www.atimes.com/atimes/Front_Page/EH14Aa01.html, last accessed, September 10, 2007.
42. In the 1990s, Africa reportedly had some ninety different PMCs present, providing security to oil and mining companies—not to mention the PMCs to whom United States military training has been outsourced during the 1990s. See David Isenberg, "Soldiers of Fortune Ltd," Center for Def. Info. Monograph, Nov. 1997, available at http://0-www.totse.com.library.newcastle.edu.au:80/en/politics/us_military/armylove.html (last visited July 10, 2007); Sebastian Mallaby, Editorial, Paid to Make Peace, Wash. Post, June 4, 2001, at A19 (noting British company Lonrho's hiring of a PMC outfit to secure and protect cotton field Lonrho had purchased).
43. Matthew Quirk, "Private Military Contractors: A Buyer's Guide," *Atlantic Monthly*, September 2004, at 39, available at http://0-www.theatlantic.com.library.newcastle.edu.au:80/doc/prem/200409/quirk.
44. P. W. Singer, "Corporate Warriors: The Rise of the Privatized Military Industry and Its Ramifications for International Security," *International Security*, 26 (2003), 186.
45. See J. C. Zarate, "The Emergence of a New Dog of War," pp. 81–2.
46. J. Weisman and A. Reddy, "Spending on Iraq Sets Off Gold Rush," *Washington Post* October 9, 2003.
47. "Bush's secret army – The USA hires contract soldiers to fight in Iraq", June 9, 2004, *Jane's Security News* www.janes.com/security/international_security/news/fr/fr040609_1_n.shtml, last accessed, September 1, 2007.
48. P. W. Singer, "War, Profits and the Vacuum of Law: Privatised Military Firms and International Law," *Columbia Journal of Transnational Law*, 42 (2004), 521, p. 522.

49. This was the case in Sierra Leone and Papua New Guinea due to a perceived lack of capacity, expertise, experience, and professionalism. Thus, the most controversial PMCs are those which provide military training and even combat services to their clients. See Tina Garmon, "Domesticating International Corporate Responsibility," 330–31.
50. "Bush's secret army – The USA hires contract soldiers to fight in Iraq," June 9, 2004, *Jane's Security News*.
51. Mark Calaguas, "Military Privatization: Efficiency or Anarchy?" *Chicago-Kent Journal of International and Comparative Law*, 6 (2006) 58, p. 60.
52. In 2002, the United Kingdom's Foreign and Commonwealth Office published a report that examines the scope of PMC military services and the potential utility that PMCs offer to states and international organizations: Green Paper: Private Military Companies Options for Regulation, House of Commons, 20 Cong. Rec. 577 (2001/2002), p. 18.
53. Ibid., para. 10.
54. Ibid.
55. Ibid.
56. Ibid., para. 11.
57. *Frontline*, "Who are the Contractors?" (June 21, 2005), available at http://www.pbs.org/wgbh/pages/frontline/shows/warriors/contractors/companies.html (last visited July 7, 2007).
58. Michael N. Schmitt, "Humanitarian Law and Direct Participation in Hostilities by Private Contractors or Civilian Employees," *Chicago Journal of Int'l Law*, 5 (2005), 511, 513.
59. P. W. Singer, *Corporate Warriors: The Rise of the Privatized Military Industry* (2003), 110–13. Singer, "The Ultimate Military Entrepreneur," 91.
60. P. W. Singer, "Corporate Warriors: The Rise of the Privatized Military Industry and Its Ramifications for International Security," 186, pp. 216–19.
61. Ibid.
62. E. Krahmann, "Private Military Services in the UK and Germany," 277.
63. C. Lehnardt, *Private Military Companies and State Responsibility* (No. 2007/2) (New York: Institute for International Law and Justice, 2007).
64. A. E. Cha and R. Merle, "Line Increasingly Blurred Between Soldiers and Civilian Contractors," *Washington Post* (May 13, 2004).
65. P. W. Singer, "War, Profits, and the Vacuum of Law," pp. 542–3.
66. Mark Calaguas, "Military Privatization: Efficiency or Anarchy?" p. 59; *Frontline*, Frequently Asked Questions (June 21, 2005), available at http://0-www.pbs.org.library.newcastle.edu.au:80/wgbh/pages/frontline/shows/warriors/faqs/ (last visited May 7, 2007).
67. See generally James R. Davis, *Fortune's Warriors* (Douglas & McIntyre, Vancouver, Canada 2002), 74.
68. See generally James R. Davis, *Fortune's Warriors*.
69. James R. Davis, *Fortune's Warriors* 68–9 (extract is not verbatim but edited by the authors).
70. Isenberg, "A Fistful of Contractors", p. 15.
71. Ibid., p. 24.
72. D. Brooks, "Private military service providers: Africa's welcome pariahs," in Bachelor (ed.), *Guerres D'Afrique* (vol. 10) (CRES: Centre de Recherches Entreprises et Societes, 2002).
73. S. Chesterman and C. Lehnardt, "Introduction," in Chesterman and Lehnardt (eds.), *From Mercenaries to Market: The Rise and Regulation of Private Military Companies* (Oxford: Oxford University Press, 2007), pp. 2–3.

74. "Iraq revokes security contractor license after shootout", *Reuters* (September 15, 2007).
75. S. Rayment, "'Trophy' video exposes private security contractors shooting up Iraqi drivers," *The Telegraphy* (November 26, 2005). Video available at http://video.google.com/videoplay?docid=4993996875456348938&q=Aegis.
76. P. W. Singer, "Corporate Warriors," pp. 101–3.
77. K. Jennings, "Armed Services: Regulating the Private Military Industry," p. 15.
78. C. Ortiz, "The Private Military Company: An Entity at the Center of Overlapping Spheres of Commercial Activity and Responsibility," in Jäger, Thomas and Kümmel, Gerhard (eds.), *Private Military and Security Companies: Chances, Problems, Pitfalls and Prospects* (Leiben, Netherlands: Vs Verlag, 2007), pp. 60–1.
79. S. Chesterman and C. Lehnardt, "Introduction," p. 3.
80. D. J. Brooks, "The Business End of Military Intelligence: Private Military Companies," *Military Professional Intelligence Bulletin* (1999), n. 1.
81. F. Schreier and M. Caparini, *Privatising Security*, p. 34.
82. Ibid., pp. 32–43.
83. Ibid., p. 43.
84. S. Chesterman and C. Lehnardt, "Introduction," p. 4.
85. F. Schreier and M. Caparini, *Privatising Security*, p. 44.
86. K. O'Brian, "What should and what should not be regulated?" in Chesterman and Lehnardt (eds.), *From Mercenaries to Market.*
87. M. David Dragics, "CACI International Inc. CAI Unscheduled Material Events (8-K) Exhibit 99".
88. CACI, CACI in Iraq "truth will out" (2007). Retrieved August 30, 2007, from http://www.caci.com/iraq_news.shtml.
89. D. Hastings, "Iraq Contractors Accused in Shootings" (August 11, 2007). Retrieved August 25, 2007, from http://www.washingtonpost.com/wp-dyn/content/article/2007/08/11/AR2007081100655_pf.html.
90. K. Sengupta, "The real story of Baghdad's Bloody Sunday," *The Independent* (September 21, 2007).
91. C. Bourge, "Mercenary as Future Peacekeeper?" (August 26, 2003).
92. D. Hastings, "Iraq Contractors Accused in Shootings." Retrieved August 25, 2007, from http://www.washingtonpost.com/wp-dyn/content/article/2007/08/11/AR2007081100655_pf.html.
93. R. Brodsky, "Senate Dems Hear Whistleblower Claims of Abuse" (2007), from http://www.govexec.com/dailyfed/0907/092107rb1.htm.
94. United States Senate Committee on the Judiciary. "Combating War Profiteering: Are We Doing Enough to Investigate and Prosecute Contracting Fraud and Abuse in Iraq?" One Hundred Tenth Congress, First Session, March 20, 2007 Serial No. J–110–20.
95. G. Turbiville Jr., "Outlaw Private Security Firms: Criminal and Terrorist Agendas Undermine Private Security Alternatives," *Global Crime and Justice*, 7 (2006) 561. This article notes 11,000 PSCs, employing 165,000 personnel and having 71,000 weapons in Russia as of 1999.
96. A. Sherman, "Forward unto the Digital Breach: Exploring the Legal Status of Tomorrow's High-Tech Warriors," *Chicago Journal of International Law*, 5 (2004), 335, p. 337.
97. K. Bredemeier, "Iraq: Thousands of Private Contractors Support US Forces in Persian Gulf," *Washington Post* (March 3, 2003) (quoting Peter Singer).
98. A. E. Cha and R. Merle, "Line Increasingly Blurred Between Soldiers and Civilian Contractors."

99. Ibid.
100. Quoted in *Wikipedia: The Free Encyclopedia*, available at http://www.wikipedia.org/wiki/CACI (last visited June 19, 2006).
101. A. Verlöy and D. Politi, "Contracting Intelligence: Department of Interior Releases Abu Ghraib Contract" (2004). Retrieved July 28, 2004, from http://www.publicintegrity.org/wow/report.aspx?aid=361&sid=100.
102. Rebuilding Iraq: Actions Still Needed to Improve the use of Private Security Providers, GAO-06-865T released June 13, 2006, p. 2.
103. J. Christoff, Stabilizing and Rebuilding Iraq: Coalition Support and Intentional Donor Commitments: GAO-0-828T (2007).
104 J. K. Elsea, *Private Security Contractors in Iraq: Background, Legal Status and Other Issues*. Updated July 11, 2007, CSR Report for Congress, Congressional Research Service, p. 3.
105. *Frontline*, Frequently Asked Questions (June 21, 2005), available at http://0-www.pbs.org.library.newcastle.edu.au:80/wgbh/pages/frontline/shows/warriors/faqs/ (last visited May 7, 2007).
106. See J. C. Zarate, "The Emergence of a New Dog of War," pp. 81–2.
107. T. Garmon, "Domesticating International Corporate Responsibility," 325, p. 327.
108. E. W. Orts, "War and the Business Corporation," *Vanderbilt Journal of International Law*, 35 (2002), 549, pp. 556–7.
109. J. C. Zarate, "The Emergence of a New Dog of War," p. 77.
110. Ibid., p. 78.
111. Ibid., p. 78.
112. For a crisp, concise analysis see J. N. Maogoto and B. Sheehy, "Contemporary Private Military Firms Under International Law: An Unregulated 'Gold Rush'," *Adelaide Law Review*, 26 (2006), 245.
113. J. N. Maogoto, *State Sovereignty and International Criminal Law*.
114. The General Assembly, International Convention against the Recruitment, Use, Financing and Training of Mercenaries, 44/34 Cong. Rec. 306 (1989). *International Convention against the Recruitment, Use, Financing and Training of Mercenaries*, GA Res 44/34, UN GAOR, Annex, 306.
115. The difficulty in so distinguishing lies in the fact that combat and noncombat roles are invariably linked making any distinction between the two somewhat arbitrary.
116. D. Shearer, "Outsourcing War," pp. 68–9; see also Commission on Human Rights, *Report on the Question of the Use of Mercenaries as a Means of Violating Human Rights and Impeding the Exercise of the Right of Peoples to Self-Determination*, UN ESCOR, [24] UN Doc E/CN.4/1998/31 (1998) (prepared by Enrique Bernales Ballesteros).
117. Many PMCs are actually divisions or subsidiaries of such prominent businesses as Northrop-Grumman, Booz Allen Hamilton, the Carlyle Group, and Bechtel. See J. D. Michaels, "Beyond Accountability: The Constitutional, Democratic, and Strategic Problems with Privatizing War," *Washington University Law Quarterly*, 82 (2004), 1001, p. 1023.
118. "Blood and treasure: Mercenaries", *Economist*, November 4, 2006, 381 (8502), p. 77.
119. The industry is not limited to mega-corporations. One company on the S&P small cap index, Cubic Corporation, has focused on electronic defense systems and training to its great benefit. Cubic Corporation's profits "rose 41% in fiscal 2002," and its stock price tripled between 1999 and 2003.

120. "The Baghdad boom; Mercenaries" *Economist*, March 27, 2004, 370 (8368), p. 29.
121. Hossein-Zadeh, I. "Why the US Is Not Leaving Iraq: The Booming Business of War Profiteers" Global Research—January 12, 2007. Retrieved; www.globalpolicy.org.
122. M. Sapone, "Have Rifle with Scope, Will Travel," p. 12.
123. Ibid., p. 10.
124. J. C. Zarate, "The Emergence of a New Dog of War," pp. 93–103.
125. M. Sapone, "Have Rifle with Scope, Will Travel," pp. 19–20.
126. C. J. Rosky, "Force, Inc.: The Privatization of Punishment, Policing, And Military Force in Liberal States," *Connecticut Law Review*, 36 (2004), 879, p. 984.
127. See e.g. D. Kassebaum, "A Question of Facts—The Legal Use of Private Security Firms in Bosnia," *Columbia Journal of Transnational Law*, 38 (2000), 581–602; J. C. Zarate, "The Emergence of a New Dog of War," pp. 93–103.
128. See *DOD, Regulation 5000.2-R, Mandatory Procedures for Major Defense Acquisition Programs (MDAPS) And Major Automated Information System (MAIS) Acquisition Programs* (2002) available at http://dod5000.daumil/DOCS/DoDI%205000.2-signed%20(May%2012,%202003).doc (visited June 15, 2006).
129. G. L. Campbell, "Contractors on the Battlefield: The Ethics of Paying Civilians to Enter Harm's Way and Requiring Soldiers to Depend upon Them," paper presented at the Joint Services Conference on Professional Ethics, Springfield, VA (2000, 27–28 January).
130. H. M. Howe, "Global Order and the Privatization of Security," p. 7.
131. J. O. McGinnis, "The Decline of the Western Nation States and the Rise of the Regime of International Federalism," *Cardozo Law Review*, 18 (1996), 903, p. 905; A.-M. Slaughter, *A New World Order* (Princeton: Princeton University Press, 2004).
132. Or at least since Wallenstein's private army. See P. W. Singer, "The Ultimate Military Entrepreneur," 6–15.
133. P. W. Singer, "Corporate Warriors," pp. 186 and 209.
134. It should be noted that many PMCs act in support of UN humanitarian endeavors.
135. Reference the involvement of Executive Outcomes in Sierra Leone. See S. Kiley, "Leone Faces Aid Cut Over Apartheid Soldiers," *The Times* (July 19, 1995), available at LEXIS (classified as "News & Business, Major World Newspapers").
136. See chapter 5 of this book which discusses the role of PMCs in the Balkans and the litigation regarding activities by interrogators in Abu Ghraib prison in Iraq. See also J. N. Maogoto, "Watching the Watchdogs: Holding the UN Accountable for International Humanitarian Law Violations of the 'Blue Helmets'," *Deakin Law Review*, 5 (2000), 47, p. 51.

2 The Corporate Form and the Private Military Corporation

1. The company's website offers no further information about its legal identity, directors, or shareholders. It identifies itself merely as "Blackwater USA." "XI Trials of War Criminals Before the Nuremberg Military Tribunals under Control Council" (unpublished manuscript, 1948).
2. Ibid.
3. Ibid.
4. Ibid.
5. Ibid., http://www.blackwaterusa.com/copyright.html
6. Ibid., http://www.blackwaterusa.com/new/index.html

7. J. Franklin, "US contractor recruits guards for Iraq in Chile," *Guardian* (March 5, 2004).
8. MPRI, "About MPRI—Taking Expertise Around the World" (2005). Retrieved April 2, 2007, from http://mpri.com//site/about.html.
9. MPRI, Activities www.mpri.com/about/activities.htm cited in D. Kassebaum, "A Question of Facts," 581–602.
10. www.mpri.com
11. See state supported killing using PMCs in V. Newell and B. Sheehy, "Corporate Militaries and States: Actors, Interactions and Reactions," *Texas International Law Journal*, 41 (2006), pp. 67–101, and for examples of corporately employed PMC murders see Coca-Cola's use of right wing paramilitaries in Colombia in Sinaltrainal v. Coca-Cola Co, 256 1345 (SD Fla. 2003).
12. "Call to investigate shooting of scientist," *Newcastle Herald* (March 13, 2006), concerning the killing of 72-year old professor, Kays Juma, of the Faculty of Agriculture, University of Baghdad, on March 25, 2006, p. 16.
13. AEGIS Defense Services Ltd., "AEGIS Specialist Risk Management" (2007). Retrieved September 10, 2007.
14. D. Brooks, *Ruthless Humanitarianism: Why Ignoring the Private Security Option in Darfur is a Mistake* (n.d., from http://www.goodmagazine.com/section/Provocations/ruthless_humanitarianism).
15. If one accepts M. Jensen's view of the corporation. M. C. Jensen, "Value Maximization, Stakeholder Theory, and the Corporate Objective Function," *European Financial Management Review*, 7 (2001), 297.
16. P. W. Singer, *Corporate Warriors*, p. 43.
17. Ibid., p. 47.
18. Ibid.
19. J. U. Bauer, Report on United Nations Commission on Human Rights Fifty-third Session: United Nations Commission on Human Rights (1997). Quoted in P. W. Singer, *Corporate Warriors*, p. 188.
20. See, for example, P. Agee, *CIA Diary: Inside the Company* (Harmondsworth: Penguin Books, 1975).
21. J. G. Hill, "Public Beginnings-Private Ends-Should Corporate Law Privilege the Interests of Shareholders?," *International Corporate Law*, 9 (2000), 21.
22. Clearly, whose good was being considered in these trading companies is an issue. It seems hardly likely that the good of the indigenous people whose land was being invaded was considered, nor yet the well-being of the majority of the sailors or settlers. Nevertheless, following the political line, public good here is as discussed by the government.
23. R. P. Austin and I. M. Ramsay, *Ford's Principles of Corporations Law*, 13 (Australia: LexisNexis Butterworths, 2005), p. 32. Bold added.
24. M. Friedman, "The Social Responsibility of Business Is to Increase Its Profits," *New York Times* (September 13, 1970).
25. See discussion in B. Sheehy, "The Trouble with Stockjobbers: the South Sea Bubble, the Press and the Legislative Regulation of the Markets," *Newcastle Law Review* (forthcoming).
26. See discussion in R. Grantham, "The Doctrinal Basis of the Rights of Company Shareholders," *Cambridge Law Journal*, 57 (1998) 554–8, pp. 557–8.
27. B. Sheehy, "The Trouble with Stockjobbers."
28. R. Grantham, "The Doctrinal Basis of the Rights of Company Shareholders," p. 559.
29. See D. J. H. Greenwood, "Introduction to the Metaphors of Corporate Law," *Seattle Journal of Social Justice*, 4 (2006), 18, pp. 9–12. See also, B. Sheehy,

"Scrooge—The Reluctant Stakeholder: Theoretical Problems in The Shareholder-Stakeholder Debate," *University of Miami Business Law Review*, 14 (2005), pp. 193–241, ibid.

30. W. Bratton, "The 'Nexus of Contracts' Corporation: A Critical Appraisal," *Cornell Law Review*, 74 (1989a), 412–452, pp. 433–4.
31. W. Laufer, *Corporate Bodies and Guilty Minds: The Failure of Corporate Criminal Liability* (Chicago: University of Chicago Press, 2006), pp. 48–51.
32. Ibid., pp. 52–67. See also D. J. H. Greenwood, "Introduction to the Metaphors of Corporate Law."
33. A. Alchian and H. Demsetz, "Productions, Information Costs, and Economic Organization," *American Economic Review*, 62 (1972), 777, pp. 10–11.
34. D. J. H. Greenwood, "Introduction to the Metaphors of Corporate Law," p. 9.
35. R. P. Austin and I. M. Ramsay, *Ford's Principles of Corporations Law*, pp. 25–7.
36. F. H. Easterbrook and D. R. Fischel, *The Economic Structure of Corporate Law* (Cambridge: Harvard University Press, 1991).
37. Ibid.
38. This ideal state has been called "panglossian" in a review of Easterbrook and Fischel's in the Harvard Law Review titled, "Dr. Pangloss meets the Coase Theorem," *Harvard Law Review*, 105 (1992), 1408–13.
39. S. Bottomley, "From Contractualism to Constitutionalism: A New Framework for Corporate Governance," *Sydney Law Review*, 19 (1997), 277–313.
40. Ibid., p. 281.
41. These regulatory suggestions will be discussed in greater detail later in the chapter.
42. The failure of recognition of the corporate entity is seen as a major obstacle to law enforcement vis-à-vis corporate criminal law. W. Laufer, *Corporate Bodies and Guilty Minds*.
43. Quoted in J. Scahill, "Bush's Shadow Army," *Nation* (April 2, 2007).
44. B. Sheehy, "Corporations And Social Costs: The Wal-Mart Case Study," *Journal of Law & Commerce*, 24 (2004), pp. 1–55.
45. L. E. Mitchell (ed.), *Progressive Corporate Law* (vol. 7) (Boulder: Westview Press, 1995).
46. Promising work although still developing, and which has attracted considerable attention is M. Blair and L. Stout, "A Team Production Theory of Corporate Law," *Virginia Law Review*, 85 (1999), 247.
47. This is not an uncontroversial statement. It forms the basis for the general stakeholder debate. See B. Sheehy, "Scrooge—The Reluctant Stakeholder" pp. 193–241.
48. L. Cata Backer, *Comparative Corporate Law: United States, European Union, China and Japan* (Durham, NC: Carolina Academic Press, 2002), pp. 1129–304 argues for these two but adds a "duty of disclosure." This latter duty is not well recognized outside of the USA. For the Australian and New Zealand position see J. Farrar, *Corporate Governance: Theories, Principles, and Practice*, 2nd edn (Melbourne: Oxford University Press, 2005), pp. 103–6.
49. M. Eisenberg, "Corporate Law and Social Norms," *Columbia Law Review*, 99 (1999), 1253, pp. 1265–78, in L. Cata Backer, *Comparative Corporate Law*, pp. 1130–9.
50. See discussion in B. Sheehy, "Scrooge—The Reluctant Stakeholder", pp. 193–241.
51. L. Cata Backer, *Comparative Corporate Law*, pp. 1183–212.
52. Ibid., pp. 1156–83.

53. R. Grantham, *The Limited Liability Of Company Directors* (Research Paper No. 07–03) (Brisbane: The University of Queensland, 2007).
54. R. Grantham, "The Doctrinal Basis of the Rights of Company Shareholders," R. Grantham, "Attributing Responsibility to Corporate Entities: A Doctrinal Approach," *Company and Securities Law Journal*, 19 (2001), pp. 168–180.
55. See discussion in J. Farrar, *Corporate Governance*, pp. 336–47.
56. See discussion in B. Sheehy, "Shareholders, Unicorns and Stilts: An Analysis of Shareholder Property Rights," *Journal of Corporate Law Studies*, 6 (2006), pp. 165–212.
57. By Limited Liability Act, 18 & 19 c133 (1855) in the UK.
58. Interestingly, some institutional shareholders have become activists in various areas of interest including socially responsible investing among other things.
59. See, for example, the comments of T. Lanza, CEO of L-3 Communications, a Lockheed spin-off PMC in "L-3 Communications Announces Acquisition of MPRI," *Business Wire* (July 18, 2000).
60. E. Schrader, "US Companies Hired to Train Foreign Armies," *Los Angeles Times* (Sunday, April 14, 2002).
61. Office of Management and Budget, "Department of Defense" (2005, February 12, 2007). Retrieved February 14, 2007, from http://www.whitehouse.gov/omb/budget/fy2005/defense.html.
62. P. W. Singer, *Corporate Warriors*, pp. 84–5.
63. See, for example, "L-3 Communications Announces Acquisition of MPRI."
64. Salomon v Salomon Co., 2 232 [1895] in the UK & Commonwealth and Santa Clara County v. Southern Pacific Railroad Company, 118 394 1886 in the USA.
65. R. Tomasic, S. Bottomley and R. McQueen, *Corporations Law in Australia* (Canberra: The Federation Press, 2002), pp. 44–5, L. Cata Backer, *Comparative Corporate Law*, pp. 1064–77.
66. R. Tomasic, S. Bottomley and R. McQueen, *Corporations Law in Australia*, pp. 45–7, L. Cata Backer, *Comparative Corporate Law,* pp. 1077–97.
67. United States v Milwaukee Refrigerator Transit Co., 142 247 1905, p. 255.
68. This corporate law doctrine comes from equity, which identifies a fraud upon a power as a breach of duty pursuant to a power of appointment. Discussed in Ngurli Ltd. v McCann, 425 1953, 438–440.
69. These activities were not limited to corporations, but often were partnerships and trusts. This issue concerning the involvement of the corporate entity in misdeeds is illuminatingly discussed in D. Litowitz, "Are Corporations Evil?," *University of Miami Law Review*, 58 (2004), 811. Some aspects of other vehicles are discussed in F. O. Stover and S. P. Hamill, "The LLC Versus LLP Conundrum: Advice for Businesses Contemplating the Choice," *Alabama Law Review*, 50 (1999), 813–847.
70. At least in the Australian context. For empirical evidence, see I. Ramsay and D. Noakes, "Piercing the Corporate Veil in Australia," *Company and Securities Law Journal*, 19 (2001), 250.
71. Daimler Co. v Continental Tyre and Rubber Co. (Great Britain) Ltd., 2 307 [1916].
72. Collet v. American Nat'l Stores, Inc., 708 273 (Mo. Ct. App. 1986), p. 284.
73. I. Ramsay and D. Noakes, "Piercing the Corporate Veil in Australia,".
74. Ibid.
75. A thoughtful approach discussing the specific problems with the PMC market, such as lack of true competition and transparency, are discussed in D. Avant, "The emerging market for private military services and the problems of regulation," in Chesterman and Lehnardt (eds.), *From Mercenaries to Market.*

76. Records of private contractor deaths are difficult to find. One compilation by the Iraq Coalition Casualty Count can be found at http://icasualties.org/oif/Civ.aspx.
77. See, for example, the discussion of the history of corporate occupational safety laws in the USA in H. Zinn, *The Twentieth Century: A People's History*, 1 (New York: Harper Perennial, 2003), pp. 38–39.
78. A. Belcher, "Corporate Killing as a Corporate Governance Issue," *Corporate Governance An International Review*, 10 (2002), 47–54.
79. See, for example, the Zeebrugge ferry disaster of 1987.
80. See, for example, the James Hardie scandal in Australia.
81. See the discussion in N. Foster, "Personal Liability of Company Officers for Corporate Occupational Health and Safety Breaches: Section 26 of the Occupational Health and Safety Act 2000 (NSW)," *Australian Journal of Labour Law*, 18 (2005), pp. 107–135.
82. See, for example, the scandal caused by the revelation of one of the houses owned by the CEO of James Hardie, located in California overlooking the beach and valued at $3.0 million.
83. This is the matter of fraud in contract, fundraising, or for some types of environmental damage in some jurisdictions.
84. J. Kwok, "Armed Entrepreneurs: Private Military Companies in Iraq," *Soviet Legacies*, 28 (2006), pp. 12–18.
85. R. Verkaik, "British Army pays £1m to Iraqi families," *Independent* (December 3, 2005).
86. K. Bisset, "Iraqis given secret payments," *Daily Telegraphy* (April 9, 2007).
87. Marc Galasco, former US Defense Intelligence officer, and now Senior Military Analyst with Human Rights Watch, quoted in Human Rights Watch, "Iraq: US Data on Civilian Casualties Raises Serious Concerns" (2007). Retrieved September 10, 2007, from http://hrw.org/english/docs/2007/04/12/iraq15687_txt.htm.
88. S. Fainaru and S al-Izzi, "US Security Contractors Open Fire in Baghdad: Blackwater Employees Were Involved in Two Shooting Incidents in Past Week," *Washington Post* (May 27, 2007) A01.
89. A detailed and helpful summary of the case can be found at MPRI, "About MPRI – Taking Expertise Around the World" (2005). Retrieved April 2, 2007, from http://mpri.com//site/about.html.
90. D. J. Callahan and M. P. Miles, "Blackwater Heavies Sue Families of Slain Employees for $10 Million in Brutal Attempt to Suppress Their Story" (June 8, 2007). Retrieved September 1, 2007, from http://www.alternet.org/story/53460/.
91. "no body to be kicked and no soul to be damned" is the saying long attributed to the poet Edward Thurlow. In 1612, Justice Edward Coke said: "They (corporations) cannot commit treason, nor be outlawed, nor excommunicated, for they have no souls". Suttons Hospital Case, 10 32b 1612.
92. Undoubtedly the best book on the subject of corporate criminality is the recent work, W. Laufer, *Corporate Bodies and Guilty Minds*. Corporations have been held criminally liable for manslaughter in R. v. P&O European Ferries (Dover) Ltd, 93 72 1991. For an Australian perspective, see N. Foster, "Personal Liability of Company Officers for Corporate Occupational Health and Safety Breaches," pp. 107–135.
93. This concern is what drives the recent corporate governance debate.
94. This is the effect of the Sarbanes-Oxley legislation in the USA.
95. The exception is in military activity as between soldiers of opposing forces.

96. R. v. Huggins, 92 518 1730), pp. 522–3, R. Grantham, "Attributing Responsibility to Corporate Entities," p. 171. For a thorough review of corporate criminal liability, see W. Laufer, *Corporate Bodies and Guilty Minds*, pp. 3–43.
97. R. v. Nelson Group Services (Maintenance) Ltd. 331 [1998].
98. Both the UK and Australia have attempted to create a unique form of offense that is corporate criminal responsibility. Criminal convictions have been obtained in several cases against corporate officers. See, for example, R. v. Kite, 2 295 [1996], and R. v. Denbo Pty Ltd. and Timothy Ian Nadenbousch, Unreported (SC Vic 1994) respectively. Kite's employer OLL Ltd. was also convicted of manslaughter. In determining criminal liability, Australia's Crime Code, Pt. 2.5, s. 12 requires the mens rea to be present among the management.
99. For one approach to the problem, see S. Chesterman, "The Corporate Veil, Crime and Punishment: R v Denbo Pty Ltd and Timothy Ian Nadenboush," *Melbourne University Law Review*, 19 (1994), 1064–1073.
100. See discussion in M. Olthoff, 'Beyond the form-should the Corporate Veil be Pierced?," *UMKC L. Rev*, 64 (1995), 311.
101. Similar tests can be found in the UK, Canadian and Australian case law.
102. W. Laufer, *Corporate Bodies and Guilty Minds*.
103. Sometimes referred to as a war of attrition.
104. W. Laufer, *Corporate Bodies and Guilty Minds*.
105. Sometimes referred to as a war of attrition.
106. M. Ezzati and A. Lopez, "Estimates of global mortality attributable to smoking in 2000," *The Lancet*, 362 (2003), pp. 847–852.
107. World Health Organization, "Why is tobacco a public health priority?" (2007). Retrieved March 21, 2007, from http://www.who.int/tobacco/en/.
108. WHO studies note the movement of big tobacco into the 3rd world. www.who.int/tobacco/health_impact/en/.
109. M. S. Givel and S. A. Glantz, "Tobacco lobby political influence on US state legislatures in the 1990s," *Tobacco Control*, 10 (2001), 124–134.
110. J. Maogoto and B. Sheehy, "Torturing the Rule of Law: USA and the Post 9-11 World," *St. John's Journal of Legal Commentary*, 21 (2007), pp. 689–725.
111. D. Isenberg, "A Fistful of Contractors," British American Security Information Council, 2004, p. 12.
112. A hand summary of these remedies is available in the article by military lawyer P. Carter, "How to Discipline Private Contractors: What Consequences Do the Companies Involved in Abu Ghraib Face?" (May 4, 2004). Retrieved April 1, 2007, from http://www.slate.com/id/2099954.
113. MPRI, "About MPRI – Taking Expertise Around the World" (2005). Retrieved April 2, 2007, from http://mpri.com//site/about.html.
114. P Spiegel, "No Contractors Facing Abu Ghraib Abuse Charges," *Financial Times* (FT) (August 9, 2005).
115. It is conceded by corporate law scholars that multinational corporations are out of control. See, for example, J. Dine, *The Governance of Corporate Groups* (Cambridge: Cambridge University Press, 2001). By this statement scholars mean that governments cannot impose their wills on corporate groups. Consider for example the James Hardie scandal in which the corporation reorganized moving its offices from Australia to the Netherlands to avoid liability for billions of dollars in asbestos related claims. L. M. LoPucki, "The Death of Liability," *Yale Law Journal*, 106 (1996), 1. See also, J. J. White, "Corporate Judgment Proofing: A Response to Lynn LoPucki's The Death of Liability," *Yale Law Journal*, 107 (1998), 1363. One of the most notorious mass corporate

killings occurred in India. Union Carbide operated a chemical plant in Bhopal, India. As a result of inadequate supervision on maintenance matters, some 2,660 people were killed and 30,000–40,000 injured. J. Cassels *The Uncertain Promise of Law: Lessons from Bhopal* (Toronto: University of Toronto Press Incorporated, 1993). recording the Indian court's estimates for settlement purposes. The event, which occurred on December 2, 1984, some twenty-two years later still has legal issues outstanding. The Indian court's efforts to have the American CEO of the Indian subsidiary extradited to face legal proceedings have been thwarted by the USA at every step. It is clear that the Union Carbide case is a disaster from every angle except the corporate angle. The final settlement reached with the Indian government was a mere $470 million on a case many suggested was worth at least $3.3 billion. See discussion in J. Cassels, *The Uncertain Promise of Law.*

116. N. C. Seddon and M. P. Ellinghaus, *Cheshire and Fifoot's Law of Contract*, 8th edn (Chatswood, NSW: LexisNexis Butterworths, 2002), 18.1, p. 839.
117. Noted as an illegal contract in Ibid., 18.16, p. 849.
118. Ibid., p. 856.
119. Ibid., [emphasis added].
120. Ibid., 18.33, p. 867.
121. W. Laufer, *Corporate Bodies and Guilty Minds,* see in particular, chapter 2.
122. W. Bratton, "The Nexus of Contracts Theory of the Firm: A Critical Examination," *Cornell Law Review*, 74 (1989b), 407.
123. B. Sheehy, "The Trouble with Stockjobbers."
124. See the excellent discussion in W. Laufer, *Corporate Bodies and Guilty Minds*, chapter 1.
125. Ibid., and J. Richter, *Holding Corporations Accountable* (London and New York Zed Books, 2001); J. Dine, *The Governance of Corporate Groups.*
126. J. Richter, *Holding Corporations Accountable.*
127. E. W. Orts, "Corporate Governance, Stakeholder Accountability, and Sustainable Peace: War and the Business Corporation." Notes omitted.
128. Discussed in W. Laufer, *Corporate Bodies and Guilty Minds*. See also the background section to the 1996 Report of the Defence Industry Initiative on Business Ethics and Conduct http://www.itcilo.it/english/actrav/telearn/global/ilo/guide/defence.htm#Background%20of%20the%20Defense%20Industry%20Initiative. R. Weber, *Swords into Dow Shares: Governing the Decline of the Military-Industrial Complex* (Boulder, CO: Perseus, 2001).
129. T I UK, Defense against Corruption (unpublished manuscript) (London, 2006). See also W. Laufer, *Corporate Bodies and Guilty Minds*, R. Weber, *Swords into Dow Shares*, pp. 32–33.
130. Sommer, "Whom should the corporation serve? The Berle-Dodd Debate revisited sixty years later," *Delaware Journal of Corporate Law*, 16 (1991), 33.
131. C. A. H. Wells, "The Cycles of Corporate Social Responsibility: An Historical Retrospective for the Twenty-first Century," *Kansas Law Review*, 51 (2002), 77.
132. I have written on this elsewhere in B. Sheehy, "Scrooge—The Reluctant Stakeholder," pp. 193–241.
133. B. Sheehy, "Corporations and Social Costs," pp. 1–55.
134. Ibid.
135. D. J. H. Greenwood, "Introduction to the Metaphors of Corporate Law," p. 3.
136. A. A. Berle and G. C. Means, *The Modern Corporation and Private Property* (New York: Harcourt, Brace & World, 1968).
137. D. J. H. Greenwood, "Introduction to the Metaphors of Corporate Law," p. 3.

138. See, for example, discussion of Executive Outcomes political connections and USA Vice-President Dick Cheney in P. W. Singer, *Corporate Warriors*, pp. 101–8 and pp. 138–41, respectively.
139. Ibid., pp. 80–82.
140. Ibid., pp. 104–115.
141. An excellent introductory textbook is J. Farrar, *Corporate Governance*.
142. Discussed in chapter 10 "Contractual Dilemmas," P. W. Singer, *Corporate Warriors*, pp. 151–68; R. Weber, *Swords into Dow Shares*.
143. For example, see discussion of Brown & Root & Halliburton in P. W. Singer, *Corporate Warriors*, pp. 136–8.
144. D. Isenberg, "A Fistful of Contractors," British American Security Information Council, 2004, pp. 39–40.
145. Sandline International, *Private Military Companies—Independent or Regulated?* 1998.
146. D. R. Desai, "Have Your Cake and Eat It Too," 825.
147. R. Weber, *Swords into Dow Shares*, p. 183.
148. Singer makes a suggestion that an approved list of PMCs be assembled and provided for PMCs registered. P. W. Singer, *Corporate Warriors*. Singer's discussion focuses on an audit body, rather than the disclosure requirements proposed here.
149. S. Fainaru and S. al-Izzi, "US Security Contractors Open Fire in Baghdad."
150. Singer notes employees provided by DynCorp as too old, too fat, and as unqualified to work on aircraft although employed as such. P. W. Singer, *Corporate Warriors*, pp. 154 and 156.
151. Ibid., p. 222.
152. R. Weber, *Swords into Dow Shares*, pp. 177–182.
153. P. Zumbansen, and D. Saam. "The ECJ, Volkswagen and European Corporate Law: Reshaping the European Varieties of Capitalism," *German Law Journal* 8 (2007), 11.
154. E. Krahmann, "Private Military Services in the UK and Germany," 277.
155. See, for example, D. Isenberg, "A Fistful of Contractors," British American Security Information Council, 2004, pp. 46–47; and K. Jennings, "Armed Services: Regulating the Private Military Industry" (No. Fafo Report-532, 2007).
156. R. Weber, *Swords into Dow Shares*.
157. P. W. Singer, "Wars, Profits, and the Vacuum of Law," p. 546.
158. These guidelines, such as the Geneva Convention, have suffered severe setbacks as a result of the USA's clear breach and disregard of its obligations in Guantanamo and Abu Ghraib.
159. Certainly one can predict the howling of bankers and other financiers whose contributions finance the acquisition of combat helicopters and other weaponry. But why should they be exempted from liability if any other contributor is not?
160. D. Montgomery, "Pipeline to Justice: Burmese Activist Has the Attention of the White House and the World," *Washington Post* (August 13, 2003).
161. A list of the petitioners can be found at http://www.feinstein.org/own/corporatecharterrevocation.html. A small demonstration took place at the Loyola Law School in Los Angeles when the Attorney General Lockyer attended to deliver as speech. http://www.corpwatch.org/article.php?id=269
162. R. Benson, *Challenging Corporate Rule: The Petition to Revoke Unocal's Charter as a Guide to Citizen Action* (New York: Apex Press, 1999). Unocal was taken to court unsuccessfully on the use of forced labor in Burma, Doe v. Unocal, 110

1294 (C.D. Cal. 2000) and appeal December 3, 2001, US 9th Circuit Court of Appeals.

163. See N. Foster, "Personal Liability of Company Officers for Corporate Occupational Health and Safety Breaches," pp. 107–135. Opposing the view of increased director's liabilities, see R. Baxt, "The necessity for appropriate reform," in Adams, Bristow and Cannings (eds.), *Collapse Incorporated: Tales, Safeguards and Responsibilities of Corporate Australia.* (Sydney: CCH Australia Limited, 2001) 325–52, p. 325.
164. B. Garratt, *The Fish Rots from the Head: The Crisis in Our Boardrooms—Developing the Crucial Skills of the Competent Director* (London: Profile Books, 2003), p. 3; N. Kendall and A. Kendall, *Real World Corporate Governance: A Programme for Profit-enhancing Stewardship* (London, United Kingdom: Pitman Publishing Corp., 1998), pp. 9–10. See also discussion in J. du Plessis, J. McConvill and M. Bagaric, *Principles of Contemporary Corporate Governance* (Cambridge: Cambridge University Press, 2005).
165. For example, see the Australian legislation, Corporations Act, Cth (2001), s. 206.
166. C. Rodriguez-Gavarito, "Nike's Law: The Anti-Sweatshop Movement, Transnational Corporations, and the Struggle Over International Labor Rights in the Americas," in Santos and Rodriguez-Gavarito (eds.), *Law and Globalization from Below* (Cambridge: Cambridge University Press, 2005).
167. See Singer's classification, P. W. Singer and J. M. Olin, "Corporate Warriors: The Rise and Ramifications of the Privatized Military Industry," *International Security*, 26 (2001/2002), 16–19.
168. The Company Law of the People's Republic of China (1999), articles 68 and 69. Adopted at the Fifth Session of the Standing Committee of the Eighth National People's Congress,...and promulgated as Presidential Decree No. 29 of the People's Republic of China on December 25, 1999, effective as of the same day.

3 The State, Control of Violence, and the Private Military Corporation

1. R. Pound, "Law and the State: Jurisprudence and Politics," *Harvard Law Review*, 57 (1944), 1193–236.
2. J. Maogoto, *International Criminal Law and State Sovereignty*, chapter 1. See also S. Neff, *Friends But No Allies: Economic Liberalism and the Law of Nations* (New York: Columbia University Press, 1990), chapter 1.
3. Montevideo Convention on the Rights and Duties of States 1933 (1936).
4. C. Warbrick, "States and Recognition in International Law," in Evans (ed.), *International Law* (Oxford: Oxford University Press, 2003), pp. 205–6.
5. J. Maogoto, *International Criminal Law and State Sovereignty*, pp. 18–19.
6. C. Warbrick, "States and Recognition in International Law," pp. 213–14. Discussed in context in A. Anghie, "Finding the Peripheries: Sovereignty and Colonialism in Nineteenth-Century International Law," *Harvard International Law Journal*, 40 (1999), 1.
7. J. Bodin (ed.), *Les Six Livres de la Republique*, 1962). Cited and discussed in J. Maogoto, *International Criminal Law and State Sovereignty*, pp. 8–11.
8. J Maogoto, *International Criminal Law and State Sovereignty*, p. 9.
9. Ibid., p. 14 (italics omitted). As Maogoto acknowledges, this traditional view of sovereignty is being challenged on several fronts. An insightful comment is I. Simonovic, "Relative Sovereignty of the Twenty First Century," *Hastings International & Comparative Law Review*, 25 (2002), 372.

10. Green Paper: Private Military Companies Options for Regulation, House of Commons, 20 Cong. Rec. 577 (2001/2002), available at http://www.fco.gov.uk/Files/KFile/mercenaries,0.pdf [hereinafter Green Paper]. A Green Paper is a policy discussion paper drafted by the Executive but authorized for publication by the Parliament. The aim of a Green Paper is to promote public debate and to inform policy development.
11. M. Weber, *The Theory of Social and Economic Organization* (New York: Oxford University Press, 1947) p. 154.
12. "The Bill of Rights," (1688).
13. J. Maogoto, *International Criminal Law and State Sovereignty*, pp. 15–31.
14. Of course, international law also recognizes principles capable of running contrary to the state monopoly on violence, such as the right to self-determination of peoples within state boundaries or across state boundaries.
15. P. Singer, "The Ultimate Military Entrepreneur," *Military History*, Spring (2003b), 1.
16. P. Singer, *Corporate Warriors*, pp. 29–31.
17. For a general review, see E. A. Nordlinger, *Soldiers in Politics: Military Coups and Governments* (Englewood Cliffs: Prentice Hall, 1977); for a more critical examination focused on a specific case, arguing among other things that a military coup is part of the normal political process, see J. S. Fitch, *The Military Coup d'État as a Political Process: Ecuador, 1948–1966* (Baltimore, MD: Johns Hopkins, 1977).
18. See recent examples, discussion in P. Singer concerning the effectiveness of various PMCs in Africa where their role was limited to providing strategic advice to smaller, but ultimately successful troops. P. Singer, *Corporate Warriors*.
19. An excellent resource on the arms trade is publications section of the British American Security Information Council website. For a summary review of weaponry and perceived threats see British American Security Information Council, "Weapons Trade Publications" (2007). Retrieved February 21, 2007.
20. "Arsenals" in "The Oxford Companion to Military History" (2003). Retrieved August 27, 2007.
21. Ibid.
22. I. Mount, D. H. Freedman and M. Maier, "The New Military Industrial Complex: To arm for digital-age war, the Pentagon has turned to a new generation of defense contractors. The hardware is impressive. It's also deadly." *Business 2.0* (2003).
23. P. Towell, S. Daggett and A. Belasco, *Defense: FY 2008 Authorization and Appropriations*: Congressional Research Service (CRS), 2007, cited in S. M. Kosiak, "Comparison of the FY 2008 House and SASC Defense Authorization Bills" (2007). Retrieved August 28, 2007, from http://www.csbaonline.org/4Publications/PubLibrary/U.20070813.Comparison_of_the_/U.20070813.Comparison_of_the_.pdf.
24. P. Stålenheim, C. Perdomo and E. Sköns, "Military expenditure," in *SIPRI Yearbook 2007* (Oxford: Oxford University Press, 2007) 267–297, p. 267.
25. J. Freier, "Arms and the Terrorist," *The Journal of International Security*, 9 (2005); see also P. Singer, *Corporate Warriors*, ch. 5, pp. 73–88.
26. Marsh, "Two Sides of the Same Coin? The Legal and Illegal Trade in Small Arms," *The Brown Journal of World Affairs*, 9 (2002), 219, p. 223. See the detailed and well-researched article of Amnesty International, *A Catalogue of Failures: G8 Arms Exports and Human Rights Violations* (May 19, 2003).
27. Marsh, "Two Sides of the Same Coin? The Legal and Illegal Trade in Small Arms," p. 223.

28. See discussion in P. Williams, "Transnational Organized Crime and International Security," in Gamba and Meek (eds.), *Society under Siege: Crime, Violence and Illegal Weapons* (vol. 1), (Pretoria, SA: Institute for Security Studies, 1997), R. T. Naylor, "The Rise of the Modern Arms Black Market and the Fall of Supply-side Control," in *Society under Siege*, and A. F. Musah and R. Castle, "Eastern Europe's Arsenal on the Loose: managing light weapons flow to conflict zones" (May 1998). Retrieved September 5, 2007, from http://www.basicint.org/pubs/Papers/BP26.htm.
29. The reader is referred to the vast literature on this area, perhaps starting with web accessible resources at the British American Security Information Council, http://www.basicint.org/WT/wtindex.htm, Oxfam's 2003 report "A Catalogue of Failures: G* Arms Exports and Human Rights Violations", http://web.amnesty.org/library/index/engior300032003 and various publications from the Stockholm International Peace Research Institute: www.sipri.org.
30. S. Chan and W. Safran, "Public Opinion as a Constraint against War: Democracies' Response to Operation Iraqi Freedom," *Foreign Policy Analysis*, 2 (2006), 137.
31. See discussion in J. N. Maogoto, *State Sovereignty and International Criminal Law*.
32. United States v. Emerson, 270 203 (5th Cir. 2001), holding that the right is individual, and Nordyke v. King, 319 1185 (9th Cir. 2003), that the right is collective. For discussion, see R. Hardaway, E. Gormley and B. Taylor, "The Inconvenient Militia Clause of the Second Amendment: Why the Supreme Court Declines to Resolve the Debate over the Right to Bear Arms," *St. John's Journal of Legal Commentary*, 16 (2002), 99.
33. R. Hardaway, E. Gormley and B. Taylor, "The Inconvenient Militia Clause of the Second Amendment."
34. E. H. Monkkonen, "History of Urban Police," *Crime and Justice*, 15 (1992), 547, p. 549.
35. C. Edwards, "Democratic Control of Police: How 19th Century Political Systems Determine Modern Political Structures," paper presented at the History of Crime, Policing and Punishment Conference convened by the and held in Canberra, (December 9–10, 1999), p. 2; and generally, C. Edwards, *Changing Policing Theories for 21st century societies*, 2nd edn (Leichhart: Federation Press, 2005).
36. See, for example, the survey in D. Dixon, *Law in Policing: Legal Regulation and Police Practices* (Oxford: Clarendon Press, 1997).
37. M. Lipson, "Private Security: A Retrospective," *Annals of the American Academy of Political and Social Science*, 498 The Private Security Industry: Issues and Trends. (1988) 11, p. 15.
38. D. Dixon, *Law in Policing*.
39. P. Stenning, *Private Policing—Some Recent Myths, Developments and Trends*: Law Commission of Canada, 2006, p. 149.
40. Ibid., p. 148.
41. J. Freeman, "Extending Public Law Norms Through Privatization," *Harvard Law Review* 116 (2003), p. 1287.
42. P. Singer, *Corporate Warriors*.
43. National Commonwealth Audit, "Report to the Commonwealth Government (Australia)" (1996).
44. J. E. Stiglitz, *Globalization and its Discontents* (New York: Norton, 2002), pp. 53–61.
45. P. Singer, *Corporate Warriors*; see Singer's discussion of the composition of the market, pp. 78–80.

46. A. Markusen, "The Case against Privatizing National Security," *Governance: The International Journal of Policy, Administration and Institutions*, 16 (2003), 471, p. 471.
47. Ibid., and P. Singer, *Corporate Warriors*, p. 157.
48. Refer to the debate over privatization of public water utilities in South Africa (the question of "Public Private Partnerships in Water and Sanitation"), as reproduced in a compilation of news articles and commentary accessible on "The Water Page" website, http://www.thewaterpage.com/ppp_debate.htm (last visited October 27, 2005).
49. C. P. L. M. Lynch, "Testimony of California Public Utilities," paper presented before the US Senate Commerce, Science & Transportation Committee (March 15, 2002).
50. "Chunnel may 'cost taxpayers millions'," *BBC News* (March 28, 2001).
51. For example, governments have been required to bring plants and services up to particular standards to render them marketable; further, it is not uncommon for state-owned enterprises to be sold at prices set well below value. M. Hossain and J. Malbon (eds.), *Who Benefits from Privatisation?* (Taylor & Francis Group, 1998). See, for example, A. Brown, "The Economics of Privatisation: Case Study of Australian Telecommunications," in Hossain and Malbon (eds.), *Who Benefits from Privatisation?* (Taylor & Francis Group, 1998).
52. B. Sheehy, "Scrooge the reluctant Stakeholder," *U. of Miami B.L.R.* (2005).
53. P. Singer, *Corporate Warriors*, pp. 49–51.
54. Ibid., p. 50.
55. Ibid., pp. 55–7.
56. See, for example, H. Zinn, *A People's History of the United States* (New York: HarperCollins Publisher Inc., 1980), pp. 11–12.
57. For example, the private aspect of the supply chain of military hardware (the "military industrial complex") has forged a longstanding relationship between states and private companies and is one facet of the nascent defense market. In this context, consider the competition between Boeing and Lockheed Martin to be the preferred supplier of fighter jets during the Cold War.
58. A. Markusen, "The Case against Privatizing National Security," *Governance*, p. 476.
59. B. Yeoman, "Soldiers of Good Fortune," *The Independent Weekly, INDY.* (2003).
60. D. D. Avant, "Privatizing Military Training," *Foreign Policy in Focus*, 5 (2000).
61. Ibid.
62. D. Avant, "Private Military Companies and the Future of War" (2006). Retrieved September 5, 2007, from http://www.fpri.org/enotes/200604.military.avant.privatemilitarycompanies.html.
63. D. H. Rumsfeld, "Transforming the Military," *Foreign Affairs*, May/June (2002).
64. The privatization of global water services has resulted in "huge profits [for the private corporations], higher prices for water, cut-offs to customers who cannot pay, little transparency in their dealings, reduced water quality, bribery, and corruption." M. Barlow and T. Clarke, "Water Privatization: The World Bank's Latest Market Fantasy" (2004).
65. One current well known example is the situation in Myanmar (formerly Burma), where an invidious military dictatorship, calling itself SLORC (the State Law and Order Restoration Council), maintains its iron grip on power, despite the tireless agitation of Nobel Peace Prize laureate Daw Aung San Suu Kyi, and the selfless sacrifices of countless martyrs. See Ms. Suu Kyi's website, Daw Aung San Suu Kyi's pages, "Daw Aung San Suu Kyi." Retrieved February 12, 2007, from www.dassk.org.

66. W. Blum, *Killing Hope: U.S. Military and CIA Interventions since World War II*, (Monroe ME: Common Courage Press, 1995).
67. Including sexual slavery, prostitution and illegal arms trade. Discussed in P. Singer, *Corporate Warriors*, p. 222.
68. For a narrative of the events, see the account of the barrister involved in proceedings in the USA, G. Robertson, *The Justice Game* (Sydney: Random House Australia (Pty) Ltd, 1999), pp. 242–62.
69. R. Weber, *Swords into Dow Shares.*
70. P. Singer, *Corporate Warriors*, pp. 165–6.
71. Ibid., p. 151.
72. Ibid., pp. 152–4.
73. Ibid.
74. C. Lehnardt, *Regulating the private commercial military sector* (New York: Institute for International Law and Justice, New York University School of Law, n.d.), p. 8.
75. P. Singer, *Corporate Warriors*, pp. 154–7.
76. Examples of such acts are too numerous to mention. One can look at investigations ongoing into contractors in Iraq, Defence Industry Initiate reports, or for a broader discussion see in Ibid., pp. 151–68 and chapters 2 and 4 of this volume.
77. *Combatting War Profiteering: Are we doing enough to investigate and prosecute contracting fraud and abuse in Iraq?* (2007), pp. 1–2.
78. Ibid., the OIG's report, Appendix 3, p. 7.
79. Ibid., p. 4.
80. A. Markusen, "The Case against Privatizing National Security," *Governance.*
81. Ibid., p. 493.
82. One is tempted to recall the Thirty Years War and the manner in which the Holy Roman Emperor Ferdinand turned to the financier and mercenary Albrecht Eusebius Wenzel von Wallenstein. P. Singer, "The Ultimate Military Entrepreneur," *Q. J. Mil Hist*, Spring (2003b), 1.at 9.
83. P. Singer, *Corporate Warriors*, p. 157.
84. Ibid., pp. 157–8.
85. D. Isenberg, "A Fistful of Contractors," British American Security Information Council, 2004, p. 31.
86. Ibid., p. 70.
87. A. Markusen, "The Case against Privatizing National Security," *Governance*, p. 19.
88. This relationship between state and corporation has come under considerable scrutiny and subjected to serious challenge by the development of multinational corporations. See discussion, for example, in I. Simonovic, "Relative Sovereignty of the Twenty First Century."
89. P. Singer, *Corporate Warriors*, pp. 165–6.
90. E. Krahmann, "Private Military Services in the UK and Germany," p. 28.
91. W. Laufer, *Corporate Bodies and Guilty Minds*, pp. 32–3.
92. F. Schreier and M. Caparini, *Privatising Security*, p. 52.
93. Ibid.
94. The balance of this section, Control of the PMC—Contracting is from the V. Newell and B. Sheehy.
95. M. McNamara, "Contestability and Incentives," 81 Canberra Bulletin of Public Administration 2, 81, 7, 8.
96. Ibid.
97. Ibid.
98. The PNG government did not pursue this payment option. Ibid., pp. 294–5 (citing a government inquiry).

99. Joint Committee on Foreign Affairs, Parliament of Australia, Defence and Trade, "Bougainville: The Peace Process and Beyond" (1999). Retrieved March 29, 2007, chapter 2, para. 22–37.
100. D. J. Brooks, "The Business End of Military Intelligence: Private Military Companies."
101. See, for example, insurance costs for PMC employees, noted in Isenberg page 25.
102. P. Singer, *Corporate Warriors*, p. 187.
103. Ibid., p. 118.
104. Ibid., p. 55.
105. G. Turbiville Jr., "Outlaw Private Security Firms," 561.
106. Aristotle, *On Rhetoric: A Theory of Civic Discourse* (Oxford: Oxford University Press, 1991).
107. S. W. I. Jennings, *The Law and the Constitution 45*, 1959.
108. N. S. Marsh, "Int'l Comm'n of Jurists," *The Rule of Law in a Free Society-Report of the International Congress of Jurists* (1959), p. 313.
109. R. Peerenboom (ed.), *Asian Discourses of Rule of Law: Theories and Implementation of the Rule of Law in Twelve Asian Countries, France and the U.S.* (1 ed.), (Oxford: RoutledgeCurzon, 2004), p. 2.
110. Prosecuting an action in this context is very difficult for a variety of reasons. The law may, in straightforward terms, prohibit a government from declaring war or using its military without democratic approval—but a court may not consider a PMC contract as falling within its scope. Consider, for example, the various efforts made to litigate questions related both to the Vietnam and Iraq wars in US courts, as well as the concerted attempts by governments to pervert and avoid applicable laws. J. Maogoto and B. Sheehy, "Torturing the Rule of Law: USA and the Post 9-11 Legal World," *St. John's J. of Legal Commentary*, 21 (2007), pp. 689–725.
111. S. G. Brennan, "The Purpose and Scope of Judicial Review," in Taggart (ed.), *Judicial Review of Administrative Action in the 1980's: Problems and Prospects* (Oxford: Oxford University Press, 1986), p. 19.
112. S. de Smith, H. Woolf and J. Jowell, *de Smith's Judicial Review of Administrative Action*, 4th edn (London: Sweet & Maxwell, 1980), p. 3.
113. S. A. Mason, "The High Court as Gatekeeper," *Melbourne University LR*, 24 (2000) 784, p. 788.
114. See, for example, H. W. Ballantine, "Constitutional Limitations on the War Powerq," *Viginia Law Review*, 3 (1918), 721–729.
115. Ibid.
116. The Constitution of the United States of America (1776).
117. T. Franck, "The United States Constitution in its Third Century: Foreign Affairs: Distribution of Constitutional Authority: Rethinking War Powers: By Law or by 'Thaumaturgic Invocation'?," *A.J.I.L.* 83 (1989), 766.
118. United States v. American Tel. & Tel. Co., 567 121 (D.C. Cir. 1977), p. 128.
119. Chicago & Southern Air Lines, Inc. v. Waterman S. S. Corp., 333 103 1948, p. 111.
120. See discussion in J. K. Elsea, M. J. Garcia and T. J. Nicola, *Congressional Authority to Limit U.S. Military Operations in Iraq* (Washington: Congressional Research Service, 2007), p. 14.
121. Council of Civil Service Unions v Minister for the Civil Service 374 (House of Lords, 1985).
122. Joint Committee on Foreign Affairs, Parliament of Australia, Defence and Trade., "Bougainville: The Peace Process and Beyond" (1999). Retrieved March 29, 2007. Ch. 2 para. 25 (September 27, 1999), available at http://www.aph.gov.au/house/committee/jfadt/bougainville/BV_chap2.htm.

123. S. Dinnen, R. May and A. Regan (eds.), *Agreement for the Provision of Military Assistance between the Independent State of Papua New Guinea and Sandline International* (Canberra: Research School of Pacific and Asian Studies, Australian National University (ANU), 1997) at para. 4.1 (assigning Papua New Guinea's contractual responsibilities). The agreement delegated far-reaching military command authority to Sandline's personnel:

    Immediately on signing this agreement the state automatically grants to Sandline and its personnel all approvals, permissions, authorizations, licenses and permits to carry arms, conduct its operations and meet its contractual obligations without hindrance, including issuing instructions to PNG defense forces personnel to co-operate fully with Sandline commanders and their nominated representatives. All officers and personnel of Sandline assigned to this contract shall be enrolled as Special Constables, but hold military ranks commensurate with those they hold within the Sandline command structure and shall be entitled to give orders to junior ranks as may be necessary for the execution of their duties and responsibilities.

124. The director of the Forum was arrested as a result of its opposition to the Sandline initiative. See Ibid., p. 287.
125. Virginia Newell suggested this sharp turn of phrase.
126. J. Yoo, "Using Force," *University of Chicago Law Review*, 71 (2004), 729, p. 735. Shared by M. A. Murphy, "A 'World Occupation' of the Iraqi Economy? How Order 39 Will Create a Semi-Sovereign State," *Connecticut Journal of International Law*, 19 (2004), 445.
127. W. Blum, *Killing Hope: US Military and CIA Interventions Since World War II.*
128. M. Foucault, "Neitzche, Genealogy and History," in Rabinow (ed.), *The Foucault Reader* (New York: Pantheon, 1984), p. 85.
129. For a brief history of the reliance of states on mercenaries, see J. –C. Zarate, "The Emergence of a New Dog of War," pp. 76–156.
130. For example, the company website stated the company would only undertake projects on behalf of internationally recognized governments (preferably those that are democratically elected), international institutions like the UN, and internationally recognized liberation movements. http://www.sandline.com/company/index.html (cached webpage).
131. E. Bernales Ballesteros, *Report on the Question of the Use of Mercenaries as a Means of Violating Human Rights and Impeding the Exercise of the Right of People to Self Determination*: UN Econ & Soc Council, 1998, para. 50, reads:

    The fact that a Government hires mercenaries or turns to "qualified" companies that provide mercenary services for its own defence and to strengthen positions during armed conflicts should not be invoked in claiming that its action is legal. A Government is endowed with legitimacy in order to work within its constitutional framework and that of the international treaties to which it is a party. Under no circumstances, however, may they use the power entrusted to them to engage in acts that are contrary to self-determination, to jeopardize the independence and sovereignty of the State itself or to consent to acts that may do irreparable harm to the life and security of the inhabitants.

132. Green Paper: Private Military Companies Options for Regulation, House of Commons, 20 Cong. Rec. 577 (2001/2002) p. 15.
133. D. Shearer, "Outsourcing War," *Foreign Policy*, Fall (1998) 68–69, p. 80.
134. E. Bernales Ballesteros, *Report on the Question of the Use of Mercenaries as a Means of Violating Human Rights and Impeding the Exercise of the Right of People to Self Determination*, at para. 50. A similar quotation from a later report by the

Rapporteur is cited in the Green Paper, Green Paper: Private Military Companies Options for Regulation, House of Commons, 20 Cong. Rec. 577 (2001/2002) p. 15. Mr. Ballesteros's comment posits the illegality of mercenary activity in particular, not all PMC undertakings.

135. Green Paper: Private Military Companies Options for Regulation, House of Commons, 20 Cong. Rec. 577 (2001/2002) p. 15.
136. Ibid., p. 5.
137. "Africa US PMC: Private Military Companies Washington's Use of Private Companies is Challenging AU Precepts," *Africa Research Bulletin*, 44 (April 2007), 17024.
138. R. Reid and M. Lee, "Diplomatic Convoys Curtailed in Iraq" (September 18,). Retrieved September 18, 2007, from http://news.yahoo.com/s/ap/20070918/ap_on_re_mi_ea/iraq.
139. D. McClemore, "DynCorp Wants to Hire Temporary Agents, but Officials Say They Don't Need the Help" (September 6, 2007). Retrieved September 10, 2007, from http://www.dallasnews.com/sharedcontent/dws/news/texassouthwest/stories/090607dntexbprecruiting.35ff674.html#.
140. See Isenberg (2004), pp. 39–40.
141. D. Isenberg, "A Fistful of Contractors," British American Security Information Council, 2004, p. 39.
142. J. Scahill, "A Very Private War," *Guardian* (2007b, August 1, 2007).
143. D. J. Brooks, "The Business End of Military Intelligence: Private Military Companies," p. 3.
144. Ibid. Brooks does note the competence of the Botswana forces and a number of unspecified other forces. D. Brooks, "Private military service providers: Africa's welcome pariahs," p. 3.
145. D. Brooks, *Ruthless Humanitarianism: Why ignoring the private security option in Darfur is a mistake* (n.d., from http://www.goodmagazine.com/section/Provocations/ruthless_humanitarianism).
146. R. Ulam Weiner, "Peace Corp. As the international community dithers over Darfur, private military companies say they've got what it takes to stop the carnage, if only someone would hire them," *Boston Globe* (2006).
147. A. Leander and R van Munster, "Private Security Contractors in the debate about Darfur: Reflecting and Reinforcing Neo-Liberal Governmentality," *International Relations*, 21 (2006), 201.
148. J. Scahill, "Bush's Shadow Army."
149. A. Leander, *Regulating the Role of PMCs in Shaping Security and Policy*, (Copenhagen: Copenhagen Business School, n.d.), p. 26.
150. J. K. Elsea, *Private Security Contractors in Iraq: Background, Legal Status, and Other Issues* (Washington: Congressional Research Service, 2007). In her report, Elsea cites or refers to Brooks (ten times), Peter Singer (six times), Deborah Avant (twice), Simon Chesterman (once), and Fred Schreier (once).
151. A. Leander and R van Munster, "Private Security Contractors in the debate about Darfur."
152. J. Harding, "Background briefing on Diamond Mercenaries of Africa" (1996), quoted in A. F. Musah, "Privatization of Security, Arms Proliferation and the Process of State Collapse in Africa," *Development and Change*, 33 (2002), 911, p. 11.
153. D. Brooks, "Creating the Renaissance Peace: The Utilisation of Private Companies for Peacekeeping and Peace Enforcement Activities in Africa," paper presented at the Africa Institute of South Africa's 40th Anniversary Conference, Pretoria, South Africa (2000a, May 30–June 2, 2000), p. 8.

154. D. Brooks, "Hope for the 'Hopeless Continents': Mercenaries", *Traders: Journal for the Southern African Region*, 3 (2000b), pp. 1–37.
155. D. Brooks, "Private military service providers: Africa's welcome pariahs," p. 6.
156. D Brooks, "Hope for the 'Hopeless Continents': Mercenaries," p. 4.
157. J. Astill, "British mercenaries find a new ferocity in Ivory Coast: Shunned by the west, soldiers of fortune scent new opportunities in Africa," *Guardian* (February 22, 2003).
158. A. Markusen, "The Case against Privatizing National Security," *Governance*, p. 485.
159. D. Isenberg, "A Government in Search of Cover: PMCS in Iraq," paper presented at the Market Forces: Regulating Private Military Companies, New York (March 23–24, 2006), lists several examples, pp. 5–6.
160. M. Small, "Privatisation of Security and Military Functions and the Demise of the Modern Nation-State in Africa," 1 (2006) discusses this in detail.
161. D. Isenberg, "A Fistful of Contractors," British American Security Information Council, 2004, makes this theme of costs and benefits central to his work.
162. P. Singer, *Corporate Warriors*, p. 218 ("The rationale for using PMCs instead of official covert action is that they give the cover of plausible deniability that public forces lack. If an operation goes awry, the activities of a firm are easier for a government to deny and the blame simpler to shift.").
163. B. Yeoman, "Soldiers of Good Fortune,". Yeoman notes the reaction of Congresswoman Jan Schakowsky (D-Ill): "Under a shroud of secrecy, the United States is carrying out military missions with people who don't have the same level of accountability.... We have individuals who are not obligated to follow orders or follow the Military Code of Conduct. Their main obligation is to their employer, not to their country."
164. M. Staff, *Additional Information for Hearing on Private Security Contractors*: Committee on Oversight and Government Reform, 2007, p. 3.
165. J. Scahill, "Bush's Shadow Army."
166. Ibid.
167. B. Debusmann, "In Outsourced U.S. Wars, Contractor Deaths Top 1,000" (July 3, 2007). Retrieved August 1, 2007, from http://news.yahoo.com/s/nm/20070703/wl_nm/usa_iraq_contractors_dc. It is important to avoid equating contractors with private security workers. The statistic cited is not limited to security contractors. The actual figures are simply not available.
168. Reported on The Intelligence Daily, "The Nation's Jeremy Scahill on the Impact of Private Military Contractors on the Conduct of the Iraq War" (May 12, 2007). Retrieved Septebmer 10, 2007, from http://www.inteldaily.com/?c=138&a=1973.
169. Quoted in J. Scahill, "Bush's Shadow Army."
170. Where a PMC is being paid by a company, group, or individual, then one may posit that a nonstate entity is intervening in the affairs of a state contrary to its wishes.
171. Of course, where sovereignty is contested—as in many institutionally and economically weak countries that have recently confronted internal upheavals (such as Rwanda and the Democratic Republic of Congo)—the issue becomes which group within the state is rightfully able to request external assistance.
172. "Defence Contractors: Military Industrial Complexities," *Economist*, 366 (2003) see also P. Singer, "War, Profits, and the Vacuum of Law" 521–42, p. 523.
173. J. Christoff, *Stabilizing and Rebuilding Iraq: Coalition Support and International Donor Commitments: GAO-07-827T* (Washington: U.S. Government Accountability Office, 2007). See also P. Dombrowski and R. A. Payne, "Global Debate and the

Limits of the Bush Doctrine," *International Studies Perspectives*, 14 (2003), 395. For an evaluation see S. Patrick, "Beyond Coalitions of the Willing: Assessing U.S. Multilateralism," *Ethics & International Affairs*, 17 (2003), 37.

174. Noted as such in J. K. Elsea, *Private Security Contractors in Iraq: Background, Legal Status, and Other Issues* (Washington: Congressional Research Service, 2007), pp. 25–6; and P. Singer, *The Private Military Industry and Iraq: What Have We Learned and Where to Next?* (Geneva: Geneva Centre for the Democratic Control of Armed Forces, 2004a), p. 6.
175. M. Staff, *Additional Information for Hearing on Private Security Contractors*: Committee on Oversight and Government Reform, 2007), p. 2.
176. J. K. Elsea, *Private Security Contractors in Iraq: Background, Legal Status, and Other Issues* (Washington: Congressional Research Service, 2007), p. 3.
177. Ibid., p. 4.
178. M. Staff, *Additional Information for Hearing on Private Security Contractors*: Committee on Oversight and Government Reform, 2007), p. 2. J. K. Elsea, *Private Security Contractors in Iraq: Background, Legal Status, and Other Issues* (Washington: Congressional Research Service, 2007). Several months later still holds a 20,000 figure.
179. R. Norton-Taylor, "Fears over huge growth in Iraq's unregulated private armies," *Guardian* (October 31, 2006).
180. J. Christoff, *Stabilizing and Rebuilding Iraq: Coalition Support and International Donor Commitments: GAO-07-827T.* (Washington: US Government Accountability Office, 2007).
181. D. Isenberg, "A Fistful of Contractors," British American Security Information Council, 2004, p. 28.
182. J. K. Elsea, *Private Security Contractors in Iraq: Background, Legal Status, and Other Issues* (Washington: Congressional Research Service, 2007), p. 25, P. Singer, *The Private Military Industry and Iraq*, p. 10.
183. J. Kwok, "Armed Entrepreneurs: Private Military Companies in Iraq."
184. P. Singer, "War, Profits, and the Vacuum of Law,"521–42., pp. 522–3. These services are described in J. Kwok, "Armed Entrepreneurs: Private Military Companies in Iraq.", and D. Isenberg, "A Fistful of Contractors," British American Security Information Council, 2004.
185. J. McCarthy, "Letters from the Frontline," *Newcastle Herald* (September 18, 2004), p. 4 (citing an email from Grant Cook).
186. Ibid.
187. Ibid.
188. For example—in April 2004, to coordinate PMC security services by controlling personnel quality—the Coalition Provisional Authority took steps to ensure that all PMCs operating in Iraq were registered with the Ministry of the Interior, and that PMC personnel registered the serial numbers of their weapons and disclosed their rules of combat engagement. M. P. Flaherty and D. Priest, "Iraq: More Limits Sought for Private Security Teams," *Washington Post* (April 13, 2004).
189. R. Reid and M. Lee, "Diplomatic Convoys Curtailed in Iraq" Retrieved September 18, 2007, from http://news.yahoo.com/s/ap/20070918/ap_on_re_mi_ea/iraq.
190. D. Isenberg, "A Government in Search of Cover: PMCS in Iraq," paper presented at the Market Forces: Regulating Private Military Companies, New York (March 23–24, 2006), p. 11.

191. That the Iraq invasion furthers US foreign policy can be inferred from the manner in which the US government has justified the invasion. Stated objectives have changed over time: from ridding the world of Saddam Hussein; to removing weapons of mass destruction; to fighting the good fight against terrorism; to promoting democracy. The unstated foreign policy objectives remain objects of supposition but certainly include securing access to a stable oil supply and exerting geopolitical influence in the Middle East.
192. P. Singer, *The Private Military Industry and Iraq*, p. 10.
193. S. Chan and W. Safran, "Public Opinion as a Constraint against War: Democracies' Response to Operation Iraqi Freedom."
194. P. Chatterjee, "Darfur Diplomacy: Enter the Contractors," *CorpWatch* (October 21, 2004). Available at: http://www.corpwatch.org/article.php?id=11598.
195. Ibid.
196. Ibid.
197. "Africa US PMC: Private Military Companies Washington's use of private companies is challenging AU precepts," *Africa Research Bulletin*, 44 (April 2007), 17024.
198. Ibid.
199. "Profile of DynCorp" (2007). Retrieved September 17, 2007.
200. "US firm to turn south Sudan rebels into soldiers," *Sudan Tribune* (August 12, 2006).
201. Ibid.
202. Ibid.
203. P. Chatterjee, "Darfur Diplomacy: Enter the Contractors."
204. Mr. Chatterjee attributed this conclusion to an anonymous official. Ibid.
205. "Africa-US Private Military Companies," *Africa Research Bulletin: Political, Social and Cultural Series*, 44 (2007), 17204.
206. Noted in the context of Australian foreign policy in G. Smith and D. Lowe, "Howard, Downer and the Liberal's Realist Tradition," *Australian Journal of Politics and History*, 51 (2005), 495.
207. B. Simpson, "Solidarity in an Age of Globalization: The transnational movement for East Timor and U.S. foreign policy," *Peace & Change*, 29 (2004), 453.
208. Ibid., p. 454.
209. N. Wheeler and T. Dunne, "East Timor and the new humanitarian interventionism," *International Affairs*, 77 (2001), 805, p. 807 ff.
210. Ibid., p. 810.
211. G. Smith and D. Lowe, "Howard, Downer and the Liberal's Realist Tradition," pp. 464–5, and a theme in N. Wheeler and T. Dunne, "East Timor and the new humanitarian interventionism."
212. Chubb Security Holdings Australia Ltd. (part of Chubb PLC, which is now a business unit of United Technologies Corporation).
213. Countries like Australia and New Zealand had sent contingencies of their Armed Forces to secure East Timor from internal and external threats.
214. As a postscript to Australia's use of Chubb in East Timor, the Trade Union Confederation of Timor Lorosae complained in 2003 that Chubb was one of the worst employers in East Timor, due to its record of nepotism.
215. Summarized in the report of the House Committee on Foreign Affairs, "East Timor" Senate Committee on Foreign Relations and the House Committee on International Relations, *Country Reports on Human Rights Practices for 2002* (Washington2002), pp. 786–7.
216. B. Yeoman, "Soldiers of Good Fortune."

217. Ibid. The person cited was US State Department official Bennet Freeman.
218. D. Sanger, "Playing the Trade Card," *New York Times* (1997), p. C1.
219. Started under the CPA, see M. A. Murphy, "A 'World Occupation' of the Iraqi Economy? How Order 39 Will Create a Semi-Sovereign State," *Connecticut Journal of International Law*, 19 (2004), 445 and A. K. Audi, "Iraq's New Investment Laws and the Standard of Civilization: A Case Study on the Limits of International Law," *Georgetown Law Journal*, 93 (2004), 335. For broader discussion, see K. E. Boon, "'Open for Business': International Financial Institutions, Post-conflict Economic Reform and the Rule of Law," *New York University Journal of International Law & Policy*, 39 (2007), 513.
220. See N. Chomsky and R. W. McChesney, *Profit Over People: Neoliberalism & Global Order*, 1 (New York: Seven Stories Press, 1999), pp. 68–72 (asserting that US exportation of American "values" is simply a facade that allows American oversight); see also H. Zinn, *A People's History of the United States* (charting recourse to Wilsonian idealism as a cloak for predatory foreign policy initiatives). See discussion in C. B. D. Grant, *U.S. Military Expertise for Sale: Private Military Consultants as a Tool of Foreign Policy* (US Army War College, 1998).
221. K. Silverstein, "Obiang's Banking Again: State Department and Washington insiders help a dictator get what he wants," *Harper's Magazine* (August 9, 2006).
222. A. Smoltczyk, "Rich in Oile, Poor in Human Rights: Torture and Poverty in Equatorial Guinea," *Der Spiegel* (August 28, 2006).
223. N. Hughes, "Democracy and Imperial Rivalry in Equatorial Guinea," *Review of African Political Economy*, 23 (1996), 442.
224. K. Silverstein, "Obiang's Banking Again: State Department and Washington insiders help a dictator get what he wants," *Harper's Magazine* (August 9, 2006).
225. B. Yeoman, "Soldiers of Good Fortune."
226. D. Kassebaum, "A Question of Facts," pp. 581–2.
227. P. Singer, *Corporate Warriors*, p. 31. D. Kassebaum, "A Question of Facts," pp. 581–2.
228. P. Singer, *Corporate Warriors*, p. 31.
229. D. Kassebaum, "A Question of Facts," note 227, p. 582.
230. Ibid.
231. Ibid., p. 583.
232. F. Schreier and M. Caparini, *Privatising Security*, p. 137.
233. Ibid.
234. Ibid., p. 138.

4 National Regulation of Private Military Companies

Parts of this chapter were drawn from earlier research which was incorporated into a co-authored article: V. Newell and B. Sheehy, "Corporate Militaries and States," pp. 67–101. The section introducing regulation was drawn from B. Sheehy, "Rethinking Securities Regulation: A Comparative Study of ASC, NYSE and SGX," *The Corporate Governance Law Review*, 2 (2006), p. 191.

1. T. Daintith, "The Executive Power Today: Bargaining and Economic Control," in Jowell and Oliver (eds.), *The Changing Constitution* (1985) cited in C. Graham, "Self-Regulation," in Richardson and Genn (eds.), *Administrative Law and Government Action* (Oxford: Oxford University Press, 1995).
2. P. P. Craig, *Administrative Law*, 4th edn (Sydney: Thomson Sweet & Maxwell, 2003), 29–38.

3. Ibid., 38–42.
4. This move away from direct legislative control has prompted comment. See, for example, S. Bottomley, "Where did the law go? The delegation of Australian corporate regulation," *Australian Journal of Corporate Law*, 15 (2003), 11.
5. Ibid., n. 119, 329.
6. See the sophisticated analysis of regulation particularly as it applies to environmental matters in N. Gunningham, P. W. Grabosky and D. Sinclair, *Smart Regulation: Designing Environmental Policy* (Oxford: Oxford University Press, 1998).
7. Discussed in T. Wilkins and T. E. Hunt, "Agency Discretion and Advances in Regulatory Theory: Flexible Agency Approaches Toward the Regulated Community as a Model for the Congress-Agency Relationship," *George Washington Law Review*, 63 (1995), 479, especially 492–8 et passim. These authors note a newer trend in which a voluntary preventative approach is taken as opposed to correcting current known problems or retribution type action.
8. The "Better Regulation Guide" (1998) of Cabinet Office of the UK identifies eleven alternatives in regulation: (1) do nothing: not every problem can be solved by government regulation, (2) review current regulation to determine whether regulation can improve or is the cause of the problem, (3) improve information to address information asymmetry problems, (4) introduce voluntary scheme, (5) consider code of practice with legal effect, (6) request industry to self-regulate, (7) use economic incentives, (8) consider risk-based insurance, (9) classic command and control regulation, (10) license the problematic activity, and (11) use international regulation. Quoted in Ibid., 31–2. A broader discussion on the limits of regulation can be found in I. Maitland, "The Limits of Business Self-Regulation," *California Management Review*, 27 (1985) 132.
9. There are at least six general reasons agencies are developed: (1) as a buffer between the public interests and politically motivated interference from the government, (2) escaping traditional governmental weaknesses, (3) bringing the appropriate specialists to the problem, (4) spread power, (5) create an smoother, accessible, specialized office to address matters, and (6) avoid creating too many direct bureaucrats. Identified by "Public Policy and Private Interests: The Institutions of Compromise," in Hague, Mackenzie and Barker (eds.) (1975) 362, cited in P. P. Craig, *Administrative Law*, 119, 92.
10. P. P. Craig, *Administrative Law*, 264–5.
11. C. Graham, "Self-Regulation," in Richardson and Genn (eds.), *Administrative Law and Government Action*, 199–202.
12. P. P. Craig, *Administrative Law*, 331.
13. Ibid., 345–9.
14. See, V. Haufler, *A Public Role for the Private Sector: Industry Self-Regulation in a Global Economy* (Washington, DC: Carnegie Endowment for International Peace, 2001).
15. N. Gunningham, P. w. Grabosky and D. Sinclair, *Smart Regulation: Designing Environmental Policy*, 159–63.
16. A. McColl, "The Not-So-White Companies: PMF's & Perceptions of Legitimacy," paper presented at the Critical Management Studies, University of Cambridge (2007, July 4–6, 2005).
17. B. Purchase, "The Political Economy of Voluntary Codes," in Webb (ed.), *Voluntary Codes: Private Governance, the Public Interest and Innovation* (Ottawa: Carelton Research Unit for Innovation, Science and Environment, 2004), p. 81.

18. Ibid., p. 82.
19. N. Gunningham, P. w. Grabosky and D. Sinclair, *Smart Regulation: Designing Environmental Policy*, 159.
20. D. Brooks, "Creating the Renaissance Peace," paper presented at the Africa Institute of South Africa's 40th Anniversary Conference, Pretoria, South Africa (May 30–June 2, 2000), p. 9.
21. We are taken aback by the audacity of the PMC/PSC industry in naming their industry association the International Peace Operations Associations and their reference to the "peace and stability industry". We appreciate that certain companies within the PMC/PSC industry are trying to put their best foot forward and emphasize their ability to be a force for good in a conflict ridden world, but to suggest that IPOA members are peace operatives (or the implicit suggestion that PMCs are motivated by a desire to secure peace rather than profit) is insincere. We were reminded of George Orwell's 1946 essay, "Politics and the English Language," where he warns that, "Political language…is designed to make lies sound truthful and murder respectable and to give an appearance of solidity to pure wind": G. Orwell, *The Collected Essays:Journalism and Letters of George Orwell* (New York: Harcourt Brace Jovanovich, 1968). A more contemporary attack on such cynical misappropriation and devaluing of words for the purpose of obfuscation can be found in D. Watson, *Watson's Dictionary of Weasel Words, Contemporary Clichés, Cant & Management Jargon* (Australia: Knopf, 2004).
22. Surprisingly, the private security industry is not referred to as the private peace consultants industry.
23. I P O A (IPOA), "State of the Peace & Stability Operations Industry Survey 2006" (2006). Retrieved February 4, 2007, from http://ipoaonline.org/php/index.php?option=com_content&task=view&id=103&Itemid=110.
24. I P O A (IPOA), "Civilian Contractors in Iraq: Accountability and the Uniform Code of Military Justice" (2007). Retrieved February2, 2007, from http://ipoaonline.org/php/index.php?option=com_content&task=view&id=104&Itemid=80.
25. I P O A (IPOA), *International Peace Organisation Association Code of Conduct*, 2001, from http://ipoaonline.org/php/index.php?option=com_content&task=view&id=100&Itemid=108[4.1].
26. Ibid.
27. The reference to the Convention against Torture can be found in the nonbinding preface to the Code, along with the revised version of [1.3]. Is it possible that the IPOA and its members baulked at including a binding obligation to abide by the Convention against Torture and preferred a nonbinding recommendation in the preface to the Code? Alternatively, the IPOA and its members may simply have realised that [1.3] conflicted with other clauses of the Code.
28. I P O A (IPOA), "International Peace Organisation Association Code of Conduct", 2001, from http://ipoaonline.org/php/index.php?option=com_content&task=view&id=100&Itemid=108.
29. Public security is the term used to refer to security services provided by a host government. The Voluntary Principles acknowledge that companies are sometimes required to reimburse states for public security services.
30. H R US Department of State: Bureau of Democracy, and Labor, Voluntary Principles on Security and Human Rights (unpublished manuscript) (Washington, DC, 2001) p. 6. The principles are unhelpfully presented in a dot point format rather than being numbered.
31. Ibid., p. 9.

32. Amnesty International, "Voluntary Principles for Security and Human Rights" (2006). Retrieved February 11, 2007, from http://www.web.amnesty.org/pages/ec-voluntaryprinciples-eng.
33. "Niger Ten Years On: Injustice and Violence Haunt the Oil Delta, 2005" (2005). Retrieved February 17, 2007, from http://web.amnesty.org/library/Index/ENGAFR440222005?open&of=ENG-352.
34. Ibid.
35. "Lessons from the Voluntary Principles on Security and Human Rights" (November 3, 2005). Retrieved April 1, 2007, from www.bsr.org/BSRConferences/2005/materials/2005_BSR_Conference_Voluntary-Principles.pdf.
36. Amnesty International et al., "Joint Statement of Non-Governmental Organizations on Results of the January 2006 Plenary Session" (2006). Retrieved February 17, 2007, from http://www.humanrightsfirst.org/workers_rights/issues/vp/index.htm.
37. Ibid.
38. J. Sherman, "Options for Promoting Corporate Responsibility in Conflict Zones: Perspectives from the Private Sector," *International Peace Academy Report*, 3 (2002).
39. G. Ebbeck, "Mercenaries and the 'Sandline Affair,'" *Australian Defence Force Journal*, 113 (1998), p. 5–23.
40. Quoted in D. Isenberg, "A Fistful of Contractors," British American Security Information Council, 2004, p. 44.
41. E. Krahmann, "Private Military Services in the UK and Germany," 277.
42. Australian Parliament: Joint Standing Committee on Foreign Affairs, and Trade, "Bougainville: The Peace Process and Beyond," (1999), chapter 2, para. 25 and 77.
43. G. Ebbeck, "Mercenaries and the 'Sandline Affair,'" p. 16.
44. The PNG Government "suspended" the contract on March 20, 1997 subject to a judicial inquiry, and later argued during arbitration with Sandline regarding payment of the outstanding contract sum that the contract had been frustrated in that performance was, given political developments, no longer possible.
45. A. Regan and S. Dinnen, "The Sandline Affair: a Chronology of Significant Events," in Dinnen, May and Regan (eds.), *Challenging the State: The Sandline Affair in Papua New Guinea* (Canberra: Research School of Pacific and Asian Studies, Australian National University (ANU), 1998), 16–17.
46. The matter was the subject of an international arbitration ruling handed down in Australia on October 9, 1998, Sandline International Inc. v. Papua New Guinea, 117, 552–93.
47. S. Dorney, *The Sandline Affair* (Sydney: ABC Books, 1998), p. 177.
48. S. Dinnen, R. May and A. Regan (eds.), *Agreement for the Provision of Military Assistance between the Independent State of Papua New Guinea and Sandline International* (Canberra: Research School of Pacific and Asian Studies, Australian National University (ANU), 1997), in A. Regan and S. Dinnen, "The Sandline Affair: a Chronology of Significant Events," in Dinnen, May and Regan (eds.), *Challenging the State,* pp. 178–88 (Appendix). The agreement delegated far-reaching military command authority to Sandline's personnel:

    > Immediately on signing this agreement the State automatically grants to Sandline and its personnel all approvals, permissions, authorizations, licenses and permits to carry arms, conduct its operations and meet its contractual obligations without hindrance, including issuing instructions to PNG defence

forces personnel to co-operate fully with Sandline commanders and their nominated representatives. All officers and personnel of Sandline assigned to this contract shall be enrolled as Special Constables, but hold military ranks commensurate with those they hold within the Sandline command structure and shall be entitled to give orders to junior ranks as may be necessary for the execution of their duties and responsibilities.

49. See S. Dinnen, "Militaristic Solutions in a Weak State: Internal Security, Private Contractors, and Political Leadership in Papua New Guinea," *Contemporary Pacific*, 11 (1999) 279, pp. 294–5.
50. Ibid., citing a government inquiry.
51. A. Regan and S. Dinnen, "The Sandline Affair: A Chronology of Significant Events," in Dinnen, May and Regan (eds.), *Challenging the State*, p. 11. Also, Mr Justice Andrew suggested that Sandline may had hidden objectives when entering the contract with the PNG government that related to the Panguna mine: J. Andrew, *Report of the Commission of Inquiry into the Engagement of Sandline International*, 1997, para. 6.72 and 4.34.
52. International Covenant on Civil and Political Rights GA res. 2200A (XXI)-UN Doc. A/6316, 21 (1966), *International Covenant on Civil and Political Rights*, art. 1.
53. Australian Parliament: Joint Standing Committee on Foreign Affairs, and Trade, "Bougainville: The Peace Process and Beyond" (1999), para. 2.59–2.89.
54. P. Khareen, "Executive Outcomes—A corporate Conquest 'Reference,'" in Cilliers and Mason (eds.), *Peace, Profit or Plunder: The Privatization of Security in War-Torn African Societies* (Capetown: Institute for Security Studies, 1999), pp. 84 and 93.
55. V. Newell and B. Sheehy, "Corporate Militaries and States," p. 76.
56. A. M. Taguba, "Article 15–6 Investigation of the 800th Military Police Brigade" (2004). Retrieved February 12, 2007, from www.npr.org/iraq/2004/prison_abuse_report.pdf.
57. CACI deny that any of their staff were involved in the incidents of abuse photographed at Abu Ghraib but acknowledge some wrong dong by three of their employees at Abu Ghraib at some other time: "Frequently Asked Questions about CACI." Retrieved February 13, 2007, from http://www.caci.com/main_faq.shtml. Comments by Janis Karpinski, who had been in charge of the Abu Ghraib prison, suggest that only Titan employees appeared in the photographs of abuse from Abu Ghraib: M. Cohn, "Interview with Janis Karpinski: Abu Ghraib General Lambastes Bush Administration" (2005). Retrieved February 12, 2007, from http://www.truthout.org/docs_2005/082405Z.shtml.
58. M. Cohn, "Interview with Janis Karpinski: Abu Ghraib General Lambastes Bush Administration" (2005). Retrieved February 12, 2007, from http://www.truthout.org/docs_2005/082405Z.shtml.
59. CACI states that it did not provide contract services in Guantanamo Bay or Afghanistan but it does not comment on whether it employed interrogators with experience in those locations. CACI has confirmed that the majority of its interrogators were ex-military: CACI website.
60. M. Cohn, "Interview with Janis Karpinski: Abu Ghraib General Lambastes Bush Administration" (2005). Retrieved February 12, 2007, from http://www.truthout.org/docs_2005/082405Z.shtml.
61. CACI vehemently rejects loose references to it being a mercenary pointing to its 45 year of service to the US and describing itself a "national asset for national missions." It does not address the issue of whether or not it is rightly to be categorised as a PMC.

62. For example, CACI has stated that the interrogation services they provided at Abu Ghraib accounted for only 1 percent of its revenue in 2003: "Frequently Asked Questions about CACI." Retrieved February 13, 2007, from http://www.caci.com/main_faq.shtml.
63. Those services that only the military, or a person, acting under the authority of the military, could provide.
64. "Frequently Asked Questions about CACI." Retrieved February 13, 2007, from http://www.caci.com/main_faq.shtml.
65. J. K. Elsea, *Private Security Contractors in Iraq: Background, Legal Status, and Other Issues* (Washington: Congressional Research Service, 2007), p. 19.
66. Ibid., See discussion and review of legislation and precedents, pp. 17–24.
67. Zagorin, "The Abu Ghraib Cases: Not Yet Over," *Time* (August 29, 2007). For an article that surveys the possible options for prosecution of private contactors involved with abuses at Abu Ghraib, see A. H. de Wolf, "Modern Condottieri in Iraq: Privatizing War from the Perspective of International and Human Rights Law," *Indiana Journal of Global Studies*, 13 (2006), 315. See also, "Private Military Contractors." Retrieved February 13, 2007, from http://www.amnestyusa.org/business/pmc/HousePartyToolKit.pdf. P. Singer, "The Law Catches up to Private Militaries, Embeds" (January 3, 2007). Retrieved August 30, 2007, from http://www.defensetech.org/archives/ 003123.html.
68. *The Heavily Armed Private U.S. Military-Contrators in Iraq*, United States of America Congress (2007).
69. P. W. Singer, "War, Profits, and the Vacuum of Law," 521. p. 524.
70. Green Paper: Private Military Companies Options for Regulation, House of Commons, 20 Cong. Rec. 577 (2001/2002).
71. Ibid.
72. Ibid. See also, J. C. Zarate, "The Emergence of a New Dog of War," 75, p. 77.
73. J. C. Zarate, "The Emergence of a New Dog of War," 75, p. 80; See also, Green Paper: Private Military Companies Options for Regulation, House of Commons, 20 Cong. Rec. 577 (2001/2002), p. 14.
74. P. W. Singer, "War, Profits, and the Vacuum of Law," 521, p. 524.
75. J. C. Zarate, "The Emergence of a New Dog of War," 75, p. 76. The US, South Africa, UK, and Israel are the preferred bases for PMCs.
76. Ibid.
77. Ibid. p. 77–8.
78. P. W. Singer, "War, Profits, and the Vacuum of Law," 521, pp. 534–7.
79. Ibid.
80. C. Lehnardt, *Private Military Companies and State Responsibility* (No. 2007/2) (New York: Institute for International Law and Justice, 2007), pp. 6 ff.
81. A. E. Cha and R. Merle, "Line Increasingly Blurred Between Soldiers and Civilian Contractors."
82. These regulatory triggers were expounded by an Expert Committee convened in Geneva in January 2001 to discuss, among other things, problems arising from the current definition of a mercenary under international law. It concluded that there was a need for a broader definition of a mercenary that addressed motive, purpose, payment, type of action, and nationality. See also, E. B. Ballesteros, *Commission on Human Rights, Report on the Question of the Use of Mercenaries as a Means of Violating Human Rights and Impeding the Exercise of the Right of the Peoples to Self Determination* (No. Doc E/CN.4/1998/31), p. 120: "General Assembly resolution 52/112 requested the

Secretary-General to invite Governments to make proposals towards a clearer definition of mercenaries".

83. Marsh, "Two Sides of the Same Coin? The Legal and Illegal Trade in Small Arms," pp. 222–3.
84. P. Wilson, "Saudi arms deal puts Blair back in the spotlight," *The Weekend Australian* (September 22–23, 2007), 16.
85. *International Convention against the Recruitment, Use Financing and Training of Mercenaries* opened for signature on December 4, 1989, 2163 UNTS 75, art. 1 (entered into force on 20 October 2001) ('Convention on Mercenaries').
86. See, UN Working Group on Use of Mercenaries, "Media Release at the Conclusion of its Visit to Peru" (Press Release, February 5, 2007): "The Working Group is aware that the ways in which some private security companies recruit people in countries with high unemployment to provide security services in areas of armed conflict contributes to new forms of mercenarism." Note that the Commission on Human Rights ended the mandate of the Special Rapporteur in April 2005 and has since established a Working Group comprising five regional independent experts. There has been some suggestion that this move was the result of the Rapporteur, Shaista Shameem's, moves to open up dialog with the PMC industry and her outspoken warnings to re-examine the relevance of the term "mercenary" because "this derogatory term is completely unacceptable and is too often used to describe fully legal and legitimate companies engaged in vital support operations for humanitarian peace and stability operations": V. Ghebali, "The United Nations and the Dilemma of Outsourcing Peacekeeping Operation," in Bryden and Caparini (eds.), *Private Actors & Security Governance* (Geneva: Democratic Control of Armed Forces, 2006), p. 218.
87. In force generally from October 20, 2001, in accordance with article 19(1) following the deposit of the 22nd instrument of ratification.
88. As at February 2007 the signatories to the Convention on mercenaries were: Azerbaijan, Barbados, Belarus, Belgium, Cameroon, Costa Rica, Croatia, Cuba, Cyprus, Georgia, Guinea, Italy, Liberia, Libyan Arab Jamahiriya, Maldives, Mali, Mauritania, Moldova (Republic of), New Zealand, Qatar, Saudi Arabia, Senegal, Seychelles, Suriname, Togo, Turkmenistan, Ukraine, Uruguay, and Uzbekistan.
89. See New Zealand, Parliamentary Debates (Hansard), House of Representatives, November 5, 2006 and June 29, 2006; Report on Mercenary Activities (Prohibition) Bill, Foreign Affairs, Defence and Trade Committee, 82–3 Cong. Rec. (2004).
90. Ibid.
91. Ibid., s. 5.
92. Ibid., ss. 7–11.
93. Ibid., s. 2.
94. Ibid., s. 5(3).
95. See, for example the Australian employed by an American PMC in Iraq who was engaged to protect a convoy who reported firing to neutralize the insurgents, radicals, and criminals who were attacking; {Newell, 2007 #34}.
96. {Stuff.Com.NZ., 2007 #35}.
97. Arms Export Control Act, 22 2751–99 (2000). *Arms Export Control Act,* 22 U.S.C. §§ 2751–99 (2000); C. Walker and D. Whyte, "Contracting Out War?: Private Military Companies Law and Regulation in the United Kingdom," *International and Comparative Law Quarterly*, 54 (2005) *International Traffic in Arms Regulations,*

22 C.F.R. §§ 120–30 (2005). See also, P. W. Singer, "War, Profits, and the Vacuum of Law," 521, p. 533.

98. D. D. Avant, "Privatizing Military Training Foreign Policy in Focus," *Foreign Policy in Focus*, 5 (2000).
99. C. Walker and D. Whyte, "Contracting Out War," 22 C.F.R. §§ 123.15.
100. C. Holmqvist, "Private Security Companies: The Case for Regulation," *Stockholm International Peace Research Institute*, 9 (2005), 51.
101. Green Paper: Private Military Companies Options for Regulation, House of Commons, 20 Cong. Rec. 577 (2001/2002).
102. P. W. Singer, "War, Profits, and the Vacuum of Law," 521, p. 533.
103. See discussion in chapter 3.
104. C. Holmqvist, "Private Security Companies," p. 51.
105. "President Bush Delivers State of the Union Address," *The White House* (January 2007).
106. E. Krahmann, "Private Military Services in the UK and Germany," 277.
107. Reconstruction and Stabilization Civilian Management Act of 2006 (2006), s. 2.
108. Ibid., s. 7.
109. Ibid., s. 11.
110. S A P Parliamentary Monitoring Group, Prohibition of Mercenary Activities and Regulation of Certain Activities in Country of Armed Conflict Bill: Finalisation, Protected Disclosures Act: Practical Guidelines for Employees (unpublished manuscript, 2006).
111. G. Bell, *South Africa Mercenary Ban Spurs Security Fears* (August 22, 2006 from http://today.Reuters.com/News/Crises/Article.aspx?storyId+L16396423.
112. See discussion in S A P Parliamentary Monitoring Group, Prohibition of Mercenary Activities and Regulation of Certain Activities in Country of Armed Conflict Bill: Finalisation, Protected Disclosures Act: Practical Guidelines for Employees (unpublished manuscript, 2006); R. Taljaard, "Implementing South Africa's Regulation of Foreign Assistance Act," in Bryden and Caparini (eds.), *Private Actors & Security Governance* Geneva: Democratic Control of Armed Forces, 2006, p. 172.
113. R. Taljaard, "Implementing South Africa's Regulation of Foreign Assistance Act," pp. 169–70, reminds us of the history of animosity between the ANC controlled South African Government and the PMC industry which is largely staffed with apartheid-era personnel.
114. Ibid., p. 169.
115. Regulation of Foreign Military Assistance Act, 15 (1998). *Regulation of Foreign Military Assistance Act* 15 of 1998 § 1 (providing a definition of "mercenary activity").
116. See M. Malan and J. Cilliers, Mercenaries and Mischief: The Regulation of Foreign Military Assistance Bill (unpublished manuscript, 1997).
117. Ibid., Sections 3 and 4 of the Memorandum on the Objects of the Regulation of Foreign Military Assistance Bill, 1997 makes clear that it was the South African Government's intention to bring the provision of military services by South African individuals and companies into line with the regulations that were already in place governing the transfer of arms.
118. Ibid.
119. See, for example, D. D. Avant, *The Market for Force* (Cambridge, New York: Cambridge University Press, 2005), p. 162; P. W. Singer, "War, Profits, and the Vacuum of Law," 521, 521ff.

120. R. Taljaard, "Implementing South Africa's Regulation of Foreign Assistance Act," p. 171.
121. P. W. Singer, "War, Profits, and the Vacuum of Law," 521, 521ff.
122. See, R. Taljaard, "Implementing South Africa's Regulation of Foreign Assistance Act," 174ff.
123. Ibid.
124. Thabo Mbeki, State of the Nation Address, Second Joint sitting of the third Democratic Parliament (unpublished manuscript) (Cape Town, South African, 2005).
125. K. Olaniyan, *Submission to the Portfolio Committee on Defence, South African Parliament*: Amnesty International, 2005.
126. M. Pothier, Submission to the Portfolio Committee on Defence, South African Parliament, 2005.
127. The original Bill was numbered B42-2005 while the revised Bill is numbered B42B-2005.
128. See, L. Le Roux, "Anti-Mercenary Bill Will Hamper Humanitarian Work," *The Institute for Security Studies—Integrated Regional Information Network* (2006, 30 August).
129. S A P Parliamentary Monitoring Group, Prohibition of Mercenary Activities and Regulation of Certain Activities in Country of Armed Conflict Bill: Finalisation, Protected Disclosures Act: Practical Guidelines for Employees (unpublished manuscript, 2006), s. 2.
130. Ibid., s. 1and 3.
131. R. Taljaard, "Implementing South Africa's Regulation of Foreign Assistance Act," p. 173.
132. S A P Parliamentary Monitoring Group, Prohibition of Mercenary Activities and Regulation of Certain Activities in Country of Armed Conflict Bill: Finalisation, Protected Disclosures Act: Practical Guidelines for Employees (unpublished manuscript, 2006), s. 5.
133. The Bill passed through the Parliamentary Portfolio Committee on Defence on August 15, 2006 and the Select committee on Security and Constitutional Affairs on November 1, 2006.
134. Section 14 of the Bill will repeal the *Regulation of Foreign Military Assistance Act 1998*.
135. Section 1: the definition of armed conflict includes, "a situation in a regulated country proclaimed as such in terms of section 6."
136. Regulation of Foreign Military Assistance Act (UK), Preamble (1998), [Preamble] *Regulation of Foreign Military Assistance Act 1998 (UK)*, No. 18912, Preamble.
137. Green Paper: Private Military Companies Options for Regulation, House of Commons, 20 Cong. Rec. 577 (2001/2002).
138. Ibid. p. 26.
139. Ibid.
140. Ibid.
141. Secretary of State for Foreign & Commonwealth Affairs, *Ninth Report of the Foreign Affairs Committee, Private Military Companies: Responses of the Secretary of State for Foreign & Commonwealth Affairs* (UK: State for Foreign & Commonwealth Affairs, 2001/2002).
142. Ibid., p. 4; "The availability of reputable companies to provide support [for peacekeeping and humanitarian deployments] means that the UK may be in a better position than might otherwise be the case to respond positively to requests to take part in such operations."

143. See, J. C. Zarate, "The Emergence of a New Dog of War," pp. 76–8 for general comments on the close links between PMCs and the militarily advanced countries in which these PMCs form.
144. C. Walker and D. Whyte, "Contracting Out War?," pp. 658–61.
145. D. U. D. S. Rumsfeld, *Times* (March 31, 2003).
146. See, E. Krahmann, "Regulating military and Security Services in the European Union," in Bryden and Caparini (eds.), *Private Actors & Security Governance*, D. U. D. S. Rumsfeld, *Times* (March 31, 2003).
147. A. Bearpark and S. Schultz, "The Regulation of the Private Security Industry and the Future of the Market," in Chesterman and Lehnardt (eds.), *From Mercenaries to Market.*
148. "Regulation—An ArmorGroup Perspective" (September 27, 2004). Retrieved February 27, 2007, from http://www.armorgroup.com/mediacentre/publications/?year= 2004.
149. Ibid., pp. 4–5.
150. See, C. Walker and D. Whyte, "Contracting Out War?," pp. 655–7.
151. K. Jennings, "Armed Services: Regulating the Private Military Industry" (No. Fafo Report-532, 2007), p. 12.

5 Private Military Firms under International Law

1. P. W. Singer, "Corporate Warriors," 86, p. 214.
2. America has frequently used private contractors to transport terrorism suspects to countries known to practice torture. See S. M. Hersh *Chain of Command: The Road from 9/11 to Abu Ghraib* (New York: HarperCollins Publishers, 2004), p. 53.
3. L. Dickinson, "Government for Hire: Privatizing Foreign Affairs and the Problem of Accountability under International Law," *William & Mary Law Review*, 47 (2005), 135, pp. 152–3.
4. See e.g. D. Kassebaum, "A Question of Facts," 581–602; J. C. Zarate, "The Emergence of a New Dog of War," pp. 76–156.
5. P. W. Singer, *Corporate Warriors.*
6. Ibid.
7. See e.g. Mohed Omer Beshir, *Mercenaries in Africa* (Addis Ababa: OAU, 1972) 5.
8. GA Res 2395, UN GAOR, 23rd sess, 1730th mtg, UN Doc A/7352, 8 (1968).
9. GA Res 2395, ibid.
10. GA Res 2465, UN GAOR, 23rd sess, 1751st mtg, UN Doc A/L.560/Rev. 1, A/L.561/Add.1, A/L.563.
11. GA Res 2465, ibid.
12. GA Res 2548, UN GAOR, 24th sess, 1829th mtg, UN Doc A/L.581/Add.1 (1969).
13. GA Res 2548, ibid.
14. GA Res 2548, ibid.
15. *Implementation of the Declaration on the Granting of Independence to Colonial Countries and Peoples*, GA Res 2708 (XXVI), UN GAOR, 25th sess, 1929th mtg, UN Doc A/Res/2708 (1970).
16. GA Res 2625 (XXV), UN GAOR, 25th sess, 1883rd mtg, UN Doc A/8082 (1970).
17. GA Res 2708, ibid.
18. GA Res 2727 (XXV), UN GAOR, 25th sess, 1921st mtg, UN Doc A/Res/2727 (1970).
19. GA Res 3103, UN GAOR, 28th sess. Supp. No. 30, UN Doc A/9030 (1973).
20. GA Res 3103, ibid.
21. It was this initiative which led to the adoption of a convention in 1989—*International Convention against the Recruitment, Use, Financing and Training of*

Mercenaries, GA Res A/44/34, UN GAOR, 44th sess, 72nd mtg (1989) (Convention on Mercenaries).
22. GA Res A/44/34, ibid.
23. M.-F. Major, "Mercenaries and International Law," *Georgia Journal of International and Comparative Law*, 22 (1992) 103, p. 126.
24. See UNSC Res, UN SCOR, 2314th mtg, UN Doc S/Res/496 (1981); GA Res 51, UN GAOR, 44th sess, 78th mtg, UN Doc A/RES/44/51 (1989) (referring to the 1988 attempted invasion of Maldives); GA Res 31, UN GAOR, 49th sess, 83rd mtg, UN Doc A/Res/49/31 (1995) (emphasizing the vulnerability of small states to the external threat of mercenaries and "[c] ondemning all such acts of aggression"); GA Res 33, UN GAOR, 45th sess, 44th mtg para. 17, UN Doc A/Res/45/33 (1990); GA Res 79, UN GAOR, 44th sess, 78th mtg P 34, UN Doc A/Res/44/79 (1989) (interposing the term "mercenaries" with "armed terrorists"); The General Assembly condemns the continued recruitment and use of mercenaries "for the purpose of destabilizing and overthrowing the Governments of African States and of other developing States and fighting against the national liberation movements of peoples struggling for the exercise of their right to self-determination." GA Res 89, UN GAOR, 46th sess, 74th mtg, UN Doc A/Res/46/89 (1992).
25. GA Res 89, ibid.
26. GA Res 89, ibid.
27. J. C. Zarate, "The Emergence of a New Dog of War," 76–156, p. 133.
28. Ibid., p. 133.
29. See Organization of African Declaration on the Activities of Mercenaries in Africa, reprinted in E. Robert, J. Cesner and J. H. Brant, "Law of the Mercenary: An International Dilemma," *Capital University Law Review*, 6 (1990), 365, pp. 365–6.
30. O. A. Unity, "Organization of African Unity Convention for the Elimination of Mercenaries in Africa," *OAU Doc CM/433/Rev. L.*, Annex 1 (1972a).
31. See P. Mourning, "Leashing the Dogs of War: Outlawing the Recruitment and Use of Mercenaries," *Virginia Journal of International Law*, 22 (1992), 589, pp. 600–1.
32. O. A. Unity, "Organization of African Unity Convention for the Elimination of Mercenaries in Africa."
33. UN ESCOR, 44th sess, UN Doc E/CN.4/1988/14 (1988).
34. O. A. Unity, "Organization of African Unity Convention for the Elimination of Mercenaries in Africa," art. 1, § 2.
35. Article I defined mercenaries as any nonnationals employed by a person, group or organization whose aim is: (a) to overthrow by force of arms or by any other means the government of the Member State of the Organization of African Unity, (b) to undermine the independence, territorial integrity or normal working of the institutions of the said State, (c) to block by any means the activities of any liberation movement recognized by the Organization of African Unity (Ibid).
36. J. C. Zarate, "The Emergence of a New Dog of War," 76–156, pp. 77 and 127.
37. M. Sapone, "Have Rifle with Scope, Will Travel," pp. 36–7.
38. C. Wrigley, "The Privatisation of Violence: New Mercenaries and the State" (1999). Retrieved April 1, 2007, from http://www.caat.org.uk/publications/government/mercenaries-1999.php [October 10, 2006].
39. O. A. Unity, "Organization of African Unity Convention for the Elimination of Mercenaries in Africa," *OAU Doc CM/433/Rev. L.*, Annex II Rev. 3 (1972b).
40. The aims of the Convention are expressed in its preamble. GA Res A/44/34, UN GAOR, 6th Comm, 44th sess, 72nd plen mtg Annex, Agenda Item 144, UN Doc A/44/766 (1989) reprinted in UN GAOR, 44th sess, Supp. No. 49, UN Doc A/44/49, 306 (1990) (Convention against Mercenaries).

41. GA Res A/44/34, ibid.
42. GA Res A/44/34, ibid, articles 2 and 3.
43. J. C. Zarate, "The Emergence of a New Dog of War," 76–156, pp. 77 and 79.
44. *Report of the Ad Hoc Committee on the Drafting of an International Convention against the Recruitment, Use, Financing and Training of Mercenaries*, UN GAOR, 42nd sess, Supp. No. 43, UN Doc A/42/43 (1987).
45. The aims of the Convention are expressed in its preamble. See GA Res A/44/34, ibid.
46. GA Res A/44/34, ibid, articles 6, 8, 9, 10, 12, 15.
47. See UN ESCOR, Comm'n.Hum.Rts., 47th sess, Agenda Item 9, UN Doc E/CN.4/1991/14 35 (1990).
48. Article 9 of GA Res A/44/34, ibid, which outlines the jurisdiction of states over the crime of mercenarism, stipulates that a state shall have jurisdiction when the offense is committed in its territory (or on board a ship or aircraft registered in that state) and when the offense is committed by any of its nationals.
49. GA Res A/44/34, ibid, art. 1(1) (e).
50. T. S. Milliard, "Overcoming Post-Colonial Myopia: A Call To Recognize And Regulate Private Military Companies," *Military Law Review*, 176 (2003), 1, p. 11.
51. P. W. Singer, "War, Profits and the Vacuum of Law," 521, p. 533.
52. *Convention on Mercenaries*, ibid, art. 1 (2).
53. T. S. Milliard, "Overcoming Post-Colonial Myopia," pp. 75–6.
54. H. R. Library, "Hague Convention: Respecting the Rights and Duties of Neutral Powers and Persons in Case of War on Land," *Marten Nouveau Recueil*, 3 (1907) [36 Stat. 2310–31 and 1 Bevans 654–68].
55. Ibid., [Preamble].
56. Ibid., art. 4.
57. Ibid., art. 6.
58. I. L. Oppenheim, "International Law," in Lauterpacht (ed.) (8 ed., Essex: Longman, 1955) p. 365.
59. Ibid., p. 365.
60. T. S. Milliard, "Overcoming Post-Colonial Myopia," p. 21.
61. I. L. Oppenheim, "International Law," p. 365.
62. T. S. Milliard, "Overcoming Post-Colonial Myopia," p. 21.
63. See F. Hampson, "Mercenaries: Diagnosis before Prescription," *Netherlands Yearbook of International Law*, 3 (1991), 1 p. 7.
64. Of course, the rules embodied in Hague Law are equally humanitarian and equally concerned with protection of the person. However, because Geneva Law explicitly provides for the sick, wounded, shipwrecked, and prisoners it is more often thought of as the fullest expression of humanitarian law.
65. According to A. P. V. Rogers, *Law on the Battlefield* (Manchester: Manchester University Press, 1996) p. 8: "Taking a direct part in hostilities must be more narrowly construed than making a contribution to the war effort, and it would not include taking part in arms production or military engineering works or military transport."
66. Protocol Additional to the Geneva Conventions of August 12, 1949, and Relating to the Protection of Victims of International Armed Conflicts, 1125 (1977) (Additional Protocol I), art. 47 (defining mercenaries and denying them prisoner of war status).
67. Additional Protocol I, ibid, art. 49.
68. Additional Protocol I, ibid, art. 47 (defining mercenaries and denying them prisoner of war status).

69. M. Sapone, "Have Rifle with Scope, Will Travel," p. 37.
70. See E. B. Ballesteros, *Report on the Question of the Use of Mercenaries as a Means of Violating Human Rights and Impeding the Exercise of the Right of Peoples to Self-Determination* (No. UN Doc E/CN.4/1997/24): Commission Resolution 1995/5 and Commission Decision 1996/113, 1997).
71. D. Kassebaum, "A Question of Facts," p. 589.
72. *Additional Protocol I*, ibid, art. 47(2) (c), cl. 1.
73. *Additional Protocol I*, ibid, art. 47(2) (c), cl. 2.
74. *Report of the Committee of Privy Counselors Appointed to Inquire into the Recruitment of Mercenaries* (1976) (*The Diplock Report*), para. 7.
75. *The Diplock Report*, ibid, 10.
76. Foreign and Commonwealth Office of the United Kingdom, *Green Paper: Private Military Companies Options for Regulation, House of Commons (2001–2002)*, (London2001), para. 6.
77. Additional Protocol I, ibid, art. 47(2) (b) states that a mercenary is any person who "does, in fact, take a direct part in hostilities [.]"
78. *Official Records of the Diplomatic Conference on the Reaffirmation and Development of International Humanitarian Law Applicable in Armed Conflicts* (No. XV: International Humanitarian Law, 1977), para. 25, p. 454.
79. See C. Pilloud, Y. Sandoz, B. Zimmerman, C. Swinarski and E. de Preux, Junod, "International Committee of the Red Cross: Commentary on the Additional Protocols of 8 June 1977 to the Geneva Conventions of 12 August 1949," *Journal of Peace Research*, 24 (1987), 326 p. 579.
80. M. Sapone, "Have Rifle with Scope, Will Travel," p. 39.
81. See e.g. M. E. Guillory, "Civilianizing the Force: Is the United States Crossing the Rubicon?," *Air Force Law Review*, 51 (2001), 11 pp. 11–12 (citing J. O. Tamayo, "Privatizing War: U.S. Civilians Taking Risks in Colombia Drug Mission," *Wilmington Morning Star*, A1 (2001)).
82. Additional Protocol I, ibid, art. 49.
83. Additional Protocol I, ibid, art. 47, § 1(f).
84. See B. H. Brady, "Notice Provisions for US Citizen Contractor Employees Serving with the Armed Forces of the United States in the Field: Time to Reflect Their Assimilated Status in Government Contracts," *Military Law Review*, 147 (1995), 1 p. 2.
85. G. Best, *Humanity in Warfare* (New York: Columbia University Press, 1980), p. 375.
86. J. C. Zarate, "The Emergence of a New Dog of War," 76–156, pp.124–5.
87. E. B. Ballesteros, *Report on the Question of the Use of Mercenaries as a Means of Violating Human Rights and Impeding the Exercise of the Right of Peoples to Self-Determination* (No. UN Doc E/CN.4/1997/24): Commission Resolution 1995/5 and Commission Decision 1996/113, 1997, pp. 85–6.
88. Quoted in T. S. Milliard, "Overcoming Post-Colonial Myopia," 1 p. 76.
89. *Protocol Additional,* ibid.
90. GA Res A/44/34, ibid.
91. P. Singer, "War, Profits, and the Vacuum of Law,"521–542 p. 531.
92. A-F Musah and K. Fayemi (eds.), *Mercenaries: An African Security Dilemma.* (London: Pluto Press, 2000), quoted in P. W. Singer, "Corporate Warriors," 86 p. 44.
93. The US led the "coalition," aided by a small group of supportive countries that included the UK, Australia, and Poland.
94. See "Agreement between the Department of the Interior and CACI Premier Technology, Inc". (2000). Retrieved April 1, 2007, from http://0-www.publicintegrity.org.library.newcastle.edu.au:80/docs/wow/CACI_ordersAll.pdf [15 June 2006].

95. Department of the Army, *Inspector Gen., Detainee Operations Inspection* (2004) 19–20, 87–9.
96. L. Hurst, "The Privatization of Abu Ghraib," *Toronto Star* (2004), F3.
97. *Difference Relating to the Immunity from Legal Process of a Special Rapporteur of the Commission on Human Rights (Advisory Opinion)*: International Court of Justice ICJ, 1999. Rep para. [62], [March 14, 2006].
98. See for U N UN-GAOR, "Draft Articles on the Responsibility of States for Internationally Wrongful Acts," in *Yearbook of International Law Commissions* (vol. II), 2001, p. 43, art. 4.
99. Ibid., in art. 7.
100. International Humanitarian Law documents render the state liable for private acts of its armed forces. This would include, for example, an assault by a soldier while on leave inside occupied territory: *Convention (IV) respecting the Laws and Customs of War on Land*, The Hague, October 18, 1907, art. 3; Protocol Additional to the Geneva Conventions of 12 August 1949, and relating to the Protection of Victims of International Armed Conflicts (unpublished manuscript, 1977), art. 91—a party to the conflict "shall be responsible for all acts by persons forming part of its armed forces."
101. M. Huber, Arbitral Award on British Claims in the Spanish Zone of Morocco (unpublished manuscript); M. Sassòli, "State responsibility for violations of international humanitarian law," *International Review of the Red Cross*, 846 (2002), 401.
102. C. de Than and E. Shorts, *International Criminal Law and Human Rights* (London: Sweet & Maxwell, 2003), p. 15.
103. *Responsibility of States for Internationally Wrongful Acts*, UN GAOR, 53 Sess. (2001), articles1 and 2.
104. Prosecutor v Tadic (ICTFY Appeals Chamber 1999), 96.
105. J. Crawford, *The International Law Commission's Articles on State Responsibility — Introduction, Text and Commentaries* (Cambridge: Cambridge University Press 2003), art. 5, para. 1.
106. See Daphne Barak-Erez, "A State Action Doctrine for an Age of Privatization," 45 Syracuse L. Rev. 1169 (1995).
107. {Lehnardt, 2007 #605}, p. 7–11.
108. See, for example, *Convention on the Prevention and Punishment of the Crime of Genocide*, adopted December 9, 1948, S. Exec. Doc. O, 81- 1 (1949), 78 UNTS 277.
109. See, for example *United States v Krauch, VI (US Mil. Trib. VI 1952).*
110. S. R. Ratner, "Corporations and Human Rights: A Theory of Legal Responsibility," *Yale Law Journal*, 111 (2001), 443 pp. 477–88.
111. N. Jägers, "The Legal Status of the Multinational Corporation under International Law," in Addo (ed.), *Human Rights Standards and the Responsibility of Transnational Corporations* (The Hague: Kluwer Law International, 1999), p. 262.
112. ICJ, *Military and Paramilitary Activities in and against Nicaragua (Nicaragua v United States of America) (Merits)* (unpublished manuscript, 1986).
113. Ibid., pp. 64–5.
114. Ibid., para. 115.
115. Ibid., para. 75–80.
116. Ibid., para. 86.
117. Ibid., p. 139. However, the court did agree that US support for the *contras* was in principle a breach of the prohibition on the threat or use of force against the

political independence and territorial integrity of a state (In breach of *Charter of the United Nations*, art 2(4).

118. Ibid., pp. 64–5.
119. S. M. Malzahn, "State Sponsorship and Support of International Terrorism: Customary Norms of State Responsibility," *Hastings International and Comparative Law Review*, 26 (2002), 83, pp. 100–1. The assertion is also made in K. Highet, "Evidence, the Court, and the Nicaragua Case," *American Journal of International Law*, 81 (1987), 1, pp. 40–1.
120. M. Gibney, K. Tomaševski and J. Vensted-Hansen, "Transnational State Responsibility for Violations of Human Rights," *Harvard Human Rights Journal*, 12 (1999), 267, p. 287.
121. Noam Chomsky discusses US involvement in Nicaragua with particular attention to its political motivations throughout his book: N. Chomsky, *What Uncle Sam Really Wants* (Tucson: Odonian Press, 1993), especially pp. 100–4 and 270–8.
122. Prosecutor v. Tadic (ICTFY Appeals Chamber 1999).
123. Ibid., paragraphs [115]–[116].
124. Ibid., para. [120].
125. Ibid. para. [137].
126. C. de Than and E. Shorts, *International Criminal Law and Human Rights*, p. 19.
127. D. Jinks, "State Responsibility for the Acts of Private Armed Groups," *Chicago Journal of International Law*, 4 (2003), 83, p. 89.
128. The Chamber also noted that the actions of private groups who are not connected to the military are only attributable to a state only if "specific instructions concerning the commission of that particular act had been issued" by the state, or the state "publicly endorsed or approved *ex post facto*" the conduct: Prosecutor v. Tadic (ICTFY Appeals Chamber 1999), para. [137].
129. S. R. Ratner, "Corporations and Human Rights," p. 466.
130. See Ibid. for some interesting arguments.
131. For example, in May 2004, the UN Special Rapporteur on the right to food wrote to the CEO of Caterpillar Inc. warning that allowing the delivery of its bulldozers to the Israeli army for use in Gaza and the West Bank might involve complicity or acceptance on the part of the company to "actual and potential violation of human rights." A copy of the letter is available at U Indymedia, "UN Warns Caterpillar May be Implicated in Human Rights Violations" (2004). Retrieved June 14, 2005, from http://www.indymedia.org.uk/en/regions/oxford/2004/06/293546.html.
132. The UN Human Rights Commission passed a new resolution in 2004 to extend the responsibility of rights beyond governments to nonstate actors. The letter written by Special Rapporteur Jean Ziegler to Caterpillar was the first action taken under this resolution. See: Anon., "Bulldozer Maker Warned on Rights," *Sydney Morning Herald* (June 18, 2004), 15.
133. Ratner agrees, S. R. Ratner, "Corporations And Human Rights," p. 469.
134. International Covenant on Civil and Political Rights opened for signature December 16, 1966, 999 U.N.T.S. 171.
135. See International Covenant on Civil and Political Rights, Human Rights Comm., Views of the Human Rights Committee under article 5, paragraph 4, of the Optional Protocol to the International Covenant on Civil and Political Rights (Communication No. 5/1977), UN Doc. CCPR/C/7/D/5/1977 (August 15, 1979); International Covenant on Civil and Political Rights, Human Rights Comm., Views of the Human Rights Committee under article 5, paragraph 4, of

the Optional Protocol to the International Covenant on Civil and Political Rights (Communication No. 74/1980), U.N. Doc. CCPR/C/18/D/74/1980 (March 23, 1983); International Covenant on Civil and Political Rights, Human Rights Comm., Views of the Human Rights Committee under article 5, paragraph 4, of the Optional Protocol to the International Covenant on Civil and Political Rights (Communication No. 124/1982), U.N. Doc. CCPR/C/22/D/124/1982 (July 24, 1984).

136. See International Covenant on Civil and Political Rights, Human Rights Comm., Views of the Human Rights Committee under article 5, paragraph 4, of the Optional Protocol to the International Covenant on Civil and Political Rights (Communication No. 5/1977), UN Doc. CCPR/C/7/D/5/1977 (August 15, 1979); International Covenant on Civil and Political Rights, Human Rights Comm., Views of the Human Rights Committee under article 5, paragraph 4, of the Optional Protocol to the International Covenant on Civil and Political Rights (Communication No. 74/1980), UN Doc. CCPR/C/18/D/74/1980 (March 23, 1983); International Covenant on Civil and Political Rights, Human Rights Comm., Views of the Human Rights Committee under article 5, paragraph 4, of the Optional Protocol to the International Covenant on Civil and Political Rights (Communication No. 124/1982), UN Doc. CCPR/C/22/D/124/1982 (July 24, 1984); International Covenant on Civil and Political Rights, Human Rights Comm., Views of the Human Rights Committee under article 5, paragraph 4, of the Optional Protocol to the International Covenant on Civil and Political Rights (Communication No. 1020/2001) [emphasis added].

137. Convention against Torture and Other Cruel, Inhuman, or Degrading Treatment or Punishment opened for signature December 10, 1984, 1465 U.N.T.S. 85.

138. See Office of the High Commissioner for Human Rights, Comm. against Torture, Concluding Observations of the Committee against Torture: Israel, para. 257, UN GAOR, 52nd Sess., Supp. No. 44, U.N. Doc. A/52/44 (May 9, 1997).

139. Convention against Torture and Other Cruel, Inhuman, or Degrading Treatment or Punishment opened for signature December 10, 1984, 1465 U.N.T.S. 85 [emphasis added].

140. *XI Trials of War Criminals Before the Nuremberg Military Tribunals under Control Council* (1948), p. 1259. Quoted in: S. E. Hendin, "Command Responsibility and Superior Orders in the Twentieth Century—A Century of Evolution," *Murdoch University Electronic Journal of Law*, 10 (2003), 1, p. 2.

141. W. H. Parks, "Command Responsibility for War Crimes," *Military Law Review*, 62 (1973), 1 pp. 2–4.

142. Grotius wrote, for example: "The State or the Superior Powers are accountable for the Crimes of their Subjects, if they know of them, and do not prevent them, when they can and ought to do so." H. Grotius, *De Jure Belli ac Pacis (On the Law of War and Peace)*, 1625). Quoted in: L. C. Green, "Command Responsibility In International Humanitarian Law," *Transnational Law & Contemporary Problems*, 5 (1995), 319 p. 321.

143. The Nuremberg Charter, for example, specified that acting in an official capacity for government did not relieve individuals of responsibility: *Nuremberg Charter*, art. 7; J. N. Maogoto, *War Crimes and Realpolitik: International Justice From World War I to the 21st Century* (Colorado: Lynne Rienner Publishers, 2004),p. 99.

144. At the Nuremberg trials nongovernmental civilians such as the directors of manufacturing works were convicted of war crimes based on their superiority to the criminal perpetrators. Fredrich Flick, for example, a prominent steel

industrialist, was held to have had "knowledge and approval" of criminal enslavement of civilians and prisoners of war: Prosecutor v Delalic (ICTY 1998), Para. 388 (generally referred to as the "Celebici Case") [360].

145. I. Bantekas, "The Contemporary Law of Superior Responsibility," *American Journal of International Law*, 93 (1999), 1.
146. W. J. Fenrick, "Some International Law Problems Related to Prosecutions Before the International Criminal Tribunal for the Former Yugoslavia," *Duke Journal of Comparative and International Law*, 6 (1995), 103, pp. 117–18.
147. Protocol Additional to the Geneva Conventions of August 12, 1949, and Relating to the Protection of Victims of International Armed Conflicts, 1125 (1977).
148. M. Lippman, "Humanitarian Law: The Uncertain Contours of Command Responsibility," *Tulsa Journal of Comparative and International Law*, 9 (2001), 1, p. 52.
149. S. E. Hendin, "Command Responsibility and Superior Orders in the Twentieth Century—A Century of Evolution," *Murdoch University Electronic Journal of Law*, 10 (2003), 1, p. 31.
150. The actual text of 7(3) reads: The fact that any of the acts referred to in articles 2 to 5 of the present Statute was committed by a subordinate does not relieve his superior of criminal responsibility if he knew or had reason to know that the subordinate was about to commit such acts or had done so and the superior failed to take the necessary and reasonable measures to prevent such acts or to punish the perpetrators thereof.
151. For example, L. A. Bohn, "Proceeding with Caution under article 28: An Argument to Exempt Non-Governmental Civilians from Prosecution on the Basis of Command Responsibility," *Eyes on the ICC*, 1 (2004) 1.
152. G. R. Vetter, "Command Responsibility of Non-Military Superiors in the International Criminal Court (ICC)," *Yale Journal of International Law*, 25 (2000), 89 p. 103.
153. Y. Sandoz, C. Swinarski and B. Zimmerman (eds.), *ICRC Commentary on the Additional protocols of 8 June 1977 to the Geneva Conventions of 12 August 1949*. (Geneva: International Committee on the Red Cross, 1987), p. 1013.
154. See L. A. Bohn, "Proceeding with Caution under Article 28."
155. In *Celebici*, for example, the ICTFY concluded that post-World War II the eschewal of the word "commander" in favor of the broader "superior", led inevitably to the conclusion that "[a]rticle 7(3) extends... *also to individuals in non-military positions of superior authority*": paragraphs [355]–[363] [emphasis added].
156. *Celebici Case*, see n. 144 of this chapter, para. [354].
157. Prosecutor v. Kayishema and Ruzindana (ICTR 1999) [216] reiterated in para. [220].
158. For example, the Rwandan mayor, Akayesu, attracted criminal culpability only for his *direct* role aiding and abetting genocide, as the Chamber found an insufficient subordinate/superior relationship between Akayesu and the Interahamwe (the armed local militia who perpetrated the crimes). This was despite Akayesu considerable *de facto* authority over the perpetrators and his status as the most powerful person in the village. See Ibid.,(visited June 15, 2005).
159. *Celebici Case*, above n. 151, para. [363].
160. *Rome Statute of the International Criminal Court, 183/9* (1998) reprinted in 37 ILM 999, articles 28(1) (a) and 28(2) (a).

161. ICRC, Report of the International Committee of the Red Cross on the Treatment by the Coalition Forces of Prisoners of War and Other Protected Persons by the Geneva Conventions in Iraq During Arrest, Internment and Interrogation (February 2004). Retrieved April 1, 2007, from www.cbsnews.com/htdocs/pdf/redcrossabuse.pdf p. 12, para. [25] [January 5, 2005].
162. To this date there has been: The Taguba Report, The Fay Report A. R. Jones and G. R. Fay, "Investigation of Intelligence Activities at Abu Ghraib" (23 August 23, 2004). Retrieved April 1, 2007, from http://www.defenselink.mil/news/Aug2004/d20040825fay.pdf [March 13, 2006], The Schlesinger Report and the US Senate Armed Services Committee Hearing on the Treatment of Iraqi Prisoners.
163. See, for example: The Fay Report, Ibid. (p. 15. As Stephen Cambone, undersecretary of Defense told the US Senate Armed Services Committee Hearing on the Treatment of Iraqi Prisoners: "What took place in the prison, we have all said, exceeded the regulations, laws and laws of war, convention of the Geneva Convention and everything else." U S A S Committee, "Rumsfeld Testifies Before Senate Armed Services Committee," *Washington Post* (May 7, 2004).
164. J. Borger, "U.S Military in Torture Scandal," *Guardian* (April 30, 2004).
165. The Schlesinger Report confirmed five detainee deaths as a result of interrogation. 23 more deaths are under investigation.
166. G. Ifill, S P o t I L f H R Horton and J. A. L. G. Le Moyne, "Accounting for Abuse," *PBS Newshour, PBS (USA)* (August 25, 2004).
167. The Fay report was one of at least seven inquiries that were completed related to the abuse or deaths of prisoners in Iraq and Afghanistan: A. R. Jones and G. R. Fay, "Investigation of Intelligence Activities at Abu Ghraib" (August 23, 2004). Retrieved April 1, 2007, from http://www.defenselink.mil/news/Aug2004/d20040825fay.pdf.
168. M. Cohn, "Command Responsibility: Playing Politics With Torture", *Truthout* (August 29, 2004).
169. Yoram Dinstein, The Conduct of Hostilities under the Law of International Armed Conflict 24 (2004); see also Prosecutor v. Furundzija, Case No. IT-95-17/1-T, Judgment, para. 153 (December 10, 1998); Prosecutor v. Kunarac, Case Nos. IT-96-23-T & IT-96-23/1-T, Judgement, para. 497 (February 22, 2001); see also 1 Jean-Marie Henckaerts & Louise Doswald-Beck, Customary International Humanitarian Law 318 (2005).
170. Geneva Convention Relative to the Treatment of Prisoners of War articles 13, 130; August 12, 1949, 6 U.S.T. 3316, 75 U.N.T.S. 135. See also Geneva Convention Relative to the Protection of Civilian Persons in Time of War, art. 147, August 12, 1949, 6 U.S.T. 3516, 75 U.N.T.S. 287 [hereinafter Geneva Convention on Civilians].
171. Antenor Hallo de Wolf, "Modern Condottieri in Iraq: Privatizing War from the Perspective of International and Human Rights Law," *Indiana Journal of Global Legal Studies* 13 (2006), 315, 338.
172. International Covenant on Civil and Political Rights art. 7, opened for signature December 16, 1966, 999 U.N.T.S. 171 [hereinafter ICCPR] ("No one shall be subjected to torture or to cruel, inhuman or degrading treatment or punishment.").
173. According to the Human Rights Committee:

> [t]he text of article 7 [of the ICCPR] allows of no limitation. The Committee also reaffirms that, even in situations of public emergency such as those referred to in article 4 of the Covenant [ICCPR], no derogation from the provision of

> article 7 is allowed and its provisions must remain in force. The Committee likewise observes that no justification or extenuating circumstances may be invoked to excuse a violation of article 7 for any reasons, including those based on an order from a superior officer or public authority.

International Human Rights Instruments, Compilation of General Comments and General Recommendations Adopted by Human Rights Treaty Bodies, para. 3, at 151 (General Comment No. 20 on article 7: Prohibition of Torture, or Other Cruel, Inhuman or Degrading Treatment or Punishment), U.N. Doc. HRI/GEN/1/Rev.7 (May 12, 2004) [hereinafter General Comments].

174. Convention against Torture and Other Cruel, Inhuman, or Degrading Treatment or Punishment art. 1, opened for signature December 10, 1984, 1465 U.N.T.S. 85 [hereinafter Convention against Torture]. Convention against Torture, supra note 85, art. 2(2).
175. Fay Report, A. R. Jones and G. R. Fay, "Investigation of Intelligence Activities at Abu Ghraib" (2004, 23 August). Retrieved April 1, 2007, from http://www.defenselink.mil/news/Aug2004/d20040825fay.pdfp.7; See also "Intelligence Officer Counters England: Private at Abu Ghraib prison portrayed as disobedient, bawdy," *Associated Press* (August 2004). [April 1, 2007] (Private Lyndie England claimed she was ordered to use humiliation to get Iraqi detainees to talk); R. J. Smith, "Soldiers Vented Frustration, Doctor Says; Psychiatrist Studied Interviews With Guards Accused of Abusing Iraqi Detainees," *Washington Post* (May 24, 2004). (Specialist Charles Graner's lawyer also claimed that Graner abused detainees on orders from military intelligence officials.)
176. E. McCarthy, "CACI Defense Contracts Hazy on Civilian Authority: Language Reserves Direction for Military," *Washington Post* (July 29, 2004), E05.
177. The Fay Report for example classifies the contractors as part of the Military Intelligence personnel.
178. *U S A S Committee,* "Rumsfeld Testifies Before Senate Armed Services Committee."
179. *Fay Report,* A. R. Jones and G. R. Fay, "Investigation of Intelligence Activities at Abu Ghraib" (August 23, 2004). Retrieved April 1, 2007, from http://www.defenselink.mil/news/Aug2004/d20040825fay.pdfp.48.
180. Antenor Hallo de Wolf, "Modern Condottieri in Iraq," 344–5 (2006).
181. *Fay Report,* Ibid. p. 52.
182. Caci International Inc/DE 8-K For5/27/04 EX-99, http://www.secinfo.com/dfww.111.d.htm Last accessed, September 10, 2007.
183. U S A S Committee, "Rumsfeld Testifies Before Senate Armed Services Committee."
184. Bantekas, "The Contemporary Law of Superior Responsibility."
185. A. Verlöy and P. Daniel, "Windfalls of War—U.S Contractors in Iraq and Afghanistan: Private Contractors" (2004). Retrieved April 1, 2007, from http://www.publicintegrity.org/wow/report.aspx?aid=328 [January 3, 2006].
186. See the press release issued by CACI, confirming that the company had indeed supplied contractors for interrogation purposes in Iraq. Press Release, CACI International Inc., CACI Interrogator Contract with the U.S. Army to continue (May 25, 2004), available at http://www.caci.com/about/news/news2004/05_25_04_2_NR.html (last visited August 1, 2007).
187. The Corfu Channel Case (United Kingdom v. Albania), Judgement (Merits), April 9, 1949, ICJ Reports 1949, pp. 4, 23.

188. {O'M., 1985 #606}.
189. {Singer, 2004 #178}, p. 544.
190. {Singer, 2004 #178}, p. 544.
191. {Singer, 2004 #178}, p. 546.
192. {Singer, 2004 #178}.
193. S. Brayton, "Outsourcing War: Mercenaries and the Privatization of Peacekeeping," *Journal of International Affairs*, 55 (2002), 303, pp. 308–12.
194. See E. W. Orts, "War and the Business Corporation," pp. 556–7.
195. The Westphalian model of state-dominated warfare represents "trinitarian warfare," a principle whereby the government directs the war, a state-controlled army fights the war, and the people suffer; M van Creveld, *The Transformation of War* (New York: Free Press, 1991), p. 207.
196. See A. K. Sacharoff, "Note, Multinationals in Host Countries: Can They Be Held Liable Under the Alien Tort Claims Act for Human Rights Violations?," *Brooklyn Journal of International Law*, 23 (1998), p. 929.
197. P. W. Singer, "War, Profits and the Vacuum of Law," 521, p. 525.
198. T. Garmon, "Domesticating International Corporate Responsibility," 325, p. 339.

Conclusion: Taming the Wild Dogs

1. Extracted from Professor Deborah Avant's concise synthesis in her paper, "The Market for Force: Exploring the Privatization of Military Services," paper prepared for discussion at the Council on Foreign Relations Study Group on the *Arms Trade and the Transnationalization of the Defense Industry: Economic versus Security Drivers,* accessible at http://www.cfr.org/public/armstrade/privmil.html (visited September 30, 2004).
2. E. W. Orts, "Corporate Governance, Stakeholder Accountability, and Sustainable Peace: War and the Business Corporation," *Vanderbilt Journal Transnational Law,* 35 (2002), 549, pp. 556–7.

Bibliography

Legislation

Arms Export Control Act, 22 2751-99 (2000).
Concerning the war powers of Congress and the President (1973).
Corporations Act, Cth (2001).
Difference Relating to the Immunity from Legal Process of a Special Rapporteur of the Commission on Human Rights (Advisory Opinion): International Court of Justice (ICJ, 1999).
International Traffic in Arms Regulations, 22 120-30 (2005).
Limited Liability Act, 18 & 19 c133 (1855).
Military Extraterritorial Jurisdiction Act (2000).
Montevideo Convention on the Rights and Duties of States 1933 (1936).
Official Records of the Diplomatic Conference on the Reaffirmation and Development of International Humanitarian Law Applicable in Armed Conflicts (No. XV): International Humanitarian Law (1977).
Protocol Additional to the Geneva Conventions of 12 August 1949, and Relating to the Protection of Victims of International Armed Conflicts, 1125 (1977).
Reconstruction and Stabilization Civilian Management Act of 2006 (2006).
Regulation of Foreign Military Assistance Act (UK), Preamble (1998).
Responsibility of States for Internationally Wrongful Acts, UN GAOR, 53 Sess. (2001).
Rome Statute of the International Criminal Court, 183/9 (1998).
'The Bill of Rights', (1688).
The Company Law of the People's Republic of China (1999).
Trials of War Criminals before the Nuremberg Military Tribunals under Control Council.

Table of cases

Chicago & Southern Air Lines, Inc. v. Waterman S.S. Corp. (1948) 333 US 103.
Collet v. American Nat'l Stores, Inc. (1986) 708 S.W.2d 273 (Mo. Ct. App. 1986).
Council of Civil Service Unions v. Minister for the Civil Service [1985] AC 374, House of Lords.
Daimler Co. v. Continental Tyre and Rubber Co (Great Britain) Ltd [1916] 2 AC 307.
Doe v. Unocal (2000) 110 F. Supp. 2d 1294, C.D. Cal.
Minister of Arts, Heritage and Environment v. Peko-Wallsend Ltd (1987) 15 FCR 274, Fed Ct.
Ngurli Ltd. v. McCann (1953) 90 CLR 425.
Prosecutor v. Delalic (1998) (Case IT-96-21-T).
Prosecutor v. Jean-Paul Akayesu (1998) (Case ICCTR-96-4-T).
Prosecutor v. Kayishema and Ruzindana (1999) (Case ICTR-95-1-T).
Prosecutor v. Tadic (Case IT-94-1) (Appeals Chamber 1999) I.L.M. 1518.
R. v. Denbo Pty Ltd and Timothy Ian Nadenbousch, Unreported (SC Vic 1994).
R. v. Huggins (1730) 92 Eng. Rep. 518.
R. v. Kite [1996] 2 Cr. App. 295.

R. v. Nelson Group Services (Maintenance) Ltd [1998] 4 All ER 331.
R. v. P&O European Ferries (Dover) Ltd (1991) 93 Cr App Rep 72.
Salomon v. Salomon & Co. [1897] AC 232.
Sandline International Inc. v. Papua New Guinea (1998) 117 I.L.R. 552 (Arb. Tribunal) 593.
Santa Clara County v. Southern Pacific Railroad Company (1886) 118 US 394.
Sinaltrainal v. Coca-Cola Co (2003).256 F. Supp 3d 1345, (SD Fla.)
Suttons Hospital Case (1612).10 Co. Rep.32b.
United States v. Emerson (2001) 270 F.3d 203 (5th Cir.)
United States v. Krauch (1952) 8 CCL No. 10, Trials (US Mil. Trib. VI 1948).
United States v. Milwaukee Refrigerator Transit Co. (1905).142 Fed 247.
United States v. American Tel. & Tel. Co. (1977) 567 F.2d 121 (D.C. Cir.)

Newspaper and Internet sites

"Agreement between the Department of the Interior and CACI Premier Technology, Inc." (2000). Retrieved April 1, 2007, from http://0-www.publicintegrity.org.library.newcastle.edu.au:80/docs/wow/CACI_ordersAll.pdf.
CACI "Frequently Asked Questions about CACI." Retrieved February 13, 2007, from http://www.caci.com/main_faq.shtml.
"Call to Investigate Shooting of Scientist," *Newcastle Herald* (March 13, 2006).
"Chunnel May Cost Taxpayers Millions," *BBC News* (March 28, 2001).
Cohn, M., "Command Responsibility: Playing Politics with Torture," *Truthout* (August 29, 2004).
Cohn, M., "Interview with Janis Karpinski: Abu Ghraib General Lambastes Bush Administration" (2005). Retrieved February 12, 2007, from http://www.truthout.org/docs_2005/082405Z.shtml.
Debusmann, B., "In outsourced U.S. wars, contractor deaths top 1,000" (July 3, 2007). Retrieved August 1, 2007, from http://news.yahoo.com/s/nm/ 20070703/wl_nm/usa_iraq_contractors_dc.
"Defence Contractors: Military Industrial Complexities," *Economist*, 366 (March 27, 2003).
Defense Industry Initiative *1996 Annual Report to the Public and the Defense Industry*, Defense Industry Initiative DII, 1997.
Difference Relating to the Immunity from Legal Process of a Special Rapporteur of the Commission on Human Rights (Advisory Opinion): International Court of Justice (ICJ, 1999).
DynCorp, "Profile of DynCorp (2007)." www.dyncorp.com Retrieved September 17, 2007.
Fainaru, S., & al-Izzi, S., "U.S. Security Contractors Open Fire in Baghdad: Blackwater Employees Were Involved in Two Shooting Incidents in Past Week," *Washington Post* (May 27, 2007) A01.
Flaherty, M. P., & Priest, D., "Iraq: More Limits Sought for Private Security Teams," *Washington Post* (April 13, 2004).
Franklin, J., "US Contractor Recruits Guards for Iraq in Chile," *Guardian* (March 5, 2004).
Friedman, M., "The Social Responsibility of Business Is to Increase Its Profits," *New York Times* (September 13, 1970).
Human Rights Watch, "Iraq: US Data on Civilian Casualties Raises Serious Concerns (2007)." Retrieved September 10, 2007, from http://hrw.org/english/docs/2007/04/12/iraq15687_txt.htm.

Hurst, L., "The Privatization of Abu Ghraib," *Toronto Star* (May 16, 2004), F3.

Ifill, G., Horton, & Le Moyne, J. A. L. G., "Accounting for Abuse," *PBS Newshour*, PBS (USA), (August 25, 2004).

"Intelligence Officer Counters England: Private at Abu Ghraib Prison Portrayed as Disobedient, Bawdy," *Associated Press* (August 4, 2004).

"L-3 Communications Announces Acquisition of MPRI," *Business Wire* (July 18, 2000).

"Lessons from the Voluntary Principles on Security and Human Rights" (November 3, 2005). Retrieved April 1, 2007, from www.bsr.org/BSR Conferences/2005/materials/2005_BSR_Conference_Voluntary-Principles.pdf.

Mandatory Procedures for Major Defense Acquisition Programs (MDAPS) and Major Automated Information System (MAIS) Acquisition Programs, (2002). Department of Defense, 5000.2-R http://dod5000.daumil/DOCS/DoDI%205000.2-signed%20(May%2012,%202003).doc [15 June 2006].

Mount, I., Freedman, D. H., & Maier, M., "The New Military Industrial Complex: To Arm for Digital-Age War, the Pentagon Has Turned to a New Generation of Defense Contractors. The hardware is Impressive. It's Also Deadly," Business 2.0 (March, 2003).

"Niger Ten Years On: Injustice and Violence Haunt the Oil Delta, 2005" (2005). Retrieved February 17, 2007, from http://web.amnesty.org/library/Index/ENGAFR440222005?open&of=ENG-352.

Norton-Taylor, R., "Fears Over Huge Growth in Iraq's Unregulated Private Armies," *Guardian* (October 31, 2006).

"President Bush Delivers State of the Union Address," *The White House* (2007, January).

"Private Military Contractors." Retrieved February 13, 2007, from http://www.amnestyusa.org/business/pmc/HousePartyToolKit.pdf.

"Regulation – An ArmorGroup Perspective" (September 27, 2004). Retrieved February 27, 2007, from http://www.armorgroup.com/mediacentre/publications/?year=2004.

Sandline International, "Private Military Companies – Independent or Regulated?," 1998.

Sandline, "Should the Activities of Private Military Companies Be Transparent?," (1998). Retrieved September 10, 2007, from www.sandline.com/white/transparency.doc.

Scahill, J., "A Very Private War," *Guardian*, (2007b, August 1, 2007).

Scahill, J., "Bush's Shadow Army," *Nation*, (April 2, 2007).

Schrader, E., "U.S. Companies Hired to Train Foreign Armies," *Los Angeles Times*, (Sunday, April 14, 2002).

Silverstein, K., "Obiang's Banking Again: State Department and Washington Insiders Help a Dictator Get What He Wants," *Harper's Magazine* (August 9, 2006).

Smith, R. J., "Soldiers Vented Frustration, Doctor Says; Psychiatrist Studied Interviews with Guards Accused of Abusing Iraqi Detainees," *Washington Post* (May 24, 2004).

Smoltczyk, A., "Rich in Oil, Poor in Human Rights: Torture and Poverty in Equatorial Guinea," *Der Spiegel* (August 28, 2006).

Taguba, A. M., "Article 15-6 Investigation of the 800th Military Police Brigade" (2004). Retrieved February 12, 2007, from www.npr.org/iraq/2004/ prison_abuse_report.pdf.

Tamayo, J. O., "Privatizing War: U.S. Civilians Taking Risks in Colombia Drug Mission," *Wilmington Morning Star*, A1 (February 26, 2001).

"The Nation's Jeremy Scahill on the Impact of Private Military Contractors on the Conduct of the Iraq War" (May 12, 2007). Retrieved September 10, 2007, from http://www.inteldaily.com/?c=138&a=1973.

"US Firm to Turn South Sudan Rebels into Soldiers," *Sudan Tribune* (August 12, 2006).

Verkaik, R., "British Army Pays £1m to Iraqi Families," *Independent* (December 3, 2005).

General

Africa US PMC, Private Military Companies Washington's Use of Private Companies is Challenging AU Precepts," *Africa Research Bulletin*, 44 (April 2007), 17024.

Agee, P., *CIA Diary: Inside the Company* (Harmondsworth: Penguin Books, 1975).

Alchian, A., & Demsetz, H., "Productions, Information Costs, and Economic Organization," *American Economic Review*, 62 (1972), 777.

Amnesty International, *A Catalogue of Failures: G8 Arms Exports and Human Rights Violations*, (May 19, 2003).

Amnesty International, "Voluntary Principles for Security and Human Rights" (2006). Retrieved February 11, 2007, from http //www.web.amnesty.org/pages/ec-voluntaryprinciples-eng.

Amnesty International et al., "Joint Statement of Non-Governmental Organizations on Results of the January 2006 Plenary Session" (2006) Retrieved February 17, 2007, from http://www.humanrightsfirst.org/workers_rights/issues/vp/index.htm.

Andrew, J., *Report of the Commission of Inquiry into the Engagement of Sandline International*, (1997). Joint Standing Committee on Foreign Affairs, Defence and Trade, Canberra, Australian Parliament.

Anghie, A., "Finding the Peripheries: Sovereignty and Colonialism in Nineteenth-Century International Law," *Harvard International Law Journal*, 40 (1999), 1.

Anon., "Bulldozer Maker Warned on Rights," *Sydney Morning Herald* (June 18, 2004), 15.

Aristotle, *The Politics* (Cambridge: Cambridge University Press, 1988).

Aristotle, *On Rhetoric: A Theory of Civic Discourse* (Oxford: Oxford University Press, 1991).

Audi, A. K., " Iraq's New Investment Laws and the Standard of Civilization: A Case Study on the Limits of International Law," *Georgetown Law Journal*, 93 (2004), 335.

Austin, R. P., & Ramsay, I. M., *Ford's Principles of Corporations Law*, 13th edn (Australia: LexisNexis Butterworths, 2005).

Australian Parliament: Joint Standing Committee on Foreign Affairs, D., and Trade, 'Bougainville: The Peace Process and Beyond', (1999).

Avant, D. D., "The Emerging Market for Private Military Services and the Problems of Regulation." In S. Chesterman & C. Lehnardt (eds.), *From Mercenaries to Market: The Rise and Regulation of Private Military Companies* (New York: Oxford University Press, 2007).

Avant, D. D., *The Market for Force* (Cambridge, New York: Cambridge University Press, 2005).

Avant, D. D., "Private Military Companies and the Future of War" (2006). Retrieved September 5, 2007, from http://www.fpri.org/enotes/200604.military.avant privatemilitarycompanies.html.

Avant, D. D., "Privatizing Military Training Foreign Policy in Focus," *Foreign Policy in Focus*, 5 (2000).

Ballantine, H. W., "Constitutional Limitations on the War Powerq," *Viginia Law Review*, 3 (1918), 721–729.

Bantekas, I., "The Contemporary Law of Superior Responsibility," *American Journal of International Law*, 93 (1999), 1.

Barlow, M., & Clarke, T., *Water Privatization: The World Bank's Latest Market Fantasy* (Ottawa, Ontario, Canada, Polaris Institute, 2004).

Bauer, J. (UN representative for ARTICLE 19) *Report on United Nations Commission on Human Rights Fifty-third Session*, United Nations Commission on Human Rights, 1997.

Baxt, R., "The Necessity for Appropriate Reform." In J. Adams, A. Bristow & J. e. a. Cannings (eds.), *Collapse Incorporated: Tales, Safeguards and Responsibilities of Corporate Australia* (Sydney: CCH Australia Limited, 2001), 325–352.

Bearpark, A., & Schultz, S., "The Regulation of the Private Security Industry and the Future of the Market." In S. Chesterman & C. Lehnardt (eds.), *From Mercenaries to Market: The Rise and Regulation of Private Military Companies* (Oxford: Oxford University Press, forthcoming).

Belcher, A., "Corporate Killing as a Corporate Governance Issue," *Corporate Governance: An International Review*, 10 (2002), 47–54.

Bell, G., *South Africa Mercenary Ban Spurs Security Fears* (August 22, 2006, from http://today.Reuters.com/News/Crises/Article.aspx?storyId+L16396423.

Benson, R., *Challenging Corporate Rule: The Petition to revoke Unocal's charter as a guide to citizen action* (New York: Apex Press, 1999).

Berle, A. A., & Means, G. C., *The Modern Corporation and Private Property* (New York: Harcourt, Brace & World,, 1968).

Bernales Ballesteros, E., *Report on the Question of the Use of Mercenaries As a Means of Violating Human Rights and Impeding the Exercise of the Right of People to Self Determination* (UN Econ & Soc Council, 1998).

Best, G., *Humanity in Warfare* (New York: Columbia University Press, 1980).

Blackwater, "Blackwater USA." Retrieved April 1, 2006, from http://www.blackwaterusa.com/.

Blair, M., & Stout, L., "A Team Production Theory of Corporate Law," *Virginia Law Review*, 85 (1999), 247.

Blum, W., *Killing Hope: US Military and CIA Interventions since World War II* (Monroe ME: Common Courage Press, 1995).

Bodin, J. (ed.). *Les Six Livres de la Republique,* Trans. Kenneth Douglas McRae (Cambridge, MA: Harvard University Press, 1962).

Bohn, L. A., "Proceeding with Caution under Article 28: An Argument to Exempt Non-Governmental Civilians from Prosecution on the Basis of Command Responsibility," *Eyes on the ICC*, 1 (2004), 1.

Bolton, P., & Scharfstein, D. S., "Corporate Finance, the Theory of the Firm, and Organization," *Journal of Economic Perspectives, American Economic Association*, 12 (1998), 95–114.

Boon, K. E., "'Open for Business': International Financial Institutions, Post-Conflict Economic Reform and the Rule of Law," *New York University Journal of International Law & Policy*, 39 (2007), 513.

Borger, J., "U.S. Military in Torture Scandal," *Guardian* (April 30, 2004).

Bottomley, S., "From Contractualism to Constitutionalism: A New Framework for Corporate Governance," *Sydney Law Review*, 19 (1997), 277–313.

Bottomley, S. "Where Did the Law Go? The Delegation of Australian Corporate Regulation," *Australian J. of Corporate Law*, 15 (2003), 1.

Brady, B. H., "Notice Provisions for U.S. Citizen Contractor Employees Serving with the Armed Forces of the United States in the Field: Time to Reflect Their Assimilated Status in Government Contracts," *Military Law Review*, 147 (1995), 1.

Bratton, W., "The Nexus of Contracts Theory of the Firm: A Critical Examination," *Cornell Law Review*, 74 (1989), 407.

Bratton, W., "The 'Nexus of Contracts' Corporation: A Critical Appraisal," *Cornell Law Review*, 74 (1989), 407.

Brayton, S., "Outsourcing War: Mercenaries and the Privatization of Peacekeeping," *Journal of International Affairs*, 55 (2002), 303.

Bredemeier, K., "Iraq: Thousands of Private Contractors Support US Forces in Persian Gulf War," *Washington Post* (March 3, 2003).

Brennan, S. G., "The Purpose and Scope of Judicial Review". In M. Taggart (ed.), *Judicial Review of Administrative Action in the 1980's: Problems and Prospects* (Oxford: Oxford University Press, 1986).

British American Security Information Council, "Weapons Trade Publications" (2007). Retrieved February 21, 2007.

Brooks, D., *Ruthless Humanitarianism: Why ignoring the private security option in Darfur is a mistake* (n.d., from http://www.goodmagazine.com/section/Provocations/ruthless_humanitarianism).

Brooks, D., "The Business End of Military Intelligence: Private Military Companies," *Military Professional Intelligence Bulletin* (1999).

Brooks, D., "Creating the Renaissance Peace: The utilisation of private companies for peacekeeping and peace enforcement activities in Africa," paper presented at the Africa Institute of South Africa's 40th Anniversary Conference, Pretoria, South Africa, (2000a, May 30–June 2, 2000).

Brooks, D., "Hope for the 'Hopeless Continents': Mercenaries," *Traders: Journal for the Southern African Region*, 3 (2000b).

Brooks, D., "Private Military Service Providers: Africa's Welcome Pariahs". In L. Bachelor (ed.), *Guerres D'Afrique* (vol. 10): CRES: Centre de Recherches Entreprises et Societes, 2002.

Brown, A., "The Economics of Privatisation: Case Study of Australian Telecommunications." In M. Hossain & J. Malbon (eds.), *Who Benefits from Privatisation?* (vol. 16) (London: Taylor & Francis Group, 1998).

Bush, G. W. "President Bush Delivers State of the Union Address," The White House (2007, January).

Cahlink, G. A., "Send in the Contractors," *Journal of Air Force Association.*, 86 (2003).

Campbell, G. L., "Contractors on the Battlefield: The Ethics of Paying Civilians to Enter Harm's Way and Requiring Soldiers to Depend upon Them," paper presented at the Joint Services Conference on Professional Ethics, Springfield, VA (January 27–28, 2000).

Capps, R., "Crime without punishment," *Salon* (June 27, 2002).

Carter, P., "How to Discipline Private Contractors: What Consequences Do the Companies Involved in Abu Ghraib Face?" (May 4, 2004). Retrieved April 1, 2007, from http://www.slate.com/id/2099954.

Cassels, J., *The Uncertain Promise of Law: Lessons from Bhopal* (Toronto: University of Toronto Press Incorporated, 1993).

Cata Backer, L., *Comparative Corporate Law: United States, European Union, China and Japan* (Durham, NC: Carolina Academic Press, 2002).

Cha, A. E., & Merle, R., "Line Increasingly Blurred between Soldiers and Civilian Contractors," *Washington Post* (May 13, 2004).

Chan, S., & Safran, W., "Public Opinion as a Constraint against War: Democracies' Response to Operation Iraqi Freedom," *Foreign Policy Analysis*, 2 (2006), 137.

Chatterjee, P., "Darfur Diplomacy: Enter the Contractors," *Special to CorpWatch* (October 21, 2004).

Chatterjee, P., & Thompson, A. C., "Private Contractors and Torture at Abu Ghraib, Iraq," *Special to CorpWatch* (May 7, 2004).

Chesterman, S., "The Corporate Veil, Crime and Punishment: R v Denbo Pty Ltd and Timothy Ian Nadenboush," *Melbourne University Law Review*, 19 (1994), 1064–1073.

Chomsky, N., *What Uncle Sam Really Wants* (Tucson: Odonian Press, 1993).

Chomsky, N., *Failed States: The Abuse of Power and the Assault on Democracy* (Crows Nest: Allen & Unwin, 2006).

Chomsky, N., & McChesney, R. W., *Profit Over People: Neoliberalism & Global Order*, (New York: Seven Stories Press, 1999).

Christoff, J., *Stabilizing and Rebuilding Iraq: Coalition Support and International Donor Commitments: GAO-07-827T.* (Washington: U.S. Government Accountability Office, 2007).

"Chunnel May cost taxpayers millions,", *BBC News* (March 28, 2001).
Coase, R. H., "The Nature of the Firm," *Economica,* IV (1937), 386–405.
Coase, R. H., "The Problem of Social Cost," *Journal of Law and Economics,* 3 (1960), 1–44.
Cohan, J. A., "Legal War: When Does It Exist, and When Does It End?" *Hastings International & Comparative Law Review*, 27 (2004), 221.
Cohn, M., "Command Responsibility: Playing Politics With Torture," *Truthout* (August 29, 2004).
Cohn, M., "Interview with Janis Karpinski: Abu Ghraib General Lambastes Bush Administration" (2005). Retrieved February 12, 2007, from http://www.truthout.org/docs_2005/082405Z.shtml.
Collier, R., "Iraq; Global Security Firms Fill in As Private Armies," *San Francisco Chronicle* (March 28, 2004).
Combatting War Profiteering: Are We Doing Enough to Investigate and Prosecute Contracting Fraud and Abuse in Iraq? United States Senate, Committee on Senate Judiciary (March 20, 2007).
Committee, U. S. A. S., "Rumsfeld Testifies before Senate Armed Services Committee," *Washington Post* (May 7, 2004).
Craig, P. P., *Administrative Law,* 4th edn (Sydney: Thomson Sweet & Maxwell, 2003).
Daintith, T., "The Executive Power Today: Bargaining and Economic Control". In J. Jowell and D. Oliver, *The Changing Constitution,* 4th edn. (Oxford: Oxford University Press).
Daw Aung San Suu Kyi's pages, "Daw Aung San Suu Kyi." Retrieved February 12, 2007, from www.dassk.org.
De Smith, S., Woolf, H., & Jowell, J., *De Smith's Judicial Review of Administrative Action,* 4th edn (London: Sweet & Maxwell, 1980).
De Than, C., & Shorts, E., *International Criminal Law and Human Rights* (London: Sweet & Maxwell, 2003).
De Wolf, A. H., "Modern Condottieri in Iraq: Privatizing War from the Perspective of International and Human Rights Law," *Indiana Journal of Global Studies*, 13 (2006), 315.
Debusmann, B., "In Outsourced U.S.Wars, Contractor Deaths Top 1,000" (July 3, 2007). Retrieved August 1, 2007, from http://news.yahoo.com/s/nm/20070703/wl_nm/usa_iraq_contractors_dc.
"Defence Contractors: Military Industrial Complexities," *Economist*, 366 (March 29, 2003).
Dickinson, L., "Government for Hire: Privatizing Foreign Affairs and the Problem of Accountability under International Law," *William & Mary Law Review*, 47 (2005), 135.
Dine, J., *The Governance of Corporate Groups* (Cambridge: Cambridge University Press, 2001).
Dinnen, S., "Militaristic Solutions in a Weak State: Internal Security, Private Contractors, and Political Leadership in Papua New Guinea," *Contemporary Pacific*, 11 (1999), 279.
Dinnen, S., May, R., & Regan, A. (eds), *Agreement for the Provision of Military Assistance between the Independent State of Papua New Guinea and Sandline International* (Canberra: Research School of Pacific and Asian Studies, Australian National University (ANU), 1997).
Dixon, M., & McCorquodale, R., *Cases and Materials on International Law*, 4th edn. (Oxford: Oxford University Press, 2003).
Dombrowski, P., & Payne, R. A., "Global Debate and the Limits of the Bush Doctrine," *International Studies Perspectives*, 14 (2003), 395.
Dorney, S., *The Sandline Affair* (Sydney: ABC Books, 1998).
"Dr. Pangloss Meets the Coase Theorem," *Harvard Law Review*, 105 (1992), 1408–1413.

Du Plessis, J., McConvill, J., & Bagaric, M., *Principles of Contemporary Corporate Governance* (Cambridge: Cambridge University Press, 2005).

Easterbrook, F. H., & Fischel, D. R., *The Economic Structure of Corporate Law* (Cambridge: Harvard University Press, 1991).

Ebbeck, G., "Mercenaries and the 'Sandline Affair,'" *Australian Defence Force Journal*, 113 (1998), 5–23.

Edwards, C., "Democractic Control of Police: How 19th Century Political Systems Determine Modern Political Structures," paper presented at the History of Crime, Policing and Punishment Conference convened by and held in Canberra, Canberra (December 9–10, 1999).

Edwards, C., *Changing Policing Theories for 21st Century Societies*, 2nd edn (Leichhart: Federation Press, 2005).

Eisenberg, M., "Corporate Law and Social Norms," *Columbia Law Review*, 99 (1999), 1253.

Elsea, J. K., *Private Security Contractors in Iraq: Background, Legal Status, and Other Issues* (Washington: Congressional Research Servive, 2007).

Elsea, J. K., Garcia, M. J., & Nicola, T. J., *Congressional Authority to Limit U.S. Military Operations in Iraq* (Washington: Congressional Research Service, 2007).

Evans, M. (ed.) *International Law* (Oxford: Oxford University Press, 2003).

Ezzati, M., & Lopez, A., "Estimates of Global Mortality Attributable to Smoking in 2000," *The Lancet*, 362 (2003), 847–852.

Farrar, J., *Corporate Governance: Theories, Principles, and Practice*, 2nd (Melbourne: Oxford University Press, 2005).

Fenrick, W. J., "Some International Law Problems Related to Prosecutions before the International Criminal Tribunal for the Former Yugoslavia," *Duke Journal of Comparative and International Law*, 6 (1995), 103.

Fitch, J. S., *The Military Coup d'État As a Political Process: Ecuador, 1948–1966* (Baltimore: Johns Hopkins, 1977).

Flaherty, M. P., & Priest, D., "Iraq: More Limits Sought for Private Security Teams," *Washington Post* (April 13, 2004).

Flounders, S., "Bosnian Refugees – Pawns in the 'Great Game': A new U.S. – CIA War." In L. Foerstel (ed.), *Creating Surplus Populations: The Effect of Military and Corporate Policies on Indigenous Peoples* (Washington, DC: Masionneuve Press, 1996).

Foerstel, L. E., *Creating Surplus Populations: The Effects of Military and Corporate Policies on Indigenous Peoples* (Washington, DC: Maisonneuve Press, 1996).

Foreign and Commonwealth Office of the United Kingdom, *Green Paper: Private Military Companies: Options for Regulation 2001–2002* (2002).

Foster, N., "Personal Liability of Company Officers for Corporate Occupational Health and Safety Breaches: Section 26 of the Occupational Health and Safety Act 2000 (NSW)," *Australian Journal of Labour Law*, 18 (2005), 107–135.

Foucault, M., "Neitzche, Genealogy and History." In P. Rabinow (ed.), *The Foucault Reader* (New York: Pantheon, 1984).

Franck, T., "The United States Constitution in Its Third Century: Foreign Affairs: Distribution of Constitutional Authority: Rethinking War Powers: By Law or by 'Thaumaturgic Invocation'?" *American Journal of International Law*, 83 (1989), 766.

Franklin, J., "US contractor recruits guards for Iraq in Chile," *Guardian* (March 5, 2004).

Freeman, J., "Extending Public Law Norms through Privatization," *116 Harvard Law Review* (2003), 1285.

Freier, J., "Arms and the Terrorist," *The Journal of International Security*, 9 (2005).

Friedman, M., "The Social Responsibility of Business Is to Increase Its Profits," *New York Times* (September 13, 1970).

Garmon, T., "Domesticating International Corporate Responsibility: Holding Private Military Firms Accountable under the Alien Tort Claims Act," *Tulane Journal of International and Comparative Law*, 11 (2003), 325.

Garratt, B., *The Fish Rots from the Head: The Crisis in Our Boardrooms – Developing the Crucial Skills of the Competent Director* (London: Profile Books, 2003).

Ghebali, V., "The United Nations and the Dilemma of Outsourcing Peacekeeping Operation." In A. Bryden & M. Caparini (eds.), *Private Actors & Security Governance* (Geneva: Democratic Control of Armed Forces, 2006).

Gibney, M., Toma_evski, K., & Vensted-Hansen, J., "Transnational State Responsibility for Violations of Human Rights," *Harvard Human Rights Journal*, 12 (1999) 267.

Givel, M. S., & Glantz, S. A., "Tobacco Lobby Political Influence on US State Legislatures in the 1990s," *Tobacco Control*, 10 (2001), 124–134.

Graham, C., "Self-Regulation." In G. Richardson & H. Genn (eds.), *Administrative Law and Government Action* (Oxford: Oxford University Press, 1995).

Grant, C. B. D., *U.S. Military Expertise for Sale: Private Military Consultants as a Tool of Foreign Policy* (U.S. Army War College, 1998).

Grantham, R., "The Doctrinal Basis of the Rights of Company Shareholders," *Cambridge Law Journal*, 57 (1998), 554–588.

Grantham, R., "Attributing Responsibility to Corporate Entities: A Doctrinal Approach," *Company and Securities Law Journal*, 19 (2001), 168–180.

Grantham, R., "The Limited Liability Of Company Directors" (No. Research Paper No. 07-03) (Brisbane: The University of Queensland, 2007).

Green, L. C., "Command Responsibility in International Humanitarian Law," *Transnational Law & Contemporary Problems*, 5 (1995), 319.

Green Paper: Private Military Companies Options for Regulation, House of Commons, 20 Cong. Rec. 577 (2001/2002).

Greenwood, D. J. H., "Introduction to the Metaphors of Corporate Law," *Seattle Journal for Social Justice*, 4 (2005), 273–295.

Grotius, H., *De Jure Belli ac Pacis (On the Law of War and Peace)*, 1625.

Guillory, M. E., "Civilianizing the Force: Is the United States Crossing the Rubicon?" *Air Force Law Review*, 51 (2001), 11.

Gunningham, N., Grabosky, P., & Sinclair, D., *Smart Regulation: Designing Environmental Policy* (Oxford: Oxford University Press, 1998).

Hampson, F., "Mercenaries: Diagnosis before Prescription," *Netherlands Yearbook of International Law*, 3 (1991), 1.

Hardaway, R., Gormley, E., & Taylor, B., "The Inconvenient Militia Clause of the Second Amendment: Why the Supreme Court Declines to Resolve the Debate over the Right to Bear Arms", *St. John's Journal of Legal Commentary*, 16 (2002), 99.

Harding, J. (Writer) (1996). "Background briefing on Diamond Mercenaries of Africa." Radio National (Australia) August 4.

Haufler, V., *A Public Role for the Private Sector: Industry Self-Regulation in a Global Economy* (Washington, DC: Carnegie Endowment for International Peace, 2001).

Hendin, S. E., "Command Responsibility and Superior Orders in the Twentieth Century – A Century of Evolution," *Murdoch University Electronic Journal of Law*, 10 (2003), 1.

Hersh, S. M., *Chain of Command: The Road from 9/11 to Abu Ghraib* (New York: HarperCollins Publishers, 2004).

Hersh, S. M., "Torture at Abu Ghraib: American Soldiers Brutalized Iraqis. How far up does the responsibility go?" *The New Yorker* (October 5, 2004).

Highet, K., "Evidence, the Court, and the Nicaragua Case," *American Journal of International Law*, 81 (1987), 1.

Hill, J. G., "Public Beginnings-Private Ends-Should Corporate Law Privilege the Interests of Shareholders?" *International Corporate Law*, 9 (2000), 21.

Holmqvist, C., "Private Security Companies: The Case for Regulation", *Stockholm International Peace Research Institute*, 9 (2005), 51.

Hossain, M., & Malbon, J. (eds.), *Who Benefits from Privatisation?* (vol. 16) (London: Taylor & Francis Group, 1998).

Huber, M., "Arbitral Award on British Claims in the Spanish Zone of Morocco". Unpublished manuscript.

Hughes, N., "Democracy and Imperial Rivalry in Equatorial Guinea," *Review of African Political Economy*, 23 (1996), 442.

Hurst, L., "The Privatization of Abu Ghraib," *Toronto Star* (2004) F3.

(ICJ), I. C. o. J., "Military and Paramilitary Activities in and against Nicaragua (Nicaragua v. United States of America) (Merits). Unpublished manuscript, 1986.

(ICRC), I. C. o. R. C., *Report of the International Committee of the Red Cross on the Treatment by the Coalition Forces of Prisoners of War and Other Protected Persons by the Geneva Conventions in Iraq During Arrest, Internment and Interrogation* (2004, February). Retrieved April 1, 2007, from www.cbsnews.com/htdocs/pdf/redcrossabuse.pdf.

Ifill, Gwen; Horton, Scott (President of the International League for Human Rights), and Le Moyne, John (Army Lt. Gen.), "Accounting for Abuse," *PBS Newshour, PBS (USA)* (August 25, 2004).

Indymedia, U., "UN Warns Caterpillar May Be Implicated in Human Rights Violations" (2004). Retrieved June 14, 2005, from http://www.indymedia.org.uk/en/regions/oxford/2004/06/293546.html.

International Covenant on Civil and Political Rights GA res. 2200A (XXI)-UN Doc. A/6316, 21 (1966).

(IPOA), I. P. O. A., *International Peace Organisation Association Code of Conduct* (2001, from http://ipoaonline.org/php/index.php?option=com_content& task=view&id=100&Itemid=108).

(IPOA), I. P. O. A., "State of the Peace & Stability Operations Industry Survey 2006" (2006). Retrieved February 4, 2007, from http://ipoaonline.org/php/index.php?option=com_content&task=view&id=103&Itemid=110.

(IPOA), I. P. O. A., "Civilian Contractors in Iraq: Accountability and the Uniform Code of Military Justice" (2007). Retrieved February 2, 2007, from http://ipoaonline.org/php/index.php?option=com_content&task=view&id=104&Itemid=80.

Isenberg, D., *A Fistful of Contractors: The Case for a Pragmatic Assessment of Private Military Companies in Iraq*: British American Security Information Council, 2004.

Isenberg, D., "A Government in Search of Cover: PMCS in Iraq," paper presented at the Market Forces: Regulating Private Military Companies, New York, (March 23–24, 2006).

Jägers, N., "The Legal Status of the Multinational Corporation under International Law." In M. K. Addo (ed.), *Human Rights Standards and the Responsibility of Transnational Corporations* (The Hague: Kluwer Law International, 1999).

Jayasuriya, K., "The Rule of Law and Governance in the East Asian State," *The Australian Journal of Asian Law*, 1 (1999), 107–123.

Jennings, K., "Armed Services: Regulating the Private Military Industry" (No. Fafo Report-532) 2007.

Jennings, S. W. I., *The Law and the Constitution* (1959).

Jensen, M. C., "Value Maximization, Stakeholder Theory, and the Corporate Objective Function," *European Financial Management Review*, 7 (2001), 297.

Jinks, D., "State Responsibility for the Acts of Private Armed Groups," *Chicago Journal of International Law*, 4 (2003), 83.

Jones, A. R., & Fay, G. R., "Investigation of Intelligence Activities at Abu Ghraib" (August 23, 2004). Retrieved April 1, 2007, from http://www.defenselink.mil/news/Aug2004/d20040825fay.pdf.

Joo, T. W., "Corporations Theory and Corporate Governance Law". In T. W. Joo (ed.), *Contract, Property, and the Role of Metaphor in Corporations Law* (Durham, NC: Carolina Academic Press, 2004) 520.

Kassebaum, D., "A Question of Facts – The Legal Use of Private Security Firms in Bosnia," *Columbia Journal of Transnational Law*, 38 (2000), 581–602.

Kendall, N., & Kendall, A., *Real World Corporate Governance: A Programme for Profit-Enhancing Stewardship* (London, United Kingdom: Pitman Publishing Corp., 1998).

Khareen, P., "Executive Outcomes – A corporate Conquest 'Reference'". In J. Cilliers & P. Mason (eds.), *Peace, Profit or Plunder: The Privatization of Security in War-Torn African Societies* (Capetown: Institute for Security Studies, 1999).

Kiley, S., "Leone Faces Aid Cut Over Apartheid Soldiers," *Times* (July 19, 1995).

Kosiak, S. M., "Comparison of the FY 2008 House and SASC Defense Authorization Bills" (2007). Retrieved August 28, 2007, from http://www.csbaonline.org/4Publications/PubLibrary/U.20070813.Comparison_of_the_/U.20070813.Comparison_of_the_.pdf.

Krahmann, E., "Private Military Services in the UK and Germany: Between Partnership and Regulation," *European Security*, 14 (2005), 277.

Krahmann, E., "Regulating Military and Security Services in the European Union." In A. Bryden & M. Caparini (eds.), *Private Actors & Security Governance* (Geneva: Democratic Control of Armed Forces, 2006).

Kwok, J., "Armed Entrepreneurs: Private Military Companies in Iraq," *Soviet Legacies* 28 (2006); Reprinted in Harvard International Review, http://www.harvardir.org/articles/1366/.

Laufer, W., *Corporate Bodies and Guilty Minds: The Failure of Corporate Criminal Liability* (Chicago: University of Chicago Press, 2006).

Le Roux, L., "Anti-Mercenary Bill Will Hamper Humanitarian Work," *The Institute for Security Studies – Integrated Regional Information Network* (August 30, 2006).

Leander, A., "The Commodification of Violence, Private Military Companies, and African States." Retrieved October 2, 2004, from http://www.sandline.com/hotlinks/Leander_03-02.pdf.

Leander, A., *Regulating the Role of PMCs in Shaping Security and Policy* (Copenhagen: Copenhagen Business School, n.d.).

Leander, A., & van Munster, R., "Private Security Contractors in the Debate about Darfur: Reflecting and Reinforcing Neo-Liberal Governmentality," *International Relations*, 21 (2006), 201.

Lehnardt, C., *Regulating the Private Commercial Military Sector*(New York: Institute for International Law and Justice, New York University School of Law, n.d.).

Lehnardt, C., Private Military Companies and State Responsibility, (No. 2007/2). (New York: Institute for International Law and Justice, 2007).

Lewicki, R., Barry, B., Saunders, D., & Minton, J., *Negotiation*, 4th edn (Sydney: Macmillan, 2005).

Library, H. R., "Hague Convention: Respecting the Rights and Duties of Neutral Powers and Persons in Case of War on Land," *Marten Nouveau Recueil*, 3 (1907).

Lippman, M., "Humanitarian Law: The Uncertain Contours of Command Responsibility," *Tulsa Journal of Comparative and International Law*, 9 (2001), 1.

Lipson, M., "Private Security: A Retrospective," *Annals of the American Academy of Political and Social Science*, 498 The Private Security Industry: Issues and Trends (1988), 11.

Litowitz, D., "Are Corporations Evil?" *University of Miami Law Review*, 58 (2004), 811.

LoPucki, L. M., "The Death of Liability," *Yale Law Journal*, 106 (1996), 1.

Lynch, C. P. L. M., "Testimony of California Public Utilities," paper presented at the Before the U.S. Senate Commerce, Science & Transportation Committee (March 15, 2002).

Lyons, G., & Mastandune, M., "Beyond Westphalia? State Sovereignty and International Intervention." Unpublished manuscript, 1995.

Major, M.-F., "Mercenaries and International Law," *Georgia Journal of International and Comparative Law*, 22 (1992), 103.

Malan, M., & Cilliers, J., "*Mercenaries and Mischief: the Regulation of Foreign Military Assistance Bill.*" Unpublished manuscript, 1997.

Malzahn, S. M., "State Sponsorship and Support of International Terrorism: Customary Norms of State Responsibility," *Hastings International and Comparative Law Review*, 26 (2002), 83.

Maogoto, J. N., "Watching the Watchdogs: Holding the UN Accountable for International Humanitarian Law Violations of the 'Blue Helmets,'" *Deakin Law Review*, 5 (2000), 47.

Maogoto, J. N., *State Sovereignty and International Criminal Law: Versailles to Rome* (Ardsley, NY: Transnational Publishers, Inc., 2003).

Maogoto, J. N., *International Criminal Law and State Sovereignty: Versailles to Rome* (New York: Transnational Publishers Inc., 2003).

Maogoto, J. N., *State Sovereignty and International Criminal Law: Versailles Rome* (New York: Transnational Publishers Inc., 2003).

Maogoto, J. N., *War Crimes and Realpolitik: International Justice from World War I to the 21st Century* (Colorado: Lynne Rienner Publishers, 2004).

Maogoto, J. N., & Sheehy, B., "Torturing the Rule of Law: USA and the Post 9-11 Legal World," *St. John's J. of Legal Commentary* (manuscript on file with author) (forthcoming).

Maogoto, J. N., & Sheehy, B., "Contemporary Private Military Firms under International Law: An Unregulated 'Gold Rush,'" *Adelaide Law Review*, 26 (2006), 245.

Markusen, A., "The Case against Privatizing National Security," *Governance: The International Journal of Policy, Administration and Institutions*, 16 (2003), 471.

Marsh, N., "Two Sides of the Same Coin? The Legal and Illegal Trade in Small Arms," *The Brown Journal of World Affairs*, 9 (2002), 219.

Marsh, N. S., *The Rule of Law in a Free Society* (New Delhi: International Congress of Jurists, 1959).

Mason, S. A., "The High Court as Gatekeeper," *Melbourne University LR*, 24 (2000), 784.

Mbeki, T., *State of the Nation Address, Second Joint Sitting of the Third Democratic Parliament* (Cape Town, South African, 2005).

McCarthy, E., "CACI Defense Contracts Hazy on Civilian Authority: Language Reserves Direction for Military," *Washington Post* (July 29, 2004) E05.

McCarthy, J., "Letters from the Frontline," *Newcastle Herald* (September 18, 2004).

McClemore, D., "DynCorp Wants to Hire Temporary Agents, but Officials Say They Don't Need the Help" (2007, September 6, 2007). Retrieved September 10, 2007, from http://www.dallasnews.com/sharedcontent/dws/news/texassouthwest/stories/090607dntexbprecruiting.35ff674.html#.

McColl, A., "The Not-So-White Companies: PMF's & Perceptions of Legitimacy," paper presented at the Critical Management Studies, University of Cambridge (2007, July 4–6, 2005).

McNamara, M., "Contestability and Incentives," *Canberra Bulletin of Public Administration*, 81 (1996), 7.

Michaels, J. D., "Beyond Accountability: The Constitutional, Democratic, and Strategic Problems with Privatizing War," *Washington University Law Quarterly*, 82 (2004), 1001.

Milliard, T. S., "Overcoming Post-Colonial Myopia: A Call to Recognize and Regulate Private Military Companies," *Military Law Review*, 176 (2003), 1.

Mitchell, L. E. (ed.). *Progressive Corporate Law* (vol. 7) (Boulder: Westview Press, 1995).

Monkkonen, E. H., "History of Urban Police," *Crime and Justice*, 15 (1992), 547.

Montevideo Convention on the Rights and Duties of States 1933 (1934) 165 L.N.T.S. 19.

Montgomery, D., "Pipeline to Justice: Burmese Activist Has the Attention of the White House and the World," *Washington Post* (August 13, 2003).

Morris, C. (ed.). *The Social Contract Theorists: Critical Essays on Hobbes, Locke and Rousseau* (Lanham, MD: Rowman Littlefield Publishers, 1999).

Mount, I., Freedman, D. H., & Maier, M., "The New Military Industrial Complex: To Arm for Digital-Age War, the Pentagon Has Turned to a New Generation of Defense Contractors. The Hardware is Impressive. It's Also Deadly". *Business 2.0*, (2003).

Mourning, P., "Leashing the Dogs of War: Outlawing the Recruitment and Use of Mercenaries," *Virginia Journal of International Law*, 22 (1992), 589.

MPRI, "About MPRI – Taking Expertise Around the World" (2005). Retrieved April 2, 2007, from http://mpri.com//site/about.html.

Murphy, M. A., "A 'World Occupation' of the Iraqi Economy? How Order 39 Will Create a Semi-Sovereign State," *Connectticut J. Int'l L.*, 19 (2004), 445.

Musah, A. F., "Privatization of Security, Arms Proliferation and the Process of State Collapse in Africa," *Development and Change*, 33 (2002), 911.

Musah, A. F., & Castle, R., "Eastern Europe's Arsenal on the Loose: Managing Light Weapons Flow to Conflict Zones (1998, May 1998). Retrieved September 5, 2007, from http://www.basicint.org/pubs/Papers/BP26.htm.

Musah, A.-F., & Fayemi, K. (eds), *Mercenaries: An African Security Dilemma* (London: Pluto Press, 2000).

National Commission of Audit, *Report to the Commonwealth Government (Australia)* 13th edn (1996).

Naylor, R. T., "The Rise of the Modern Arms Black Market and the Fall of Supply-Side Control." In V. Gamba & S. Meek (eds), *Society Under Siege: Crime, Violence and Illegal Weapons* (vol. 1) (Pretoria, S.A.: Institute for Security Studies, 1997).

Neff, S., *Friends but No Allies: Economic Liberalism and the Law of Nations* (New York: Columbia University Press, 1990).

Newell, V. (Writer) (2007). Radio National Australian Broadcasting Commission (Radio) , February 12, 2007. In ABC (Producer), *Perspective*. Australia.

Newell, V., & Sheehy, B., "Corporate Militaries and States: Actors, Interactions and Reactions," *Texas International Law Journal*, 41 (2006), 67–101.

Nordlinger, E. A., *Soldiers in Politics: Military Coups and Governments* (Englewood Cliffs: Prentice-Hall, 1977).

Office of Management and Budget, "Department of Defense" (2005, February 12, 2007). Retrieved February 14, 2007, from http://www.whitehouse.gov/omb/budget/fy2005/defense.html.

O'M., R. L., "Applying the Critical Jurisprudence of International Law to the Case Concerning Military and Paramilitary Activities in and against Nicaragua," *Virginia Law Review*, 71 (1985), 1183.

Olaniyan, K., *Submission to the Portfolio Committee on Defence, South African Parliament*. Amnesty International, 2005.

Olthoff, M., "Beyond the Form-Should the Corporate Veil be Pierced?" University of Missouri-Kansas City Law Review, 64 (1995), 311.

Oppenheim, I. L., "International Law." In H. Lauterpacht (ed.) 8 ed. (Essex: Longman, 1955).

Organization, W. H., "Why Is Tobacco a Public Health Priority?" (2007). Retrieved March 21, 2007, from http://www.who.int/tobacco/en/.

Orts, E. W., "Corporate Governance, Stakeholder Accountability, and Sustainable Peace: War and the Business Corporation," *Vanderblit Journal of Transnational Law*, 35 (2002), 549.

Orts, E. W., "War and the Business Corporation," *Vanderbilt Journal of International Law*, 35 (2002), 549.

Orwell, G., *The Collected Essays: Journalism and Letters of George Orwell*, (New York: Harcourt Brace Jovanovich, 1968).

Palmer, L., "Court Challenge to Mercenaries," *Sydney Morning Herald* (February 28, 1997).

Parks, W. H., "Command Responsibility for War Crimes," *Military Law Review*, 62 (1973), 1.

Parliament of Australia, Joint Standing Committee on Foreign Affairs, Defence and Trade, Canberra "Bougainville: The Peace Process and Beyond" (1999). Retrieved March 29, 2007.

Parliamentary Monitoring Group, S. A. P., "Prohibition of Mercenary Activities and Regulation of Certain Activities in Country of Armed Conflict Bill: Finalisation, Protected Disclosures Act: Practical Guidelines for Employees." Unpublished manuscript, 2006.

Patrick, S., "Beyond Coalitions of the Willing: Assessing U.S. Multilateralism," *Ethics & International Affairs*, 17 (2003), 37.

PBS, "Private Warriors" (2005). Retrieved April 2, 2007, from http://www.pbs.org/wgbh/pages/frontline/shows/warriors/.

PBS, "High-Risk Contracting Business" (2005). Retrieved April 1, 2007, from http://www.pbs.org/wgbh/pages/frontline/shows/warriors/contractors/highrisk.html.

Peerenboom, R. (ed.). *Asian Discourses of Rule of Law: Theories and Implementation of the Rule of Law in Twelve Asian Countries, France and the U.S* (1 ed.) (London, New York: RoutledgeCurzon, 2004).

Phinney, D., "Iraq Contractor Accused of Offshore Shell Game," *Special to CorpWatch*, (October 14, 2004).

Pilloud, C., Sandoz, Y., Zimmerman, B., Swinarski, C., & de Preux, E., Junod, S., "International Committee of the Red Cross: Commentary on the Additional Protocols of 8 June 1977 to the Geneva Conventions of 12 August 1949," *Journal of Peace Research*, 24 (1987), 326.

Pothier, M., *Submission to the Portfolio Committee on Defence, South African Catholic Bishop's Conference*, (November 1, 2005).

Pound, R., "Law and the State: Jurisprudence and Politics," *Harvard Law Review*, 57 (1944), 1193–1236.

Purchase, B., "The Political Economy of Voluntary Codes". In K. Webb (ed.), *Voluntary Codes: Private Governance, the Public Interest and Innovation* (Ottawa: Carleton Research Unit for Innovation, Science and Environment, 2004).

Ramsay, I., & Noakes, D., "Piercing the Corporate Veil in Australia," *Company and Securities Law Journal*, 19 (2001), 250.

Ratner, S. R., "Corporations and Human Rights: A Theory of Legal Responsibility," *Yale Law Journal*, 111 (2001), 443.

Raz, J., *The Authority of Law: Essays on Law and Morality* (Oxford: Oxford University Press, 1979).

Regan, A., & Dinnen, S., "The Sandline Affair: A Chronology of Significant Events." In S. Dinnen, R. May & A. Regan (eds), *Challenging the State: The Sandline Affair in*

Papua New Guinea (Canberra: Research School of Pacific and Asian Studies, Australian National University (ANU), 1998), 16–17.

Reid, R., & Lee, M., "Diplomatic Convoys Curtailed in Iraq" (2007, September 18, 2007). Retrieved September 18, 2007, from http://news.yahoo.com/s/ap/20070918/ap_on_re_mi_ea/iraq.

Report on Mercenary Activities (Prohibition) Bill, Foreign Affairs, Defence and Trade Committee, 83-2 Cong. Rec.(2004).

Richter, J., *Holding Corporations Accountable* (London and New York: Zed Books, 2001).

Robert, E., Cesner, J., & Brant, J. H., "Law of the Mercenary: An International Dilemma," *Capital University Law Review*, 6 (1990), 365.

Robertson, G., *The Justice Game* (Sydney: Random House Australia (Pty) Ltd, 1999).

Rodriguez-Gavarito, C., "Nike's Law: The Anti-Sweatshop Movement, Transnational Corporations, and the Struggle Over International Labor Rights in the Americas." In B. D. S. Santos & C. Rodriguez-Gavarito (eds), *Law and Globalization from Below* (Cambridge: Cambridge University Press, 2005).

Rogers, A. P. V., *Law on the Battlefield* (Manchester: Manchester University Press, 1996).

Rome Statute of the International Criminal Court, 183/9 (1998).

Rone, J., "Displacement Related to Human Rights Abuses and Aid Manipulation by the Military Parties to the War in Southern Sudan." In L. Foerstel (ed.), *Creating Surplus Populations: The Effect of Military and Corporate Policies on Indigenous Peoples* (Washington, DC: Masionneuve Press, 1996).

Rosky, C. J., "Force, Inc.: The Privatization of Punishment, Policing, and Military Force in Liberal States," *Connecticut Law Review*, 36 (2004), 879.

Rumsfeld, D. "Transforming the Military," *Foreign Affairs*, May–June (2002).

Sacharoff, A. K., "Note, Multinationals in Host Countries: Can They Be Held Liable under the Alien Tort Claims Act for Human Rights Violations?" *Brooklyn Journal of International Law*, 23 (1998), 927.

Salaam, "Guns for Hire" (2003). Retrieved February 12, 2007, from http://www.salaam.co.uk/themeofthemonth/january03/intelligence160304.htm.

Sandoz, Y., Swinarski, C., & Zimmerman, B. (eds), *ICRC Commentary on the Additional protocols of 8 June 1977 to the Geneva Conventions of 12 August 1949* (Geneva: International Committee on the Red Cross, 1987).

Sanger, D., "Playing the Trade Card," *New York Times* (February 17, 1997).

Sapone, M., "Have Rifle with Scope, Will Travel: The Global Economy of Mercenary Violence," *California Western Journal of International Law Journal*, 30 (1999), 5.

Sassòli, M., "State Responsibility for Violations of International Humanitarian Law," *International Review of the Red Cross*, 846 (2002), 401.

Scahill, J., "Bush's Shadow Army," *Nation* (2007a, April 2, 2007).

Scahill, J., "A Very Private War," *Guardian* (2007b, August 1, 2007).

Schrader, E., "U.S. Companies Hired to Train Foreign Armies," *Los Angeles Times* (Sunday, April 14, 2002).

Schreier, F., & Caparini, M., *Privatising Security: Law, Practice and Governance of Private Military and Security Companies* (No. Occasional Paper - 6) (Geneva: Geneva Centre for the Democratic Control of Armed Forces (DCAF), 2005).

Sebok, A. J., "What Tort Claims, if Any, Can Be Brought by the Inmates Who Were Tortured in Iraq?" *Findlaw* (May 17, 2004).

Secretary of State for Foreign & Commonwealth Affairs, *Ninth Report of the Foreign Affairs Committee, Private Military Companies: Responses of the Secretary of State for Foreign & Commonwealth Affairs* (UK: State for Foreign & Commonwealth Affairs, 2001/2002).

Seddon, N. C., & Ellinghaus, M. P., *Cheshire and Fifoot's Law of Contract*, 8th edn (Chatswood, NSW: LexisNexis Butterworths, 2002).
Shearer, D., "Outsourcing War," *Foreign Policy*, Fall (1998), 68–69.
Sheehy, B., "Corporations and Social Costs: The Wal-Mart Case Study," *Journal of Law & Commerce*, 24 (2004), 1–55.
Sheehy, B., "Scrooge – The Reluctant Stakeholder: Theoretical Problems in the Shareholder-Stakeholder Debate," *University of Miami Business Law Review*, 14 (2005), 193–241.
Sheehy, B., "Shareholders, Unicorns and Stilts: An Analysis of Shareholder Property Rights," *Journal of Corporate Law Studies*, 6 (2006), 165–212.
Sheehy, B. "Re-Thinking Securities Regulation: A Comparative Study of ASX, NYSE, and SGX" *Corporate Governance Law Review* 2 (1) (2006), 191–244.
Sheehy, B., "The Trouble with Stockjobbers: The South Sea Bubble, the Press and the Legislative Regulation of the Markets," *Newcastle Law Review*, 10 (forthcoming).
Sherman, A., "Forward Unto the Digital Breach: Exploring the Legal Status of Tomorrow's High-Tech Warriors," *Chicago Journal of International Law*, 5 (2004), 335.
Sherman, J., "Options for Promoting Corporate Responsibility in Conflict Zones: Perspectives from the Private Sector," *International Peace Academy Report*, 3 (2002), 335.
Silverstein, K., "Obiang's Banking Again: State Department and Washington Insiders Help a Dictator Get What He Wants," *Harper's Magazine* (2006, August 9, 2006).
Simonovic, I., "Relative Sovereignty of the Twenty First Century," *Hastings International & Comparative Law Review*, 25 (2002), 372.
Simpson, B., "Solidarity in an Age of Globalization: The Transnational Movement for East Timor and U.S. Foreign Policy," *Peace & Change*, 29 (2004), 453.
Singer, P., "The Law Catches Up to Private Militaries, Embeds" (3 January 3, 2007). Retrieved August 30, 2007, from http://www.defensetech.org/ archives/003123.html.
Singer, P., "The Private Military Industry and Iraq: What Have We Learned and Where to Next?" (Geneva: Geneva Centre for the Democratic Control of Armed Forces, 2004a).
Singer, P., "The Ultimate Military Entrepreneur," *Quarterly Journal of Military History*, Spring (2003), 1.
Singer, P., *Corporate Warriors: The Rise of the Privatized Military Industry* (Ithaca, NY and London: Cornell University Press, 2003).
Singer, P., "Corporate Warriors: The Rise and Ramifications of the Privatized Military Industry," *International Security*, 26 (2001), 86.
Singer, P., "The Ultimate Military Entrepreneur." *MHQ: Quarterly Journal of Military History*, 15 (2003), 6–15.
Singer, P., "Have Guns, Will Travel," *The New York Times* (July 21, 2003).
Singer, P., *Warriors for Hire in Iraq* (Washington, DC: The Brookings Institution, 2004).
Singer, P., "Outsourcing the War with More Private Contractors Dying and Disappearing in Iraq, Some Begin to Question the Rules of Engagement" (2004, April 16, 2004). Retrieved October 12, 2004, from http://www.autonoomcentrum.nl/nieuwe_oorlog/privat2.htm.
Singer, P., "War, Profits, and the Vacuum of Law: Privatised Military Firms and the International Law," *Columbia Journal of Transnational Law*, 42 (2004), 521.
Singer, P., & Olin, J. M., "Corporate Warriors: The Rise and Ramifications of the Privatized Military Industry," International Security, 26 (2001/2002), 16–19.
Small, M., "Privatisation of Security and Military Functions and the Demise of the Modern Nation-State in Africa," ACCORD Occasional Paper Series, 1(2) (2006).

Smith, G., & Lowe, D., "Howard, Downer and the Liberal's Realist Tradition," *Australian Journal of Politics and History*, 51 (2005), 495.

Smith, R. J., "Soldiers Vented Frustration, Doctor Says; Psychiatrist Studied Interviews with Guards Accused of Abusing Iraqi Detainees," *Washington Post* (May 24, 2004).

Smoltczyk, A., "Rich in Oil, Poor in Human Rights: Torture and Poverty in Equatorial Guinea," *Der Spiegel*, (2006, August 28, 2006).

Sommer, "Whom Should the Corporation Serve? The Berle-Dodd Debate Revisited Sixty Years Later," *Delaware Journal of Corporate Law*, 16 (1991), 33.

Spiegel, P., "No Contractors Facing Abu Ghraib Abuse Charges," *Financial Times (FT)*, (August 9, 2005).

Stålenheim, P., Perdomo, C., & Sköns, E., "Military Expenditure." In *SIPRI Yearbook 2007* (Oxford: Oxford University Press, 2007), 267–297.

Stenning, P., *Private Policing–Some Recent Myths, Developments and Trends* (Law Commission of Canada, 2006).

Stiglitz, J. E., *Globalization and Its Discontents* (New York: Norton, 2002).

Stover, F. O., & Hamill, S. P., "The LLC Versus LLP Conundrum: Advice for Businesses Contemplating the Choice," *Alabama Law Review*, 50 (1999), 813–847.

Stuff.Com.NZ., "Mercenary Back in NZ after Jail Stint" (2007). Retrieved March 20, 2007, from http://www.stuff.co.nz/3996431a11.html.

Taguba, A. M., "Article 15-6 Investigation of the 800th Military Police Brigade" (2004). Retrieved February 12, 2007, from www.npr.org/iraq/2004/prison_abuse_report.pdf.

Taljaard, R., "Implementing South Africa's Regulation of Foreign Assistance Act". In A. Bryden & M. Caparini (eds), *Private Actors & Security Governance* (Geneva: Democratic Control of Armed Forces, 2006).

Tamayo, J. O., "Privatizing War: U.S. Civilians Taking Risks in Colombia Drug Mission," *Wilmington Morning Star*, A1 (2001).

The General Assembly, International Convention against the Recruitment, Use, Financing and Training of Mercenaries, 44/34 Cong. Rec. 306 (1989). Tomasic, R., Bottomley, S., & McQueen, R., *Corporations Law in Australia* (Canberra: The Federation Press, 2002).

"The Nation's Jeremy Scahill on the Impact of Private Military Contractors on the Conduct of the Iraq War" (2007, May 12, 2007). Retrieved September 10, 2007, from http://www.inteldaily.com/?c=138&a=1973.

"The Oxford companion to military history" (2003). Retrieved August 27, 2007.

Towell, P., Daggett, S., & Belasco, A., *Defense: FY 2008 Authorization and Appropriations* (Congressional Research Service (CRS), 2007).

Ulam Weiner, R., "Peace Corp. As the International Community Dithers Over Darfur, Private Military Companies Say They've Got What It Takes to Stop the Carnage, if Only Someone Would Hire Them," *Boston Globe*, (April 26, 2006).

UK, T. I., "Defense against Corruption." Unpublished manuscript (London, 2006).

UN-GAOR, U. N., "Draft Articles on the Responsibility of States for Internationally Wrongful Acts". In *Yearbook of International Law Commissions* (vol. II), 2001.

US Dept of Justice, 25 September 2001, *The President's Constitutional Authority to Conduct Military Operations against Terrorists and Nations Supporting Them*, http://www.usdoj.gov/olc/warpowers925.htm.

"US Firm to Turn South Sudan Rebels Into Soldiers," *Sudan Tribune* (August 12, 2006).

Van Creveld, M., *The Transformation of War* (New York: Free Press, 1991).

Verlöy, A., & Daniel, P., "Windfalls of War – U.S. Contractors in Iraq and Afghanistan: Private Contractors" (2004). Retrieved April 1, 2007, from http://www.publicintegrity.org/wow/report.aspx?aid=328.

Verlöy, A., & Politi, D., "Contracting Intelligence: Department of Interior Releases Abu Ghraib Contract" (2004). Retrieved July 28, 2004, from http://www.publicintegrity.org/wow/report.aspx?aid=361&sid=100.

Vetter, G. R., "Command Responsibility of Non-Military Superiors in the International Criminal Court (ICC)," *Yale Journal of International Law*, 25 (2000), 89.

Waldron, J., "Is the Rule of Law and Essentially Contested Concept (in Florida)," *Law and Philosophy*, 21 (2002), 137–164.

Walker, C., & Whyte, D., "Contracting Out War?: Private Military Companies Law and Regulation in the United Kingdom," *International and Comparative Law Quarterly*, 54 (2005), 651–690.

Warbrick, C., "States and Recognition in International Law." In M. Evans (ed.), *International Law* (Oxford: Oxford University Press, 2003).

Watson, D., *Watson's Dictionary of Weasel Words, Contemporary Clichés, Cant & Management Jargon* (Australia: Knopf, 2004).

Webber, M., *The Theory of Social and Economic Organization* (New York: Oxford University Press, 1947).

Weber, R., *Swords into Dow Shares: Governing the Decline of the Military-Industrial Complex* (Boulder, CO: Perseus, 2001).

Weisman, J., & Reddy, A., "Spending on Iraq Sets Off Gold Rush," *Washington Post*, (9 October 9, 2003).

Wells, C. A. H., "The Cycles of Corporate Social Responsibility: An Historical Retrospective for the Twenty-first Century," *Kan. L. Rev.*, 51 (2002), 77.

Wheeler, N., & Dunne, T., "East Timor and the New Humanitarian Interventionism," *International Affairs*, 77 (2001), 805.

Whincop, M., *Corporate Governance in Government Corporations* (England: Ashgate Publishing Ltd, 2004).

White, J. J., "Corporate Judgment Proofing: A Response to Lynn LoPucki's The Death of Liability," *Yale Law Journal*, 107 (1998), 1363

Wilkins, T., & Hunt, T. E., "Agency Discretion and Advances in Regulatory Theory: Flexible Agency Approaches toward the Regulated Community as a Model for the Congress-Agency Relationship," *George Washington Law Review*, 63 (1995), 479.

Williams, P., "Transnational Organized Crime and International Security." In V. Gamba & S. Meek (eds), Society Under Siege (vol. 1) (Pretoria, SA: Institute for Security Studies, 1997).

Wilson, P., "Saudi arms deal puts Blair back in the spotlight," The Weekend Australian (September 22–23, 2007), 16.

Wrigley, C., "The Privatisation of Violence: New Mercenaries and the State" (1999). Retrieved April 1, 2007, from http://www.caat.org.uk/publications/government/mercenaries-1999.php.

Yeoman, B., "Soldiers of Good Fortune," *The Independent Weekly, INDY.* (July 23, 2003).

Yoo, J., "Using Force," *University of Chicago Law Review*, 71 (2004), 729.

Zarate, J. C., "The Emergence of a New Dog of War: Private International Security Companies, International Law, and the New World Disorder," *Stanford Journal of International Law*, 34 (1998), 75.

Zinn, H., *A people's history of the United States* (New York: HarperCollins Publisher Inc., 1980).

Zinn, H., *The Twentieth Century: A People's History*, 1 (New York: Harper Perennial, 2003).

Index

K

L

M

R

S